CONTEMPORARY ISSUES OF THE SEMIOTICS OF LAW

Oñati International Series in Law and Society

A SERIES PUBLISHED FOR THE OÑATI INSTITUTE FOR THE SOCIOLOGY OF LAW

Titles in this Series

Social Dynamics of Crime and Control: New Theories for a World in Transition edited by Susannah Karstedt and Kai Bussmann

Criminal Policy in Transition edited by Andrew Rutherford and Penny Green

Making Law for Families edited by Mavis Maclean

Poverty and the Law edited by Peter Robson and Asbjørn Kjønstad

Adapting Legal Cultures edited by Johannes Feest and David Nelken

Rethinking Law Society and Governance: Foucault's Bequest edited by Gary Wickham and George Pavlich

Rules and Networks edited by Richard Appelbaum, Bill Felstiner and Volkmar Gessner

Women in the World's Legal Professions edited by Ulrike Schultz and Gisela Shaw

Healing the Wounds edited by Marie-Claire Foblets and Trutz von Trotha

Imaginary Boundaries of Justice edited by Ronnie Lippens

Family Law and Family Values edited by Mavis Maclean

Contemporary Issues of the Semiotics of Law edited by Anne Wagner, Tracey Summerfield and Farid Samir Benavides Vanegas

The Geography of Law: Landscapes, Identity and Regulation edited by Bill Taylor

Contemporary Issues of the Semiotics of Law

Cultural and Symbolic Analyses of Law in a Global Context

Edited by

Anne Wagner, Tracey Summerfield and
Farid Samir Benavides Vanegas

Oñati International Series in Law and Society

A SERIES PUBLISHED FOR THE OÑATI INSTITUTE
FOR THE SOCIOLOGY OF LAW

•HART•
PUBLISHING

OXFORD AND PORTLAND OREGON
2005

Published in North America (US and Canada)
by Hart Publishing
c/o International Specialized Book Services
920 NE 58th Avenue, Suite 300
Portland, OR 97213-3786
USA
Tel: +1 503-287-3093 or toll-free: (1) 800-944-6190
Fax: +1 503 280 8832
E-mail: orders@isbs.com
Web Site: www.isbs.com

Hart Publishing is a specialist legal publisher based in Oxford, England. To order further copies of this book or to request a list of other publications please write to:

Hart Publishing, Salter's Boatyard, Folly Bridge, Abingdon Road,
Oxford, OX1 4LB
email: mail@hartpub.co.uk
Telephone: +44 (0)1865 245533 Fax: +44 (0)1865 794882

WEB SITE http//:www.hartpub.co.uk

British Library Cataloguing in Publication Data
Data Available

ISBN 1-84113-545-3 (cloth)
ISBN 1-84113-546-1 (paper)

Typeset by Compuscript
Printed and bound in Great Britain by
Lightning Source UK Ltd

Contents

Biographical Notes vii

Introduction Law's Garden of Forking Paths by Anne Wagner, Tracey Summerfield and Farid Samir Benavides Vanegas 1

Part I: The Interpretation and Pertinence of Law in the Global Age 17

1 Refugee Meanings by Ian Duncanson 19
2 Citizens, Immigrants, Anarchists and Other Animals by Annabelle Mooney 35
3 The Dialogistic Nature of Brazil's Arbitration Law 9.307/96 by Celina Frade 57
4 Constitutional 'Communarchy': A Constitution with Chinese Characteristics by Deborah Cao 71
5 The Quest for Certainty in Recent US Constitutional Scholarship: Original Intent and the Practice of Constitutional 'Creativity' by Frederick P Lewis 85
6 Celebrity as Authority in Law by John Brigham and Jill Meyers 95
7 Writing Around the Censor: Gypsies, Thieves, and Rebels in Early Modern Spain by William Pencak 113

Part II: Cultural and Symbolic Analyses of the Law in Context 125

8 Subversion in the World of Order: Legal Deconstruction as a Rhetorical Practice by Joanna Jemielniak 127
9 The Substantive Issue and the Rhetoric of the Abortion Debate in Ireland by Sophie Cacciaguidi-Fahy 141
10 Wealth of Terms—Scarcity of Justice? Term Formation in Statutory Definitions by Richard Foley 165
11 Enduring Signs and Obscure Meanings: Contested Coats of Arms in Australian Jurisdictions by Richard Mohr 179
12 Critical Race Reggae: The Sound of a Narrative by Aaron RS Lorenz 197
13 Cromer's Olde England and the Dome's New Britain: Two Same/Different Imageries of the Law of Britain's Empire by Ronnie Lippens 213

14 Law in the Age of Images: The Challenge of Visual Literacy
by Christina O Spiesel, Richard K Sherwin, Neal Feigenson 231

Selected Bibliography 257
Index 267

Biographical Notes

Farid Benavides studied Law and Philosophy in Colombia. Then he did a Masters in Penal Systems and Social Problems in Barcelona. He is currently studying a PhD in Political Science at the University of Massachusetts, Amherst. He recently published a book on the constitution of the concept of nation in Victorian London and has written on questions related to human rights, postcolonial theory, and development.

John Brigham is a professor in the Political Science Department of the University of Massachusetts, Amherst. He is the author of *Constitutional Language* (1978), *The Cult of the Court* (1987) and *The Constitution of Interests* (1996).

Sophie Cacciaguidi-Fahy is a Lecturer in Law (Legal French) at the National University of Ireland, Galway. Her research interests include Law and Language, Legal Semiotics and Intercultural Legal and Business Communication.

Deborah Cao is a senior lecturer affiliated with the School of Languages and Linguistics and the Socio-Legal Research Centre, Griffith University, Brisbane, Australia. She was educated in China and Australia in interpreting and translation, linguistics, and law. She has published in the areas of translation theory, Chinese legal translation and legal language, and semiotic study of Chinese law. Her forthcoming book is entitled *Chinese Law: A Language Perspective*, to be published by Ashgate.

Ian Duncanson has taught at Newcastle upon Tyne Polytechnic, the University of Keele and La Trobe University. He has been a visiting scholar at the University of Edinburgh, Carleton University, Cardiff Law School, Southern Cross University, and at the Australian Studies Centre, University of British Columbia. Currently he is Research Associate at the Institute of Postcolonial Studies, University of Melbourne, and Adjunct Associate Professor in the Faculty of Law, Griffith University. He was the founder of the annual Australian Law and Society and Australian and New Zealand Law and History conferences, both now in their second decades, and has published in the areas of law and history, law and social theory, jurisprudence and legal education. Ian is presently working on a project that examines the connection between the more authoritarian turn in British imperialism following the loss of the American colonies and the evolution of positivism, hierarchy and sovereignty in common law's relation to its subjects.

Neal Feigenson is a Professor of Law at Quinnipiac University School of Law, where he teaches Torts, Civil Procedure, and Evidence as well as Visual Persuasion in the Law; he is also a Research Affiliate in the Yale University Department of Psychology. Professor Feigenson's research interests include the application of social and cognitive psychology to legal decision making and the role of visual communication and rhetoric in law. He is the author of *Legal Blame: How We Think and Talk about Accidents.* Other recent and forthcoming publications include 'New Visual Technologies in Court: Directions for Research' (with Meghan Dunn), forthcoming in *Law and Human Behavior*; 'Emotions, Risk Perceptions, and Blaming in 9/11 Cases,' forthcoming in *Brooklyn Law Review*; and 'The Role of Emotions in Comparative Negligence Judgments' (with Jaihyun Park and Peter Salovey) (2001) 31 *Journal of Applied Social Psychology* 576.

Richard Foley is a lecturer in English at the Language Centre of the University of Lapland in Rovaniemi, Finland. His work includes ESP courses for law students, translation from Finnish into English, and responsibilities related to the University's program in Legal Linguistics. He is currently a PhD candidate in the Faculty of Law, where his research focuses on modality, terminology, and translation in the EU context.

Celina Frade has a PhD in Linguistics and is Professor of Linguistics at the Faculty of Letters and Arts, Federal University of Rio de Janeiro, Brazil. As an ESP researcher, mainly legal English, she also designs and delivers ESP and legal English courses for Brazilian professionals and Law schools in Brazil.

Joanna Jemielniak is Assistant Professor at the Leon Kozminski Academy of Entrepreneurship and Management (Warsaw, Poland) and the Chair of Administrative and Legal Sciences. She specialises in legal theory. Her main area of research covers contemporary theories of legal interpretation. Currently she is a visiting researcher (Fulbright fellow) at Harvard Law School.

Frederick P Lewis is a Professor of Political Science and former Chair of the Department at the University of Massachusetts in Lowell, Massachusetts. He holds a JD degree from Harvard Law School and a PhD from Tufts University. His latest book is *The Context of Judicial Activism: The Endurance of the Warren Court Legacy in a Conservative Age.*

Ronnie Lippens is a Senior Lecturer at Keele University (UK). His research interests include imaginaries of law, peace, and justice. He has published extensively on these issues in a variety of scholarly venues.

Aaron RS Lorenz obtained his BA from California State University, Chico and MA from San Diego State University, both in Political Science. He is currently completing his PhD in Political Science at the University of Massachusetts, Amherst. Aaron teaches courses at the University of Massachusetts, Amherst in the Department of Legal Studies entitled *Lyrics and the Law* and *Law and Personal Freedom*.

Jill Meyers has a Masters Degree from the International Institute for the Sociology of Law and is a student in the Law School at the University of California, Berkeley. She has worked for the Center for Constitutional Rights.

Richard Mohr is a senior lecturer in Law at the University of Wollongong, Australia, where he coordinates postgraduate research programs. He is co-director of the Legal Intersections Research Centre at that university. The research and preparation of his paper was supported by the Public Purposes Fund of the Law Society of New South Wales (2000, 2002) and by the International Institute for the Sociology of Law, Oñati, through a research fellowship in 2001.

Annabelle Mooney is a research associate at the Centre for Language and Communication Research at Cardiff University working on globalisation, HIV and quality of life. She also works on the rhetoric of religious cults, human rights and pragmatics.

William Pencak is Professor of History at the Pennsylvania State University and served as the President of the Semiotic Society of America in 1999–2000. Among his works are *History, Signing In: Studies in History and Semiotics* (Peter Lang, 1993), *The Conflict of Law and Justice in the Icelandic Sagas* (Rodopi, 1996), and *Reclaiming a Gay Past: History and Radical Politics in the Films of Derek Jarman* (McFarland, 2002). He has edited special issues of *Semiotica* (with Brooke Williams, vol 83, 3/4, 1991) and *The American Journal of Semiotics* (vol 12, 1995 [1998]) on semiotics and history. He is also co-editor, with Cindy Palecek, of *From Absurdity to Zen: The Wit and Wisdom of Roberta Kevelson* (Peter Lang, 2002).

Richard K Sherwin is a Professor of Law and Director of the Visual Persuasion Project at New York Law School. He teaches Torts, Criminal Procedure, Lawyering, and Visual Persuasion in the Law. He recently established the New York Law School Digital Media Lab. Professor Sherwin has lectured widely in the US and abroad and made numerous media appearances discussing topics relating to law and popular culture. He is the author of *When Law Goes Pop: The Vanishing Line between Law and Popular Culture* (University of Chicago Press, 2000) in addition to numerous interdisciplinary articles and book chapters. Recent and forthcoming publications include: 'Law in Popular Culture' in *The Oxford Companion to American Law* (Oxford University Press); 'Law's Beatitude: A Post-Nietzschean Account of Legitimation,' *Cardozo Law Review*; and 'Nomos and Cinema,' (2001) 48 *UCLA Law Review*.

Christina O Spiesel is a visual artist and writer and an Adjunct Professor of Law at both Quinnipiac University School of Law and New York Law School. She teaches Visual Persuasion in the Law at both institutions. She is also a Senior Research Scholar at the Yale Law School, where she developed and taught Envisioning Law in 1998. In addition, she is a Faculty Associate of Bard College's Institute for Writing and Thinking. A veteran of many solo and group exhibitions, she has been exhibiting her art since 1972. Her published writing in art history and criticism includes work on Leonardo Da Vinci, Artemisia Gentileschi, Manet, and DeKooning. Her meditation on criticism, 'The One Who Loved My Work,' is available online at www.genders.org. Her writing on legal matters includes 'Law, Art, and the Language of Flowers' (*Proceedings of the Law and Semiotics Roundtable*, 1999) and 'Out of Time: Maximum Security and the Dark Trickster' at www. trinity.edu/org/tricksters/TrixWay/2002. She has published word/image pieces in *Chain* (2000, 2001) 7, 8.

Tracey Summerfield is a law Lecturer at the University of Western Australia. She has a PhD in Law and Communications Studies from Murdoch University. Her research interests are in issues of law and social justice, law and communication, legal semiotics and family law. She is also an administrative decision maker on child support issues for the Australian government.

Anne Wagner is a Senior Lecturer in Applied Linguistics affiliated with the Université du Littoral, Côte d'Opale, France. Her main research interests include legal language, law and semiotics, plain language, interpretation, contemporary legal theory, law and literature, legal history. She is the author of *La Langue de La Common Law* (L'Harmattan, 2002) and editor of a special issue of *The International Journal for the Semiotics of the Law*: 'The (Ab)Use of Language in Legal Discourse' (15:4, 2002). She has also published extensively on these issues in a variety of scholarly venues.

INTRODUCTION

Law's Garden of Forking Paths

ANNE WAGNER, TRACEY SUMMERFIELD AND FARID SAMIR BENAVIDES VANEGAS

I

A GARDEN OF FORKING PATHS

IN A BEAUTIFUL tale, Jorge Luis Borges writes about a garden of forking paths.[1] This is a story that can be read in different ways. It can be read as a detective novel, in which the reader is accompanying the main character in a murder investigation. But this is not the main point of the book. What is most interesting about the book is the idea of a garden of forking paths. At the beginning the reader is led to believe that the main character is looking for an actual garden where a path leads to another and so on ad infinitum. In fact, Borges is trying to show us the difference between the traditional conception of infinity and the modern idea of it, established by German mathematician Georg Cantor. According to Cantor, there is a possibility of an abstract yet real infinity. When we say that the natural numbers are infinite, we are not only saying that to any number we can add 1 and keep the count going endlessly, but also saying that in the series 1–2 there is an infinite number of numbers and if we draw a line that goes from point 1 to point 2 we are seeing actual infinity.[2] The garden of forking paths is not, then, an actual garden but an object that conveys the idea of transfinite numbers, that is, an object that has the possibility of different paths leading to an infinite number of points. In Borges, one story leads to another, and so on, until it returns to the story's beginning, keeping the paths opening endlessly. This account reminds us, as is Borges' intention, of

[1] JL Borges, *Ficciones* (Madrid, Alianza Editorial, 1976); in English: (New York, Grove Press, 1962).

[2] JA Hernandez, *Biografia del Infinito. La nocion de transfinitud the Georg Cantor y su presencia en la obra de Jorge Luis Borges* (Caracas, Comala, 2001). For different conceptions of the infinite see DR Hofstadter, *Godel, Escher, Bach: An Eternal Golden Braid* (New York, Basic Books, 1999) and AD Aczel, *The Mystery of the Aleph: Mathematics, the Kabbalah, and the Search for Infinity* (New York, Four Walls Eight Windows, 2000).

Scherezada's *Arabian Nights* where, Scherezada, the narrator, tells the story of a girl who tells stories to the Emperor in order to avoid being killed.[3]

The law can be seen from the point of view of a garden of forking paths. When we read any handbook on legal theory, we see that every theory leads to another, with some paths diverting in search of new destinies, in an endless discussion about the real nature of the law.

The papers on law contained in this collection draw on many theories, refining legal analysis. For us, the meeting point of these papers is the relationship between law and semiotics, that is, the understanding of law as a system of signs and interpretation. In fact, in the analyses of the law contained herein, we find different common grounds and we also find that the differences between the theories can have a meeting point.

In May 2002, the European and American law and semiotics groups came together in Oñati (Spain). We find in that fact a metaphor of law and semiotics as a meeting point of all those diverging paths that constitute the analysis of law.

At this forum, scholars from different parts of the world presented papers in which the relationship between law and semiotics was analysed, and papers in which this relationship provided the tool and background for different analyses. Some of the papers were published in the International Journal for the Semiotics of Law.[4] In this collection, we present other papers presented at that meeting as well as contributions from scholars connected in different ways to law and semiotics.

Different Conceptions of the Law

At the core of much legal theory has been a link between law and language. The various studies about legal language originate from classical rhetorics, where law was seen as a separate discipline. Rhetorics was the root of many studies which are now embodied within pragmatics and discourse analysis. Indeed, rhetorics conceived speech and written acts as adjuncts, and language as the contextual means through the use of semantic fluidity.[5] This analysis was destined to fit one argument into its context, insisting on persuasion and eloquence as communicative capacities.[6] Aristotle divided language into deliberative (political), forensic (legal) and epideict (panegiric) modes, according to the object of the persuasion and effect. He was not opposed to metaphors in order to enhance language, and insisted that language be transparent and

[3] Anonymous, *The Arabian Nights' Entertainment: or, The Book of a Thousand Nights and a Night: A Selection of the Most Famous and Representative of These Tales* (New York, Modern Library, 1959).

[4] (2003) 16 *International Journal for the Semiotics of Law*. Special Isssue edited by D Cao and I Duncanson.

[5] A Wagner, *La Langue de la Common Law* (Paris, L'Harmattan, 2002).

[6] R Lindon, *Le Style, l'éloquence judiciaire* (Paris, Albin Michel, 1968).

authentic, close to verbal speech and to common reality.[7] However, this movement was ephemeral. Indeed, after Aristotle, linguistics was reduced to logics, and to the study of verbal speech as a means of discourse, or of social elocution for the analysis or demonstration of necessary and unambiguous signifiers. The aim of this study was reduced to written texts with a preference for philosophy and philology over rhetorics.

In the eleventh and twelfth centuries, Roman Law was at the core of contemporary legal thinking and confirmed the authority of the text as well as the philological nature of its interpretation. The code or written statutes provided the basis of analysis by an elite more interested in interpretation than in prior times. In law, the specialised and authoritarian monologue of jurisprudence provided the foundation of the normative and formal characteristics, as well as the autonomy, of legal language.[8] Legal language was directed towards a select and privileged minority whose aim was to defend its institutional meaning and its obscure, opaque and esoteric features.[9]

Today, our conception of the law depends upon the culture of law within which we live.[10] For the purposes of this introduction we are going to mention just some of them, because they are in some way related to our discussion about the law. However, in both traditions, we find a continuum that goes from a fear of contamination from something outside the law to something in which the law is connected to politics, everyday life, and symbolical life. That is, a process in which law loses that fear of contamination, as indicated by Gény:[11]

> Le droit est une science sociale dont les règles et les moyens d'expression dépendent étroitement des mœurs, des conceptions philosophiques et religieuses, des nécessités et des possibilités économiques, etc, tous facteurs en continuel état d'évolution.[12]

Conceiving of the law as a symbol allows us to understand how that process works and how we can connect our life to the text of the law; as suggested by Roberta Kevelson:[13]

[7] See the Plain Language Movements implemented in various countries. For more information, see the following website: <http://www.clarity-international.net>.

[8] P Goodrich, *Languages of Law: From Logics of Memory to Nomadic Masks* (London, Weidenfeld and Nicolson, 1990).

[9] V Charrow and R Charrow, 'Lawyers' Views of the Comprehensibility of Legal Language' 5th Annual Colloquium on New Ways of Analyzing Variation in English (Washington DC, Georgetown University, 1976).

[10] F De Varennes, 'Law, Language and the Multicultural State' (1996) 16(3) *Language and Communication*, at 291.

[11] F Gény, *Science et Technique en Droit Positif, vol.1: III* (Paris, Recueil Sirey, 1922) at 252.

[12] 'Law is a social science in which the rules and the means of expression directly depend upon customs, philosophical and religious ideas, upon economic necessities and possibilities, etc, which are all aspects in a continual state of evolution.'

[13] R Kevelson, *The Law as a System of Signs* (New York, Plenum Press, 1988) at 4.

1. All communication is a process of exchange of meaningful signs, and signs and signs systems such as natural language mediate between communicating persons and those objects in the phenomenal, physical world of experience to which they refer.
2. All human societies have developed complex systems of both verbal and nonverbal sign systems which are not static but which evolve continuously to correspond with and to represent changing social norms and the evolving, growing social consciousness of any given community.

The Incorporation of the Outside of the Law into the Code of the Law

A distinction can be drawn in the European tradition between the Anglo-Saxon and continental traditions. Given the significance of American jurisprudence, we will discuss the American tradition as part of the Anglo-Saxon one.

In European jurisprudence, there is a concern with the relationship between the inside of law and the outside of the law. In natural law theories, for instance, there is discussion about a distinction between law and morality. This might be viewed as an issue of sovereignty and the power to command. However, it is also a question of determining what can be placed within the law and what can be said with the language of the law, that is, one of command and obedience.[14] In the natural law tradition, the law had to be read as governed by natural law: either religious values, or secular values like the Universal Declaration of Human Rights. However, the relation was one in which law was part of morality, that is, law was contaminated by morality and was nothing else but morality.[15]

Positivism attempted to sever the relationship. In driving a wedge between law and morality, it took the fear of contamination to the extreme. Law, in the positivist tradition, is the command of the sovereign who has no sovereign to obey.[16] Law's validity does not rest on an external measure.

The philosophical Neo-Kantianism of the late nineteenth century, as well as the advent of positivism, were at the core of the development and systematisation of language and law. The systematic determination of ideal speech (linguistics) and conduct (law) became the object of normative science. The studies of the time, especially those conducted by Saussure,[17] showed the importance of using the prevailing philological and exegetical conceptions of language. The study of language was—and is still today—a

[14] See N Fairclough, *Language and Power* (London, Longman, 1989).

[15] About the law in modern times see: B de Sousa Santos, *Towards a New Common Sense: Law, Science, and Politics in the Paradigmatic Transition* (New York, Routledge, 1995) and R M Unger, *Law in Modern Society: Towards A Criticism Of Social Theory* (New York, Free Press, 1977).

[16] HLA Hart, *The Concept of Law* (New York, Oxford University Press, 1961).

[17] F de Saussure, *Cours de Linguistique Générale* (Paris, Payot, 1916) at 118.

unitarian science in which signs are elements of a code, subject to conventional regulations.[18]

There is a similar dualism in the advent of legal positivism. It can be found in the distinctions between legal system and judgment, legal validity and legal signifier, and norm and its practical application. These are always in conflict, the formers being subjective and frequent, and the latters discretionary.

The linguistic theory of Saussure corresponds with the Kelsenian theory of the legal structure. For Kelsen,[19] the grammar of law is the grammar of written text, and the formal limits of legal signifiers are the object of analysis. While Saussure wrote about *langue/parole*, Kelsen drew the distinction between *validity/legal volition.*

In summary, both studies—those of the linguist and those of the legal scholar—put an emphasis on abstract verification and on scientific description achieved with minimum normative requisites. Kelsen patently negates subjectivism, the social and the individual in favour of formalism and positivism. He explained legal science as a pure and united logic of norms. In French scholarship, we find the works of Francois Gény,[20] whose analysis of the free interpretation of the law became the basis for some analyses in the Latin American and American traditions. Gény drew the distinction between *legal science* and *legal technique,* borrowed from '*le donné*' and '*le construit*' of Bergson's philosophy.[21] The former corresponds to natural law, the latter to positive law. Gény's work was dedicated to translating the given notion into a constructed one, that is, to the translation of this latent and spontaneous normativity which comes from society to a more formal and wisely organised normativity (positive law).

After the Second World War, with the critique of positivism in Germany, several authors proposed a different approach, in order to show the danger of preserving purity in the law. In a discussion famous in continental criminal law, Hans Welzel and Gustav Radbruch each proposed different approaches to the analysis of the law as a response to the horrors brought about by the law of the Nazi Regime.[22] While Welzel proposed an approach to the law from an ontological point of view, Radbruch proposed one in which universal values were taken into account within the law. To Welzel, the law had to incorporate what he called the 'ontological structures'; that is, reality had to be taken into account in the process of legislating about it.

[18] R Kevelson, *The Law as a System of Signs* (New York, Plenum Press, 1988).

[19] H Kelsen, *La Théorie Pure du Droit* (Paris, Dalloz, 1953) at 85.

[20] F Gény, *Science et Technique en Droit Privé Positif* (Paris, Recueil Sirey, 1922) vol 1, at 235.

[21] H Bergson, *Oeuvres, Essai Sur Les Données Immédiates De La Conscience, Matière Et Mémoire, Le Rire, L'évolution Créatrice, L'énergie Spirituelle, Les Deux Sourcces De La Morale Et De La Religion, La Pensée Et Le Mouvant* (Paris, Presses Universitaires de France, 1930–59).

[22] H Welzel, *Derecho penal Aleman* (Buenos Aires, Editorial Depalma, 1985) and G Radbruch, *Derecho Legal y Derecho Supralegal* (Bogota, Temis, 1986).

However, this approach did not say anything about the role of the law and the dangers of positivist approaches under a totalitarian regime.[23] For Radbruch, on the other hand, the law could not be analysed as an autonomous structure, but should be analysed with reference to external values. To Radbruch there was a supralegality that determines the status of the law. This supralegality was established in the values of the Constitution or, in today's context, in the Universal Declaration of Human Rights.

The works on law of Robert Alexy and Jurgen Habermas can be seen in this light, that is, as an incorporation of non-legal elements in the discussion of the validity of law. Unlike Kelsen, Alexy and Habermas propose an argumentative theory of law in which the validity of law is given not only for the procedure of its production but also for its respect of a supralegal system, that is the universal conception of human rights. However what makes this approach different from the natural law tradition is the fact that these are not conceptual values but are incorporated in a higher law or in the spirit of democracy.[24] To Alexy, 'the law has to incorporate the argumentative and the institutional procedure of the application of the law into a theory of the democratic constitutional state.' In his interpretation of Habermas, he shows that the law is a case of the general practical discourse, that is, it is related to a democratic ethos and to moral practices of modern democracies.[25] Unlike natural law theories, these approaches to the law do not claim that the law is just another way of describing morality, but that the law is permeated by non-legal discourses and practices.

Other authors, like Niklas Luhmann, insist on the incorporation of the outside of the law into the language of the law. Outside elements can be incorporated as long as the language and the code of the law is preserved. To Luhmann, law and legal discourse cannot be permeated by or confused with the outside of law. On the contrary, law is a subsystem of the social system that has its own binary code, that is, lawful/unlawful (recht/unrecht) and it is under this code that everything is incorporated into the law. Law and particularly the legal system are autopoietic systems but not, as in the traditional theory of systems, closed systems. To say that the legal system is autopoietic means that the law creates and recreates itself, that its code is auto-reproductive, and that law imposes its own language whenever there

[23] I Muller, *Hitler's Justice, the Courts of the Third Reich* (Cambridge, MA, Harvard University Press, 1992).

[24] R Alexy, *The Argument From Injustice, A Reply To Legal Positivism* (New York/Oxford, Clarendon Press/Oxford University Press, 2002) 127; and *A Theory of Constitutional Rights* (New York, Oxford University Press, 2002). About Habermas: M Rosenfeld and A Arato (eds), *Habermas on Law and Democracy, Critical Exchanges* (Berkeley/Los Angeles/London, University of California Press, 1998) and J Habermas, *Between Facts and Norms, Contributions a Discourse Theory of Law and Democracy* (Cambridge, Mass, MIT Press, 1996).

[25] R Alexy, 'Jurgen Habermas's Theory of Legal Discourse' in Rosenfeld and Arato (eds), 1998, above n 24, at 232.

is a relation with its outside.[26] The outside of the law is its surroundings, but once within the law it has to adopt its binary code. As is clear, this particular approach to the law is the result of the modern understanding of the state and society and, as Wallerstein would say it, is the result of taking the nation-state as the unit of analysis.[27]

The Contamination of the Law with Politics

In the American tradition, perhaps the most important analysis of the law is that of the Realists. The works of Benjamin Cardozo and Oliver Holmes are seminal in the conception of the law as politics. Cardozo, whose work was based on the ideas of Francois Gény, proposed that law is not the result of the written word in the statute but the result of real life. The law has to be interpreted in relation to everyday life, to capture its contamination by morality and politics.

This approach has been followed in the American tradition by critiques of the law like the Critical Legal Studies Movement, the Constitutive Approach and the Legal Consciousness Studies. What makes these studies interesting for us is their understanding of the law as embedded in real life, as being something other than structure. But unlike the European tradition, this kind of analysis conceived the law as being contaminated from outside and as being something else (politics, etc). The European tradition, on the other hand, saw the outside of the law as a part of the law with proper codification.

The persistent conception of a legal order that is unified and definite excluded historical and sociological considerations. Law is a social phenomenon, and in order to be recognised by society, statutes have to be intelligible and easy to understand.[28] Hart's main preoccupation was the opacity of legal language, due to his idea that law is a system of rules, interconnected lexically and only able to be understood by legal experts. Only the system is capable of interpreting the system.

Hart's philosophy of language is based on a conventional view of the referent: this referent works as a function of the emitter's intent, and one affirmation is valid only when considered with the external world. The meaning of words depends, not only on the communication being transmitted, but also on the act and intent of the speaker.[29] This idea is in complete

[26] N Luhmann, *A Sociological Theory of Law* (London/Boston, Routledge and Kegan Paul, 1985) and P Gimenez Alcover, *El Derecho En La Teoria De La Sociedad De Niklas Luhmann* (Barcelona, Instituto de Criminologia de la Universidad de Barcelona, 1993).

[27] I Wallerstein, *The End of the World as We Know It: Social Science for the Twenty First Century* (Minneapolis, University of Minnesota Press, 1999).

[28] HLA Hart, 'A Description of Responsibility and Rights' in *Essays in Logic and Language* 146–66 (1963). *Definition and Theory in Jurisprudence* (London, Clarendon Press, 1953) at 116.

[29] HLA Hart, *The Concept of Law* (London, Oxford University Press, 1961) at 58.

contradiction to the traditional idea *per genus et differentiam*. When Hart considers the problems of interpretation, he remains in between formalism (core of settled meaning) and realism (the penumbra of uncertainty).

Hart was criticised because he adopted a theory of an ingenuous language where the signifier is a fixed entity with a central and peripheral clarity, independent from the context and from the use of concepts. However, in contradictory terms, Hart also proposed a theory of legal pragmatics where the signifier is purely conventional. Indeed, the existence of the '*core of settled meaning*' is based on the functioning of the legal system. This simply means that language does not have inherent qualities. Instead, its semantic characteristic is modified according to one's perception of it. The rules and its content are clear but the contingent effect of its use is not so visible. Indeed, the penumbra reflects the indeterminate feature of the object. Moreover, from time to time and from one case to another, the idea of the meaning of some terms as being 'settled' is questionable.

According to McCormick, the structure of legal language is formed by legal institutions which are governed by overarching rules. These are divided into three types of rules: institutive (the ones which create the institution); consequential (the consequences in law of the existence of such an institution); and terminative (those which lead to the disappearance of such institutions) rules. The legal system thus represented closely resembles the syntagmatic level described by Greimas:[30] the legal subjects evolve within a vital history represented by legal states (or consequential rules) and its transformations (or institutive and terminative rules). Such transformations are finalised by means of acts, and the person who carries them to an end is given qualification and obtains competence from them. This schema, in turn, parallels Hart's rule of recognition: the institutive and terminative rules recognised the examples of these institutions as legal in the processes known by Greimas as *vérification*. McCormick's point is without any doubt positivist, because it is based on the legal validity under which authority can be established. McCormick, however, explains that public and private institutions have the same structure with distinct contents, a matter which Hart did not address.

But one of the questions that remain in this discussion about the law is 'why do people obey the law?' To positivists, the law is obeyed because it is the law; that is, it is the command of the sovereign. To those from a Marxist tradition, the law is obeyed because, as a form of ideology, people are cheated into obedience.[31] Under the concept of hegemony, some scholars have found that the law is obeyed because people see in the law a source of legitimacy for the state but also the law is seen as an instrument to convey the claims of the oppressed.

[30] AJ Greimas, '*Analyse Sémiotique d'un Discours Juridique*' in *Sémiotique et Sciences Sociales* (Paris, Seuil, 1967).

[31] A Stone, 'The Place of Law in the Marxian Structure-Superstructure Archetype' (1985) 19(1) *Law and Society Review* 39; S Spitzer, 'Marxist Perspectives in the Sociology of Law' (1983) 9 *Ann Rev Sociol* at 103.

The law is a symbolic construction and therefore rests on a variety of undertakings. What gives law its meaning is, for some, ideology, for others, the welfare of the majority. However, what is manifest is a conception of the law as a material structure that carries symbols of everyday life. The analyses that are made in the law and semiotics movements show that the law's symbolism cannot be understood by reference only to itself, a strictly 'legal' meaning. It is a symbol that conveys life, a symbol that in itself is contaminated with life, politics, morality and so on. Law and semiotics is an obvious meeting point between traditions, because it is the place where all the discussions about the law can find a common language.

II

CREATION OF THE INTERNATIONAL ROUND TABLES FOR THE SEMIOTICS OF LAW

The law and semiotics organisations are the result of the interests of scholars who wanted to analyse the law from different perspectives than those of the traditions of European and Anglo-Saxon jurisprudence. The International Round Table for the Semiotics of Law, like the merging of the studies of law and language, is itself a garden of forking paths. It has a history born of the merging of two distinct but clearly related traditions.

Bernard Jackson was the key figure in the more Greimasian oriented International Association for the Semiotics of Law (IASL). With Bernard Jackson's exceptional energy, drive and vision, the Association also began the International Journal for the Semiotics of Law (IJSL), along with Eric Landowski. Indeed, Eric Landowski's influence has also been felt in the International Journal for the Semiotics of Law being listed in English and French, and in welcoming articles and book reviews written in French. When Dragan Milovanovic became the editor of the IJSL, he tried to stay within the direction of the journal as envisioned by Bernard Jackson (with some input by Eric Landowski and Roberta Kevelson) and build on his predecessors, each of whom had made tremendous strides in the quality of the journal. His own emphasis was to expand the contributions of articles by world-wide authors. Indeed, there has been a considerable increase of more internationally oriented authors. And at least one issue per year is a special issue.

Roberta Kevelson was to be the key figure of the more Peircean oriented Round Table for Law and Semiotics. No formal journal was begun, but Roberta was to edit an annual collection of papers of the meetings, sponsored by Peter Lang Publisher under the title, Semiotics and the Human Sciences.[32]

[32] Amongst them: R Kevelson (ed), *Flux, Complexity, and Illusion, Sixth Round Table on Law and Semiotics* (New York, Peter Lang, 1992); R Kevelson (ed), *Conscience, Consensus, and Crossroads in Law, Eighth Round Table on Law and Semiotics* (New York, Peter Lang, 1993).

Even though each organisation was focused on a key philosopher in semiotics, other persuasions were encouraged in the annual meetings. Roberta Kevelson was very much like Bernard Jackson in terms of being the charismatic leader of the association. Her incredible energy, scholarly insights, support for scholars, and good humor was to make her the charismatic leader of the Roundtables.

Each organisation had an annual meeting or conference. Roberta held hers in the USA, in Reading, Pennsylvania. Bernard had his mostly in Europe. Some presenters were members of both groups. Usually, each meeting witnessed 15–22 presenters. These meetings were the occasions for incredibly intensive discussions. And most important, the exceptional energy of both Bernard Jackson and Roberta Kevelson was the key for the continuance of each organisation. Both were innovators, were 'movers', were setting history, were defining the contours of a new discipline, the 'semiotics of law.' And each was an exceptional international scholar.

A key period was when Bernard Jackson transferred the duties of publishing his various journals to Kluwer Academic Publishing Co. The energy and drive that he had was missed immediately. John Brigham at the University of Massachusetts at Amherst picked up Roberta's organisation when Roberta passed away from a heart attack. Maarten Henket was to preside over the International Association for the Semiotics of Law. Whereas the Round Tables had a hiccup and continued in the format started by Roberta, the IASL began to lose some cohesion.

At this time, concerned about the future of the IASL and also thinking in terms of institutionalising the two organisations around the ideas of its founders rather than on the founders themselves, Dragan Milovanovic (current Editor of the International Journal for the Semiotics of Law) initiated various discussions with Maarten Henket and John Brigham as to a more radical solution to the future of both organisations: a merger.

Initially, each organisation chose to continue in their independent directions. However, two years later it seemed evident that perhaps much more could be accomplished by having a merged organisation. Numerous discussions among the three of them took place along with others in each of the two organisations. After several months of discussion, they agreed to merge. The name would be 'The International Roundtable for the Semiotics of Law'. The title was an attempt to include components of each organisation.

On the drafting board were the following ideas, many of which are still being worked out: that they would rotate Presidents from Europe to America and back to Europe; that the annual conference would rotate every year from Europe to America and back to Europe; that a 6-member advisory/coordinating committee would be put in place; that one issue of the journal, of the four per year, would include selected papers from the annual conference with perhaps the current President being the Special

Issue Editor; that an annual edited book would include other papers on semiotics of law; and that at some point, by-laws would be written (regarding elections, time in office, etc). They also agreed to include IJSL as the official journal of the new organisation. Finally, at the meeting that has led to this collection, there was a commitment to ensuring that the group had a truly international make-up. This collection, for example, includes papers, not only from Europe and North America, but also from South America and Australia and includes a paper on Chinese law.

III

THIS COLLECTION: CONTEMPORARY ISSUES ON THE SEMIOTICS OF LAW

In Goodrich's book, one sentence summarises the ideas presented at the First International Round Tables for the Semiotics of Law in 2002, Oñati (Spain):

> The question of language, which must now be taken to include all the other systems of signs—of architecture, dress, geography, ceremony, aura and technology—that accompany legal tradition, that prejudge the text as a legal text, the spoken word as the word of the law, that question of language is the question of the institution.

This collection of papers investigates the institution of the law, in combination with, and as part of, a multiplicity of sign systems. If further themes can be developed around the broad focus of law and semiotics, they are, perhaps, that: firstly, law be understood as part of a global system of meaning; and, secondly, that despite the homogenising threat of globalisation, the play of legal meaning retains a socio-historical specificity. The global issues of human migration (Duncanson), human rights (Mooney), colonisation (Lippens), and the transnational power of the celebrity (Brigham and Meyers), are played out in local spaces, in the public discourses through which they are given localised representation (Cacciaguidi), in moments of activism (Lorenz), and as a tool of subversion (Pencak). The law is a rhetorical device which at once constitutes these global and local truths but which is also constituted by them.

Interpretation and Pertinence of Law in the Global Age

We live in times of globalisation. To some, from a neoliberal perspective, this is a new era in which the world has, for the first time, become truly global. To others, from a Marxist perspective, this is just a new wave of globalisation, since capitalism has inherently been of a global character since its beginnings. Whatever perspective we take, and there are consequences for the analysis, it is important to take into account the role of the law in these times of globalisation. One of the aspects of this period is the global character of capital, communications and legal instruments. But another aspect, which is analysed by one of the contributors of this volume, is the global movement of people in huge numbers. This results, in part, from the colonial history of some of their countries of origin. As some of the immigrants hold, 'we came here, because you went there'. New questions are raised by global migration: for example, the role of immigration laws, and the symbols that are behind the attraction of some countries as places of immigration. In these times, symbols become global, and the law, as a system of symbols, needs to talk in a global language if it is to achieve its purpose of being obeyed in this wider context. This global language includes symbols of immigration, danger, terrorism, human rights, and constitutionalism. These are made common through their use in everyday life. Celebrities play a central role in the everyday communication of the law. The articles of this section illustrate some of the global dimensions of the law.

In *Refugee Meanings,* Ian Duncanson analyses how the meaning of refugee has been constructed in the official discourse in Australia. He shows how this concept has become a negative one, from representing the protection of a population in need of civilisation, to a conception of the refugee as a disease, as the Other we do not want to have in our midst. Quoting Lacan, the constitution of the object can only be seen at the level of the concept, and that is precisely what he does.

In this article, Duncanson shows that in Victorian England the persecuted foreigner was seen as deserving refuge, who belonged to a race that could benefit from the civilising mission of the white man. This was the white man's burden, to protect and educate people from those races. The goal was to reform, to discipline, to incorporate the foreigners, via homogenisation, into the already unified concept of the British nation. However this meant racial purity and that is why some people, who were considered too different to be incorporated, were left outside, as a sign of the insiders' unity. As Duncanson writes:

> The view that ethnic difference or multiplicity signalled danger to political and cultural integrity was made popular in late nineteenth Australia. Aborigines and 'Chinamen' and cheap colored labor could not be constituted Australian.

The Chinese were constituted as the signifiers of the Other, of what was not-Australian. The author shows how the Australian working class received this new meaning of foreigners, and how they incorporated them in their perception of otherness.

According to Duncanson, this language of inclusion/exclusion was used to read the situation of refugees and the new term of 'asylum seekers.' As a result, these new foreigners are not considered as deserving protection, and they are now treated as a military threat, as a danger to the unified Australian nation. The refugees are left in the border, where they cannot contaminate the Australian nation. Duncanson shows how new languages, new meanings and new concepts determine not only the way we perceive reality but also the way we act according to that new perception.

In a similar vein, Annabelle Mooney's *Citizens, Immigrants, Anarchist and Other Animals* is an analysis of different narratives about human rights, which shows that the understanding of such rights can be based on the dehumanisation of subjects. Human rights are not just legal instruments; they can be rhetorical tools and instruments of political negotiation but they can also justify oppression. Mooney's article shows that the way human rights are constructed can be used for controlling immigration or criminalising protesters.

In *The Dialogistic Nature of Brazil's Arbitration Law 9.307/96*, Celina Frade analyses legislation as genre and shows that the law is a dialogue of many voices. This approach seeks to show the connections between genre, language, and context. By analysing Brazilian law, Frade treats the law as a literary text, introducing insightful ideas about the role of the law in Brazilian society as well as in the global community.

In *Constitutional 'Communarchy': A Constitution with Chinese Characteristics*, Deborah Cao analyses Joseph Raz's theory about the nature of a Constitution with particular emphasis on the Chinese case. After analysing the meaning that a constitution has in China and the limitations to its development due to the specific institutional arrangements of the Chinese government, Cao shows the links existing between liberal democracy and constitutionalism. In this paper, she shows that the transition to democracy cannot be understood just as the transformation of old institutions into new democratic ones, but that it is necessary to take into account the local culture of law and its dialectic with western institutions. In a world where liberal democracy and western ways of life are becoming dominant, it is useful to see the negotiation and new meanings that this concept acquires in a new context.

In *The Quest for Certainty in Recent US Constitutional Scholarship*, Frederick Lewis analyses the doctrine of original intent that is dominant in the conservative bloc of the US Supreme Court. According to this doctrine, in the interpretation of the Constitution the interpreter has to follow closely the original intention of the founding fathers. Instead of imposing his own conceptions about policies in some areas, the constitutional judge has to appeal to the intention that the founding fathers had when they drafted the Constitution. However, as Lewis shows, this doctrine assumes that it is possible to know the intentions of the drafters of the Constitution and that in practice there is rarely investigation into the original intention of the drafters. When there is, the final interpretation is contrary to the meaning of the Constitution. This work is reminiscent of Bakhtin's ideas about interpretation, when he said that once a text is written it does not belong to its author, and of Jauss's hermeneutic of reception.[33]

In *Celebrity and Authority in Law*, John Brigham and Jill Meyers analyse the role of celebrities in our understanding of the law. Unlike the positivist tradition that sees the state as the source of the law and the realist one that sees judges as the source of law, Brigham and Meyers show how our image of law is usually mediated through media and particularly through the statements and actions of celebrities.

In *Writing Around the Censor: Gypsies, Thieves, and Rebels in Early Modern Spain,* William Pencak shows the strategies adopted by early Spanish writers to avoid the gaze of the censor. In a country of vast contradictions the literature was no different. Though the Spanish Inquisition of the seventeenth century sought to censor writing, the result was the development of a mastery of language to disguise the writers' calls for revolt. Many masterpieces, in literature and visual art, arose from the tension. Pencak uses Greimasian and Peircean semiotic analysis and subaltern studies to examine three lesser known examples of the period: two of Cervantes' *Exemplary Stories,* 'The Little Gipsy Girl' and 'Rinconete and Cortadillo' published in 1613; and Lope de la Vega's play *Fuente Ovejuna* written between 1611 and 1618. As with so many of the papers in this collection Pencak's work is a reminder of the indexical potential of a sign, notwithstanding the restraints imposed by relevant systems of authority. In these Spanish classics, legality can stand in for non-legality, illegitimacy for legitimacy, outlaw for valor, ordinary people for heroes and heroes for brutes.

Cultural and Symbolic Analyses of the Law in Context

One of the main characters of the law is its ability to constitute the world. We know that the law is just a creation of men, but it is important to remember that it is a creation with a particular life. As some of the authors of this section show, when the law regulates a particular field, it is, at the same time, constituting it so that it may regulate it in a legal way. In this section we will see some of the ways in which the law is related to its context but also, and this is more important, the centrality of the law in the constitution of its field of operation. We see that many of the themes associated with globalisation become implicated in the law's rhetorical practice at a local level. In addition, they provide the symbols for localised moments of resistance and subversion, generating meaning production within localised contexts.

[33] M Bakhtin, *Teoria Y Estetica De La Novela, Trabajos De Investigacion* (Madrid, Taurus, 1989) and HR Jauss, *Aesthetic Experience And Literary Hermeneutics* (Minneapolis, University of Minessota Press, 1989).

In *Subversion in the World Order*, Joanna Jemielniak discusses the role of rhetorical practices in the law. In this article, she shows how we live in a rhetorical world; that is, rhetoric is an instrument for persuasion. In this analysis, the law is not just a tool that people use to convince other people about their claims, it is *the* rhetorical tool: it is not part of rhetoric, it *is* rhetoric. The law is not only the cold structure we find in legal logic, it is a literary text that has to be analysed in a hermeneutic way. As a literary text, the law tells us things about our world; it is not the command of the sovereign anymore, but the expression of our lives.

This conception of the use of rhetoric is seen in the case of abortion in Ireland. In *The Substantive Issue and the Rhetoric of the Abortion Debate in Ireland*, Sophie Cacciaguidi tells us how the legal concept of the 'substantive issue' is a term invented as a rhetorical tool in the debate on abortion in Ireland. By using rhetorical topos as legal concepts, the law reifies the world and presents it as the real world. Therefore, there is no need to convince, only a need to command. Through reification of the world by rhetorical means, the law creates a world and presents it as real. The law, as in Borges' tales, talks about a world that does not exist except through assuming its reality, thus making it real.

In *Wealth of Terms*, Richard Foley analyses the issues involved in attempting to ensure that the legislation of the European Union remains accessible in the language of the nationals of each country. This shows that the intelligibility of legislation lies not only in the art of translation and command, but also in questions of the negotiation of meaning between the different actors in the process of production and enforcement of the law.

Richard Mohr writes about coats of arms as full of meaning and as symbols of power in *Enduring Signs and Obscure Meanings: Contested Coats of Arms in Australian Jurisdictions*. Mohr shows that these coats change their meaning with the passing of time and with the context in which they are inscribed. That is, it is not enough to read the symbol in an internal way but also it is necessary to read through the context in which the symbol is presented and used. In his analysis of coat of arms in Australia, Mohr shows the associations that can exist between power and the object that symbolises it.

In *Critical Race Reggae: The Sound of a Narrative,* Aaron Lorenz analyses the law from a critical race perspective. Through the use of reggae music, Lorenz shows that this music conveys in a better way the message of the repulsion with racism and optimism for change than we find in Critical Race theories. In this text, he shows that in the rhythm of reggae music and in its lyrics, particularly in the songs of Bob Marley, there are similarities in structure and message and a firm faith in overcoming racism and eliminating oppression.

Ronnie Lippens considers British law from an Orientalist point of view in his chapter, *Cromer's Olde England and the Dome's New Britain.* Using

Cromer's images of the Empire, Lippens analyses British law and the new Dome as images of what is called 'Englishness.' He compares old and new England and shows how the New England and its images, like the New Dome, are expressions of an ex-Empire that aspires to regain its lost strength.

The emergence of a multidisciplinary approach to legal rhetoric, including visual imagery as a modern form of rhetoric, provided the platform for Christina O Spiesel, Richard K Sherwin and Neal Feigenson to develop a course 'Visual Persuasion in the Law.' Their chapter, *Law in the Age of Images: the Challenge of Visual Literacy* explains the development and outcomes of this course. In an era of interdisciplinarity, meaning-making and construction becomes more complex because of the plurality of available interpretative screens. Mass mediated images have permeated all facets of our culture, including law and legal practice, and visual imagery has provided an additional means of legal communication. 'Visual Persuasion in the Law' sought to provide students with the ability to both deploy and critically analyse visual imagery within the constraints and demands of legal argumentation. In this chapter, the writers set the scene of a space in which law and visual culture are mutually implicated. They then lead us through the work of the students and finally embark on an explanation of the methods employed to permit students to explore this world of 'polysemy and uncertainty.'

This is a collection of different essays in which the law is analysed using semiotics as the meeting points. It also shows that the semiotic approach seeks to recreate new ideas in more complex dimensions through more dynamic methods. As in Scherezada's story, this is the centre where all meet to open new paths of reflection about the law.

Part I

The Interpretation and Pertinence of Law in the Global Age

1

Refugee Meanings

IAN DUNCANSON

We do not enquire whether they be democrats or aristocrats, French, Italian or Austrian, Buonapartists or Legitimists.... We only know them to be friendless and miserable (Back Bench British MP, 1870s).

To the starving organ grinder and broom girl, the land of refuge is open to all (Foreign observer, 1870s).[1]

I

INTRODUCTION

HOW HAS THE meaning of the refugee been constructed in the story that has come to dominate official statements in Australia and those of the conservative leaders of opinion in the media? Every story, as we know, has its origins in a kind of authorial violence, one that wrests it from its background, orders it and determines that it shall take one course rather than another, contain characters of a certain quality and provenance and not others. Unexplored, therefore to that extent suppressed, alternatives remain, like refugees, traces for the reader to discover in the interstices of the text. The practice of defining, which forms an important component in official discourse,[2] typically adopts a narrative style in which the reader's authority is dependent, and in which the narrator as an un-positioned observer occludes alternative perspectives by appearing apodictically to name the world as it is. This privileged meaning determines whether or not the reader has 'understood' the text as a competent reader. But as Lacan has remarked, 'if we try to grasp in language the constitution of the object, we cannot fail to notice that this constitution is only to be found at the level of the concept,' which is always contestable as a readerly activity.[3]

[1] Quoted in B Porter, *The Refugee Question in Mid-Victorian Politics* (Cambridge, Cambridge University Press, 1979), at 2.

[2] F Burton and P Carlen, *Official Discourse: On Discourse Analysis, Government, Ideology and the State* (London, RKP, 1979) is still the classic Anglophone text in this area.

[3] J Lacan, *Ecrits: A Selection* (New York, Norton, 1977), at 150.

This paper is the third in a series concerned with different aspects of the meanings given in Australia by recent conservative federal governments and their media supporters to those who wish to seek asylum here without having first waited in squalid camps in, say Iran or Pakistan. As good positivists, government spokespersons and their media apologists first find a method that will ground the conclusion they wish to reach; and on this occasion the method involves s/citing the appropriate knowing observer, a person one has learned to think of as 'the ordinary Australian'—taking the lead from John Howard, the 2002 Prime Minister of Australia, who holds no aspiration higher than the avocation of ordinariness.[4]

The focus of the first paper was on the anxieties produced by the idea—clearly projected, for example, by repeated assertions of sovereignty, of the illegitimacy of UN human rights committees' criticism of Australian domestic policies—of the Australian nation state as nothing if not a bounded container of interior homogeneity; moreover, one perpetually threatened with loss of identity by the culturally and ethnically different outsider who persists in seeking entry and whose intrusion must be repelled to maintain the body's integrity. The paper noticed that the culture of fear of difference originating from an apparent *outside*, a culture circulating with sometimes more, sometimes less influence during Australia's short history, seemed, among other consequences, to produce an exaggeration and an elision of that *within* which cannot be the same. Aboriginal Australians, white culture's guilty secret, feature there in a narrative contradiction symptomatic of repressed guilt. On behalf of contemporary Europeans, this (white) narrative denies that later non-Aboriginal generations share any responsibility with those who preceded them for the theft of Aboriginal land that accompanied the European invasion; or for the theft of children from Aboriginal families, and their attempted destruction of Aboriginal culture during the period of attempted assimilation; or for the effects of those practices on the condition of Aborigines in the present. At the same time, however, the white story celebrates the 1915 defeat by the Turks, of the British Imperial Australia-New Zealand Army Corps at Gallipoli, as a defining national moment, an important part of a heritage to be shared by all who wish to be considered truly Australian.

In mining company propaganda of the 1980s,[5] and Prime Ministerial rhetoric twenty years later,[6] Aborigines threaten both back-yards and

[4] One may cite this mythical creature, having first sited him in a subject position with certain prospects. In a well-known cartoon, Leunig, a popular cartoonist for the Melbourne *Age*, told the story of the sighting of an ordinary Australian 'by a tourist at about 11:15 PM on Monday night' in a desolate area east of the city now rendered a secret by expert investigators: *Age* 19 April 2002.

[5] R Libby, *Hawke's Law: The Politics of Mining and Aboriginal Land Rights in Australia* (Perth, WA, UWA Press, 1990).

[6] A Markus, *Race: John Howard and the Remaking of Australia* (Sydney, Allen and Unwin, 2001).

back-grounds,[7] as the symbolic order re-constituting the subject of white Australia seems to regress to the colonial fantasy in which land was always at risk of seizure by non-Europeans. Contemporary claims by Aborigines for land rights, which are, of course, at the same time an insistence on black presence and identity, reawakens among non-indigenous Australians a guilt that is displaced on to an irrational fear about the security of suburban freeholds.[8] Ironically, the unarticulated but clear representation of the European-Australian body politic as masculine—that is, as bounded, autonomous, internally homogenous and ordered—has led to the gestation at the level of national consciousness of something quite different. The penetrating fantasy of a potent outsider—from the non-European diaspora to the apparatus of international human rights agencies—has created a pregnant awareness of something within.

The second paper[9] questioned whether the recent official response to seaborne arrivals in Australia, frequently in recent years members of persecuted groups from Afghanistan and the middle east traveling via Indonesia, might be seen psychoanalytically as a form of hysteria, given its curious lack of proportion to the small numbers of people making or intending to make landfall on the continent. Apprehension about the destruction of the self—in this case a self-estimate, at least, of a tolerant, relatively free society—may be in danger of accomplishing its own destruction—the promotion of xenophobia, suspicion and draconian internal and external security legislation. The nation-self appeared, from this perspective, as a kind of security blanket at risk, an indispensable comforter in a bewilderingly complex world, but one now threatened with confiscation by a selfish thief. Or, to put it in a more theoretically refined way, the nation might figure as a Lacanian *object*, a substitute for lost belonging, or the particular form taken by an inevitable obstacle to the return to Being and wholeness with the world, one whose enjoyment by the subject was about to be stolen. Only a moral reprobate or a criminal intending the theft of something priceless could justify the vituperation one hears from government ministers and, in official pronouncements, in which the refugee/asylum seekers are exactly who they need to be: blackmailers, bad parents, and economic refugees, profiteers at the expense of the Australian purse.[10]

[7] The threat posed to the imago of Anglo-Celts by re-visiting the issues raised by European invasion and the dispossession of Aboriginal people is discussed in M Dixon, *The Imaginary Australian: Anglo-Celts and Identity—1788 to the present* (Sydney, UNSW Press, 1999), at ch 5.

[8] Land subject to freehold and even most leasehold title is legally exempt from indigenous land claims.

[9] I Duncanson, 'Telling the Refugee Story: the "Ordinary Australian", the State of Australia' (2003) XIV *Law and Critique* at 29–43.

[10] In conservative discourse, there are 'real' refugees, who are perceived as requiring first to serve their apprenticeship as asylum seekers. In contrast, one can be branded an 'economic', fake, refugee, without qualification.

In the symbolic order of the ordinary Australian who inhabits the common sense nation state of official discourse, the coherence of which might be rendered problematic by an influx of uninvited and culturally diverse people, it is not necessary to add 'to whom?' to questions about the meaning of refugee/asylum seekers. The character and opinion of the reader can be subsumed into the privileged voice of the author. The danger asylum seekers represent is precisely to the shared culture that makes the additional question, the possibility of a diversity of readerships, unnecessary to contemplate. However, it is worth examining the homogeneity implied by this shared culture, which is asserted in order, specifically, it seems, to be placed in jeopardy by handfuls of brown people in small wooden boats.

II

CLASS AND MEANING

Without examining the practical application in Victorian Britain of the sentiment expressed by the member of the House of Commons in the introductory quotations, or the accuracy of the foreign observer's description, the meaning system in play seems clear, especially in light of Europe's perception of Britain at that time as wealthy, powerful and tolerant, and mid-Victorian Britain's (bourgeois) perception of its bourgeois self as a nation under whose matchless constitution liberty, property and the rule of law were exceptionally secure. The persecuted foreigner, rich or poor, deserves refuge. The strong, free nation that provides refuge is thereby additionally admirable. Marx might work impoverished but unhindered in the British Museum; Napoleon III might repose in a more affluent exile on a country estate. It is tempting to contrast this Christian parable of the gift—of hospitality to those in need—elevating the giver, with the Hobbesian anxieties through which the meaning of the refugee and the nation are inflected in the decades spanning the turn of the twentieth into the twenty first century. In other texts, contemporary with the quotations above, the bourgeois Victorian Englishman may understand 'foreign' to mean 'less fortunate' or, if we think of TB Macaulay's or John Stuart Mill's pedagogical plans for India, to signal persons or 'races' in need of British instruction in rationality, judgement and political wisdom.[11] But foreigners did not seem for the English gentlemen positioned as author or reader to signify quite the danger of contamination, engulfment or the extinguishment of the

[11] TB Macaulay, Speech to the House of Commons, 10 July 1833 on the government of India, in TF Ellis (ed), *Macaulay's Miscellaneous Letters and Speeches* (London, Longmans Green, 1889), at 572; JS Mill, *Representative Government*, D Thompson (ed) (Princeton NJ, Princeton University Press, 1976).

host's culture that they seem to signify in refugee narratives a century and more later.[12]

Tensions are nevertheless visible in nineteenth-century British texts, however, between the English, the not (or not yet) English and the un-English. One has only to think of that fantasy-symptom of the subordination and denial of the feminine and the native, the gothic or fearsome, hideous other of popular literature, from Conan Doyle to Bram Stoker.[13] James Vernon shows how the three categories, of English, non- and un-English, played out in the narratives of Macaulay, Maitland and Stubbs about the British constitution.[14] In the shadow of the Indian insurrection of 1857, the Jamaican rebellion at Morant Bay in 1865, agitations by working class men and feminists for the vote, and Irish 'terrorism'. Stubbs in particular, Vernon writes, was anxious to define out of the constitution of England those whose 'paternity' was not traceable to the folk customs of ancient Germanic forests. Commenting ironically on this tradition, in which the catholic Irish were not included in the celebrated constitutional 'ability of the Englishman to do as he likes,' Matthew Arnold doubted, too, that this conception of the matchless constitution could guarantee order once the British 'populace'—the working class—gained access to political participation. Strict discipline (for Arnold, in all senses of the term) and rigorous behavioral entry conditions to this constitution, principally the inculcation of culture and discipline at various social levels, would be necessary if 'sweetness and light' were to be achieved.[15] As with prisons, where the goals were both reform of the prisoner and protection of the public,

> so, too, in schools, the State has another interest besides the encouraging of reading writing and arithmetic—the protection of society...[16]

keeping disorder off the streets whilst curing the unruly tendencies of those who embodied it. Included in the white man's burden was the duty to teach exotic natives the meaning of who they were, God's children wanting the civilisation of their imperial pedagogues. The interior others, too, the subjects of new discourses about intelligence, criminality, charity and more,

[12] For British Minister, Peter Hain, not only do Muslims endanger western ways of life by refusing to assimilate, thus providing terrorist recruiting possibilities, but dark skinned members of the EU itself, governments bordering the Mediterranean, also do so with their less rigorous immigration controls: *Independent on Sunday* 19 May 2002.

[13] K Hurley, *The Gothic Body: Sexuality, Materialism and Degeneration at the Fin de Siecle* (Cambridge, Cambridge University Press, 1996); HL Malchow, *Gothic Images of Race in Nineteenth-Century Britain* (Stanford, Stanford University Press, 1996).

[14] J Vernon, 'Narrating the Constitution' in J Vernon (ed), *Re-Reading the Constitution: New Narratives in the Political History of England's Long Nineteenth Century* (Cambridge, Cambridge University Press, 1996).

[15] M Arnold, *Chaos and Anarchy*, JD Wilson (ed) (Cambridge, Cambridge University Press, 1960).

[16] M Arnold, quoted in C Baldick, *The Social Mission of English Criticism* (Oxford, Oxford University Press, 1983), at 34.

required to be taught: teaching 'them' about order, civilisation, decency keeps safe 'our' heritage:

> the working class was seen as the object for colonisation by its cultural superiors in order that 'respectable' members of the class be separated from the 'rough' residue, and the leaders of the class be made fit for a limited role in governing ... In this process, any shadows of socialist organisation were to be dispersed by the radiance of a common culture and heritage.[17]

Victorian discourse on education assumes heterogeneity of behavior, demeanor and perception among classes, and for that reason establishes border controls on entry to the nation. If English working class outsiders were to be allowed inside, the condition was their assimilation to the cultural values of their superiors, and what better sign of this new virtuous synthesis around this heritage of Englishness than that all 'inside' classes should focus on signs of deficiency in outside others—Foucault's 'bad boys,' the rough working class, fallen women and the racially deficient—who might include morons, imbeciles and other categories in the taxonomies of Victorian psychology. This is the era of the penitentiary, the Charitable Organisation Society, the Contagious Diseases Acts and the eugenics movements. Australian elites were ahead of Britain in establishing a blended class of episodic political participants, even extending voting rights, the episodic sign of political citizenship, to women after federation. The virtuous heritage available to be shared and withheld as a mark of community values here was not a literary canon, an ancient history or a matchless constitution, but racial purity. The view that ethnic difference or multiplicity signaled danger to political and cultural integrity was made popular in late nineteenth century Australia. Aborigines and 'Chinamen' and 'cheap colored labor' could not be constituted Australian.

In Stuart McIntyre's account,[18] the late colonial bourgeoisie saw business possibilities in a federation of the five colonies, which could erect tariffs against overseas manufactures. The colonial working class, by contrast, bruised by unsuccessful struggles with employers, did not share this enthusiasm. What did interest them, though, was to gain for their corner of Empire an exemption—which federation seemed to promise—from Imperial policies of the free movement of peoples within the Empire, and especially from British treaty undertakings to permit access to the Empire to Chinese subjects.

Cheap Chinese labor could be, and sometimes had been, used by employers to undermine the bargaining power of the white working class,

[17] B Doyle, *English and Englishness* (London, Routledge, 1989), at 18. The primary school text which inaugurated the journey of Margaret Drabble's protagonist from the provincial lower middle class into her metropolitan heritage forms the title of Drabble's novel, *The Radiant Way* (Harmondsworth, Penguin, 1988).

[18] S MacIntyre, *A Concise History of Australia* (Melbourne, Cambridge University Press, 1999), at 139–40.

and continued to represent a threat to them for this reason. But the question remains why this should be so in jurisdictions where wage rates and work conditions were heavily regulated by the state through courts of industrial arbitration.[19] The answer is that for the white man of the 1890s and early twentieth century, 'Chinese' was a signifier of dirt, disease, drug addiction and sexual promiscuity, characteristics disqualifying their signified subjects from entry into the constitutional, constituting zone of citizenship. Simultaneously, of course, the Chinese were recognised as frugal, honest, thrifty and hard working, habits for which they were feared as much as for their drug-induced torpor and lust. As Slavoj Zizek once observed in a discussion of ideology, the image of outsiders stealing our jobs merges so imperceptibly into the image of outsiders living off the fruits of our labor—they do both together—that we do well to be suspicious of both.

Meanings are not produced and circulated in a vacuum, texts are not read by passive recipients.[20] The 'readerly' as opposed to 'writerly' character of texts, whether, that is, they operate to open or close off possible meanings, is itself a function of the context of their reception.[21] The negative meaning of 'the Chinaman' among Australian social elites—the employers who paid them lower wages than white men, the political and legal leaders who supported discrimination against them[22]—received an uncritical reception from a working class anxious to gain inclusion in the polity on the ground of racial purity. Texts, Derrida indicates of his usage:

> do not exclude the world, reality, history, the text is not the book, it is not confined in a volume, in itself confined to the library. It does not suspend reference—to history, to the world, to reality, to being.[23]

Texts are always in context when we gain some awareness of the positioning which enables us to notice. As an important kind of context, class as a site for the production of the textual meaning of the nation should not be overlooked merely because of the premature abandonment of Marxist writing. We do not have to suppose that belief is 'read off' from a social class position, or that a 'true' homogeneous class interest can be discerned once the distortions of ideology imposed by a dominant class are transcended.

[19] Of a period only a little later, the era of the 1914–18 war, one notices how the meaning of the laborer as a member of the international working class united against capitalism was eclipsed.

[20] See P Fuery and N Mansfield, *Cultural Studies and Critical Theory* (Melbourne, Oxford University Press, 2000), at ch 3: 'The Readerly Question'.

[21] T Hawkes, *Structuralism and Semiotics* (London, Methnen, 1977). S Greenblatt, 'Towards a Poetics of Culture' in A Veeser (ed), *The New Historicism* (London, Routledge, 1989). See G Allen, *Intertextuality* (London, Routledge, 2000), at 76–89.

[22] H Irving, *To Constitute a Nation: A Cultural History of Australia's Constitution* (Melbourne, Cambridge University Press, 1997), at 159; R Joyce, *Samuel Walker Griffith* (St Lucia, Qld, University of Queensland Press, 1984).

[23] J Derrida, *Limited Inc* (Evanston, IL, Northwestern University Press, 1976), 'Afterword'.

Of course 'Chinamen' could have been perceived more strategically as thrifty and honest, and they could have been included in the system of labor arbitration, possibly to the benefit of the white working class against whom they would not have been available as competitors; but not when they were the sign of working class belonging in the nation, when they were the necessary difference that signaled the sameness of white employees and white employers.

Similarly, the asylum seeker could be a victim or a prudent evader of persecution—and the volume of conservative propaganda from government and the media suggests that anti-asylum-seeker hostility is frequently hard to maintain—but not perhaps when s/he performs the role of the federation era Chinese, and indeed more. For the notion of nation that anti-refugee discourses help sustain provides a vicious and self-sustaining circle of global exploitation by the north of the south. Marx's reserve army of labor, as illegal migrant or 'guest' worker, makes German factories and Californian orchards economic, as sweated worker underwrites the profits of multinational corporations in Indonesia and China, and as 'rogue state' citizen in the new world order tests the efficacy of the latest 'smart' weapons in conflicts which, as Baudrillard remarked, are not wars.[24] Recognising the history of the nation's production in a class compromise that also draws upon psychically appealing practices of inclusion and exclusion may assist a move toward more constructive, less exclusionary and more humane practices.[25]

If it seems paradoxical that public discussion of class, and of the implications of the separation of the ownership and control of capital from those who serve capital with their labor, should have diminished at the very time when, in consequence of capital restructuring, intellectual workers confront serious losses of control over what they do, in schools, universities and in the media,[26] the reasons are clear enough. In the post-cold war era, 'we' no longer have to convince 'them,' or the undecided, that the west encourages more curiosity and permits more critical inquiry than the others. The pretence can be abandoned that free thought and technical and other forms of progress are necessarily associated.[27]

[24] J Baudrillard, *The Gulf War Did Not Take Place* (tr by P Patton) (Indianapolis, Indiana University Press, 1995): 'the Iraqis were electrocuted, lobotomised, running toward the television journalists ... or immobilised beside their tanks ... can this be called a war?' at 67–68.

[25] If the notion of propaganda seems naively out of place in a semiotic account—and see on this point the discussion of right wing think tank material, its circulation and 'disinformation' in P Bourdieu and L Wacqant, 'On the Cunning of Imperial Reason' (1999) 16 *Theory, Culture and Society* 41—there is now a large and respectable literature on government and private interventions designed to reorient politics and economics away from the relatively redistributive, welfare and egalitarian trends established after World War II, and their effects: See the literature cited in I Duncanson, 'Unchartered Lands in an Age of "Accountability"' (1997) III *Res Publica* 3; 'The Centre May not Hold' (2001) 8 *International Journal of the Legal Profession* 69.

[26] J Derrida, 'The University in the Eye of its Pupil' (1983) Fall *Diacritics* 3.

[27] See the contributions to B Brecher, O Fleischmann and J Halliday (eds), *The University in a Liberal State* (Aldershot, Avebury Press, 1996).

III

COMMUNITY, TRADITION

In considering the foreigner and especially the refugee narratives, important theoretical and even policy insights become themselves refugees when we ignore the heterogeneity with which class infuses meaning, possibly because we fail to reflect on two crucial implausibilities in the liberal writing that seems to predominate in the mainstream of opposition thought in a conservative era. Good examples of such writing are the texts of those paradigmatic progressive liberals, Ronald Dworkin and John Rawls. Dworkin articulates the belief—ultimately perhaps, derived from Hans-Georg Gadamer, that it is possible to attribute to the population that inhabits the territory of a single political state a homogeneous, if not immediately apparent, set of beliefs, making possible a synthesis capable of generating the famous 'right answer' in cases of legal disagreement, broadly defined.[28] In his *Theory of Justice*, Rawls' equally famous 'veil of ignorance' was designed to ground a procedure for which a consensus of rational people would exist, for generating agreement about the principles of social justice.[29]

Terry Eagleton questions Gadamer's

> enormous assumption that there is a single mainstream tradition ... that history forms an unbroken continuum and ... that the prejudices which we (who?) have inherited are to be cherished ... History for Gadamer is not a place of struggle, discontinuity and exclusion, but a 'continuing chain,' an ever-flowing river, almost, one might say, a club of the like-minded. (Gadamer) cannot come to terms with the problem of ideology—with the fact that the unending dialogue of human history is as often as not a monologue of the powerful to the powerless.[30]

Slavoj Zizek criticises Rawls' theory as, in effect, an unintentional replay of quantum mechanics, in which the epistemological impossibility is asserted of possessing all the values necessary for certain knowledge of the world. In *A Theory of Justice*, justice can be calculated if one does not know one's identity, place or time. But if one does know these kinds of characteristics about oneself, the calculation of justice is then impossible.[31]

The impulse to an ultimate homogeneity, self-presence and certainty, the conviction of Oneness, even as an aspiration, might be explained in the Lacanian terms of the mirror stage, 'a drama whose internal thrust is

[28] R Dworkin, *Taking Rights Seriously* (London, Duckworth, 1977); *Law's Empire*, (London, Collins, 1986).
[29] J Rawls, *A Theory of Justice* (Oxford, Oxford University Press, 1974).
[30] T Eagleton, *Literary Theory: An Introduction* (Oxford, Blackwell, 1983), at 72–73.
[31] S Zizek, *Enjoy Your Symptom! Jacques Lacan in Hollywood and Out* (New York, Routledge, 1992), at 70–71.

precipitated from insufficiency to anticipation'[32] in the production of the 'primordial I' as an Imaginary refuge from the horror of fragmentation. In legal discourse, from which liberalism draws much of its structure, parasitic as that discourse often is on the demands of the lawyer in the office or the courtroom, fragmentation and uncertainty yield to the strategic necessity of achieving a result within a constrained economy of disagreement; but when the disciplining out of contingency and uncertainty comes to govern theoretical as well as strategic concerns, dogma and eventually intellectual paralysis, inhibit the very practical activity of evaluating the politics and political effects of what one is doing.[33] We ask what the law is, or what it means, eliding the 'for whom?' 'for whose benefit?' 'to whose detriment?'[34] The signified's tendency always to slip under the signifier, is what, in the Lacanian observation, we cannot fail to notice'. But of course we can and do forget what we cannot fail to notice, losing the creative tension that Hume noticed, between the skepticism that promotes inquiry by focusing on contingency, and the certainty one requires to, as Wittgenstein phrased it, 'go on.'

To add the further, but not ever final, addition to the question that formed the beginning of the present discussion, or perhaps to look behind the beginning and ask why we took it to be the point of origin: what is the meaning to be attached to the figure of the asylum-seeker/refugee—*for whom*? S/he is the signified of certain discourses about the nation and the state,[35] but what does s/he signify in that discourse from the perspective of, say, (to invoke Brecht)[36] a worker who reads, the literate subject who neither owns nor controls capital?

[32] J Lacan 1977 above n 3 at 4.

[33] G Spivak draws a distinction between theory and practice on the one hand, as linked activities, and strategy, in which certain arguments or assumptions might be made with an awareness of their long term limitations. Thus, strategic, like other 'essentialism is like dynamite or a powerful drug; it can be effective in dismantling unwanted structures; uncritically employed it is destructive and addictive': Lee Phillip Sipiora and Janet Atwill, 'Toward a Productive Crisis: A Response to Gayatri Spivak' www.jac.gsu.edu/jac/10.2/Articles/S.htm (accessed June 2002).

[34] As G Allen puts it in relation to ideological texts: 'The fact that signified concepts become, in the differential system of language, signifiers for other signifieds, which themselves become signifiers, must be erased if official, or what Bakhtin calls monological discourse, is to do its ideological work.' G Allen, *Intertextuality* (London, Routledge, 2000), at 32.

[35] And these vary from the apocalyptic and machismo to the relatively humane: see the *Age* 24 June 2002: 'Europe's approach a rebuff to Howard and Ruddock,' commenting on the European Seville summit's rejection of a punitive approach to the illegal asylum-seeker situation, despite an annual arrival rate 100 times that experienced in Australia.

[36] This is the worker who noticed the aporias that made official narratives 'work': 'The young Alexander conquered India/ Was he alone?/ Caesar beat the Gauls/ Did he not even have a cook with him?' B Brecht, 'A Worker Reads History,' *Selected Poems*, quoted in A Arblaster, *The Rise and Decline of Western Liberalism* (Oxford, Blackwell, 1984), at 49.

IV

THE OFFICIAL POSITIONINGS OF THE ASYLUM SEEKER: FROM CRIMINAL TO ENEMY

The term 'asylum seeker' is widely used as an official locution to describe people whose claim to refugee status has received the imprimatur of neither the United Nations High Commission for Refugees, nor the country whose asylum they seek.[37] Investigating the legitimacy or otherwise of refugee claims is often expressed as 'processing.' In a manner familiar to readers of Foucault, it soon becomes in Immigration Department statements the body of the claimant rather than his or her claim that is understood as undergoing processing, substituting for people—the friendless and the miserable of the opening quotation—a-personal substances to be transformed through the knowing manufacture of others. Government refugee texts, then, are narratives in which certain subjects are visible as interlopers of dubious authenticity with few claims to dignified treatment, and in which certain official others appear as the guardians of truth—who truly belongs in this place, among the people for whom we speak?—and overriders and underwriters of humanity: after all, as Costas Douzinas observes, the outsider has no human rights.[38]

'Australia' appears in these refugee narratives as signified, present, complete, obvious. In its completeness, in contrast to the fragmented and scattered nature of the outsiders, lies its qualification to exclude. And exclusion here implies not only the barring of friendless subjects, but also, in order to give that practice the appearance of respectability, it implies also precluding, closing off the possibility that the Australia signified in the refugee narrative's signifying act might also be the signifier of something else—perhaps a neurotic symptom. Of what kind of neurotic symptom we have a clue. The body politic of the continent is, I have suggested, produced as masculine in most of the texts about it. It has attributed to it a rationalised unity, its interior is firmly differentiated from its outside, its boundaries lawfully impenetrable.[39] Klaus Theweleit's study of one particular literature in which masculine bodies are produced—that of the soldier males of the 1920s German Freikorps—finds manifest in it a fear of unexplored emotions 'within' the body that might hamper disciplined self-control, and of the outside (especially feminine) other that might threaten the subject's

[37] Interestingly, it seems only to be applied to predominantly brown people in predominantly white countries. One speaks, for example of 'refugee camps' in Pakistan and Iran, not 'asylum seeker camps'.

[38] C Douzinas, *The End of Human Rights: Critical Legal Thought at the Turn of the Century* (Oxford, Hart Publishing, 2000).

[39] I Duncanson, 'Mr Hobbes Goes to Australia: Law, Politics and Difference' (2000) 13 *International Journal for the Semiotics of Law* 279; 'The Racial (Re)turn: Coloring Human Rights in Australia' (2002) *Griffith Law Review* (forthcoming).

self-sufficiency.[40] Perhaps the textual privileging of the signified, Australia, in conservative and government literature about refugees, also signifies a neurotic anxiety that this body politic is not self-sufficient and in control, but is, actually, in-continent.

Two discrete but imbricated discourses about refugees have been produced by government policy, and supported by its conservative media allies. Beginning a decade or so ago, asylum seekers who arrived without visas were detained for the often long periods taken to determine their claims, subjected to degrading treatment in poor conditions, usually in remote camps in environmentally harsh areas. The theme of contagion forms a kind of matrix, the unarticulated center around which the policies were oriented. BSE ('mad cow disease'), foot and mouth disease and the unbid migration of Asian people, all seemed to require careful quarantining to avoid the pollution of the order within. Newly arrived people at the camps were separated from earlier detainees to prevent their thwarting the state's immune system by learning about the requirements of the UN Refugee Convention or the availability of legal advice and help. Distance, razor wire and high fences separated the regimes of confinement from domestic scrutiny, preventing the infection of officially delegated dis-infection procedures by humanitarian or civil rights discourses.

The alien character of the prisoners was emphasised in selective, sometimes deceptive, reports from government sources, reports often then amplified in the tabloid press, of bizarre, exotic behavior: the sewing together of lips during hunger strikes; self mutilation; the throwing of children into the sea and deliberate sinking of boats to 'blackmail' the navy into landing the families in Australia. Asylum seekers' faces, otherwise dangerous signs of common humanity with Australians, were ordered by the Defense department not to be displayed publicly in photographs under the department's jurisdiction. In these official narratives, the sewn-up can only be spoken for, the obscured face cannot be seen to see. There are chilling similarities, in the concealment of imprisoned subjects' bodies and the re-presentation of them in de-humanised forms, to the policies of fascist governments and the 'clash of civilisations' rhetoric which represents Islam in the popular media as a less evolved culture than that of the 'west.' The consequences, too, are similar. Thus the disbelief, among even educated and generally well-informed Australians, in the stories that lawyers and civil rights workers tell about brutality and treatment close to torture in the camps, results not merely from convictions about the tendency of Australians to decent (ie *decentia*: 'fitting') behavior but from the stories

[40] Klaus Theweleit, *Male Fantasies* (2 vols) (Minneapolis, University of Minnesota Press, 1987, 1989). The report of the UN special envoy on human rights, Justice Bhagwati (*Age* 2 August 2002) on the sub-prison conditions endured by detainees, including children, in the asylum-seeker detention camp at Woomera, South Australia, was condemned by federal government spokesmen and 'moderate' critics alike as 'unhelpfully' emotional.

about the in-decency (as the dictionary has it, the impropriety, or we might say, the lack of proper being (here)) of the prisoners. Bizarre behavior, bizarre treatment, try credulity and tire curiosity.[41]

The discourse of contamination by the un-Australian alien was successfully re-framed in August 2001—before the terrorist attacks on New York and Washington DC. Once designated criminals and associates of criminals and subjected to the regime of a private prison company, asylum seekers in late 2001 became a military threat, to be repelled from the country's boundaries by Australia's military. During the late 1990s, sporadic attempts had been made by the Immigration Department to conflate the phenomena from which asylum seekers sought escape—persecution, assassination and terror from state or state-approved sources—with the escapees themselves. If they had been drafted into the military in their home states, it was implied that they could well be terrorists, if they had been interrogated by the police in their country of origin, they were 'known to the security services.' People's provenance in disordered lands still implied contagion, but this re-framing converted from signs of the criminal law violated, to signs of imminent invasion. The conversion was complete when the events of August 2001 intersected with another re-framing, which had been under way since the new federal government took office in 1996. Until then, Australia had been an international 'good citizen',[42] encouraging NGO participation in UN human rights discussions and cooperating in the drafting of conventions. In the new government's reframing of the situation with particular reference to the ethnic origins of human rights committees,[43] Australia's potency and self-control is threatened by the invasive oversight of UN human rights committees and 'special interest group' NGOs whose evaluations and criticisms of government policy cross the frontiers that demarcate sovereign self-possession. Interestingly, much of the media work preparing this new direction has

[41] As the old Tom Paxton song has it, 'We didn't know,' said the burgomeister/ 'About the camps on the edge of town ... We heard the cattle cars, it's true/ And maybe they carried a Jew or two/They woke us up as they rattled through/ But what did you expect us to do?.. ': Tom Paxton, 'We Didn't Know,' on 'Ain't That News' Elektra Records (1965). See R Manne, 'The tragedy of indifference,' *Age* 24 June 2002: The Australian navy knew that a grossly overloaded boat 'in poor condition,' according to Coastwatch intelligence sources on 18 October 2001, was on its way from Indonesia to Australian waters, but no search and rescue mission was initiated. 353 people died, 44 were rescued by Indonesian fishing boats on 23 October 2001. Defence's 'callous indifference' to Middle Eastern asylum seekers is plain from its inaction, Manne writes. On 22 October 2001, its only action was to note that the boat must have sunk: He quotes the Navy taskforce memorandum of that date concerning the boat: 'Not spotted yet, missing, grossly overloaded, no jetsam spotted...' .

[42] See the discussion in A Markus, 2001 above n 6 at 108 and following.

[43] *Age* 4 1 2000: the Foreign Minister drew attention to the committee's including Pakistani, Cuban, Ecuadorian, Chinese and Romanian members. At one level the objection seems to be that these countries have poor human rights records. At another level, since technically the members are there, not as representatives of their governments' policies, but of the UN, the Minister's unease seemed connected to ethnicity and the impropriety of brown people criticising white governments' treatment of other brown people—Aborigines and refugees.

been done by writers also obsessed with the necessity for restoring traditional patterns of domestic authority, asserting, for example, the unnatural lives experienced by children bereft of mothers (because mothers work) or of fathers (because mothers have driven them away by initiating divorce); and the silencing by censorship (castration) of men by feminists unnaturally occupying public space.[44]

In August 2001, asylum seekers in this frame of events spearheaded a violation of Australia by UN committees, unrepresentative NGOs and ignorant and often ethnically inappropriate foreign critics. A Norwegian container ship, the Tampa, rescued more than 400 men, women and children, mainly Iraqis and Afghanis on their way from Indonesia to Australian waters without visas, when their boat began to sink. The master of the Tampa proposed to disembark the people he had rescued. Defining the threat performatively by the nature of its response, before sending medical supplies, the government sent elite combat troops to the ship. Bellicose election speeches from Prime Minister John Winston Howard, urging a possibly bewildered population to do its patriotic duty against an unclearly quantified foreign threat, echoed, farcically, the 'we will fight them on the beaches ... we will never surrender' of his hero, Winston Churchill.[45] Along with the survivors of a second nearby sinking, the Tampa passengers were coerced on to military transports and conveyed to Pacific island client states for 'processing.' Guided missile warships now guard the continent from incursions by Muslims in small wooden fishing boats. The refugee as a sign of that from which s/he seeks refuge, as a hostile foreign menace, has acquired an additional, spurious, and, for the federal government, fortunate, plausibility in the wake of the US 'war on terrorism.'

V

THE BARRED SUBJECT OF THE REFUGEE

The official story bars the refugee-subject at the border. On the threshold, or apprehended within, s/he has no human face in the official pictures and no human rights in the official gazettes. Like the Gothic fantasies aroused by the repressed and subordinated, the horror lies both in her hideous form and in the beguiling appearance s/he is able to assume. S/he is the Antoinette[46] made dangerous and self-destructive Bertha Mason in the

[44] I Duncanson 2000 above n 39.

[45] Howard's endlessly repeated election campaign promise, 'We will decide who comes to this country and the manner of their coming' was supplemented with his response to the Tampa rescuees: 'those people will never set foot on Australian soil. Never.' Quoted in G Rundle, 'The Opportunist: John Howard and the Triumph of Reaction' (2001) 3 *Quarterly Essay* 26.

[46] J Rhys, *The Wide Sargasso Sea* (New York, Norton, 1982); C Bronte, *Jane Eyre* (1847) (Harmondsworth, Penguin, 1966).

white rejection of her claims to equal worth. As Rochester, in Brontes' novel, enriched by her family's wealth, seems to owe her nothing, so the north owes nothing to the south. Nothing about the presence requires an explanation except the threat it represents to sanity and order. Like the Bronte novel, the refugee story begins with a danger whose etiology is not explained, and yet the refuge of another origin can be discerned.

At one level, there is a human being, a third world subject from a former northern colony. For capital this being signifies either cheap overseas labor, a higher return on investment for funds exported to regimes whose disciplinary methods may secure docile employees; or it may signify exploitable legal or super-exploitable illegal immigrant labor whose contribution may be to facilitate the production of goods or services where the demand for profits from shareholders or for cheap services from domestic employers makes ordinary local workers impracticable from capital's point of view. In any of these cases, success for capital depends upon rigorous border control. Human rights in the workplace, where they have not been subverted at 'home,' must not be allowed to infect overseas sites. Immigrants must remain quarantined from the benefits available to locals in order to maintain their status as 'flexible'—low-paid and easily dismissible; and local workers may police this frontier themselves to the extent that in-comers are successfully wielded as a threat to living standards.

The refugee at the threshold as critical origin sends another beginning into refuge. So long as this figure lends appeal to calls for a national unity that obscures politically those differences of interest that are producing unprecedented inequalities of access to social resources, political questions will not be asked. Whilst those seeking refuge are conceded the role of besiegers, internal differences and the exigencies of 'national security' can erode multiple layers of political controversy and multiple sites and issues of contestation. Politics is maneuvered into monologic, monotonal and monochrome conditions, the famous Thatcherite 'there is no alternative,' even where that leads into radically authoritarian economies of control. And here we come to the paradox of globalisation. Border control and the strong security state are precisely the conditions in which the erosion of local values is made possible. The state can avoid responsibilities by appealing to irresistible forces only where it is strong enough to preclude alternatives.

But while it is in the interests of capital and its directly political agents—Australia and Papua New Guinea and the US role in Chile, of course come to mind here—to maintain cheap labor in insecure conditions, often under repressive and unstable governments from which they are obliged on occasions, and when they can, to escape, it is not in the long term interests of those not in control of capital. For them, one could say, the refugee means, not a danger to their nation's identity or security, or to their jobs, but a failure well documented by writers like Chomsky to hold first world politicians accountable for the instabilities they create elsewhere in the world in the short term interests of capital. The dream of some liberal writers that a virtuous synthesis of political values can be accomplished in nation states is doomed to failure, or to pointless abstraction: the end of ideology means the politics of no choice, and it permits the substitution of panics such as that surrounding the discussion of refugees, for a politics with a constructive outcome.

2

Citizens, Immigrants, Anarchists and Other Animals

ANNABELLE MOONEY

I

INTRODUCTION

THE UNITED KINGDOM Human Rights Act 1998 (HRA) came into effect October 2000. In many ways, this has been a welcome piece of legislation, requiring public bodies to conform to the rights contained in the European Convention on Human Rights. While the legislation incorporates into domestic law a European convention, one can still take cases to the European Court of Human Rights should domestic remedies be exhausted. Further, under international law, the status of nation states is such that they retain sovereignty over their territories. This is as one would expect and perhaps prefer. However, in some cases, the powers of the state, whether realised primarily through legislation or the judiciary, distinguish between those who are afforded rights and those who are not. While these mitigations of rights are justified in appropriate legal terms, the way in which this is done indicates a hierarchy of people with respect to their access to rights. In short, the case of immigration law is clearly one where national sovereignty takes precedence over abuses of some human rights. While this is not in itself controversial, with respect to the way this hierarchy might work in other domains, it is essential to see how this is done.

For this reason, I will spend some time dealing with immigration law, and how 'reasonableness' and 'proportionality,' both legal terms of art, are dispensed by the courts. These terms, as well as principles of human rights law, allow and sometimes compel judicial exercise of discretion. Secondly, I will examine newspaper reportage from May Day protests in London,[1] particularly those in 2001 where arguably a number of human rights violations

[1] May Day was designated an international labor day by the International Socialist Congress of 1899, but now is used as an occasion for anti-capitalism and anti-globalisation demonstrations.

occurred. These potential violations were not foregrounded as an issue by the press—rather the protestors are represented as animals participating in threatening, undemocratic behaviour. It should then be clear that one does not access human rights under the HRA but *legal* human rights. To have access to such rights one needs to be a credible citizen. One also has to have a 'reasonable' case. I suggest that these legal human rights are at risk from media representations such as those around May Day protests. Further, I argue that sustained representation in the mass media threatens to render some people and their causes unreasonable. Representations, such as those presented in the mass media, cannot but inform the discretionary actions of the courts. In these cases, representations include the discourses around certain groups, photographs of them and the value of certain lexical terms.

The examination of the law around immigration may seem unrelated to the representation of protestors. The portrayal of immigrants in the press, and racism generally, has been adequately covered elsewhere.[2] Human rights law is as yet to come into direct conflict with the May Day protests. But gatherings of this kind, often in relation to what are understood as the negative aspects of globalisation, are on the increase. As will be discussed, the nature of the protests and protestors is often misunderstood.[3] It seems to me that it is only a matter of time before such conflicts arise. The UK Terrorism Act 2000 is underpinned exactly by concerns with safety of the general public and with interests of a 'democratic' society. This legislation grants extensive powers, especially with respect to suspension of an individual's rights if s/he is suspected of being involved in terrorist activity. Indeed, it is not inconceivable that this Act could be used against the protestors discussed below.[4] Thus the examination of immigration law is to show what

[2] The former in, for example, O Santa Ana, '"Like an Animal I was Treated": Anti-immigrant Metaphor in US Public Discourse' (1999) 10(2) *Discourse and Society* 191–224; the latter extensively by, for example, van Dijk. See TA Van Dijk, *Racism and the Press* (London, Routledge, 1991).

[3] See for example N Klein, *Fences and Windows: Dispatches from the Front Lines of the Globalization Debate* (New York, Picador, 2002).

[4] For example, the definition of terrorism is as follows:

> (1) In this Act 'terrorism' means the use or threat of action where—
> (a) the action falls within subsection (2),
> (b) the use or threat is designed to influence the government or to intimidate the public or a section of the public, and
> (c) the use or threat is made for the purpose of advancing a political, religious or ideological cause.
>
> (2) Action falls within this subsection if it—
> (a) involves serious violence against a person,
> (b) involves serious damage to property,
> (c) endangers a person's life, other than that of the person committing the action,
> (d) creates a serious risk to the health or safety of the public or a section of the public, or
> (e) is designed seriously to interfere with or seriously to disrupt an electronic system.

has happened. Examination of the representation of protestors is to prefigure what may well happen in terms of prioritising public order over human rights. Should cases around these protests reach the courts, and a body of judgments be available for scrutiny, it will be too late.

There are two further things to add at this point. Firstly, this analysis would be enriched by a detailed consideration of media theory. As the representations of protestors here are largely (though not exclusively) uniform, there is little room for challenging the negative representation of protestors. It is taken as a given. I do not mean to suggest that audiences are passive or that producers of the media are conspiratorial. It is the effect of this apparent uniformity on the judiciary's consideration of what 'public opinion' is that is of primary concern.

Secondly, the link between the two parts of this paper, immigrants and protestors, is certainly one of access to human rights. However, there is a further connection which is less prosaic. Santa Ana's work[5] on the representation of immigrants in the US finds that they are often referred to as animals. The protestors too are portrayed and treated as animals. This is hardly co-incidence as animals have no *human* rights. The two very different examples have been chosen in part to show that we need to ask questions not only about certain groups being denied rights, but about the operation of such rights in general.

II

LIMITED BY THE LAW

It is worth noting at the outset that European Convention rights (and as articulated in the HRA) are limited by 'the law'; indeed there is no such thing as an absolute right. This is as we might expect in legislation and indeed in any society. The HRA requires that courts interpret legislation (as much as possible) such that it is consistent with the HRA. However, it is possible to legislate clearly in contravention of rights of the HRA. In such cases, the Court is able to issue a statement of incompatibility. Naturally, because of separation of powers, the Court cannot simply amend the law.[6]

But the question remains, how far do these Articles go in protecting what we consider to be fundamental rights? Is there indeed a difference between the lawful deprivation of a right and cases where we can consider that the right does not apply? This is something akin to the difference between circumstances in any case being a complete defence or being mitigating circumstances. This difficulty is partly accounted for in the notion

[5] Santa Ana, 1999 above n 2.

[6] For a fuller outline of these procedures and the effects of the HRA generally, see J Wadham and H Mountfield, *Blackstone's Guide to the Human Rights Act 1998* (London, Blackstone, 1999).

of 'proportionality.' With respect to the notion of 'proportionality' in *B v SSHD* the Court of Appeal notes that proportionality:

> [in] essence amounts to this: a measure which interferes with a Community or human right must not only be authorised by law but must correspond to a pressing social need and go no further than is strictly necessary in a pluralistic society to achieve its permitted purpose; or, more shortly, must be appropriate and necessary to its legitimate aim.[7]

These are important legal and semantic questions. It is in the realm of proportionality that justification for mitigation of rights is made.

It is worth stressing again that legal rights have a chance of succeeding only if there is legislative ambiguity ie that it is in fact possible to read legislation as conforming to the HRA. In *R v SSHD ex parte Pierce,* Lord Hoffman notes:

> Parliamentary sovereignty means that Parliament can, if it chooses, legislate contrary to fundamental principles of human rights. The Human Rights Act 1998 will not detract from this power. The constraints upon its exercise by Parliament are ultimately *political*, not legal (emphasis added).[8]

Thus there are three limitations to the rights under the Act. The first is that there must be some ambiguity, the second is that the resulting decision (upholding the right) must be in line with the law, and finally, the result must be proportionate. These limitations have their basis in the HRA, conventions of international law and domestic case law. These limitations are effected through the legal concepts of reasonableness and proportionality. While these *prima facie* have 'common sense' meanings, within this legal context they are realised in specific ways.

III

IMMIGRANTS AND OTHERS

This is not a paper only recounting or accounting for the law. The point is to show how when human rights come into conflict with national immigration laws, the latter always win. How they triumph is of particular significance for other groups. Indeed, the triumph often results in the judiciary stating that there has not been an abrogation of rights, when what in fact is the case is that the abrogation is considered legitimate because of competing interests. The selection of the United Kingdom is not a singling out. While people are theoretically equal before the law, society and the law impose their own differentiation before judgements are made. The law,

[7] [2000] 2 CMLR 1086 at 17.
[8] [1998] AC 539.

partly by retelling the 'facts',[9] prepares the field, as it were, and it is not always a level one.

The mitigation and effective suppression of human rights in the face of immigration law is possible if it is 'reasonable' and 'proportionate'.[10] What counts as reasonable is considered an 'objective' test as we shall see, yet no specific criteria are given. As noted previously and elsewhere[11] it seems to me that mass media representation cannot but impact on what is considered 'reasonable' in a judicial context. Reasonably, the judiciary is given certain discretion. Part of the difficulty (and interest) in dealing with notions of what is 'reasonable' and 'proportionate' is the fact that the terms have both common-sense definitions as well as legal ones.

Further, the process of presenting arguments and decisions in a legal context is subject to particular forces. Mathewson notes that the

> description of events must be tailored to the law against which they will be measured, even as the law is itself re-articulated with reference to those events.[12]

Immigrants and those without official permission to enter or remain in a country are subject to limitations. There is no question that nation states are sovereign and that they should, and indeed are, able to make decisions about their own lands and citizens in their best interests. With respect to immigration law, the European Court of Human Rights is clear about a State's right to have an immigration policy:

> So far as the ECHR is concerned, the jurisprudence makes clear that it is legitimate for a State to have an immigration policy and the mere fact that its implementation will interfere with family life [for example] does not render unlawful every such act of implementation.[13]

Singh for example, notes that 'the power of a state to control who may enter its territory has traditionally been regarded as an essential aspect of its sovereignty.'[14] Further, this control provides:

[9] See BS Jackson, 'Narrative Theories in Legal Discourse' in C Nash (ed), *Narrative in Culture: The Use of Storytelling in the Sciences, Philosophy and Literature* (London, Routledge, 1990), at 23–50.

[10] This would seem to be a case of Alexy's balancing of principles. See R Alexy, *A Theory of Legal Argumentation: The Theory of Rational Discourse as Theory of Legal Justification*, R Adler and N MacCormack (trans) (Oxford, Oxford University Press, 1989).

[11] A Mooney, 'Human Rights, Linguistics and the Law: The UK and Beyond' (2002) 15 *International Journal for the Semiotics of Law* 389.

[12] GC Mathewson, 'Outdoing Lewis Carroll: Judicial Rhetoric and Acceptable Fictions' (1998) 12 *Argumentation* 233 at 239.

[13] *R v SSHD, ex parte Peter Isiko Susan and Shemy Isiko* [2001] HRLR 15 at para 8.

[14] R Singh, *The Future of Human Rights in the United Kingdom* (Oxford, Hart Publishing, 1997) at 91.

> an important means to pursue such governmental goals as the detection of crime ... the prevention of terrorism, and (perhaps most controversially) the protection of the domestic labour markets and the social security systems from those who are regarded as being outsiders and therefore as not having full claims on the community's resources.[15]

Regardless of the UK's right to control immigration, it is clear that some people have more of a right to be in the UK than others. It is exactly the 'other', outsiders, who do not have 'full claims on the community's resources.' I hasten to add that this is typical of many countries. Nonetheless, certain characteristics deprive people of the right to stay in the UK. Singh perceptively remarks:

> At the end of the twentieth century, there is a danger that we are setting up an exceptional system of law where there is a privileged caste of European citizens [101] those who are nations of Member States, while those who are nationals of third countries, and who are lawfully settled in a Member State, remain in a real sense second-class citizens.[16]

The problem appears to be even more severe and less clear than this. Those in a position to lawfully settle in a Member State may be second class citizens. But the gulf between these people and those who may not even enter the EU, or who may be readily deported, is far greater.

R (on the application of Mahmood (Amjad)) v SSHD,[17] (Mahmood) is one of the foundational cases for balancing immigration law with the right to family and private life. The applicant, Mr Mahmood, had entered the UK illegally but at the time of the Secretary of State's decision been married for under two years to a UK resident and had two children. Because of the way in which the right to family and private life is phrased in the Convention (and thus in the HRA), it is applied:

> except such as in accordance with the law and is necessary in a democratic society in the interests of national security, public safety or the economic well-being of the country for the prevention of disorder and crime, for the protection of health or morals, or for the protection of the rights and freedoms of others.[18]

The Court held that to not require an entry clearance from the applicant would:

> in the absence of exceptional circumstances justifying the waiver, disrupt and undermine firm immigration control because it would be manifestly unfair to other would-be entrants seeking entry clearance in their country of origin.[19]

[15] *Ibid.*
[16] Singh, above n 14, at 100–1.
[17] [2001] HRLR 14.
[18] Article 17.
[19] Para 23.

Whether Mahmood had a right to abode because of his marriage is not at issue. The right has to be secured in the normal way; that is, by procuring entry clearance in his country of original residence.

There are two tests given in this case, described as being on a 'sliding scale' such that:

> the graver the impact of the decision in question upon the individual affected by it, the more substantial the justification that would be required.[20]

The first test is the conventional Wednesbury[21] test of reasonableness:

> On this model the court makes no judgment of its own as to the relative weight attached to this or that factor taken into account in the decision-making process; it is concerned only to see that everything relevant and nothing irrelevant has been considered, and that a rational mind has been brought to bear by the Secretary of State in reaching the decision.[22]

On this first test, Mahmood's application was dismissed. The second approach involves consideration of the human right involved and thus proof that it is not being interfered with or that the interference is proportionate.[23] This relies on a settled principle of common law:

> It is that the intensity of review in a public law case will depend on the subject-matter in hand; and so in particular any interference by the action of a public body with a fundamental right will require a substantial objective justification.[24]

It was clear to the Court that the right to family life had been interfered with, though no error of law had occurred in terms of the first test (vis-à-vis the Secretary of State's decision). In terms of proportionality, Laws LJ (May LJ concurring) commented, 'it is simply unfair that he [the applicant] should not have to wait in queue like everyone else.'[25] That the applicant should have to undergo this process (of 'queuing') before arriving in the UK is not regarded as an effect on rights disproportionate to the purpose of immigration legislation, even though this resulted in a breach of the right to family life.

It is here that the common sense meanings of proportionate and legal meanings collide. Even though Mahmood has an arguable right to be in the UK by virtue of his marriage, the law allows deportation so that Mahmood

[20] Para 19.
[21] (1948) 1 KB 223.
[22] Cited in *Mahmood*, above n 17, at 277.
[23] *Mahmood*, above n 17 at 277.
[24] *Mahmood*, above n 17 at 278.
[25] *Mahmood*, above n 17 at 281.

can fulfil application processes in his native country. From a practical point of view, and especially considering costs to himself and the state, this does seem extreme. However, this view at least recognises that the right to family and private life will be compromised.

The Master of the Rolls takes a slightly different route to the same conclusion. He explicitly invokes an objective test:

> When anxiously scrutinising an executive decision that interferes with human rights, the court will ask the question, applying an objective test, whether the decision maker could reasonably have concluded that interference was necessary to achieve one or more of the legitimate aims recognised by the Convention.[26]

Further:

> the deportation of the appellant is necessary in the interests of an orderly and fair control of immigration and ... his right to respect for his family life was not violated.[27]

Thus the Master of Rolls considers that because the violation is proportionate, the violation did not occur. This, it seems to me, is the central problem.

Thus three things are considered. Firstly, whether the Secretary of State acted rationally and secondly, whether the right in question has been violated. It is well worth noting that this will not be the case if the action falls within the exceptions provided for in the Convention (and now in the HRA). To clarify, it is possible that the right is extinguished because of conditions specified in the HRA. However (and finally), if a right has been violated or interfered with, one has to consider whether this is proportionate with the aims of the legislation at hand.

As the Secretary of State is democratically accountable for decisions, the judiciary cannot 'substitute its own decision.'[28] The Secretary of State is required only to 'examine ... all the facts of the case.'[29] Yet because the decision has to be a 'rational' one, the Court may examine 'the underlying facts rigorously to see if they *compelled* a different decision' (emphasis added).[30] Though the use of 'compel' suggests a singular outcome (and implies that the facts somehow speak for themselves) there are in fact a 'range of reasonable responses' to issues raised.[31]

The question of proportionality is also said to have an objective answer. Three cases concerning appeals on medical grounds render this objectivity

[26] *Mahmood*, above n 17 at 287.
[27] *Mahmood*, above n 17 at 294.
[28] *R (on the application of Samaroo) v SSHD* [2001] IMM AR 324.
[29] *Ibid.*
[30] *R v SSHD ex p Jagot*, [2000] Imm AR 414.
[31] *Ibid.*

somewhat opaque. In *R (on the application of Njai) v SSHD*[32] the Court held that permission to remain should be granted on the basis of 'credible medical evidence' that the applicant would suffer due to not being able to obtain appropriate medication in the Gambia for schizophrenia. 'Therefore, there existed compelling humanitarian considerations to justify granting N leave to remain.'[33]

On the other hand, an applicant who argued that his mental health was at risk should he be returned to Malta was denied permission to remain:

> While there was some evidence that his repatriation would cause some stress, it was not sufficient to justify finding that his repatriation would constitute inhuman treatment.[34]

Arguably more serious, in *K v SSHD*, an HIV-positive citizen of Uganda suffering from AIDS was refused permission to remain:

> To accept that submission [that lack of treatment would be inhuman or degrading treatment] would be to adopt a rule that any country without a health service which was available free of charge to all people within its boundaries would be a place to which it would be inhuman and degrading to send someone.[35]

It was considered that treatment in Uganda was available, even though it was clear that the applicant would not be able to afford it. However, access to treatment is exactly what was considered in a case of deportation; *R v SSHD ex p Cardoso*.[36] It was found that the applicant '*would receive* adequate treatment in Brazil' (emphasis added). In the former case, it would appear that deportation is not so much a breach of Article 3 of the HRA (prohibition of torture) which it seems to be referring to, but rather of right to life. Further, if K (the applicant above) was receiving anti-retro viral treatment, which seems likely (as he was suffering from AIDS) this is possible grounds for an asylum application (though obviously this is quite a separate matter).

As noted, some case law appears to conflate the violation of rights with the justification for this on the grounds of proportionality. In *R (on the application of Savas (Mehmet Ali)) v SSHD* it was held that:

> Art 8 [of the HRA; the right to privacy and family life] was not infringed by a decision to return S, a Kurdish asylum seeker married to a UK citizen, to Germany as the interference with his right to family life under Art 8 was

[32] (2000) WL 33122384.
[33] *Ibid.*
[34] *R (on the application of X) v SSHD* (2000) 56 BMLR 180.
[35] [2001] Imm AR 11.
[36] [2000] Imm AR 1.

> outweighed by the public interest in maintaining an effective system of immigration control.[37]

This case considered the likely decision of Germany, the fact that the applicant could still appeal to the European Court, and that now married, the interruption to family life was temporary.[38] Thus the right (Article 8) was 'not infringed' only because the interference with the right was outweighed by the public interest. This appears to be a conflation of reasonableness and proportionality.

In *R (on the application of Kariharan) v SSHD,* the Auld LJ notes:

> if a claimant has a valid human rights claim to stay when he makes it, he is entitled to do so whatever the status of the decision designed to remove him; he has a section 65 entitlement.[39]

Here, section 65 refers to the Immigration And Asylum Act (1999), which in turn refers to the HRA. Thus the pertinent question is what amounts to a 'valid human rights claim'?[40] As just noted, it seems that a 'valid claim' does not include cases which are excluded by the provisions of the Convention. Further, a 'valid claim' on human rights grounds needs to trump the public interest supporting immigration law generally.

Sometimes the same outcome is effected by different phrasing. In *Miller v Leeds Magistrates Court*[41] the Court held that:

> the purpose of such an order [to stop football fans travelling to matches] was to protect the general public from football violence, not to inflict punishment on the individuals concerned.

It would perhaps be possible to frame the aforementioned cases in the same way. For example, 'the *aim* is not to deprive the individual of right to family life, rather the *intention* is to protect immigration law.' Words are the basis of law; words with particular felicity conditions and legitimacy standing behind them. If we are to accept this legitimacy, words need to be consistently and carefully used. From the small amount of case law examined, it is not clear when a right is being violated (and this considered justifiable) and when the violation is deemed not to have occurred because of the justifiability of the violation.

The rhetoric of 'balancing' suggests that one can partially have a right. Certainly no rights are absolute, either legally or logically. However to say

[37] [2001] EWHC Admin 1062.

[38] See also for example *Sayaniar v Immigration Appeal Tribunal* [2001] EWHC Admin 390; *Ahmed (Nasim) v SSHD* 2001 SC 705; *R v SSHD ex p Hakansoy* [2001] Imm AR 16; *R v SSHD ex p Cardoso* [2000] Imm AR 1.

[39] [2002] EWCA Civ 1102 para 24.

[40] *Ibid.*

[41] [2001] EWHC Admin 554.

a right has to be 'balanced' against policy matters suggests that the right remains operative. Clearly it does not. I suggest, in a small attempt to urge consistency and transparency, firstly that the rights in the HRA be called 'legal human rights'—as this is what they properly are—and secondly that violation and proportionality be dealt with separately and clearly.

I now turn to nationals from countries not covered by the ECHR *apropos* Singh's argument in relation to 'castes' of people. If one comes from a state which is not a signatory to the Convention, the HRA is less easy to apply. In *R (on the application of Ullah) v Special Adjudicator*,[42] the applicant claimed he would be persecuted on the basis of his Ahmadi religion if deported to Pakistan. While there was support for persecution of Ahmadis, the applicant and his family had not experienced to 'any serious degree some of the problems that many Ahmadis in Pakistan'[43] had. The application was refused as the denial of rights in the home country had to be a 'flagrant denial.' Further:

> The main purpose of the European Convention on Human Rights [1050] was to protect individuals from arbitrary intervention by the signatory states. Any positive obligation to provide protection from interference by third parties was far more limited than the obligation of a signatory state not to interfere with the individual's rights and freedoms.[44]

Further, as the applicant was from a non-signatory state, Pakistan, the UK court would have no assistance in determining the breach of the right and may indeed apply standards 'more stringent than would be appropriate in the particular circumstances in Pakistan.'[45] Seemingly if the persecution originates with the state (though it is not clear that this is the case) the state would not consider such persecution a breach of any kind of right. This, one would suspect, would also be the case with regimes committing acts of torture or genocide. This, however, does not speak against asylum claims. It does seem reasonable to conclude, that given persecution of Ahmadis in Pakistan is well documented, the applicant would experience such persecution should he return, even if he had not to date.[46]

[42] QBD (Admin Ct) Administrative Court, [2002] EWHC 1584.
[43] *Ibid.*
[44] *Ibid*, pp 1049–50.
[45] *Ibid.*
[46] As with some other cases, this seems to come close to an asylum issue. The Home Office notes:

> To be granted asylum under the 1951 UN Refugees Convention it is necessary to demonstrate a well founded fear of persecution because of race, religion, nationality, membership of a particular social group or political opinion. Alternatively, asylum seekers can be granted 'exceptional leave to remain,' a discretionary grant of leave made by the Home Secretary, allowing a person to stay in the UK for a limited period of time. (http://www.ind.homeoffice.gov.uk/default.asp?pageid=91 [accessed 19/12/02]).

Indeed, given the clear distinction between aliens and nationals, it is not clear why the HRA is applied in the former cases at all. Given that even those who have a right to remain in the UK, on the grounds of marriage to a citizen for example, are required to conform to the technical requirements (that is, obtaining an entry clearance) in the interests of protecting immigration law, it is not clear that the HRA ever overrides it. At the same time, the 'objective' and 'reasonable' criteria are not always transparent. This certainly vitiates the notion that law should operate in predictable ways.

IV

PROTESTS AND ANARCHISTS

The portrayal of a group of victims in the press recently goes some way in showing how it is possible to deny humans human rights with little or no controversy. It is important to note that in this case (as far as I am aware) no legal action has taken place.[47] Thus the examination of representation here does not come directly up against legal questions in an active sense. Rather, the media coverage is examined to show how it shapes itself (or can be understood) in relation to human rights without actually broaching the topic. The examples given here come from a cross-section of the press: *The Guardian*, *The Daily Telegraph* and BBC online news coverage. In examination of the following representations, issues covered in relation to immigration law are directly relevant. In the case of the protestors, deprivation of rights would be justified in the interests of *democracy* and *public safety*. That is, disregarding the human rights of the protestors would be easily justifiable as proportionate to legislative aims in the areas of safety and security (under the Terrorism Act for example).

During the May Day protests in London in 2001 a large number of people were detained in a city location in the rain, unable to leave, with no access to food, refreshment or any kind of relief:

> By 3 PM, the morale of everyone gathered was low. They were wet, tired, hungry, and those who smoked had run out of roll-ups. It was clear that the vast majority were little more than part-time protesters, not least because many of them wore branded training shoes.[48]

The representation here of protestors as 'part-time' suggests that they were not serious; that they were trespassing on *protest land* they were not fit for. It also invokes a discourse of employment, 'part-time' routinely being used

[47] However, Liberty, a human rights group, did write to the Metropolitan police asking it to apologise for the detention. See www.liberty-human-rights.org.uk.

[48] 'Branded trainers' presumably means Nike, Adidas, Reebok and so forth. *BBC Online* 1/5/01.

in an employment frame. This is not surprising given the original underpinnings of May Day activities. Implicit is the accusation that the protestors do not work in *normal spheres* but take protest action as *employment*. An image of students is also implicit in this representation. They are a section of society regarded as uniquely privileged to partake in such activities as protests (albeit part time) and stereotypically consumers of roll-up cigarettes and also perhaps branded clothing.

The importance of branded clothing is, of course, that the protest concerned (if it can be understood as having a single *voice*; indeed, even if one can consider that this was a *single protest*) globalisation, specifically the economics and politics and effects of such things as multinationals. This is not the place to consider what globalisation means.[49] Yet, the many concerns of the protestors would be one place to start in unravelling what people understand by *globalisation* (and by this I mean not what academics and politicians understand by globalisation). For the purposes here, it is sufficient to note that this was not a single protest with a single voice but covered such things as pollution, human rights, multi-national economics, third world debt, the decline of the welfare state and poverty.

Regardless of the socio-economic profile of the protestors, they were not allowed to leave the area in which they were contained for up to six hours. Upon leaving, personal details were taken, images recorded (something only legally allowed if there are grounds to suspect a crime has been committed) and some film confiscated:

> As the evening wore on, the police strictly controlled the release of protestors from Oxford Circus. According to eyewitnesses, the demonstrators were only allowed out one at a time and many had their photographs taken by police cameramen. Officers are only supposed to do this when there are strong grounds to suspect a person has been involved in criminality.... Protestors also complained about the indiscriminate use of stop and search powers.[50]

The protestors are shown as a force which needs to be 'controlled,' released 'one at a time' as though police were fearing a human flood. The discourse here does pay some attention to the question of rights. Eyewitnesses vouch for the way in which protestors were treated, as well as the protestors' own 'complaints.' There is, however, no explicit identification of rights abuses. This text is from *The Guardian*, a well known left of centre daily. It is thus not surprising that these issues are raised. Nonetheless, even this paper participates in construction of the 'anarchist' or 'spiky' in contrast to the 'fluffy', the latter being the harmless, 'part time protestor.' Likewise, the *Telegraph* reports, 'There were plenty of 'fluffies'—protestor speak for

[49] 'Globalization' could mean whatever the user wants it to mean. See C Turenne Sjolander, 'The Rhetoric of Globalization: What's in a Wor(l)d?' (1996) 51 *International Journal* 603.

[50] See N Hopkins, V Dodd and R Allison, 'Police Trap for Protestors' *The Guardian* 2 May 2001 [accessed 2 July 2001].

peaceful demonstrators—and a few anarchists, known as 'spikies'.'[51] While described as two ends of a spectrum (soft/harmless vs hard/harmful), the oppositional lexicalisation serves to reify and stereotype anyone with reservations about aspects of globalisation into one of the two camps.[52] It is clear that anarchists are dangerous and that fluffies are not (as the lexeme suggests). There is thus no credible anti-global space to be occupied.

The police announced beforehand that there would be a zero tolerance approach to violence:

> A 'zero tolerance' police operation which involved corralling thousands of protestors in a tight, strictly marshalled cordon around the West End of London last night led to accusations of unlawful detention at the end of another May Day marked by occasional violence and vandalism.[53]

One of the most noted comments was the damage to property caused by the protestors:

> Metropolitan Police Authority Chairman Lord Harris, 'The police tactic of containment in and around the flashpoint of Oxford Street to avoid serious injuries to innocent people and damage to property proved to be the right one.'
>
> 'They [60 protestors let out at 10 PM] overturned a car, smashed shopfronts with rocks and other missiles, targeting firms including the Royal Bank of Scotland, Abbey National, Barclays Bank, Coffee Republic and Habitat, and attempted to set fire to a Tesco store.
>
> The protest is estimated to have cost London's businesses up to £20m in lost revenue as dozens of businesses were forced to shut with repair and policing costs also being considerable.[54]

The representation here is of a volatile situation, a 'flashpoint', with potential 'serious injuries to innocent people.' This suggests that the protestors are guilty of something (in opposition to 'innocent people'). The 'zero-tolerance' approach articulated further affirms this. Incidentally, the emphasis on damage to property is greater than damage to people.

Notwithstanding the prolonged confinement of the protestors, the small number of protestors (60 out of about 5,000) responsible for violence later in the evening was touted as justification for the earlier corralling. This is clearly post-hoc justification. The argument is akin to stating that to contain a lion and poke chairs in his face is justified on the basis of the lion's subsequent anger:

[51] S Laville, D Millward and T Hardin, 'Police Tactics Stop Anarchists from Passing Go' (2 May 2001) *Electronic Telegraph* [accessed 2 July 2001].
[52] See for example, http://www.guardian.co.uk/mayday/graphic/0,7367,480801,00.html [accessed 19 December 2002].
[53] See Hopkins *et al* 2001.
[54] BBC News online 2 May 2001.

London Mayor Ken Livingstone condemned the Tottenham Court rampage: This appalling vandalism shows the decision to contain the protestors was right ... The immediate turn to violence on dispersal indicates that this was the core objective of the organisers.[55]

That Mr Livingstone can describe any 'core objectives' or indeed 'organisers' misrepresents the nature of the protest and the protestors. His statement appears to be an attempt to re-frame the actions of the protestors in discourse and ideologies which they eschew.

This deprivation of rights is implicitly justified in the media through representing the protesters as animals and therefore not with access to ***human*** rights. Protestors were 'herded' and 'corralled' into Oxford Circus where they were 'penned.'[56] The *Daily Telegraph* reports that 'May Day 2001 was a signal triumph for the forces of law and order.'[57] The event was billed as a battle, with 'scruffy black-clad' anarchists on one side and police protecting law abiding citizens on the other.[58]

We see in the following tension between the two views of the protest with battle imagery ('stand-off') but with protestors 'unable to escape' signalling their detention:

Five hundred demonstrators were blockaded by police, 10 deep, near Euston station. In a two-hour stand-off, the demonstrators, many on bicycles, were corralled in the rain unable to escape. Eventually they were allowed to leave in small groups. Each individual was subjected to a body search under Section 60 of the Criminal Justice Act.[59]

'Stand-off' suggests that the demonstrators were dangerously armed, that they were armoured and on horseback rather than 'bicycles.'

At other points, the representation of the *danger* that the protestors represent is almost comical. *The Telegraph* reports that in one *confrontation* outside a disused bacon factory:

police seized white boiler suits, used by the Wombles protest group, body armour made from foam, Monopoly maps detailing targets for the protest and several broken table legs to be used as weapons. Inside, all the rooms were clearly marked, including one called the 'bomb factory.'[60]

If we begin at the end of this paragraph, we find the idea implicit in the preceding descriptions; the suggestion that the protestors are armed and

[55] BBC News online 2 May 2001.
[56] D Greaves, J Steele, S Laville, T Harding and D Millward, 'Police Quell May Day Threat' *Electronic Telegraph* 2 May 2001 [accessed 2 July 2001].
[57] S Laville *et al*, see above n 51.
[58] *Ibid.*
[59] Hopkins *et al* 2 May 2001.
[60] *Ibid.*

dangerous. To note that all rooms were clearly marked is hardly sinister; for doors to be labelled, *kitchen*, *bathroom* and so on is hardly subversive activity. To describe foam as any kind of 'armour' is curious, and the suggestion appears to be that 'white boiler suits' are somehow dangerous as we are told that they were 'seized.' On the topic of table legs, 'several' hardly seems a significant number unless one is dealing with ballistic missiles. Indeed, this is exactly the point and exactly why the 'bomb factory' is mentioned at the end. If the items seized had been grenades, machines guns and ammunition, the text would be routine and justifiable. Further, protestors who protect themselves with foam seem unlikely to actually be making bombs. But dealing with the protestors as though they are dangerous terrorists, implicitly justifies use of extreme measures (arguably now enshrined in various anti-terrorism legislation).

The confrontation outside this 'bomb factory' began with 'eight anarchists' holding hands, 'forming a circle and performing a parody of a Morris dance.' When the 'anarchists returned to base' they scattered flower petals as they went. That the media coverage can simultaneously belittle the anarchists and treat them as a serious violent threat depends on the depiction of deviance. Difference becomes at once ludic, ludicrous and threatening.

People were warned to stay away from the protests. Tony Blair, Prime Minister said:

> I believe people in Britain are tolerant, outward-looking, inclusive. But I believe too that there are indeed limits to that tolerance. It is likely we will see the limits of tolerance being challenged again tomorrow, in the so-called 1 May demonstrations.[61]

The limits of British tolerance appear to fall in line with the tolerance of the press. Where this cycle begins is not at issue here, though it deserves further consideration. The press then purports to speak for the majority of citizens; the police act for it. Blair goes so far as to question the very name of the day, 'so-called', thus attempting to erase any credibility. It should be noted that Blair's *beliefs* about Britain's tolerance are just that, pending further evidence. He purports to speak for the British but thus excludes all those participating in the protests.

I am not arguing that vandalism and damage to people and property should be allowed. But to assume that people are guilty before a crime is even effected is a gross deprivation of rights. Further, the *general public* seems not to understand the reason for the protests at all; and it is worth being clear that these were protests (plural), occurring on the same day in the same places. There was no May Day mastermind co-ordinating the entire operation. Indeed, it is ironic that the police were so concerned about protecting property when this cuts to the core of what was at stake in the

[61] BBC News online 30/4/01.

protest. Using terms like 'anarchist' (who are known as 'spikies') as well as the more benign 'fluffies' alienates people from other people; the 'serious' protestors from the 'part-time' ones; protestors from the 'general population'; the 'guilty' from the 'innocent.'

The coverage of May Day (2002) events took a different and somewhat more derisive turn. In preparation, '[M]ore than 5,000 police were on the streets of London or being held in reserve' but 'the mood appeared different.'[62] One protestor is quoted as saying 'We've been walking round in circles for hours ...What is the point of this?'[63] The press representation continues in this theme describing protestors as 'milling about' or chanting 'radical' and 'bizarre' slogans. The same newspaper reports that trouble did erupt 'as darkness fell.' The implications of this need hardly be raised. '[P]olice in riot gear surrounded around 200 protestors ... in Soho.'[64] As in 2001, section 60 of the Criminal Justice Act 1994 was invoked with protestors searched and photographed before leaving. The police were instructed to film and follow protestors. In oblique comment to the day, Tony Blair was reported as remarking:

> If you have got something to say, say it democratically. Come out and vote, but don't end up trying to beat the place up because your politics aren't the politics shared by the vast majority of people.[65]

However given that the first protest of the day was at the trial of 'seven members of the anti-capitalist Wombles group [who] are on trial for public order offences after one of them allegedly made an obscene gesture at a police van in Oxford Street last October'[66] it seems that Blair might be overstating the case. Further, to suggest that protesting, or 'beat[ing] the place up' (to use Blair's curious transformation), is not democratic begs the question as to what the right to association and free speech actually mean. Certainly violence against people or property is not a right. However, Blair suggests that such violence was the sole aim of the protest.[67] Blair also implies that democracy is not interested in minority views.

[62] J Wilson, P Kelso and J Vasagar, 'A Skirmish in Mayfair' *The Guardian* 2 May 2002 [accessed 16 August 2002].

[63] *Ibid.*

[64] N Hopkins, P Kelso, J Wilson and J Vasagar, 'Peace in Paris, Skirmishes in the Streets of London' *The Guardian* 2 May 2002 [accessed 16 August 2002].

[65] *Ibid.*

[66] *Ibid.*

[67] Articles 10 and 11 in the HRA (UK).

While not possible here, press coverage of the Countryside Alliance demonstration in London September 2002 focussed on celebrities and politicians present. Statements from the government reported in the press supported the general contention that rural UK needs support. Disturbingly, this was also a demonstration with anti-democratic elements. Further, the main purpose of the demonstration was to support the continuation of fox hunting. The media represented the group as generally far more liberal than it actually is. See Z Williams, 'Hypocrisy is on the March' *The Guardian* 24 September 2002 [accessed 10 October 2002].

V

PRESS AND PRESSURE

It is acceptable in law to balance up human rights with other considerations. In the case of May Day Protests, this would be in the interests of protection of property and peace in the capital. It should be clear that I don't think this is acceptable. Certainly in the case of the 2001 'riots', as mentioned, it is not clear that there would have been any violence from the protestors had they not been so detained by the police. However, the most dangerous action in relation to the protests was undoubtedly the mass media representation of them.

I do not want to suggest that it is the responsibility of the press to educate the public about all matters in the world. However, this kind of sustained media representation informs public opinion. It is exactly this public opinion which in turn eventually informs the legislature and the judiciary. The narrative construction of events that the media performs is also performed in the courtroom and in the very handing down of judgements.[68]

It is extremely difficult to prove beyond a doubt that one thing leads to the other notwithstanding assertions such as 'Law is among the dominant institutions entwined with the mass media'[69] and the various models of media influence.[70] I argue rather that there is a credible space for such influence, especially in the field of human rights. Boutros Boutros-Ghali has commented that 'Member States [of the UN] never take action on a problem unless the media takes up the case.'[71] Thus the agendas of those who control the media dictate the agenda of justice. '[T]hose with power are those who can determine the very definition of news. Power also rests with those whose voices and perspectives are heard the most.'[72]

Language is a medium of the press and the law. Words in judgments cannot be accidental which is to say, that because of precedent and legal interpretation generally, they will not be accidental. A slip of the pen is not insignificant though it may for a time be quiescent. In the case of immigrants in particular, press coverage and the treatment that they receive at law appear to be moving closer.

The representation of immigrants and asylum seekers is well documented and need not be detailed here.[73] Santa Ana's work on the representation

[68] See Jackson, above n 9, 1990.

[69] RV Ericson, 'Mass Media, Crime, Law and Justice' (1999) 31(3) *The British Journal of Criminology* 219, at 223.

[70] See generally D McQuail, *Mass Communication Theory: an Introduction* (London, Sage, 1983).

[71] R McCorquodale and R Fairbrother, 'Globalization and Human Rights' (1999) 21(3) *Human Rights Quarterly* 735 at 759.

[72] MD Alleyne, *International Power and International Communication* (London, MacMillan, 1995), at 67–68.

[73] See for example Santa Ana, 1999; AC Mehan, 1993; TA Van Dijk, 1987 and 1991.

of immigrants in American press focuses exactly on their depiction as animals. This dovetails nicely with the representation of protestors as animals and with the effacing of human-ness in this metaphorical transformation. Animals do not deserve human rights; nor do non-citizens, nor do those citizens who upset other citizens. The case of discrimination on the bases of possession of cultural capital is even clearer when one considers some legitimate modes of entry to the UK.[74]

Santa Ana's work draws extensively on cognitive linguistics, particularly Lakoff and Johnson's work on metaphor.[75] The representations created by the press

> are not written to be read as creative fiction. They are taken by the reading public as more-or-less factual descriptions of the political and social events and statements of the day.[76]

Essentially this means that the 'reading public' do not submit their newspapers to the scrutiny that academics do. The dehumanising effect of this is that 'immigrants are portrayed as less than human.'[77]

Central to the Lakoff and Johnson understanding of metaphor is that it is part of a conceptual system. It is not simply stylistic transformation of *literal* language. The 'power of prose metaphor'[78] in the mass media is that they do not usually draw attention to themselves.

Van Dijk argues that the mass media is the 'most pervasive' printed form and arguably the 'most influential.'[79] Yet, arguments about the influence of the mass media on public opinion do not need to be irrefutably established for there still to be a connection to legal discourse. The mass media at least 'reflects the embodied basic values of the dominant political order.'[80] Van Dijk also notes that '[f]undamental norms, values, and power arrangements are seldom explicitly challenged in the dominant news media.'[81] Further, the power of these views may also be explained by the equivalence that metaphor creates.[82] The conceptual integration, or blending, that Fauconnier and Turner (among others) discuss, can be understood as acceptance of the terms of metaphor, and more importantly, of the equivalence (cf. similarity) between these people and animals.

[74] Two recent schemes include the 'Highly Skilled Migrant Program' and a program for Innovators (essentially entrepreneurs).
[75] See for example, *Metaphors We Live By* (Chicago, University of Chicago Press 1980).
[76] Santa Ana 1999 above n 2 at 198.
[77] *Ibid*, at 202.
[78] *Ibid*, at 217.
[79] TA Van Dijk, 'Structure of Discourse and Structures of Power' (1989) 12 *Communications Yearbook* 18 at 42.
[80] Santa Ana 1999 above n 2 at 217.
[81] Van Dijk 1989 above n 79 at 43.
[82] See Fauconnier, Gilles and Mark Turner, 'Conceptual Integration Networks' (1998) *Cognitive Science* 22(2): 133–87.

The mass media represents and arguably influences the dominant values of society. The discourse that Santa Ana deals with, political discourse, 'is constructed interactively, over time and across interlocutors.'[83] Certainly the same can be said of case law. Singh, however, argues that 'Judges are not susceptible to the same day-to-day pressures that politicians are' such as re-election.[84] Thus, 'Judges can take a more long term view, drawing on the enduring values of our society such as equality and fairness.'[85] This assertion, that the judiciary are only concerned with equality and fairness and not with policy and political issues (such as the protection of the labour market and the social security system mentioned in a later chapter) is somewhat idealistic and flatly contradicted by the examination of immigration law above.

I am not suggesting that the judiciary are intentionally biased. But if we know anything at all about culture, epistemology and representation, we know that complete objectivity eludes us. Supreme Court Justice Robert Jackson's often cited words are relevant here. 'We are not final because we are infallible, but we are infallible only because we are final.'[86]

In the case of human rights in particular, such bias, or rather understanding of local culture and values, is provided for by the European Court of Human Rights.[87] This margin is not unlimited:

> The view taken by their respective laws of the requirements of morals varies from time to time and from place to place, especially in our era which is characterised by a rapid and far-reaching evolution of opinions on the subject. By reason of their direct and continuous contact with the vital forces of their countries, State authorities are in principle in a better position than the international judge to give an opinion on the exact content of these requirements as well as on the 'necessity' of a [754] 'restriction' or 'penalty' intended to meet them. ... Nevertheless, it is for the national authorities to make the initial assessment of the reality of the pressing social need implied by the notion of 'necessity' in this context.[88]

The 'necessity' refers to that which is:

> necessary in a democratic society in the interests of public safety, for the protection of public order, health or morals, or for the protection of the rights and freedoms of others.[89]

Thus decisions are based on local and subjective judgements as well as the rule of law. I do not mean to suggest that the effect of media coverage

[83] Santa Ana 1999 above n 2 at 195.
[84] Singh 1997 above n 14 at 50.
[85] *Ibid.*
[86] *Brown v Allen* (1953) 344 US 433, 540.
[87] *Handyside v United Kingdom* (1976) 1 EHRR 733.
[88] *Handyside v United Kingdom* at 753–54.
[89] Human Rights Act UK 1998.

is immediate or even as 'rapid' as the European Court suggests. Rather, the values articulated over a period of time either become or reflect dominant values in society. The judiciary is expected and required to take heed of such values in certain discretionary areas.

It is clear that the voices we hear from the media generally do not consider protests (or immigrants)[90] as part of a democratic society. The British Prime Minister certainly does not. While the law states clearly that pluralism, tolerance and broadmindedness are the values of democratic society,[91] white boiler suits seem to be considered beyond the pale. Indeed, case law also affirms that '[f]reedom of expression constitutes one of the essential foundations of' democratic society.[92]

Decisions that prioritise immigration law, or 'democratic value' (in the case of the May Day protests), over human rights essentially efface the humanity of applicants just as surely as corralling protestors. The re-reading that I propose is rather than understanding human rights as balanced against other considerations, we should understand that they simply do not apply because of a clash with law. As it stands, the two are not considered separately but together. It is time they parted company.

[90] Cf Santa Ana 1999 above n 2.
[91] *Handyside v United Kingdom* at 737, para 49.
[92] *Ibid.*

3

The Dialogistic Nature of Brazil's Arbitration Law 9.307/96

CELINA FRADE

I

INTRODUCTION

LAW IS AN area of human activity where differences between peoples, nations and cultures can be enormous because legislation (law-making) tends to be 'an accumulation of idiosyncratic historical developments and native traditions.'[1] The primary nature of legislation is to regulate social behaviour by means of words in one of two ways: it commands or empowers. Thus the law sets up two categories of 'legal illocutionary act': while mandatory illocutionary acts impose an obligation to act or not to act, discretionary illocutionary acts confer a power that may or may not be exercised.[2] On the other hand, the binding force of legislative text is attached to a linguistic formulation that, once enacted, 'exists indefinitely or until repealed', and its authority is reinforced and given continuity by an assumption that their words are 'continually speaking'.[3]

In the two main contemporary legal systems—common law and civil law—legislation is the largest and the most powerful source of law and appears in several forms of texts, or genres, such as enacted laws (Acts of Parliament, statutes or normative acts), and judicial decisions, formulated in a 'contextually dependent fuzzy language.'[4]

In order to gain status as a 'valued symbol', legislation must be 'petitioned' for within the legal discursive system itself by means of well-established and regulated procedures and also must 'pass discursive texts', as

[1] R Hiltunen, *Chapters on Legal English: Aspects Past and Present of the Language of the Law* (Helsinki, Suomalainen Tiedeakatemia, 1990), at 12.

[2] Y Maley, 'The Language of Legislation' (1987) 16 *Language in Society* 29.

[3] *Ibid* at 38.

[4] M Dascal and J Wróblewski, 'The rational law-maker and the pragmatics of legal interpretation' (1991) 15 *Journal of Pragmatics* 437.

specified in the rules of legislative writing.[5] Once within the system, legislation is interpreted as:

> the process of continuous movement through the system, a process which both expresses the higher orders of meaning that constitute the 'social semiotic', the meaning systems of the culture and at the same time changes and modifies the system itself as well.[6]

Thus, to say that a 'text' has meaning as legislation is to relate it specifically to a legal universe of discourse as distinct from others, and thus to interpret it in terms of legal norms and assumptions about the nature of meaning.[7] And meaning is both context-dependent and a product of social contextualised practices.

As a genre, legislation is a way of (inter)acting, of producing social life in the semiotic mode and is usually associated with a series of relatively stable agreements, historically constituted, approved by the legal community. The result is not only a particular kind of text but also specific processes of production, distribution and interpreting[8] which may display permissible variations across each legal system's usage and socio-cultural and political factors.

This article approaches the dialogistic nature of Brazil's Arbitration Law 9.307/96[9] (hereinafter 'the Law') under the context of civil law tradition. Legislation seems to be a suitable locus for the study of dialogism in legal language. As opposed to monologism, which assumes individuals and cultures to be analytical primes, the dialogist (also dialogical) approach to discourse (text and genre) and communication takes '*actions and interactions*, eg the discursive practices, *in their contexts* as basic units.'[10] Generally used to refer to talk in face-to-face interaction, the term 'dialogue' can be extended to define any representations in writing, including types of interaction through language or other semiotic means.

However monological and asymmetrical legislation seems to be, it is filled with '*dialogic overtones*' manifested, at the micro level, as the interplay among the various *voices* and, at the macro level, as a response to

[5] C Bazerman, 'Performatives constituting value: the case of patents' in BL Gunnarsson, P Linell and B Nordberg (eds), *The Construction of Professional Discourse* (London and New York, Longman, 1997), 44 at 45.

[6] MAK Halliday, *Language as Social Semiotic: The Social Interpretation of Language and Meaning* (London, Edward Arnold, 1978), at 137.

[7] This consideration was taken following Halliday's example with literary texts: *ibid.*

[8] N Fairclough, *Discurso e mudança social [Discourse and social change]* (Brasília, Editora UnB, 2001a), at 161.

[9] The original text of the Law is available only in Portuguese in the issue of the Official Gazette ['*Diário Oficial*'] dated Tuesday, September 24, 1996. Due to its length it has not been attached to this article. A version in English of some of its glossed clauses is provided for a wider accessibility.

[10] P Linell, *Approaching dialogue: Talk, interaction and contexts in dialogical perspectives* (Amsterdam/Philadelphia, John Benjamins Publishing Company, 1998), at 7.

other social practices, other social groups and its socio-cultural environment, historically constituted, 'even though this responsiveness may not have assumed a clear-cut external expression.'[11] In the present context , the dialogistic properties of transnational legislation particularly reflects the attempts of states and various organisations towards uniformisation of rules and laws, such as international arbitration, to regulate trade and commerce on a global level.

The chapter is organised as follows: firstly, we address dialogism in genre and some main dialogistic properties; secondly, we analyse legal dialogism as manifested in legislation in the two contemporary legal systems; thirdly, we provide a brief overview of the latest developments of international arbitration and fourthly we illustrate our claims with an account of the dialogistic properties of the Law. We conclude suggesting further similar analyses of legal English across legal systems.

II

DIALOGISM AND GENRE

Dialogism constitutes a theoretical framework for analysing discourse (text and genre), communication and cognition and focuses on 'the contextual nature of interaction',[12] that is, it includes not only its immediate local contexts but also the relevant situational and socio-cultural contexts. The dialogistic paradigm is better understood in contrast to monologism, the dominant paradigm in the language sciences which looks upon language (and not discourse) as a code, communication as information transfer and cognition as individual information processing.[13] When we come to interpret language dialogistically, the conceptual framework is drawn from 'rhetoric rather than from logic' and the grammar is a 'grammar of choices rather than of rules.'[14]

Dialogism in genre has been addressed in rhetorical criticism,[15] linguistic anthropology,[16] interdisciplinary discourse analysis,[17] Critical Discourse

[11] M Bakhtin, 'The Problem of Speech Genres' in *Speech Genres and Other Late Essays* in C Emerson and M Holquist (eds), VW Mcgee (trans) (Austin, University of Texas Press, 1986), at 92 (author's emphasis).

[12] Linell 1998 above n 10, at 35.

[13] For a comprehensive analysis of monologism and dialogism see Linell 1998 above n 10.

[14] Halliday 1978 above n 6.

[15] KK Campbell and KH Jamieson, 'Form and genre in rhetorical criticism: an introduction' in KK Campbell and KH Jamieson (eds), *Form and genre: shaping rhetorical action* (Falls Church, VA, The Speech Communication Association, 1978) 9 at 32. CR Miller, 'Genre as a Social Action' (1984) 70 *Quarterly Journal of Speech* 151 at 167.

[16] CL Briggs and R Bauman, 'Genre, Intertextuality, and Social Power' (1992) 2 *Journal of Linguistic Anthropology* 131 at 172.

[17] Linell 1998 above n 10.

Analysis,[18] semiotics,[19] and socio semiotics.[20] The studies share insights on common dialogistic properties of genres using different terminology, such as responsiveness, intertextuality, interdiscursivity and recontextualisation; addressivity, other-orientedness and other-orientation; responsive understanding and specialised shared knowledge; and polyphony, heteroglossia and multivoicedness.

These properties are semiotic resources realised by choices of lexicogrammatical structures which stand for the 'complex matrix of contexts'[21] of the genre. Contexts, in turn, are also semiotic phenomena insofar as they are meaningful in relation to the genre and set up the framing for its adequate interpretation.

Genres are 'certain relatively stable thematic, compositional, and stylistic types of utterances' which reflect historical changes and all the changes taking place in social life.[22] Genres are quintessentially responsive insofar as they are constructed 'as a mosaic of quotations', that is, as a response to preceding and to subsequent discourses and can be repeated with varying degrees of reinterpretation.[23] Viewed in a synchronic or horizontal perspective, a genre provides 'framing devices' to shape discourse into ordered, unified, and bounded texts by means of the generation of textuality; viewed in a diachronic or vertical perspective, generic responsiveness orders discourse in historical and social terms.[24]

Bakhtin innovates when he situates the genre within history and society by introducing the status of the word as a minimum structural unit of utterance, and not of language. As a unit of language, the word, like the sentence, 'belongs to *nobody*'[25] and is devoid of expressive meaning. It is only when a word becomes a complete utterance that it becomes capable of determining the 'directly active responsive position' of the writer and the apprehension of the reader.[26] The word is spatialised in a three-dimensional 'intersection of textual surfaces' as a set of dialogical elements: that of the writer, the addressee and exterior text—contemporary or earlier cultural context.[27] Thus, the word plays the dual role of 'mediator', linking structural models to

[18] N Fairclough, *Language and Power* (London and New York, Longman, 1989). N Fairclough, *Discurso e mudança social [Discourse and social change]* (Brasília, Editora UnB, 2001a). N Fairclough, 'The Dialects of Discourse' (2001b) XIV *Textus* 2, 231 at 242.

[19] J Kristeva, *The Kristeva Reader* (London, Basil Blackwell, 1986).

[20] Halliday 1978 above n 6. G Kress and T Threadgold, 'Towards a Social Theory of Genre' (1988) 21 *Southern Review* 3, 215 at 243.

[21] P Linell, 'The power of dialogue dynamics' in I Marková and K Foppa (eds), *The Dynamics of Dialogue* (Hemel Hempstead, Harvester Wheatsheaf, 1990) 147 at 177.

[22] Bakhtin 1986 above n 11, at 64, 71 and 73. In fact, the author provides this definition for 'speech genres.' He defines 'speech' as any utterance, from a single word, the sentence to the large narrative, not as a linguistic unit but as a 'unit of speech communication' belonging to a 'particular speaking subject.'

[23] Kristeva 1986 above n 20, at 37.

[24] Briggs and Bauman 1992 above n 17.

[25] Bakhtin 1986 above n 11, at 84.

[26] *Ibid*, at 82.

[27] Kristeva 1986 above n 20, at 36.

historical and social environment and of 'regulator', controlling mutations from diachrony to synchrony, eg to generic structure.[28]

Each genre has 'its own typical conception of the addressee, and this defines it as a genre.'[29] But the specific addressee is not the only one and there may be cases in which other audiences (virtual or remote) as well are regarded as important objects of generic other-orientedness. In any event, one can only understand a genre if one accounts for the writer's attitude towards the *other's* particular 'apperceptive background of responsive understanding' and anticipation of his/her responsive reaction.[30] On the other hand, the addressee will accept the writer's and the genre's positioning and the authority of the writer so as to interpret, evaluate and ratify it as he does.[31] If audience is ignored, the genre is likely to 'rhetorically degenerate' or ultimately disappear insofar as it fails to achieve responsiveness to its perceived situational demand.[32]

Underlying the concept of dialogism is the theory of 'voice', which accounts for the presence of one or more individuals or discourse types coexisting (and also contradicting) within a particular genre. There are a number of potential relationships of voices in utterances: from one voice only, 'the hallmark of the authoritarian individual or society,'[33] for example, to the polyphonic nature of novels. In general, the many voices call on a background of shared knowledge and assumptions about the socio-cultural contexts and, more narrowly, on the shared specialised meanings for a responsive understanding to the genre.

Thus, the genre, in a dialogistic perspective, is the linguistic form of social interaction and identifies the nature of its various contexts which, in turn, 'can be revealed in the act of meaning itself.'[34] The next section offers a characterisation of what we mean by legal dialogism and its main dialogical properties as manifested in legislation.

III

LEGAL DIALOGISM

Legal systems vary according to the socio-cultural and historical origins and development they encode. There are also variations in law-making

[28] Kristeva 1986 above n 20, at 37.
[29] Bakhtin 1986 above n 11, at 95.
[30] *Ibid*, at 97.
[31] G Kress and T Threadgold 1998 above n 21, at 243.
[32] KK Campbell and KH Jamieson, 'Form and genre in rhetorical criticism: an introduction' in KK Campbell and KH Jamieson (eds), *Form and genre: shaping rhetorical action* (Falls Church, VA, The Speech Communication Association, 1978), at 25.
[33] G Cook, *The Discourse of Advertising* (London and New York, Routledge, 1992), at 183.
[34] R Hasan, 'Contexts for meaning' in JE Alatis (ed), *Language, Communication and Social Meaning Georgetown University Round Table on Languages and Linguistics 1992* (Washington, DC, Georgetown University Press, 1992), at 86.

processes and 'rhetorical thought patterns'[35] as expressed in particular conventions of description and argument in the use of law languages, including legislative writing, across (and within) legal systems. Let us exemplify these variations with a brief characterisation of the two main contemporary legal systems: the common law and the civil law.

The common law, or Anglo Saxon law, was developed in England from the time of the Norman Conquest (AD 1066) and is adopted nowadays in the United States, Australia, Canada, India and New Zealand as well. It is based on court decision, on the doctrines implicit in those judicial decisions and on customs and usages rather than on codified written laws. The fundamental principles of the common law are based on the 'gradual accumulation of individual precedents'[36] from case decisions together with individual cases. The common law has produced a legal language which is formal, detailed, technical and prolix both lexically and syntactically, revealing the great antiquity of the system. These factors partially account for the preference for explicitness and particularity and for the concern of avoiding ambiguities and misunderstandings in the legal community.

In contrast, the civil law system is based on Roman law and the canonic law (law of the Church) as codified in the French or Napoleonic Code (1894) and established in a systemic and principled legal method. Adopted in Continental Europe (except the UK) and South America, including Brazil, the civil law is framed by political histories which led to codifications of law and a 'bureaucratic view of the courts as instruments of democratic state power.'[37] he main source of law is the enactment of normative acts which are regarded as 'unilateral decisions of the competent state organ.'[38] The civil law language prefers 'generality' to 'particularity' and law is usually drafted in broad general principles and also in an intelligible and simple style. It is supposed to be understood by the ordinary citizen while, at the same time, allowing the courts to establish its details of its application in specific cases.[39]

Nevertheless, legal language usage seems to share dialogistic properties which are culturally independent and commonly associated with the profession—the responsiveness of the meanings of its terms and its pragmatic fuzziness—and which ensures 'sufficient uniformity' to allow for regular and reliable legislative interpretations.[40]

[35] HG Widdowson, *Exploration in Applied Linguistics* (Oxford, Oxford University Press, 1979), at 155.
[36] L Campbell, 'Drafting Styles: Fuzzy or Fussy?' (1996) 3 *E-Law Murdoch University Electronic Journal of Law* 2.
[37] *Ibid.*
[38] Dascal and Wróblewski 1991 above n 4, at 428.
[39] Y Maley, 'The language of legislation' (1987) 16 *Language in Society* and VK Bhatia, *Analysing Genre: Language Use in Professional Settings* (London and New York, Longman, 1993).
[40] Dascal and Wróblewski 1991 above n 4, at 434.

Responsiveness in the sense of 'overlapping references, both implicit and explicit, between texts'[41] is a most pervasive feature of legislative writing. Most legislation is context-dependent and has to be interpreted against a background of related legislation, and also applicable principles and standards across legal systems. Explicit cross-referencing acts metaphorically as a locus to 'respond' to other legal texts (or other discourses), creating a change in meaning in the 'quoting' text and its communicative contexts due to changes in socio-cultural, historical and political practices. Implicit references to broad principles and concepts may be readily understood but are not readily applied and have remote response when fit into each new context. As their applicability remains open, they allow for a 'multitude of different interpretations' and may lead to markedly different (or unwanted) outcomes in particular cases.[42]

Likewise, the vocabulary of legislation includes, on the one hand, technicality and precision of meaning encoded in technical terms and terms of art[43] and, on the other hand, flexibility and vagueness of meaning encoded in general terms and judgment words. Terms of art may refer either to the subject matter legislated (*arbitral award*) or purely legal concepts words (*equity*) and their meanings are taken for granted by the legal community. General words (*the parties, whoever*) account for the generality of the legal rule to be applied in given changing circumstances in a changing context and can be used strategically to leave it to the courts' discretion to construe and apply the rule or else to alter the law. Judgment words (*reasonably, willful*) are judged subjectively though they may rely on previous court decisions and definitions to identify behaviour to which such terms can apply in changing contexts.[44]

The contexts of legislative interpretation are construed as satisfying some presuppositions of what is shareable and shared by the law-maker and the law-interpreter/applier.[45] On the production side, the law-maker has the authority of the legislature (standing for the sovereign power) and is assumed to be a competent user of legal language and of relevant rules of legal reasoning; on the reception side, there are those subject to the legislation (the audience) and the law-interpreter/applier, who is assumed to have access to 'the following interpreter-independent realities': a legal language, the situational context of legislation, the relevant rules of legal language, a legal system and directives of legal interpretation.[46]

[41] Y Maley, 'The language of the law' in J Gibbons (ed), *Language and the Law* (London and New York, Longman, 1994), at 25.

[42] Campbell 1996 above n 37.

[43] As to D Mellinkoff, *The Language of the Law* (Boston, Little Brown and Company, 1963), at 17. A term of art is 'a technical word with specific meaning'.

[44] Maley 1987 above n 40.

[45] See also C Frade, 'The Legal Cooperative Principle: An Essay on the Cooperative Nature of Contractual Transactions' (2002) 15 *International Journal for the Semiotics of Law* 4, 338 at 343.

[46] Dascal and Wróblewski 1991 above n 4, at 435.

To sum up, in a dialogistic perspective, the fundamental assumption is that, taking into account the legal system, legal interpretation cannot be dissociated from a general intent to cover all legal relations within the national society. And also legal interpretation should be concerned with the implementation of 'the value of adequacy of law to the changing needs of life',[47] which is the case of international arbitration and the efforts of states and organisations towards the uniformity of its rules and procedures.

IV

INTERNATIONAL ARBITRATION

Generally related to economics, globalisation also concerns providing legal conditions for global trade and commerce. The growth of arbitration as an alternative form of dispute resolution to state justice has been directly related to the ever-increasing globalisation of international commerce, legal professional and legal education.[48] As states engage in international trade and commerce, the idiosyncracies of national laws are no longer able to guarantee prompt, effective and knowledgeable dispute resolution of international business disputes.[49]

In an integrated globalised economy, institutionalised kinds of transnational laws and procedures have been developed to provide for the acceptance and uniformity in the regulation of issues which cannot be provided by national laws. Thus language plays a crucial role as a semiotic means to represent the construction of uniform law and legal practices on a global level. This does not mean to oppose national to uniform law but rather to contribute to the coordinating actions between them to compensate for the lack of structure of national laws to meet global requirements. In the case of international arbitration, successful attempts towards uniformity have resulted in the emergence of several conventions and model laws to be adopted transnationally, such as the International Chamber of Commerce (ICC) in 1923 and the Model Law of the United Nations Commission on International Trade Law (UNCITRAL) of 1985.

In this context, countries which were traditionally reluctant to accept arbitration, both in domestic and international relations, such as Brazil, were encouraged to modernise their arbitration laws in order to offer an attractive and effective forum for the resolution of international conflicts.[50]

[47] Dascal and Wróblewski 1991 above n 4, at 438.

[48] DF Vagts, 'The Impact of Globalization on the Legal Profession' in M Pfeifer (ed), *The Internationalization of the Practice of Law* (The Netherlands, Kluwer Law International, 2001), at 67. H van Houtte and P Wautelet, 'International Lawyers and Uniform Law' in M Pfeifer (ed), *The Internationalization of the Practice of Law* (The Netherlands, Kluwer Law International, 2001), at 89.

[49] R Briner, 'Globalization and the Future of Courts of Arbitration' in M Pfeifer (ed), *The Internationalization of the Practice of Law* (The Netherlands, Kluwer Law International, 2001), at 68

[50] *Ibid*, at 69.

Although Brazil has been using arbitration both in foreign and domestic controversies since 1900, it was not until 1996 that a modern arbitration law—the Brazilian Arbitration Law 9.307/96—was enacted pressed by the needs of a new international legal order.

The interaction between national laws and uniform transnational laws can prove difficult but it is essentially dialogistic. Uniform laws necessarily function against the background of national rules, while, on the other hand, their application and interpretation can vary according to national courts and depend upon their legal traditions and social and economic backgrounds.[51] Partly inspired by the Spanish legislation (1988), the UNCITRAL and the provisions of both the New York Convention (1958) and the Panama Agreement (1975), the Law provides us with an example of dialogistic transnational legislation and the uneasy tension between national and uniform laws.

V

THE DIALOGISTIC LAW

On the whole, the Law follows the rules of Brazilian legislative drafting: the title contains the number and the date of the enactment, 'Law no 9307, of September 23, 1996', followed by the short title 'Provides for arbitral proceedings' and it is organised into seven chapters, forty-one articles and forty-nine paragraphs.

The successful enactment of the Law presupposes the ordinary institutional context of the Brazilian law-making process: the submission of a draft for future approval into law to the legislative, the executive and the judiciary bodies and the citizens; its sanction by the President, deputies and senators and the publication of the enacted law, mandatory to all citizens, in the Official Gazette.[52] Also, the Law provides the 'arbitral' context for the parties wishing to enter into arbitration in case of (or as a result of) contractual controversies. Both contexts are not physical constructs but 'semiotically constituted'[53] insofar as their value and identity are known respectively by the way law-maker and law-interpreter/applier interpret them and by the meanings of words and terms that are meant.

One of the most striking dialogistic properties of the Law is its multitude of *voices*—an array of institutional and social groups—in 'dialogue' with one another. The Law may be regarded both as a macro speech act, with its 'declarative' formula presented in the beginning of the document 'I make known,' and also an hybrid speech act, which combines three types of

[51] van Houtte and Wautelet 2001 above n 49, at 100.

[52] C Frade, 'Introduction to the Legal System in Brazil' in VK Bhatia, CN Candlin, J Engberg and A Trosborg (eds), *Multilingual and Multicultural Contexts of Legislation: An International Perspective* (Hamburg, Peter Lang GMBH, 2003) at 24.

[53] Hasan 1992 above n 35, at 85.

speech acts and the two performers of the act contained in this formula. Firstly, it is a declarative speech act in which the President himself 'declares' something to others. In this case, the grammatical and real subject of the sentence is the President. Secondly, the National Congress performs one of its attributions, that is, to 'decree' the law and, thirdly, the President also performs his other attribution to 'sanction' the law:

> The President of the Republic—I make known that the National Congress decrees and I sanction the following Law: (the entire text of the law that follows).

The predicate 'the following Law' is a place holder since 'the real subject, extraposed to the end of the sentence is the entire text of the law'.[54] This is the site where the many other *voices* (apart from the law-maker) that is, the parties, arbitrators, witnesses, attorneys, other arbitral institutions and the courts interact to ensure the institution, the procedures and the enforcement of arbitration.

It is worth pointing out that the *voice* of the courts is still very strong in the Law. If compared to the UNML which envisages court involvement in nine instances, the Law envisages court involvement in eleven instances. Moreover, the Law leaves it unclear if these instances are the only ones subject to court intervention, which may lead to other controversies. It still reflects the primacy of the State upon the citizens on all levels of society deeply embodied in the 'collective unconsciousness'[55] and which compels citizens to rely exclusively on the courts to solve their problems.

The interpretation of the Law, as in most Brazilian legislation, must be systematic since it is subordinated to a set of more general provisions from which it cannot and should not be dissociated. Responsiveness to prior (or subsequent) legislation is manifested, for example, in explicit references to the Code of Civil Procedure as highlighted in the clauses below:

> 14th Art. It is challenged to act as arbitrators, persons who hold, with the parties or with the litigation submitted to them, some of the relations which characterise cases of impediment or suspicion of judgments, applying to them, as the case may be, the same rights and responsibilities under the Code of Civil Procedure.
>
> Article 36. It is applied to the homologation for the recognition or enforcement of the foreign arbitral award, as it may apply, the provision under Arts 481 and 484 of the Code of Civil Procedure.

[54] D Kurzon, *It is hereby performed ... Explorations in Legal Speech Acts. Pragmatics and Beyond VII: 6* (Amsterdam, John Benjamins, 1986).

[55] P Martins, 'Arbitragem através dos Tempos. Obstáculos e Preconceitos à sua Implementação no Brasil' ['Arbitration through Times. Obstacles and Prejudice to its Implementation in Brazil'] in AN Pucci *et al* (eds), *A Arbitragem na Era da Globalização* [*Arbitration in the Era of Globalisation*] (Rio de Janeiro, Editora Forense, 1999) 35 at 67.

The 'quoted' parts of the Code are recontextualised in the Law and are used as resources in creating new meaning in the 'quoting' text, that is the Law, and its communicative context.

Words and terms, as unit of utterances, in the Law are available as 'resources with *potentials*'[56] to be interpreted interactively with contexts in routinised ways by the law-maker and the law-interpreter/applier. Thus, word meanings are relatively stable over time but, at the same time, are constantly open to negotiation and accommodation either in local (articles and paragraphs) or external contexts of legislation. The vocabulary of the Law comprises judgment words, general legal principles, technical terms and terms of art.

Judgment words have relatively stable meanings because they are subject to social and historical changes in the continuity of legal practice. This is the case of 'capable' in the following clauses which 'respond' both to the Civil Code and the Constitution:

> Article 1. Any capable person to a contract may refer to arbitration to settle litigation in relation to defeasible equity rights.

In the 1916 Civil Code, in force until January 12, 2002, a natural person was deemed 'capable' if he/she was 21 years old. According to the current Civil Code (Article 9), a person reaches his/her 'civil autonomy' at the age of 18 and is in perfect mental condition to answer for his/her actions. This means that he/she can perform all the acts of civil life, including entering into contractual transactions, without parent authorisation.

In the article below the word 'capable' is restrictive as to who is capable of acting as arbitrator. According to Article 34, Paragraph XVI of the Federal Constitution, public officers (such as judges and ministers) cannot act as arbitrators since they are prohibited from accumulating more than one paid function. However, as there is omission in the Law, it allows any safe conclusion indirectly and the issue should be defined by practice:

> Article 13. Any capable person in the parties' confidence may act as an arbitrator.

In both cases, the 'letter of the law' remains the same despite changes in social and institutional conditions, and it is the task of the law-interpreter/applier to assume a change in meaning to make the Law appropriate in the light of the current context.

The general legal principles underlined in the clauses below have achieved the status of semitechnical words and their meanings have been 'interactionally established over time, in the history of practices.'[57]

> Article 2. Arbitration may be conducted based on law or equity, at the parties' discretion.

[56] Linell 1998 above n 10, at 119 (original in italics).
[57] Dascal and Wróblewski 1991 above n 4.

> Paragraph 1. The parties may freely agree upon the rules of law that shall be applied to arbitral proceedings, provided that there is no violation to good customs and to public policy.
>
> Paragraph 2. The parties may also agree on arbitration proceedings based on general principles of law, usage and good customs and on international rules of commerce.

The term 'equity', as pragmatically used in our legal system, corresponds to the English expression 'equity' from Latin *aequitas* from *aequus* (equal). The law-interpreter/applier is authorised to judge by equity: a) in situations where the rule is not applicable any more; b) when the situation has not been predicted by the legislator; c) when the rule gets old and does not cope with the reality or d) because the application of the rule will cause imbalance between the parties.

The reference to the 'general principles of law' constitutes a long-standing tradition in international arbitration and the arbitrators decide upon universal norms used in the choice of law. The principles of 'usage and good customs' and 'public policy' are stated in Article 17 of the current Introduction Law to the Civil Code, which says that any laws, acts and sentences which offend the national sovereignty, public order and good customs are not effective in Brazil. Nonetheless, there are differences between national and international usage and customs. 'International rules of commerce' are varied and seem to hold a supranational character in a movement towards uniformity of proceedings to meet the needs of international commerce.

The Law also hosts technical terms such as 'disposable equity rights', 'adhesion contracts', 'decide *ex officio*', 'pecuniary liabilities', 'coercive measures and injunctive relief.' These terms display 'technical meanings' and are semiotic modes to 'conceptualise and classify extralinguistic realities' related to the subject matter of the Law and whose meaning are shared by the law-makers and the law-interpreter/applier.

In conclusion, the analysis of the Law in the light of its dialogical properties highlights the tension between the simultaneous application and interpretation of uniform and national rules to international arbitration in Brazil. Although in some situations it is clear that the question is covered by national rules, in others the boundary between national and uniform law is not drawn precisely creating uncertainty the very predictability which uniform law is supposed to bring.

VI

CONCLUSION

Dialogism is a theoretical framework to address discourse (text and genre), communication and cognition in relation to various contexts. Its legal counterpart—legal dialogism—is manifested in legislation across legal systems in terms of various *voices* interacting, the responsiveness of the meanings of its words and terms and its pragmatic fuzziness. In the context of globalisation, the attempts of states and organisations towards uniformity in the application and interpretation of transnational laws and regulations rely on dialogistic properties in order to cope with the tensions between national law and uniform laws. This is the case of Brazil's Arbitration Law 9.307/96 analysed in this article.

The use of dialogism in legislation raises some questions. On a local level, it provides for the contexts of local interactions and the sociocultural and legal practices established over long traditions;[58] on a global level, it provides for multiple contexts of transnational interactions and sets up the basis for new conventions in legal practice. Above all, legal practitioners must acquire a minimum awareness of the dialogistic approach in order to produce, apply and interpret legislation on all levels.

Further analysis could focus on the analyses of dialogism in other types of local and transnational legal documents (agreements, treaties and contracts) and also on the creation of uniform dialogistic conventions for the drafting of such documents.[59]

[58] Linell 1998 above n 10, at 54.

[59] See C Frade, 'Mitigating Conflict in Arbitration Clauses Through Language' (2002) 2 *LSP & Professional Communication* 18 at 25.

4

Constitutional 'Communarchy': A Constitution with Chinese Characteristics

DEBORAH CAO*

I

INTRODUCTION

IN THE LAST two decades or so, the People's Republic of China (PRC) has undergone significant changes in its political, social, economic and legal institutions and practices. In particular, there have been major efforts in the rationalisation and strengthening of the legal structure and legal institution.[1] Pertinently, some of the societal developments have been reflected constitutionally such as the incorporation of the 'socialist market economy' and 'rule of law' in the Constitution and in the changes in the lawmaking process by the national legislature, the National People's Congress (NPC). The Chinese leadership seems determined to build 'socialism with Chinese characteristics' and 'a legal system with Chinese characteristics.' This essay examines some of the Chinese characteristics already embodied in the Chinese Constitution, in particular the linguistic presence and absence of the Chinese Communist Party (CCP) in the Constitution, the relationships and tensions between constitutional norms and quasi-norms such as the CCP policies. The essay finally discusses some of the implications of the Chinese constitutional arrangements.

* The author wishes to thank Professor Michael Dowdle of City University of Hong Kong, Professor Randall Peerenboom of the UCLA Law School, and Professor Suri Ratnapala of the Law School, University of Queensland. She would also like to thank Professor Dragan Milovanovic and Professor John Brigham for their kind encouragement and advice. The research was supported by a Griffith University Research Development Grant (2002).

[1] R Peerenboom, 'Ruling the Country in Accordance with Law: Reflections in the Rule and Role of Law in Contemporary China' (1999) 11(3) *Cultural Dynamics* 315–51, at 321.

II
CHARACTERISATION OF CONSTITUTIONS

Constitutions are said to be fundamental laws. They can mean different things depending on whether they are constitutions of liberal democracy or other forms of governments.[2] Whereas the formal authority and supremacy of constitutions of democracies is strengthened by their substantive content as such constitutions provide for separation of powers and free election, the constitutions of non-democratic states such as China differ in both formal authority and substantive content.[3]

Modern constitutionalism or constitutional government in Western democracies has generally involved the notion of a civil society organised and governed on the basis of a relatively stable body of constitutional law.[4] It requires a certain type of constitution, one that limits the powers of political authorities and has the capacity to withstand momentary currents of opinion or political will through a combination of internal mechanism, supporting institutions and culture.[5] A democratic constitution embodies a conception of the fundamental rights and obligations of citizens and establishes a judicial process for adjudication of disputes.[6] It seeks to strike a balance between the rights and freedoms of the governed and the exigencies of effective government.[7] The basic features of constitutional government thus include representative democracy, rule of law, separation of powers, federalism, and human rights.[8] This, however, is not the sole meaning and purpose of a constitution because in nations with different traditions, social tensions and configurations of political powers, constitutionalism may be understood and practised differently.[9] In this connection, it has also been argued that the existing theories of constitutionalism and constitutional development are ill-equipped to explore the elements of constitutional potential in regimes that lack significant praxis of electoral democracy and/or judicial review, ie, authoritarian regimes.[10] The existing constitutional theories were developed primarily to address the problems and issues of

[2] A Chen, *An Introduction to the Legal System of the People's Republic of China* (Singapore, Butterworths, 1992), at 39.

[3] *Ibid*, at 39–40.

[4] AS Rosenbaum, *Constitutionalism: the Philosophical Dimension* (New York, Greenwood Press, 1988), at 4.

[5] S Ratnapala, 'The Idea of A Constitution and Why Constitutions Matter' (Summer 1999/2000) *Policy* 3, at 3.

[6] Rosenbaum 1998 above n 4 at 4.

[7] *Ibid.*

[8] D Beatty, *Constitutional Law in Theory and Practice* (Toronto, University of Toronto Press, 1995), at 4; see also CH McIlwain, *Constitutionalism: Ancient and Modern* (Ithaca, Cornell University Press, 1947).

[9] Rosenbaum 1998 above n 4 at 4.

[10] M Dowdle, 'Of Parliaments, Pragmatism, and the Dynamics of Constitutional Development: the Curious Case of China' (2002) 35(1) *New York University Journal of International Law and Politics* 1, at 1.

the more mature constitutional systems, which have very different concerns from those of the newly emerging constitutional systems like China, which is also an authoritarian and communist country.[11] It has also been claimed that recent history demonstrates that despite their infirmities, authoritarian regimes can contiguously evolve into more constitutional systems.[12] Thus, understanding the processes and motors that can drive such evolution would expand our understanding of the phenomenon of constitutionalism and give us insight into the sociological working of the more mature constitutional systems as well.[13]

For the purpose of this study, Raz's distinction of the thin and thick senses of constitution may serve as a constructive starting point.[14] Raz's characterisation is not meant to draw borderlines but to focus discussion, to highlight the central features of constitutions.[15] According to Raz, in the thin sense, every legal system includes a constitution. The constitution in this sense is simply the law that establishes and regulates the main organs of government, their constitution and powers, and includes law that establishes the general principles under which the country is governed, eg, democracy, if it establishes democratic organs of government and so on. In contrast, the thick sense of constitution is a combination of seven features. First, in incorporating the thin sense, the constitution defines the powers of the main branches of government. This feature identifies the constitution as constitutive of the legal and political structure which is that legal system. Second, it is meant to be of long duration, to serve as a stable framework for the political and legal institutions of the country, preserving stability and continuity in the legal and political structure, and the basic principles that guide its institutions. Third, it is enshrined in one or a small number of written documents. Fourth, it constitutes a superior law, invalidating ordinary laws that conflict with it. Fifth, the constitution is justiciable. There are judicial procedures to implement the superiority of the constitution. Sixth, it is entrenched, its amendments being more difficult to secure. Seventh, its provisions include principles of government (democracy, federalism, basic civil and political rights, etc.) that are generally held to express the common beliefs of the population about the way their society should be governed. The constitution expresses a common ideology. Furthermore, according to Raz, if the autonomous legal traditions of different countries rightly play a major part in determining their constitutional development, then a theory of the constitution cannot be based on social or economic or cultural factors as it cannot be derived from extraneous circumstances.[16] It must allow a major

[11] *Ibid*.
[12] Dowdle, above n 10, at 1–2.
[13] *Ibid*.
[14] J Raz, 'On the Authority and Interpretation of Constitution: Some Preliminaries' in L Alexander(ed), *Constitutionalism: Philosophical Foundations* (Cambridge, Cambridge University Press, 1998), 152–93.
[15] *Ibid*, at 152–53.
[16] *Ibid*.

role to internal legal considerations. So, reflections on a constitutional theory should proceed by examining the enumerated abstract central features of a constitution and their implications.[17]

III

FEATURES OF THE CHINESE CONSTITUTION

The concept and practice of constitution is admittedly a Western tradition. It was introduced to modern China around the turn of the twentieth century. However, despite the Western origin and influence, the Constitution in the PRC was and is very Chinese. The Chinese constitutional form derived from Western liberal constitutionalism. In theory, the principles of legality or the rule of law, such as the supremacy of the constitution, the equality of all persons before the law, and the independent exercise of judicial powers are reaffirmed in Chinese constitutional text, academic studies and in official opinions.[18] One noticeable feature of the Chinese Constitution is that there is a constant tension between constitutional form and substance, between potential ideal and reality, a tension between semantic constitution and constitution as a social practice.[19]

The Chinese Constitution is enshrined in a written document called *xianfa* (constitution). It defines China's political structures and prescribes rights and obligations for its citizens. In terms of the semantic meanings, *xianfa* is an imported linguistic sign and an imported legal concept and practice. The term *xianfa* (constitution) was believed to be borrowed from the Japanese.[20] The Japanese used the existing Chinese character, *xian* originally meaning 'imperial' dating back over two thousand years ago in China and *fa* meaning 'law.' *Xian* had a broader meaning in classical Chinese than when it was used by the Japanese and then by the Chinese for the Western concept of 'constitution.' In China, constitutional efforts were first manifested in legal form in 1908 when the principles of a constitutional government were articulated in the Principles of Constitution among others, aiming at transforming the Chinese body politic into a constitutional monarchy patterned after the Meiji Constitution in Japan, a kind of 'plagiarism' of the Japanese 1889 Constitution.[21] There were also numerous other attempts in the form of provisional constitutions and constitutions.[22] Now,

[17] *Ibid.*

[18] Chen 1992 above n 2 at 3.

[19] *Ibid*, at 39.

[20] Tiechuan Hao, 'Zhongguo jindai faxue liuxuesheng yu fazhi jindaihua' [China's Returned Law Students in Modern Times and Its Modern Legal Development] (1997) 6 *Faxue yanjiu* [*The CASS Law Journal*] 3.

[21] Jianfu Chen, *Chinese Law: Towards an Understanding of Chinese Law, Its Nature and Development* (The Hague, Kluwer Law, 1999), at 59.

[22] For discussions, see *ibid.*

the basic idea of *xianfa* in Chinese corresponds to that in English, ie, a constitution is a legal document with supreme legal force, setting out the basic structures of government.

In contemporary China since 1949, the Constitution and the meaning of *xianfa* have often been associated with politics. Constitutional law was once called 'law of politics', and Chinese legal academics regarded constitutional law as part of political science until recently.[23] The Chinese Constitution is both a political and a legal document; it has legal force as well as political significance.

The political association also finds an expression in the text of the Constitution. The Chinese Constitution defines the political structures of the PRC, a set of general rules and serves as a fundamental charter of organisation. It is relatively stable in that it provides a stable framework for the political institutions and basic principles that guide its institutions despite the frequent amendments (see below). Seventy-eight of the one hundred thirty-eight articles deal with state organisational structure. So, the Constitution is more of a document about state organisation than with the checks and balances of governmental powers, more with future direction of the society than the protection of fundamental rights of citizens, more with general principles than with detailed rules capable of implementation.[24] However, it does set the parameters for legal developments and administrative laws and regulations have been issued implementing various aspects of the Constitution.[25]

The Constitution consists of a preamble and four chapters. Chapter One is General Principles. In Chapter One, according to the Constitution, the PRC is a socialist state under 'the people's democratic dictatorship' (Art. 1). It establishes the general principles and other guidelines, such as the basic government and administrative structures, the general economic system and national defence, the cultural, educational, population, environmental and language policies. In Chapter Two, the Constitution lists the fundamental rights and duties of Chinese citizens. The expressly guaranteed rights include right to equality before the law, political rights and freedoms, freedom of speech, of the press, of assembly, of association, of procession, and of demonstration, religious freedom, personal freedoms, social and economic rights, cultural and educational rights etc (Arts. 35 and 36). Chapter Three concerns the structure of the state. It sets out the structures of the Chinese legislative, executive and judiciary structures. The National People's Congress (NPC) is the highest organ of state power, exercising the legislative power of the state. The NPC's powers laid down in the Constitution include amending the Constitution, making and interpreting

[23] Guanghui Wang, 'Xianfa wei genben fa zhi yanjin' [Constitution as a Basic Law and its Evolution] (2000) 2 *Faxue yanjiu* [*CASS Law Journal*] 127, at 127.

[24] Chen 1999 above n 2 at 58.

[25] *Ibid.*

basic laws, the election and removal of top officials, consideration and approval of the state budget, plans for national economic and social developments, reports on their implementation, and generally supervising the implementation of the Constitution (Arts 62–64). The NPC has a Standing Committee whose powers include law-making, interpreting the Constitution and laws, constitutional supervision and implementation, annulment of illegal administrative or local regulations (Art 67). It also prohibits the Standing Committee members from holding office in state administrative, adjudicative or procuratorial organs (Art 65). The executive and administrative powers are vested in the State Council, the highest organ of state power (Art 85). Chapter Three also provides that the people's courts exercise adjudicative power and the people's procuratorates exercise the procuratorial powers. It further provides that the courts and procuratorates shall independently exercise their powers in accordance with law and shall not be interfered with by administrative organs, social organisation or individuals (Arts 126 and 131). Chapter Four covers the National Flag, the National Emblem and the Capital.

Thus, there seems to be an explicit separation of the three branches of government in Chapter Three although the Chinese government and theoreticians always officially reject the notion of separation of powers as a Western bourgeois deception of the ruling class to control the people,[26] and despite any desirability of executive restraints, all powers are subject to the leadership of the CPC.[27]

Apart from this basic setup, the most distinctive feature of the Chinese Constitution is the entrenched status of the CCP, a kind of constitutional communism or constitutional 'communarchy'. The CCP is entrenched directly and indirectly, explicitly and implicitly, in the Constitution. The Chinese Communist Party and its ideology are supreme in Chinese law and in the Constitution. This political dominance is manifested in several levels constitutionally.

Historically, the first PRC Constitution adopted in 1954 was heavily influenced by the USSR and its communist ideology regarding constitution. One of the Soviet influences in constitutional thought was that a constitution was traditionally regarded as guidelines for the legislature. Thus, the Chinese Constitution serves as the party-state's programs for ideological guidance and as a political document that reflects government policies.[28] The constitutional provisions are dependent for their implementation on further enactment of ordinary legislation. This is indicated linguistically through the extensive use of vague and broad phrases such as 'according to

[26] Chen 1992 above n 2 at 48.
[27] *Ibid*, at 48 and 40.
[28] Xingzhong Yu, 'Citizenship, Ideology, and the PRC Constitution' in M Goldman and EJ Perry (eds), *Changing Meanings of Citizenship in Modern China* (Cambridge, Mass, Harvard University Press, 2002), 288 at 290.

law', 'within the scope of the law' and 'subject to law.' It was believed that the Chinese Constitution has no direct legal force.[29] It raises the question of one of the essential features of a constitution, ie, constitutional justificiability.

Generally speaking, the CCP has always been very prominent in the Constitution, both in letter and spirit. One of the functions of the Constitution is to ensure and consolidate state powers of the governing party, the CCP. The 1954 Constitution highlighted the leading role of the CCP in the victory won by the PRC. The 1975 Constitution, the most politicised version promulgated during the Cultural Revolution (1966–76), stipulated the subjection of the Chinese people to the absolute leadership and supremacy of the CCP. The 1982 Constitution, which is in force currently, is less direct in its reference to the CCP. It does not mention the CCP and its leading role in the main text, but in the Preamble only. This follows the practice in other socialist countries, with the actual exercise of power of the Party to be carried out through extra-constitutional methods.[30] The disappearance of the CCP in the main text of the Constitution was the result of the 1982 constitutional amendment (see below regarding the amendment). In the current Preamble where the CCP is mentioned, it reconfirms that the victories and achievements of the PRC were attained by the Chinese people under the leadership of the CCP, and that the Chinese people will continue to be led by the CCP in future endeavors to build socialism. The Preamble states that:

> Under the leadership of the Chinese Communist Party and the guidance of Marxism-Leninism, Mao Zedong Thought, and Deng Xiaoping Theory, the Chinese people of all ethnic groups will continue to adhere to the people's democratic dictatorship and the socialist road, and to uphold reform and opening to the outside world, steadily improve socialist institutions, develop a socialist market economy, promote socialist democracy, improve the socialist legal system, and work hard and self-reliantly to modernise the country's industry, agriculture, national defence and science and technology step by step to build China into a strong and prosperous, culturally advanced and democratic socialist nation.

This statement seems to be the most significant one in the Preamble, providing a common communist ideology for China and the exclusive power of the CCP to achieve that ideology. The ideology is known as the four fundamental principles, ie, to uphold socialism, people's dictatorship, the leadership of the Communist Party and the guidance of Marxism-Leninism, Mao Zedong Thought, and Deng Xiaoping Theory. These four principles are part of the constitutional guiding ideology. The four fundamental principles were laid down by the CCP and are found in the CCP Constitution.

[29] Chen 1992 above n 2; Chen 1999 above n 21.
[30] Chen 1999 above n 21.

It seems that the inclusion of the four fundamental principles and the CCP into the Constitution was not without opposition.[31] It was reported that Deng Xiaoping insisted on the inclusion of these principles, but at the same time it was recognised that the Party and the government must be separated.[32] The omission of specific provisions on Party leadership as contained in the 1975 and 1978 Constitutions seemed to reflect the CCP's realisation that it would seem more legitimate and democratic to translate its policies into law through legislation rather than the direct control of state functions by the Party.[33] The Party operates with the Constitution, rather than under or above it at least in theory. However, such deliberate omission and reduced textual presence of the CCP does not mean that the CCP is in any way less prominent or has less power or influence, as the Chinese Constitution must be read and interpreted with the CCP direction and guidance.

The four fundamental principles as found in the Preamble to the Constitution presents a major conflict both in form and substance with the idea of constitutional supremacy. The Constitution recognises the supreme legal force of the Constitution (Art 5 and the Preamble). The Constitution is regarded as the mother-law, forming the foundation of all other laws. The Constitution shall prevail over any other types of laws, rules or regulations (Art 5). No one, no parties, organisations or individuals, are to be above the Constitution and the law (Art 5), and it is now generally accepted that this applies to the CCP. Despite Article 5, in practice, as the guiding ideology of the Constitution is the Communist Party, Party and government policies can prevail over the Constitution and law. Thus, the supremacy of the CCP may mean that the Constitution and law may not be supreme where there is a conflict between the Party and the law.[34] In China, there has always been an explicit recognition, acceptance and insistence that everything must be done under the CCP leadership, either to implement the Constitution, law or any policy. The CCP enjoys exclusive control over all forms of state power, and as the ultimate source of power and legitimacy in China, it represents a higher, alternative system of authority and legitimacy.[35]

In terms of basic constitutional principles in Chinese constitutional law, they include principles of all powers belonging to the people (Art 2), the socialist public ownership as its economic system (Art 6) and promotion of socialist spiritual civilisation (Art 24), and constitutional supremacy (Art 5),

[31] Chen 1999 above n 21 at 71.
[32] See *ibid*.
[33] *Ibid*, at 71.
[34] Chen 1992 above n 2 at 39; Chen 1999 above n 21.
[35] P Keller, 'The National People's Congress and the Making of National Law' in JM Otto, MV Polak, Jianfu Chen, and Yuwen Li (eds), *Law-Making in the People's Republic of China* (The Hague, Kluwer Law International, 2000), 75, at 80–81.

as found in different sections of the Constitution. Here the implicit or indirect entrenchment of the CCP is the phrase 'socialist spiritual civilisation.' This phrase is not defined in the Constitution, but the CCP and the Chinese government define it to include the meaning of the four fundamental principles, which prominently include the leadership of the CCP.

In addition, in China, there have been no explicit legal rules or principles for constitutional interpretation used by the courts, but it has been proposed by some Chinese commentators that a general guiding principle for constitutional interpretation is the four fundamental principles.[36]

It is interesting to note that, in the Law on Legislation (2000), for the first time in the provisions of Chinese laws, the supremacy of the CCP and the four fundamental principles in Chinese lawmaking have found their legislative expression.[37] Article 3 of the Law on Legislation states that:

> Lawmaking shall observe the basic principles of the Constitution, take economic construction as its central task, follow the socialist road, adhere to the people's democratic dictatorship, uphold the leadership of the Chinese Communist Party under the guidance of Marxism, Leninism, Mao Zedong Thought and Deng Xiaoping theory, and persevere in reform and the open door policy.

This is of a similar wording to that in the Constitution Preamble, a further explicit legal entrenchment of the CCP in Chinese lawmaking. As suggested, the incorporation of the four fundamental principles into a legal provision raises a serious question about whether the Chinese law-makers now intend to make the *de facto* leadership of the CCP a *de jure* one.[38] This is not surprising, as law in China is said to be essentially the finalisation of the CCP's principles and policies.[39]

At another level, how the Constitution is amended can also illustrate the overriding power of the CCP. As the Chinese lawmakers always insist that a constitution shall only contain the fundamental and necessary provisions that can be decided at the present time, the Constitution is frequently subject to amendments. Pertinently, all the Chinese constitutional changes reflect the ideological changes of the CCP. In the fifty odd years from 1949 to 2002, the Constitution was amended eight times in addition to the four different versions. Each amendment corresponded to or resulted from wider political changes, and was proposed or approved by the Communist Party. None of the Party's proposed amendments were ever rejected by the

[36] See Bikun Jiang, *Xianfa xue* [*Constitutional Law*] (Beijing, Zhongguo zhengfu daxue chubanshe, 1999), at 81.

[37] See Jianfu Chen, 'Unanswered Questions and Unresolved Issues: Comments on the Law on Law-Making' in JM Otto, MV Polak, Jianfu Chen, Yuwen Li (eds), *Law-Making in the People's Republic of China* (The Hague, Kluwer Law International, 2000) 235, at 254.

[38] *Ibid*, at 254.

[39] Keller 2000 above n 37 at 77.

NPC. In fact, it was said that an established constitutional convention in China is that the CCP Central Committee initiates and proposes constitutional amendment.[40]

The first PRC Constitution was adopted in 1954, heavily influenced by the Soviet Union in both form and substance. The second Constitution was made in 1975 during the Cultural Revolution. Between 1966 to 1976, due to the political upheavals, the Chinese legal system and laws were largely abolished. The 1975 Constitution was a skeleton of the 1954 Constitution and it reflected Maoist triumph over Russian ideologies but nevertheless an extreme Chinese Left ideology prevailed, resembling a political manifesto than a constitution.[41] It expressly affirmed the direct rule of the Party over legislature, government and armed forces, reflecting Mao's disregard for law and constitutional constraints.[42]

The third Constitution was promulgated in 1978 when the Cultural Revolution ended, largely restoring the 1954 version. In 1982, another Constitution was adopted and it is this document currently in force, reflecting China's desire for modernising and economic development. In 1988, it was amended to legitimise the existence of the private economy. In 1993, there was another amendment, in which 'socialist market economy' replaced 'planned economy' (Art. 15), among others. In 1999, the Constitution was again amended, incorporating 'governing the country in accordance with law' (*yifa zhiguo*) and 'rule of law' (*fazhi*) (Art. 5), and 'Deng Xiaoping Theory' in the Preamble. All these were politically related changes. 1999 also saw the deletion of 'counter-revolutionary crimes' (Art. 28), an effort by the legislature and the government to reduce the political content in the Constitution as 'counter-revolutionary' was a distinctively political label.

One noteworthy change in the 1999 constitutional amendment is that it seems that wider opinions were canvassed compared with past practices. It was reported that three of the six amendments including the inclusion of 'governing the country in accordance with law', 'rule of law' and 'building a socialist rule of law state' proposed by the Communist Party to the NPC Standing Committee had originally been suggested by an individual who was a member of the NPC.[43] This may be seen as part of the wider lawmaking changes. Also unprecedented were a series of seminars given by a group of respected legal scholars in 1999 to the leaderships of the Communist Party and of the NPC, explicating their expert opinions on law and legal

[40] Chongde Xu, *Xianfa* [*Constitutional Law*] (Beijing, Zhongguo remin daxue chubanshe, 2001), at 36.

[41] Chen 1999 above n 21.

[42] *Ibid.*

[43] Hongji Mo, *Zhengfu yu gongmin xianfa bidu: Zhonghua renmin gongheguo xianfa xiuzhengan quanjing touxi* [*Compulsory Readings for the Government and Citizens: A Complete Analysis of the Chinese Constitutional Amendments*] (Beijing, Zhongguo renmin gongan daxue chubanshe, 1999).

concepts such as the 'rule of law' and 'constitutionalism.' This was in contrast to the past practices that it was always the Communist Party that dictated to everyone else what certain things must mean. These could be seen as evidence for the expanded channel of communication between the government, the legislature, and through NPC members and the wider public, to enhance the legitimacy of the government, the CCP, and law in general.

The frequent amendments of the Constitution and the occasional complete re-writes are partly related to the existing constitutional arrangements. Article 64 allows constitutional amendments by a two-thirds majority of the national legislature as opposed to referenda or other stricter amendment procedures. This is an inherent defect in the Constitution. It further weakens constitutional supremacy, as the constitution could just become another ordinary law, susceptible to easy modification or abrogation by transient holders of political powers, an idea and practice contrary to constitutionalism.[44]

IV

MAKING SENSE OF THE CHINESE CONSTITUTION

The Chinese Constitution is both a political and legal document. It enjoys supreme legal force but has yet to manifest its legal force adequately or sufficiently. It often sounds rather hollow to ordinary Chinese. Notwithstanding, one should not regard it as a purely political manifesto and ignore its legal significance. It has been argued that empirically, law increasingly matters in contemporary China.[45] So should the Constitution. Our understanding of China's constitutional developments may provide useful pointers for our study of China's legal developments. A number of implications can be drawn.

Firstly, if we measure the Chinese Constitution with reference to Raz's characterisation as alluded to earlier, we can see that the Chinese Constitution establishes the basic framework of government and defines the basic powers of government. It is relatively stable despite the constant amendments. It is not entrenched although it is more difficult to amend than other types of laws. Importantly, its justiciability is doubtful, although there are signs that more people are willing to use the Constitution to defend their rights and the courts are more willing to rely on the Constitution, directly or indirectly.[46] More importantly, the supremacy of the Constitution is often questionable

[44] Ratnapala, 1999/2000 above n 5.

[45] Peerenboom 1999 above n 1 at 341.

[46] See Gui Shen, 'Xianfa tongzhi shidai de kaishi—xianfa diyi an cunyi' [The Beginning of the Rule by the Constitution? Doubts about the 'First Constitutional Case']. www.chinalaw-info.com, 2001; Lei Wang, *Xianfa de sifahua* [*Constitutional Law Applied in Courts*] (Beijing, Zhongguo zhengfa daxue chubanshe, 2000); Jing Wu, *Xianfa yu gongmin zhijie duihua* [The Direct Dialogue between the Constitution and Citizens], *People's Daily*, 5 September, 2001: http://zgrdxw.peopledaily.com.cn.

despite the explicit written constitutional guarantee. This is where the CCP comes in. As discussed earlier, the supreme status and rule of the CCP are explicitly and implicitly entrenched in the Constitution and in practice. The Chinese Constitution indeed expresses a common ideology, ie, the communist or socialist ideology of the CCP. The entrenched supremacy of the CCP is the most distinctive feature of the Chinese Constitution. In China, CCP policies work in a quasi-legal normative fashion, competing with the constitutional norms. On the one hand, the CCP itself is not a lawmaking body or a branch of the government. On the other hand, lawmaking is the affairs of the state organs, but such lawmaking bodies are not autonomous, and instead reside under the leadership of the CCP.[47] Of direct relevance here are what have been called the 'Party norms': the political line, the polarity norms, and the policies of the Party.[48] In China, party policies normally dictate what the government does and precede the formal adoption of laws (including the amendment of the Constitution, see earlier discussion).

In this connection, it was lamented that the adoption of the notion of a socialist market economy has facilitated the further abandoning of the chineseness of Chinese law and has made the present Chinese legal discourse and legislation distinctively Western.[49] It was said that Western scholars now easily find their familiar language in Chinese law because Chinese law, in its forms, structure and methodologies, has become Western.[50] However, I see the single party dominance and the communist guiding ideology as the most distinctive Chinese characteristic in Chinese law and the Constitution. In this sense, Chinese law in essence cannot be considered Westernised. Chinese law and its constitutional law are uniquely Chinese in practice and in its fundamental principles. The quasi-legal norms of the CCP policies and the supremacy of the CCP explicitly and implicitly in the Constitution constitute the most salient characteristic of Chinese constitutional law.

Given the current health or lack thereof, of the Chinese Constitution, it is necessary to ponder the jurisprudential ramifications of constitutions in a systemic sense. In today's world where the human and societal diversity, the multiplicity of cultures and peoples and the multiplicity of laws in different contexts and texts are being highlighted, it is nevertheless important to examine the inherent legal and constitutional features of a legal system, particularly in relation to emerging or developing legal systems such as China's. Law can never be autonomous from social contexts. It is inevitably influenced by the culture, society, and the world-view of its subjects. Law is not just a set of isolated norms, rules and principles. However, an over-emphasis and over-interpretation of contextual and cultural factors may hide or disguise the

[47] Haroo Von Senger, 'Ideology and Law-Making. Law-Making in the People's Republic of China' in JM Otto, MV Polak, Jianfu Chen and Yuwen Li (eds), *Law-Making in the People's Republic of China* (The Hague, Kluwer Law International, 2000) 41, at 44.

[48] See *ibid* for further discussion.

[49] Chen 1999 above n 21 at 84.

[50] *Ibid*, at 2.

inefficiency, ineffectiveness and inherent flaws that may and indeed do exist in developing legal systems. In China's case, cultural factors, (eg, the Chinese cultural propensity or preference for generality and flexibility over legal certainty and specificity, or cultural or ideological expediency over constitutional supremacy and legal rules), must not be used to explain away the inherent defects in its legal system. In a developing legal system like China's, it is all the more important that law and legal authority, coherence and rationality of law are given sufficient consideration over extra-legal factors in China's legal development, not just in academic deliberation, but more importantly, in the development and practice of law. It is highly constructive to examine and explain why certain culture and people do things in certain ways. It is equally, if not more, constructive that, in the development of an emerging and new legal system as in China's, law and *rules* of law are made as rules and made to function as such through constitutional rule-governance. Constitutional rules ought to govern and also need to be seen to do so.

In this connection, the legal theory of ethical positivism and the idea of rule governance may provide useful philosophical as well as practical guidance and a pathway for China in its legal institutional building and constitutional development. Ethical positivism claims that given the appropriate political and legal culture, specific rule governance can have an important role to play in moving societies towards the attainment of general prosperity, effective humanity and social justice.[51] The appropriate political culture would be that of the liberal democratic system. However, ethical positivism as an aspirational model of law can be taken to serve the values of a wide range of particular philosophies, individualistic, communitarian, hedonistic or pluralist as it is morally eclectic and politically tolerant.[52] Central to ethical positivism is that a system of law ought to be a system of rules. The core limitation on legal subservience to political decision making is that political authority must be mediated by such rules and not simply a matter of ad hoc particularistic decrees or discretion.[53] With regards to constitutional law, ethical positivism requires that the rules which governments must obey have to be clear and precise to put limitations on governments.[54] Essential to this is the separation of powers, in particular the separation of the legislative and adjudicative functions.[55] Undoubtedly such a system works better with a democratic government.

In China's case, because of the expressly stated constitutional supremacy, and given the quasi-separation of legislative and executive powers and the increasing recognition of this constitutional rule, the Constitution may

[51] TD Campbell, *The Legal Theory of Ethical Positivism* (Aldershort, Dartmouth, 1996), at 9.
[52] *Ibid*, at 5.
[53] *Ibid*, at 5–6.
[54] TD Campbell, 'The Point of Legal Positivism' (1998) 9 *The King's College Law Journal* 63, at 80.
[55] *Ibid*, at 81.

contribute meaningfully to restrain the executive government. The Chinese Constitution enshrines the basic principle of constitutional supremacy. What is lacking is its actual enforcement. Similarly, in recent years, the Constitution has undergone major revisions, and numerous laws are being passed in China, but the lack of rule of law and lack of legal enforcement are so extensive that the written laws and the acts of passing laws are often viewed with a large dose of cynicism by the Chinese population. There have been talks of a crisis of faith in law because law is seen as ineffectual or unenforced resulting in disappointment or lack of trust in law on the part of the Chinese people.[56] So, legal rules starting with the constitutional rules need to be realised. Besides, the legislative efforts currently under way also need to be more vigorous and rule governed. The constitutional provisions provide the legitimate device and moral and legal ground, to devise and enforce necessary clear rules for governance and for limiting executive powers. It seems that the NPC has started to make some limited but significant headway in this regard.[57] In addition, given the vast changes in the Chinese society, China's socio-political environment has become increasingly fragmented, serving to progressively shift the locus of political discourse out of the CCP and into the constitutional arena.[58] Thus, law and the Constitution may have a very significant role to play in restraining the government and the CCP, even if this may be an 'unintended consequence' of the government and Party's efforts to restore its legitimacy in institutional and legal construction.[59] It is the government, not the totality of social and economic life, that ethical positivism wishes to further and confine through rule-governance. Moreover, as the constitutional system has its own rules for discursive engagement, this engenders an increasing constitutionalisation of political discourse and the increasing value of the unique arbitrage opportunities inherent in the constitutional apparatus.[60] Consequently, the society, as in China's case, is made to give greater political weight and attention to the normative and structural aspects that define that apparatus, resulting in an ever-growing constitutionalisation of the political environment.[61]

Finally, the Chinese Constitution carries both political meaning and legal significance. It is more than just a political document. The words in the Constitution carry and should carry legal force. Words can mean different things to different people and their absence may also carry meaning. So, to understand the Chinese Constitution, we need to read between and beyond the lines.

[56] Dingjian Cai, 'Development of the Chinese Legal System Since 1979 and Its Current Crisis and Transformation' (1999) 11(2) *Cultural Dynamics* 135.

[57] See M Dowdle, 'Constructing Citizenship: The NPC as Catalyst for Political Participation' in M Goldman and EJ Perry (eds), *Changing Meanings of Citizenship in Modern China*, (Cambridge, Mass, Harvard University Press, 2002), 330.

[58] *Ibid.*

[59] MS Tanner, *The Politics of Lawmaking in Post-Mao China: Institutions, Processes and Democratic Prospects* (Oxford, Clarendon Press, 1999), at 36.

[60] *Ibid.*

[61] *Ibid.*

5

The Quest for Certainty in Recent US Constitutional Scholarship: Original Intent and the Practice of Constitutional 'Creativity'

FREDERICK P LEWIS

> Our knowledge swims in a continuum of uncertainty and indeterminacy.
>
> (Charles Peirce)
>
> What does it mean to say we 'know' something in a world in which things happen higgledy-piggledy? ... Pierce's conclusion was that knowledge must therefore be social. It was his most important contribution to American thought.
>
> (Louis Menand)
>
> The life of the law has not been logic; it has been experience.
>
> (Oliver Wendell Holmes, Jr)

HOLMES' FAMOUS APHORISM is a semiotic statement. It tells us that at least in the Anglo-American legal tradition, legal meaning is primarily shaped by the experience of resolving actual conflicts in different contexts over time, rather than being derived from abstract reasoning processes and concepts which are then imposed upon disputes as they may arise. As applied to US constitutional law, it suggests that the meaning of broad, sweeping, often highly ambiguous constitutional phrases arises from the experience and results of political conflict throughout the history of the United States.

I

THE INSISTENCE ON ORIGINAL INTENT

Much of US semiotic and jurisprudential thought teaches the limitations of any quest for certainty as well as the necessity of looking to context and experience in understanding legal doctrine.[1] Nevertheless in recent decades, the work of a vocal group of US constitutional commentators has centered around their strenuous insistence on confining constitutional interpretation to the original intent of the framers.[2] The effort has been to show that the US Supreme Court's extensive period of judicial activism that began in the 1950s and accelerated through the 1960s and into early 1970s was wrong—that the Court abused its power by using it to excess. Most of the criticism seems prompted by a conservative ideological response to the liberal values that animated that activism. It has coincided with major changes in US national politics over the last three decades: the decay of the political coalition that provided a climate of support for the broad thrust (if not all the details) of what is usually thought of as the Warren Court revolution,[3] and the gradual coming to power of a new conservative coalition.

These critics have shared a belief that the great expansion of rights and liberties, which supporters see as the Court's major accomplishment during this period, was not really legitimate. They seek the 'correct' way to limit the expansive concepts and broad constitutional phrases that were at the center of mid-twentieth century activism. Confining constitutional interpretation to the original intent of its framers has come to be seen by them as the legitimate and appropriate way of achieving that desired limitation. The changing political climate, along with new and divisive constitutional conflicts (most notably those surrounding the abortion issue), has brought renewed energy to the controversy.

Now at first glance the original intent approach might seem to comport with Holmes' insight. It looks to the context, the particular experience that shaped understanding of constitutional language at the time a constitutional phrase was framed. But in insisting on looking only to a particular point in past time, and in refusing to consider how that context has evolved over subsequent decades and in so doing has impacted the meaning of the language, the original intent approach actually proposes an antithetical course. Once constitutional meaning is established (if it is) by seeking out the original intent two hundred or one hundred fifty years ago, it is applied to the present day by either literal application or a rigid reasoning process. The original intent approach is an effort to limit or repudiate subsequent judicial (or other) development of that meaning.

[1] See generally, L Menand, *The Metaphysical Club: A Story of Ideas in America* (New York, Farrar Straus and Giroux, 2001).

[2] Raoul Berger exemplifies the original intentionalists. His best known book is *Government by Judiciary: The Transformation of the Fourteenth Amendment* (Cambridge, MA, Harvard University Press, 1977). Other examples are: R Bork, *The Tempting of America: The Political Seduction of the Law* (New York, Macmillan, 1990); and W Berns, *Taking the Constitution Seriously* (New York, Simon and Schuster, 1987).

[3] See L Powe, *The Warren Court and American Politics* (Cambridge, MA, Harvard University Press, 2000); F Lewis, *The Context of Judicial Activism: The Endurance of the Warren Court Legacy in a Conservative Age* (Lanham, MD, Rowman and Littlefield, 1999).

Of course, as the recent case of *Bush v Gore*[4] so dramatically demonstrated, there are obvious problems associated with the aggressive exercise of judicial power in interpreting the US Constitution. The extremely close Presidential election in 2000 between then Governor George Bush of Texas and Vice-President Al Gore came down to a handful of disputed votes in the State of Florida. After extensive legal maneuvering, a limited recount of votes ordered by the Florida Supreme Court was halted by the US Supreme Court resulting in a Bush victory. Although the issue was not without legal complexities, in the eyes of many Gore supporters, the intervention by the US Supreme Court through a narrow 5–4 vote, with the Justices bitterly split on ideological lines, was an outrageous example of conservative activism motivated by blatant political expediency rather than jurisprudential principle. The wake of this decision has left many problems for the Court.

II

DIFFICULTIES WITH ORIGINAL INTENT

But there are also many difficulties with theories like original intent as they have frequently been put forward as the solution to those kinds of problems. Many sorts of objections have been raised to the insistence upon confining US constitutional interpretation to the original intent of the framers of the US Constitution. What if the framers' original intent was that we not follow their original intent? There is actually precious little reason to suppose that they expected to bind us to their precise conception of the scope of what they were doing, as distinguished from their broad and often quite general purposes.

And whatever might be said about the framers of the original US Constitution, by the mid-1860s when the three post-Civil War Reconstruction amendments to the Constitution were drafted,[5] the idea that the US Supreme Court might well be taking general phrases of the Constitution and interpreting them aggressively was well understood. In light of the detail that appears in several sections of the Fourteenth Amendment, it seems reasonable to ask: if its framers did not want the sweeping language of its Equal Protection Clause ever carried beyond specific limits (ie, no suffrage matters, no school integration), why did they not put those limits explicitly into the language of the Amendment instead of drafting a general prohibition against denial of equal protection of the laws?

[4] 531 US 98 (2000).

[5] The Thirteenth Amendment abolished slavery; the Fourteenth Amendment was designed to assure rights for the newly freed former slaves; and the Fifteenth Amendment gave them the franchise.

The likely answer is that, as politicians, proponents were more concerned with papering over issues than in highlighting them, and utilised vague language to pull together a constitutional amending majority. The various factions needed were able to get behind broad language and read into it whatever limitations, empowerments, and entitlements they sought. The supporters would have found it sufficient to say, truthfully, that given then current meanings and political contexts, the Amendment would do this and not do that. But it is difficult to imagine that most would have been shocked or surprised to find out that historical experience has shaped and altered some aspects of the meaning of their language over time.

Nevertheless, among proponents of original intent, the claim has been vigorously put forward that when constitutional language is ambiguous, following traditional principles of statutory interpretation one looks to the historical record to see what the original drafters and supporters intended. It is also advanced as the most democratic approach to interpretation since the Constitution and its amendments are to be viewed as effectively 'superstatutes' adopted by an extraordinary majority which can properly be altered only by another such extraordinary majority. The proposition that broad constitutional provisions might be appropriately approached somewhat differently from most ordinary statutes usually gains no appreciation.

Indeed, the strenuous insistence on confining constitutional interpretation to original intent often seems premised upon an almost 'fundamentalist' insistence on clarity and certainty that exists far more definitely in the minds and emotions of many of the proponents than it does in historical reality. It has been a crusade arguably more rooted in issues of psychology than in the realities of jurisprudence.

To me, the place where semiotic and jurisprudential insights most validly meet is in these notions that knowledge is ultimately social and that experience, not logic, is the life of the law. And it is in the actual US historical experience that those who quest for certainty in constitutional interpretation face their greatest challenge. For despite the insistence of the 'fundamentalists,' like it or not, there is, in fact, a long-standing US practice, arguably derived from the British, of creatively developing, often dramatically, substantive constitutional arrangements while maintaining the original forms or provisions, and it is by no means an exclusively judicial process. It frequently involves political action, sometimes judicial action, and often a combination of the two. In other words, as I have argued elsewhere,[6] the actual historical reality of US constitutionalism for over two hundred years stands in dramatic opposition to the impulse to constitutional fundamentalism.

[6] Originally in F Lewis 1999 above n 3.

III

CONFRONTING THE HISTORICAL REALITY OF CONSTITUTIONAL 'CREATIVITY'

It has been often pointed out that an examination of the written documents that are the constituents of, or nominally reflect, the constitutional and political system of Great Britain will tell one very little about its actual substantive workings.[7] In the United States too, political struggle and changing societal needs marked constitutional development from the very beginning. Indeed, the document we call the Constitution itself emerged as a major act of creative political and legal development that rather blithely disregarded existing constitutional understandings.

After all, the mandate of the convention that drafted it in 1789 was simply to propose revisions to the Articles of Confederation that had emerged from the American Revolution against British rule. The delegates chose to disregard this mandate; instead, they wrote a new Constitution with built-in ratification devices and drove it through to successful adoption regardless of technical proprieties. The US Constitution was literally born in an act of creative development of dubious formal legitimacy. It has likely survived for over two centuries in part because of the political and judicial tradition of activist creative development that has made the US Constitution a 'living' document.

Many of the best-known examples of creative constitutional development occurred early in US history and did not involve the judiciary. Without amending a document that provided for the selection of the executive by a very indirect, somewhat elitist process, creative developments produced a much more democratic, if obviously still somewhat imperfect, process. These developments included the growth of broad-based political parties, presidential nominating conventions, making figureheads of the members of the Electoral College by requiring electors to pledge to vote for their party's candidate, and the two-term presidential tradition that Franklin D Roosevelt broke and which was then finally restored by a formal constitutional amendment.

The US Civil War and the Reconstruction period that followed it, together ranging from 1860 through 1877, were marked by extraordinary constitutional 'creativity.' Although the Civil War was fought and won on the principle that no state having joined the Union could secede from it, in the period known as Reconstruction that immediately followed the War, the South was absent from Congress as a practical matter. And the Republican party, which firmly controlled Congress in its absence, was determined to press a Reconstruction agenda upon a South then under military occupation by Union troops.

[7] Going back at least as far as Bagehot. See *The English Constitution* (London, CA Watts, 1964).

President Andrew Johnson, a pro-war Democrat who came to office after the assassination of Abraham Lincoln, was prohibited from dismissing members of his cabinet and when he ignored this legislation of doubtful constitutionality, he was impeached and tried by the Congress, coming within one vote of actual removal from office. In an effort to confer civil and voting rights upon the newly freed ex-slaves, the southern states were effectively coerced into ratification of three constitutional amendments designed to accomplish these objectives. The Reconstruction era Congresses also passed a number of pieces of legislation designed to enforce these rights and to put down the growing Ku Klux Klan terror by southern whites determined to undermine Reconstruction efforts.[8]

In the presidential election of 1876, several southern states reported two sets of election returns, one set favoring the Republican candidate Hayes and the other the Democrat Tilden. A special commission was appointed and the result was an informal 'compromise.' The Republican Rutherford B Hayes was awarded the Presidency; upon taking office, he pulled the Union troops out of the South which enabled white 'redeemer' forces to regain control there. This 'compromise' was a non-judicial and largely informal constitutional settlement. It began a process that developed the then recently amended Constitution in ways that undermined much of what Reconstruction Congresses thought they were accomplishing. Over the next three decades it led to the rise of a system of strict state-imposed racial segregation throughout the South. Overall, this was a very major instance of activist, if unfortunate, constitutional development, in which the role of the judiciary was largely limited to legitimising constitutional creativity that was rooted in political and social action.[9] It lasted for decades into the mid-twentieth century until the 'compromise' and much of the ratifying judicial doctrine were finally undone by the mid-twentieth century Civil Rights Movement—a complex combination of interrelated political, social and judicial activity.

US history is filled with examples like these where existing constitutional arrangements and understandings are changed without formal amendment but through unorthodox political and social action, activist judicial interpretation, or both. A large portion of the conflict during the early decades of the twentieth century over state and federal regulation of important aspects of the evolving national industrial economy also involved creative constitutional development.

The struggle over whether the national government possessed the full power to promote and regulate a national economy culminated in President Franklin Roosevelt's attempt to 'pack' the US Supreme Court. At the beginning

[8] Some still survive. See 42 USC § 1981; 42 USC § 1983; 42 USC § 1985; 18 USC § 241; 18 USC § 242; 28 USC § 1443; 42 USC § 1994.

[9] The most infamous example of judicial action during this period was the US Supreme Court's decision in the case of *Plessy v Ferguson* 163 US 537 (1896), which legitimised the southern claim that the Fourteenth Amendment's command that the states grant every person the 'equal protection of the laws' was satisfied by the provision of public facilities that were 'separate but equal.'

of his second term in 1937, Roosevelt was faced with a Court majority that seemed likely to strike down key parts of his 'New Deal' reform legislation aimed at ameliorating the harshest effects of the Great Depression.

The US Constitution provides for the existence of the Supreme Court but it does not specify the number of Justices who will sit on it. This is established by ordinary legislation and the number can therefore be increased at any time by new ordinary legislation. Roosevelt introduced such legislation in an effort to immediately produce additional seats on the Court that he then could fill with new Justices presumably friendly to his program. Although his proposal was not in the end enacted by Congress, the pressure caused two sitting Justices to change their previous position on the extent of the national government's powers. The outcome produced a victory so decisive for those who favored expanded national governmental power that it can be viewed as a kind of 'settlement,' with both conservatives and liberals supporting it from the mid-1930s to the present day. In particular, Supreme Court decisions of the late 1930s and early 1940s[10] established a broad and sweeping view of Congress's Interstate Commerce power with little if any practical limits in the economic arena.

Recent decisions[11] have set some rather debatable restrictions on congressional utilisation of the commerce power; yet they still do not seem to threaten the fundamentals of the settlement of 1937. It is perhaps notable that President Bill Clinton's Health Care proposal of the early 1990s was denounced by its opponents in almost every possible way. But none of them suggested that if it were enacted, it would be unconstitutional. This was the case although one hazards the guess that we would be hard-pressed to locate a founding father who clearly intended Congress' powers to extend to the establishment of a program of National Health Insurance.

Finally, it is also notable that in the early 1970s, after explicitly rejecting the claim for a hundred years,[12] the post-Earl Warren Supreme Court simply announced that the persons who might not be denied the equal protection of the laws included women after all. Perhaps because the Court majority of the 1970s declined to find gender to be a 'suspect' classification,[13]

[10] From *NLRB v Jones and Laughlin Steel Corporation* 301 US 1 (1937), through to *Wickard v Filburn* 317 US 111 (1942).

[11] Most notably in *US v Lopez* 514 US 549 (1995), where the Court struck down a congressional statute banning possession of a firearm near a public school. The law had been based on the interstate commerce power. The narrow 5–4 majority basically argued that the law involves matters that are neither interstate nor commerce.

[12] See *Bradwell v Illinois*, 16 Wallace 130 (1873); *Goesaert v Cleary*, 335 US 464 (1948). The first case in which the US Supreme Court utilised the Fourteenth Amendment's Equal Protection Clause to strike down a state law that made a gender distinction was *Reed v Reed*, 404 US 71 (1971).

[13] The Court came closest in *Frontiero v Richardson*, 411 US 677 (1973) where four out of nine justices voted to make gender a suspect classification. At the time, it seemed likely that Constitution would be amended to give women a strong guarantee against discrimination. However, in the end, the proposed Equal Rights Amendment narrowly failed to be ratified by the required number of state legislatures.

which would have led to the prompt elimination of virtually all gender distinctions at law, conservative criticism of this development has been surprisingly muted. But ongoing forces of societal change, coupled with some recent judicial decisions,[14] suggest the possibility that most legal gender distinctions may not survive in the US in the long run even under what has now come to be called 'semi-suspect' analysis—an intermediate level of judicial scrutiny that for several years has allowed many gender distinctions to continue.

Each of the examples of creative constitutional development that have been set forth here and many others that could be listed are well known and much written about. Some derived primarily from political action, some from judicial action, and some from a combination of the two. But perspectives on them often imply that the examples explored are in some sense deviations from the norm. I would argue they are not—that for good or ill, creative constitutional development, whether judicially initiated or otherwise, is (in that favorite USA phrase) 'as American as apple pie.' In light of this important deeply rooted historical reality, which admittedly raises very complex questions, it is really the insistence by constitutional 'fundamentalists' on adherence to the concept of original intent that seems to be both simplistic and deviant.

IV

WILL CHAOS ENSUE?

The debate among political and constitutional theorists over finding and adhering to original intent, which has so preoccupied the US academy in recent decades has produced much passion, occasional brilliance, yet arguably little real light. Primarily, that is because this debate has centered overwhelmingly upon the expressed normative and theoretical concerns of these commentators and paid too little attention to actual US historical experience as generally understood.

Now one could hardly deny the importance of normative and theoretical concerns. But as we all go about the business of constructing and reconstructing the world through language, we may lose our way if we do so without paying sufficient self-critical attention to the inner needs that often seem to drive this process and which may be occasionally revealed.

In an interesting review[15] of Vincent Crapanzano's *Serving the Word: Literalism in America from the Pulpit to the Bench*[16] Alan Wolfe considers what the book has to say about the 'jurisprudence of original intent'[17] of

[14] *United States v Virginia et al*, 518 US 515 (1996).
[15] A Wolfe, 'The Hermeneutic Hole,' *The New Republic*, 31 January 2000, 36.
[16] (New York, New Press, 2000).
[17] A Wolfe above n 15, 38.

people like Robert Bork and Antonin Scalia. He characterises Crapanzano's strong criticism of originalism as 'missing the point.' For Wolfe, the point is that legal words are 'special' because they are meant to regulate our conduct and it is 'necessary to agree to the fiction that, for purposes of governing us, they have an unvarying meaning even if we know they cannot have an unvarying meaning.' We do this because 'the alternative is chaos.'[18]

Alan Wolfe usually has much good sense to offer on a wide variety of subjects and there is certainly some in many parts of this long review. But what he offers us most on the subject of original intentionalism is a kind of clarity; he brings to the surface and makes manifest that which, I suggest, is likely quite typical of the underlying, but unacknowledged, concerns of those who are strongly motivated to advocate or defend the original intent approach.

V

CONCLUSION

Two decades ago, Paul Brest observed about several theories of constitutional interpretation then being advanced that:

> all are vulnerable to similar criticism based on their indeterminacy, manipulability, and, ultimately, their reliance on judicial value choices that cannot be 'objectively' derived from text, history, consensus, natural rights, or any other source. No theory of constitutional adjudication can defend itself against self-scrutiny.[19]

In the end, most efforts to impose original intent upon the process of constitutional interpretation seek to avoid the fundamental problems of ambiguity and arbitrariness that inevitably lie within it. They are an attempt to keep from facing and dealing with these realities by reducing constitutional interpretation to a talismanic device. For over two hundred years these realities have been insistently reasserting themselves periodically, and constitutional meanings have shifted accordingly. To try to deny this history is to deny the life of the law and the real nature of the US Constitution.

[18] A Wolfe above n 15, 39.

[19] P Brest, 'The Fundamental Rights Controversy: Essential Contradictions of Normative Constitutional Scholarship' (1981) 90 *Yale Law Journal* 1063, at 1096.

6

Celebrity as Authority in Law

JOHN BRIGHAM and JILL MEYERS

I

INTRODUCTION

YEARS AGO STEWART Macauley encouraged us to look outside the courts to find law. Recently such an orientation has come to characterise work that is identified with Law and Society.[1] During the annual meeting of scholars operating from this framework in Budapest scholars considered various aspects of social life affected by and affecting law. The aspect of celebrity, which we think is important to law, received relatively little attention. Few papers were given directly on celebrity (if we don't count celebrity academics like Bentham, Selznick and Bourdieu);[2] this was in spite of the fact that the theme of the conference was 'law in action' and an important influence was cultural studies.[3] There were sessions that drew on celebrity indirectly. The work of the cartoonist *Felix*, a popular source in Hungary buttressed an argument about the challenges of Eastern European law in transition.[4] There was a session on the book *When Law Goes Pop*, by Richard Sherwin[5] and there were papers dealing with movies and popular culture.[6] The overwhelming majority of the work, however, was about law professors, judges, legislators, statutes and court opinions. While

[1] S Macauley, 'Non-Contractual Relations in Business: A Preliminary Study,' (1963) *American Sociological Review* 28; See also David Papke, 'How Does Law Look in the Movies' 27 *Legal Studies Forum* 439 (2003); Austin Sarat, 'The Law is All Over: Power, Resistance, and the Legal Consciousness of the Welfare Poor' *Yale Journal of Law and the Humanities* 2(2).

[2] P Robson's 'Notions of Justice in the Films of Sidney Lumet' and A Howe's 'Lindy Chamberlain: Trial by Sex, Circumstance, and Opinion' are exceptions, Annual Meeting of the Law and Society Association, Budapest, 2001.

[3] Cultural studies scholarship is important in Law and Society, and cultural studies is nearly obsessed with celebrity.

[4] See A Sajo, 'Encounters in Law,' Annual Meeting of the Law and Society Association, Budapest, 2001.

[5] *When Law Goes Pop: The Vanishing Line Between Law and Popular Culture* (Chicago and London, University of Chicago Press, 2000).

[6] See A Sarat, 'Constructing Memories of Pain: Remembrance and Revenge in *Unforgiven*' Annual Meeting of the Law and Society Association, Budapest, 2001.

there is considerable sensitivity to the idea that we might look to other parts of the culture for insight about law, celebrity is being treated by socio-legal scholars as peripheral to law and the academic discussion of it.[7] We propose that legal authority, while obviously associated with texts and the knowledge held by lawyers as to what a judge will do, is also a function of cultural forces, including celebrities traditionally thought to be outside the law.

This essay examines the extent to which celebrity has been incorporated into the contemporary system of legal authority. Recognition of the general social tendency toward the cultural authority of celebrity is evident in the work of Lawrence Friedman. He observed:

> ... celebrities have displaced other role models. When people (especially young people) adopt idols today, these idols come from the world of celebrities, rather from the world of traditional authority.[8]

We find evidence in legal scholarship and cultural commentary suggesting that this idea is gaining currency. We think displacement may be a bit extreme, at least with regard to law, but in matters like search and seizures, marriage, assault or discrimination, celebrities contribute to what we know to be the law. In this regard, we propose that it is important to incorporate celebrity into our picture of law.[9]

We work from the perspective called 'law in society' which has, in the last 30 years, expanded what scholars know to be law. Further, we develop a constitutive understanding of the authority behind law.[10] When we say a celebrity has authority in law we mean that what she or he proposes or exemplifies is, under certain circumstances, the law. That it means what law means to significant portions of the population. This form of authority is meant to operate in a fashion similar to, if not identical with, what judges or prosecutors contend that law means. By including the authority of celebrity in law we follow a shift in attention from institutional sources per se to cultural sources of law. When Oprah, for example, calls attention to the suffering of a battered wife her view has the authority to alter or

[7] Celebrity within the academy plays a role in this understanding with figures like Ronald Dworkin, Carol Gilligan and Angela Davis having special status as celebrity intellectuals. See PW Kahn, *The Cultural Study of Law: Reconstructing Legal Scholarship* (Chicago & London, University of Chicago Press, 1999).

[8] Friedman, *The Horizontal Society* (New Haven, Yale University Press, 1999): 35.

[9] 'To misunderstand the role of the popular media is to ignore the fact that the "major contemporary political issues" of today (environmental, ethnic and sexual youth movements, for instance) all arose outside the traditional public sphere. Instead of being generated through intellectual, social or political elites, they were "informed, shaped, developed and contested within the privatized public sphere of suburban media consumerism"': J Hartley, *Popular Reality: Journalism, Modernity, Popular Culture* (London and New York, Arnold, 1996) p 157, as quoted in G Turner, F Bonner, and PD Marshall, *Fame Games: the Production of Celebrity in Australia* (Cambridge, Cambridge University Press, 2000) 7.

[10] J Brigham, *The Constitution of Interests: Beyond the Politics of Rights* (NY, NYU Press, 1996).

reinforce public perception of battery. We acknowledge that this authority may not be determinative of legal meaning so we say it 'has authority' rather than that it is 'authoritative.'

We are not simply adding celebrity to the array of judges, lawyers and enforcement personnel who tell us what the law is. We contend that the authority of law is accurately understood as a function of many authorities; few, perhaps none of whom ultimately determine legal meaning on their own. Scholars, for instance, play a role in law reviews and teaching, to help determine what is law. Officials, like the clerks of courts,[11] are seen as determining in practice what counts as law even though their authority is suspect. More starkly, clerks at Kinkos will tell you that you can't Xerox money and that you have to clear copyright to make multiple copies of material. Celebrities have a place in this process precisely because we do not wish to treat meaning in law as if there is law, or legal production, and then comment on it by outsiders.

We wish to take on conventional notions of where law comes from. Though not official, the reporting of news sources is the law for most people. Gap studies such as those by McCann and Haltom have provided an accounting of the ways we can go wrong with the popular press as a source of law. Papers, even those as prestigious as *The New York Times*, clearly have their biases and slants. We don't wish to trivialise the production of law so that we say that law is no more than whatever we know. Yet, at some point law depends on how we interpret and internalise, perceive and understand a segment of the social rules. The law we are interested in has a social reality. It is in society. Celebrities significantly influence this law. Clearly only some knowledge is knowledge of law and there are hierarchies of understanding. Many people in the United States sincerely believe that they have 'a right to do whatever they want in their own home' at least until held accountable for some transgression of the law, like domestic violence. We want to base this study on the intuitive claim that what they believe to be the law is law until their view is successfully challenged or a reconceptualisation takes place.

One recent development that suggests the importance of celebrity in law is a shift in the perspective of news and other cultural constructions. There is a new self consciousness that moves reporting from claiming a detached knowledge about the world, claiming to stand outside, to knowledge or news presented from within. As Graeme Turner and his colleagues have argued,

> Coverage of celebrities within news and current affairs is widely cited as evidence of a decline in *hard* news values, the ascendancy of infotainment, and the decline of the press as an independent source of information.[12]

[11] B Yngvesson, *Virtuous Citizens, Disruptive Subjects* (NY, Routledge, 1993).
[12] Turner *et al* 2000 above n 9 at 5.

We accept this formulation that media is 'fundamentally participating in the cultural construction' of society[13] and in the process forming opinion and making law. In the socio-legal field, as in the social sciences more generally, the issue of identity and identity formation has been a concern that features mutually constitutive processes. This is our formulation of the interconnectedness one finds in law and society.[14] Our study of celebrity status in law is consistent with this concern. We draw attention to law as a social formation that resides in identity and society.

II

CELEBRITY STATUS

By celebrities we mean people who are widely known. Clint Eastwood is a celebrity, as is Madonna. We accept a version of the Turner definition coming out of cultural studies that '... anyone the public is interested in is a celebrity.'[15] This is the same definition Friedman uses when he says, 'the essence of celebrity is high visibility'.[16] A plumber may be a celebrity if he wins the lottery, performs some heroic deed or becomes a figure in a popular text whether television, movies, literature or advertising. A plumber on *Survivor* could become a celebrity. A plumber could not become a celebrity for simply being an extraordinary plumber unless she is an extraordinary plumber who gets employed to a home makeover show on television. In this sense, celebrities are famous. Some of the issues that arise from this minimal definition are considered here.

We think that it is important to note that celebrities come from various fields. Like law, this is a broad category. Entertainment and sports are sources of celebrity. Politics is another source. Business is not, generally a source of celebrity, though of course there are exceptions like media mogul Ted Turner. Generally it means visibility across a wide spectrum of national or international life. Celebrity status is consequently linked to spheres of influence. Eastwood and Madonna are known beyond the United States. Kylie Minogue and Slim Dusty have long been celebrities in Australia and were not known much beyond the boundaries of that nation (though Minogue's status changed in 2002). We focus on celebrity status that at least rises to the level of the nation.

While we are primarily interested in influences on national law, some of the most important celebrity influences are transnational. Spanish students are said to have known the law on search and seizure from watching television from the United States. This phenomenon is often discussed with the

[13] Turner *et al* 2000 above n 9 at 6.
[14] S Hall, *Critical Dialogues in Cultural Studies*, edited by K-H Chan and D Mortey (London, Rantledge, 1996).
[15] Turner *et al* 2000 above n 9 at 9.
[16] Friedman 1999 above n 8 at 27.

emphasis on how silly or paradoxical the resulting knowledge turns out to be. In a case where a Spanish citizen quotes Andy Sipowicz from *NYPD Blue* to a member of the Guardia Civil we share a concern for the welfare of the Spaniard marshalling his American television knowledge. However, what seems trivial at a superficial level begins to make more sense as we look closely at both law and celebrity to understand their constitutive relation.

Like law, the status of celebrity crosses the boundaries of groups. What is claimed for both law and celebrity transcends the pluralism of interests and issues. Celebrity and law are statuses that unite individuals into groups and groups into cultures. By their nature they are synthetic. The synthesis has many different meanings and kinds of cultural significance. For Turner and his colleagues, 'the celebrity is at their most active and significant when they mark a point of convergence' or, as Marshall puts it, when they can provide 'a bridge of meaning between the powerless and the powerful.'[17] Celebrity in this sense is political, even transformative, at least at the level of identity. Without focusing here on the political dimension, the wide recognition and consequences for group identity are clearly phenomena that involve power that is relevant to various groups, classes and society. The tension over this boundary crossing is evident with Jennifer Lopez and Tiger Woods. Jennifer Lopez justifies the word 'Nigger' in her song as incorporating a pariah category as blacks do. Part of Woods' celebrity, in addition to the fact that he is remarkably good at golf, is the fact that he is of mixed race and a person of color dominating a country club sport. In this, the contradictions as well as the range add to his celebrity rather than detracting, as they might with regard to other types of social capital. All of these examples address the boundary crossing that is at the basis of legal authority.

Scholars have proposed that the status of celebrity in contemporary cultures of the sort we are focusing on is new.[18] Our concern is to establish that this authority is an authority in law. We think that recognition of celebrity authority in this sense, as law, is new. Lawrence Friedman emphasizes the ordinary quality of modern celebrities and our familiarity with their lives. This is part of his analysis of 'horizontal societies'.[19] He says 'It is precisely the illusion of familiarity—the images, the show, the projection on the public screen that makes the celebrity what she is.'[20] This is an important

[17] Above n 12, Bonnes *et al* 2000 at 12; D Marshall, *Celebrity and Power: Fame in Contemporary Culture* (Minneapolis, University of Minnesota Press, 1997) at 124.

[18] Nick Bromell, *Tomorrow Never Knows: Rock and Psychedelics in the 1960s* (University of Chicago Press, 2001) 26 describes pop celebrities' 'appealing mix of authority, vulnerability, and trustworthiness' as 'something very new to American culture.'

[19] 'The vast audience has the allusion of a peep show: what goes on behind the scenes is revealed before their very eyes. Instead of fairy tales we have tabloids ... in which the characters are rich but ordinary, leading lives drenched in romance and scandal yet almost obsessively mundane ... Talent, luck, or tragedy or chance has anointed them. Yet at the base, there is something amazingly ordinary about them.' Above n 8 Friedman 1999 at 29.

[20] *Ibid.*

argument and one of the features that determines the nature of celebrity influence in law. Celebrity, like law, penetrates the everyday aspects of life in the United States and other industrial nations. Of course, celebrities are not really ordinary or we wouldn't be interested in them. What Friedman calls the 'paradox'[21] of difference and sameness creates a complicated and various dynamic as the heart of both the psychology of consciousness about social norms and the mechanisms of legal authority.

Scholars from Ernst Kantorowicz, Michael Rogin and Sheldon Wolin[22] to Stuart Hall and Michel Foucault, link ordinary people to celebrities through the governing structure. Kantorowicz, Rogin and Wolin explored the monarchical corollary between the body of the King and the body politic in which a sense of the sameness was part of the King's authority and the clarity of succession based on blood relations. For Hall and Foucault, the modern structure of authority has replaced the body and blood with the market and media culture as the place where the way we live is delineated. Rogin's work is an important link. His insight about the celebrity character that emerged as Ronald Reagan, the President may be extended to other aspects of the governing authority. The capacity to know, in an ordinary sense, and be 'in awe' at the same time is an element of legal authority.

Since the celebrity does not 'speak an arcane, elitist language' Friedman suggests that the 'fixity' of traditional authority has vanished.[23] In this sense his is an updated 'realist' formulation but one with a romantic view of the 'tradition' in law. For some time now the authority of law has been in the institutional structures rather than in the words of the practitioners.[24] The real meaning of the notion that the law is 'what the judge says it is' involves a shift from the texts of law to the actors in important institutions. We don't believe, at least in the societies we are talking about, that the authority of law has become weak and fluid to the point of lacking authority. Rather, the penetration of celebrity life and famous stories into the consciousness of citizens brings law home, or into the home. This penetration makes law part of identity and consciousness. Law understood in this way is anything but lacking in 'fixity'. The penetration and to a great extent the rigidity of law—at least when measured against a notion that anything goes—appears to be substantial. Indeed, the controversy, in March of 2003, over the Dixie Chicks saying they are embarrassed to come from the same state as American President George W Bush indicates one kind of consequence. Celebrity trials like that of Robert Blake in the same period indicate other, very real, consequences.

[21] *Ibid* at 35.

[22] EH Kantorowicz, *The King's Two Bodies* (Princeton, Princeton University Press, 1957); M Rogin, *Ronald Reagan, the Movie* (Berkeley, University of California Press, 1987) S Wolin, 'The People's Two Bodies' (1981) 1 *Democracy* 11–19.

[23] Friedman 1999 at 35.

[24] J Brigham, *The Cult of the Court* (Philadelphia, Temple University Press, 1987).

Timothy McVeigh became a celebrity as have many other famous criminals. McVeigh was internationally famous given the nature of his crime and his punishment. His status was partly due to his own effort, the magnitude of his crime, but it is also a function of the government's response. This was the case with Bonnie Parker and Clyde Barrow, bandits in the 1930s. Their celebrity was considerably enhanced and brought to a new generation by the movie made by Arthur Penn of their lives in the 1960s. In McVeigh's case a relatively traditional social background from the United States presented a puzzle when interpreting his crime and punishment. He became a celebrity for being condemned to death and being ordinary. Oprah Winfrey's celebrity is also ordinary in shape but extraordinary in magnitude. Oprah seems to be influential in matters of social policy like the home and family. With her book club she extended her influence to art and literature.

People in the United States are familiar with the influence of celebrities in matters of policy. These run from Barbra Streisand supporting the Clinton Presidency and *Selena* star Edward James Olmos condemning police behavior in Los Angeles to Charlton Heston symbolically heading the National Rifle Association in the United States and Ronald Reagan, Clint Eastwood and Sonny Bono holding public office.[25] The meaning and influence varies. Celebrities are highly visible in matters of social convention that have a policy dimension but around which there is a social consensus about what is good and what is bad such as divorce, domestic violence, and drinking driving. We think that the authority of celebrity is greatest and most closely associated with law where a social consensus adheres. For instance, we are used to celebrity commentary on drugs or driving while intoxicated but much less used to commentary on the status of private property or even the value of social security. This phenomenon is heightened in time of war with grave risks to the celebrity who opposes even a relatively unpopular war.

We think that political leaders are a special case. National presidents become celebrities by virtue of their office in most of the world. In addition, JFK and Ronald Reagan were celebrity Presidents. As political leaders, JFK and Ronald Reagan derived authority from their celebrity. Their celebrity status overlapped with the authority they got from institutional sources. Scholars believe that the Civil Rights Bill of 1964 in the United States would not have been passed if it has not been for the stature JFK achieved in death. The techniques Ronald Reagan learned as a celebrity entertainer clearly helped him to enhance his image as President. Bill Clinton had celebrity status as President, as an interesting personality and in his association with well known figures.

Celebrity is a relatively unstable condition compared to what we expect of authority in law. Indeed, in the lore of Anglo-American law terms like

[25] See July 2001 regarding struggle over oil reserves in Alaska.

precedent and stare decisis affirm the importance of positions that endure in spite of controversy.[26] Though not simply dependent on the marketplace, celebrity is clearly a function of markets and other volatile social forces. Commentary on an issue, a relatively passive stance, can threaten celebrity status. Ralph Nader, who became much more of a celebrity due to his run for President in 2000, seems to have diminished in significance since then. Even simply getting caught in the networks of social approbation can threaten the status of a celebrity. This is true as when mistakes are made by celebrities, such as those by George Michael in a bathroom in LA, Hugh Grant with a prostitute, or Winona Ryder shoplifting.

There are dangers to celebrity when in conflict with the law or even its ideological underpinnings. Thus, the homophobic lyrics of white rapper Eminem were both vehicle and limitation to be transcended. For basketball player rapper Alan Iverson an outlaw image is part of the celebrity and it is acceptable up to a point. Though perhaps acting out of some destructive urge, in their involvement with the law, Michael, Grant and Ryder did not seem to be in control and their celebrity status was clearly in jeopardy. Here, marginal figures, like Snoop Doggy Dog and Eminem who have a following may be able to maintain their position in society consequent to clashes with the law but Sean Coombs, though once identified with the gangster image was starting a line of clothes when his trouble with the law seemed to escalate and at least some of the outlets for his clothes seem to have become squeamish after he appeared in court. The Dixie Chicks, in a comment mocking the President of the United States on the eave of war with Iraq in 2003, seem to have risked the loyalties of their core 'country' audience.

Celebrity status is a complex social quality embedded in culture and consequently linked to law. Celebrities are not totally in control of the messages they send. The message can be counter to what an individual celebrity might intend or desire, as in the case of Hugh Grant's soliciting a prostitute. The image may endure after a celebrity has died or fallen from public consciousness. Charlie Chaplin was a celebrity whose views on Fascism, like those of Ezra Pound, caused considerable controversy. They remain legends whose status is partly affected by their identification with a discredited ideology. They may or may not take credit for their influence. They may or may not be consistent in their positions. Manu Chao the former leader of the rock band Mano Negra and son of refugees from the Spanish Civil War who had fled to France sings of the immigrant and identifies with the under class in albums like *Clandestino*. Consequently, his recording contract with the international corporation Virgin Records generated considerable criticism. His response was that he is 'not trying to rewrite the laws, just to sing.' This is an attempt to evade accountability that belies the relationship

[26] The status of celebrity is vulnerable to a degree that is greater than some other status relations, like parenthood or sainthood, particularly when it comes to involvement with law.

we are suggesting. In fact, the issue of rebellion and counter hegemonic material is particularly important to understanding the relationship between celebrity and legal authority. One of the issues in this important relationship is the role of corporations in defining and often sanitising the views of celebrities they market. But of even greater consequence is the link between powerful business enterprises and law. It is far easier to get the recorded product from Virgin Records about Manu Chao than it was from his less prominent and more idiosyncratic sources. One of the characteristics of law is the scope of authority.

Celebrity calls attention to the social quality of authority in law. A lawyer or other member of the law enforcement community can of course become a celebrity, like Johnny Cochran of OJ Simpson fame. We presume that celebrities of this sort may have even more authority than celebrities in other areas when it comes to being sources of law. Thus, the realm to which a celebrity is associated influences his or her authority in law. Similarly, celebrities entering the realm of law, whether fictional or not, may have significant legal authority. Clint Eastwood, as the character *Dirty Harry*, became associated with toughness on crime. He provided a cultural mechanism for identifying with the state as an inadequate force for law and order. The character resisted the conventions of public authority with the consent of the viewers. Philip Gourevitch's book, *We wish to inform you that tomorrow we will be killed with our families: Stories From Rwanda*, makes this point in discussing the movies *A Time to Kill* and *Sleepers*.

> [In] *A Time to Kill* ... A couple of worthless white-trash rednecks are out drinking and driving. They abduct a young black girl, rape her, torture her, and leave her corpse in a field ...The girl's father doesn't trust the local judiciary to do adequate justice, so he waits for the men to be brought in chains to the courthouse, steps out of the shadows with a shotgun, and blows them away ... [In] *Sleepers* ... kids play a prank that results in the accidental death of a passerby. They are sent to a reform school, where they are repeatedly gang raped by wardens. Then they are released. Years pass. One day, two of the original quartet encounter the warden who had been the chief tormentor in reform school, so they draw their handguns and blow him away ...

As summarised by Gourevitch the shared premise is that 'the law and the courts were so incapable of fairly adjudicating the cases in question that it wasn't worth bothering with them'.[27] This is the level at which we find it useful to associate law with celebrity.

Princess Diana was, technically, a figure in the state apparatus as Princess. But she did not seem closely linked to what we conventionally

[27] See also, 'Both movies were quite popular in America seen by many millions of citizens ...' and 'Still, I was troubled by the premise the two movies shared: that the law and the courts were so incapable of fairly adjudicating the cases in question that it wasn't worth bothering with them' at 343: P Gourevitch, *We wish to inform you...* (USA, Picador, 1999) 342–3.

think of as law. Yet, upon her death it became clear that she was associated with the identity and authority of sovereign power in England. Perhaps even more important than her policy interests in the campaign against land mines and for the rights of AIDS patients in which her compassion was a powerful cultural statement her death symbolised the deep identification of people across class and even nationality with glamour and style. And the continuing authority of that style has been sought actively to be associated with the monarchy since her death.

A celebrity judge is a tricky category in a discussion of celebrity and law. Judge Ito in OJ Simpson's criminal trial became a familiar example of a judge. He influenced perception of what it means to be a judge and to be Japanese American. Thus, a race not traditionally associated with judging in America became associated with the most prominent jurist of his time. Ito was certainly a celebrity Japanese American. As a celebrity judge all of the authority he had was initially through the law in the traditional, non-celebrity sense. His influence on the trial on the other hand was a function in part of his own celebrity and that of the trial. Ito had what we are calling authority over his court as he heard arguments and set the tone for the proceedings. When former Senator Alphonse D'mato of New York joked about Ito being Japanese the judge was reduced to a symbol of discrimination against Asian Americans. Subsequently, dissatisfaction with the acquittal became associated with what commentators claimed was Judge Ito's inability to control the trial. In becoming one of the celebrities associated with an unpopular trial his authority over law generally diminished while his significance as an example of the pitfalls of celebrity in law may have grown.

The actors are more clearly what we understand by celebrity. They will be the sort of celebrities to which we turn in contending that television and radio as well as academic and popular intellectual sources contribute to the meaning of civil and criminal codes, judicial and administrative authority, and notions about who we ought to obey. For most cultural activity that is driven by law, the action and opinion of celebrities play a significant role that is more important than academic and intellectuals have recognised. It may be more important in practice than the contributions of many legal actors to the development of the law. We are asking when and how celebrities that we see in tabloids and entertainment TV make law.

III

CELEBRITY AS A KIND OF AUTHORITY

Authority in law is not simply about judges anymore. The interpretive forms have been expanded from lawyers and judges to the character of social life more generally. John Brigham has discussed this shift as being from the courts as temples of justice to television.[28] In the sociology of law today, Susan Silbey and Patti Ewick explore the architecture of authority in their work about scientific laboratories.[29] Socio-legal scholars considering the capacity of the nation-state to direct the conduct of global corporate power, call attention to the constitutive legislation that starts corporations on their journey and the control of financial and securities markets.[30]

We don't think that there is a simple link between celebrity and traditional legal authority. Instead, we want to suggest new ways in which politics, law and public relations converge in how society is ordered today. The homophobic commentaries of Eminem and Allen Iverson were subsumed in a public relations onslaught by the music and basketball communities, which moderated the lyrics and cushioned their impact. Celebrity stature and law are worked out in a public realm as arcane in its workings as anything in the fabled legal systems of the past or the fables of Kafka. Celebrity, like legal authority, requires a place in public consciousness. Legislation does not simply need the support of the public to pass, sometimes it does and sometimes it doesn't, but legislation needs the knowledge of the public to be authoritative, to operate from consent rather than armed force.

Here we explore the overlap and interpenetration between celebrity and law emphasising the ways in which celebrity operates as authority. Max Weber taught us to consider various sources of law.[31] His traditional authority called to mind pre-modern cultures where custom and norm were relatively stable. He wrote of the rational-legal as the characteristic form of modern societies operating under the rule of law and he introduced the charismatic to delineate the power of personal presence over how people chose to act. The notion of celebrity as authority that we would like to develop here necessarily modifies the framework. It falls somewhere in between Weber's idea of rational-legal authority and charismatic authority. In fact, we argue that the more charismatic aspect of celebrity authority has entered into and perhaps altered, at least relative to Weber's perspective, the nature of rational-legal authority. Yet, Weber's social analysis, in adding a component of cultural and ideological phenomena to how we understand society, is a foundational perspective for this work.

[28] John Brigham, 'Law and Humanities: Symposium on the Image of Law(yers) in Popular Culture' (2003) *Syracuse Law Review* 58, 1165–99.

[29] P Ewick and SS Silbey, 'The Architecture of Authority,' The Law and Society Meetings, Budapest, 2001.

[30] JW Cioffi, 'Governing Globalization? The State, Law, and Structural Change in Corporate Governance' (2000) 27 *Journal of Law and Society* 572.

[31] Traditional, Rational-Legal and Charismatic. M Weber, *Basic Concepts in Sociology* (tr by HP Seder) (NY, Citadel Press, 1921/1968); HH Gerth and C Wright Mills, *From Max Weber* (NY, Bedminster Press, 1946/1959). See also C Boulanger, 'The Charisma of Law: Max Weber's Relevance for Understanding Institutional Change', Annual Meeting of the Law and Society Association, Budapest, 2001.

Friedman makes a point to distinguish a celebrity from an authority.[32] In his formulation, 'a celebrity is someone we know, or think we know, through the media, through publicity, that is, vicariously.'[33] This vicarious knowledge is a key to what Friedman calls the 'horizontal' relation he sees in society. He perceives this relation as not what it 'seems' to the participants. According to Friedman, people think that they have a relationship with celebrities but they do not really. We propose that Friedman is only partially correct here and that the horizontal relation that makes us think we know Ronald Reagan, 'Dutch', as a nice guy or Julia Roberts as a good kid is part of who they are. They are people that millions of us 'know' and as such they are celebrities. It does not seem to be significant that in some sense we do not 'really' know them. That is, it may be true that we do not know them as we know our parents or lovers but that does not make our familiarity false, it simply makes it part of the contemporary nature of celebrity.[34] Celebrities become authorities out of this relation and saying that the familiarity we feel is false is minimally relevant to the study of celebrity. It is as if we said of the authority of Moses that it was wrong for the Israelites to see him as a father figure because he was really not the father of them all. The authority of law in traditional terms is often much like the authority of celebrity that depends on familiarity. Much like Stuart Scheingold in *The Politics of Rights* we suggest that the perception of closeness is a key to the authority of celebrity.

It is essential to recognise the authority of celebrity to understand modern law. Some of this may well require recognition of a greater fluidity in law, as already noted. But we are not sure this characteristic is essential or even necessarily characteristic. We don't argue that all the certainty in law has vanished. Indeed, the very ordinary quality of celebrity status is a huge constraint. It influences how celebrities appear and the impact they have on law. While it may seem unsettling to think that internationally acclaimed death row inmate Mumia Abu-Jamal along with pop singer Madonna and Supreme Court Justice David Souter all represent sources of law, it seems to be true. We do not provide a basis for assessing which of these sources is the most influential but rather suggest that jurisprudence must include them all.[35] It would seem that Abu-Jamal, convicted in Philadelphia of killing a policeman and an international symbol of the political and racial problems associated with the death penalty as it is practiced in America, is unsettling to traditional legal authority. To the extent that 'the law' includes the fact

[32] '... the difference between a "celebrity" and an "authority" is fundamental', above n 8, Friedman 1999 at 15.
[33] *Ibid.*
[34] M Rogin, *Ronald Reagan, the Movie* (Berkeley, University of California Press, 1988). Last year Julia Roberts, who was sitting behind my son Atticus in a New York movie theater, reached down and touched his shoulder with a kind of awareness of her celebrity and its ordinariness that she explored in *Notting Hill.*
[35] In some theories of constitutional interpretation the rise in significance of judges is unsettling to a notion that the law is in the text.

of capital punishment in Pennsylvania, Abu-Jamal reminds us of its problems and presents a real threat to the idea that those convicted under it deserve their fate. Part of 'the law' is the fact that the death penalty is disproportionately applied to people of color in America, especially at the federal level, and in Abu-Jamal's celebrity may be disruptive for that practice. It is at this point of disruption or effectiveness that the role of celebrity is of interest to this study. David Souter, as a Justice of the United States Supreme Court may or may not comment on Abu-Jamal's case in his official capacity. If he does it will be an important source of law. Madonna, in the course of her career, has commented on race and the death penalty, and though she seems unlikely to comment on Mumia in an interview or as part of a performance, it is not highly unlikely—and that comment would be a source of law.

Sometimes the relationship between celebrity and law is tense and conflictual. Judges impose gag orders in order to keep defendants from becoming celebrities along the lines of Billy Sol Estes, one of the first televised trials.[36] The argument is that to celebrate and publicise a trial may deprive a defendant of due process. Defendants who start as celebrities affect the aspiration that jurors are impartial and their celebrity alters the character of the trial as we have learned from trials like that of OJ Simpson, Winona Ryder and Robert Blake. Juries have said that potential martyrdom, a form of celebrity, influenced their choice of punishment.[37] Convicted celebrities have to be segregated in prison for fear that their status might provoke attacks[38] understood by prison officials as an aspiration for celebrity on the part of the attacker.[39] Some forms of law actively resist full participation in the market. The Supreme Court in refusing to televise its oral arguments is opting for a traditional form of authority based in the text and the discourse. The justices may be successful in maintaining their niche by resisting the market. For most practitioners, to be known requires marketing or the cultivation of celebrity.

Authority is more than simply influence. Authority entails, at least to some degree, the capacity to compel. All celebrities, because they are known, become part of the way we perceive the world so we say they have influence to the extent that, in their opinions and actions we find standards for our beliefs and behavior. As in the case of law, we think that compulsion of the sort that orders people to behave a certain way is not the foundation of legal authority. More often law constitutes behaviors as expected

[36] One of the first states to allow televised trials was Texas. This policy led to televised coverage of the 1962 trial of Billy Sol Estes. It was also the basis for Estes' appeal to the United States Supreme Court. A majority (5–4) of the Court's Justices overturned Estes' conviction: *Estes v Texas*, (1965) 381 US 532.

[37] Mentioned with regard to Oklahoma City accomplice Terry Nichols in June 2001.

[38] Such an attack by a white supremacist on John Walker Lindh, 'The American Taliban,' was reported to have taken place at a medium security prison in California in March of 2003.

[39] As described to me by a guard at Folsom Prison with regard to the segregation of Erik Menendez in the Spring of 2000.

or normal so that to do otherwise would be nearly unthinkable. It is at this level that we believe celebrity compels.

There are instances in the academy, where celebrity is examined in ways that bear on it being a kind of authority. In a paper at the Budapest conference, the movie *Saving Private Ryan* became a familiar way to introduce issues surrounding the laws of war in the paper 'Trying Private Ryan: The Prosecution of Grave Breaches of the Laws of War in the Shadow of the International Criminal Court'.[40] Because of their familiarity, movies and the well-known actors that appear in them provide a kind of rhetorical authority. In the above case, when 'Saving' becomes 'Trying,' the turn of phrase is meant to evoke a familiar nod to the cleverness of the author and the familiarity of the issue. We find images and references from popular culture applied to law because they have a special resonance as recurring parts of our life. For instance, Rob McQueen's reference to 'Carl Schmitt for Corporate Lawyers: Liberalism and the Corporate Governance Debate,'[41] takes its form from the series of books heralding access to various techniques '... for Dummies' and Carl Schmitt himself has an academic currency that gives it a celebrity form.[42] Celebrity cases, both trial and appellate, have special status for scholars because others are more likely to know about them.

There are cases where the plaintiff or the defendant becomes something of a celebrity and they are treated in the media as standing in for law in a way that tells us about the meaning of celebrity. William Haltom and Michael W McCann have been working on the case of a woman who became famous because she successfully sued McDonald's when she spilled very hot coffee on herself.[43] Knowledge of the case and its initially large settlement, they feel, places undue emphasis on high damage awards and contributes to the backlash against civil liability.

IV

CELEBRITY LEGAL PRACTICE

The oak tree of the English legal landscape becomes central to Eve Darian Smith's thesis that the channel tunnel has transformed the English psyche. Looking at *The Golden Bough* of Malcolm Frasier, Darian-Smith explores

[40] W Bradford, 'Trying Private Ryan: The Prosecution of Grave Breaches of the Laws of War in the Shadow of the International Criminal Court', Annual Meeting of the Law and Society Association, Budapest, 2001.

[41] Annual Meeting of the Law and Society Association, Budapest, 2001.

[42] Schmitt's celebrity at the moment seems to come from a continuing concern about the conditions in early 20th-century Germany that produced such an aggressive society.

[43] W Haltom and MW McCann, 'Java Jive: Liebeck v McDonald's as Media Icon', Annual Meeting of the Law and Society Association, Budapest, 2001; LH Carter, 'Reconstructing Impartiality After *Bush v Gore*', Annual Meeting of the Law and Society Association, Budapest, 2001.

the image of the garden as a reference for the order in law. In contemporary culture the television is a similar place. When we turn on TV to spend time with Oprah, the Simpsons or the evening news we are going to a place from which we come to know things about law.[44]

One of the things we take from TV and other celebrity outlets is a sense of how to feel about law. In particular we learn to trust or not trust police or courts,[45] formulate notions through sitcoms such as Ally McBeal as to what it is like to be a lawyer and we learn to identify with the victim or perhaps even the defendant. In her article, 'The Oprah Dilemma,' Kathy Laster begins with a quote from Oprah to establish the significance of our recent elevation of the victim to iconic status in Western law.[46]

The centrality of law in rap or hip-hop is the sort of case that makes the issue of celebrities and law compelling. Sean 'Puffy' or 'P Diddy' Coombs' widely chronicled encounters with the law become morality plays in the public arena. On the one hand the relatively flamboyant flaunting of law in the music supports the story told by the police that Coombs fired a gun he was carrying in response to criticism from a fan at a nightclub in New York City. His defense in court however, contrary to his public message was that he did not have a gun. He was acquitted but on the basis of a very ungangster line. He lost his girlfriend at the time, Jennifer Lopez, whose celebrity began to surpass his and in a subsequent arrest for a traffic violation he (not to be confused with J Lo) was made to look foolish while contending that he was being harassed.[47] Clearly this is an arena in which celebrity and law clash and in shifting from the celebrity persona to that of defendant the authority of state law over rap image is affirmed.

In examining the contested space of law, white rapper Eminem's homophobic lyrics provide an important example. Challenging anti discrimination law while appealing to the discriminatory sensibilities of many People in the United States, Eminem's nomination for multiple Grammy Awards in 2000 drew attention to his performance. The producers of the show turned the evening into a restatement of the general norm of toleration. Eminem sang with Elton John who is publicly gay. The law that subsumed Eminem and his lyrics was the tolerance of the recording industry, the

[44] See also J Brigham, 'Architectures of Justice' (1999) 1 *Journal of Social Change and Critical Inquiry*; J Brigham, 'LA Law' in Jarvis and Joseph (eds), *Prime Time Law* (Carolina Academic Press, 1998) 21–33; 'Exploring the Attic: Courts and Communities in Material Life', *Special Issue of Law in Context on Courts, Tribunals and New Approaches to Justice*, O Mendelsohn and L Maher (eds) (Bundoora Australia, La Trobe University Press 1994) 131–155.

[45] See JL Hoffmann, 'The Confounding of Procedure and Substance: The Liebman Study and the Future of the Death Penalty in the United States', Annual Meeting of the Law and Society Association, Budapest, 2001.

[46] K Laster and E Erez, 'The Oprah Dilemma: the Use and Abuse of Victims', Annual Meeting of the Law and Society Association, Budapest, 2001.

[47] Coombs' decision to change his name to P Diddy has suffered from as well as potentially being a manifestation of diminished celebrity. Conversations on this point with Natalie Meyers have been suggestive.

same tolerance that is so important to freedom of expression. In this example the lyrics of one artist become subordinate to something larger and the celebrity source of law is not the individual but the production.

In reconsidering events like those surrounding Sean Coombs, George Michael and Hugh Grant, brushes with the law where celebrity and the legal system of courts and police interact, there is no simple correlation. While neither Coombs nor Michael seem to have gained significantly from their arrests and the publicity around their transgressions, neither have they fallen entirely. Michael as a sex symbol among teen girls may have suffered but perhaps the range of meaning we associate with homosexuality may have expanded as it did when it became public that Rock Hudson was gay.

We have suggested that the authority of celebrity is multi dimensional. The law operates on celebrities and they contribute to how we know law. The influence is no more necessarily intended than the violations of law that play such a crucial role in linking celebrity and law. We simply wish to approach law so as to provide for a multi linear exchange of meanings. The issue of authority is at least partly a function of visibility, credibility and marketability. To say that celebrity is authoritative would from time to time include celebrities saying 'this is the law' but far more often it would mean that how we understand the world in terms of celebrity would be an aspect of law. Sean Coombs submitting to court while his gangster music decries the authority of the courts is one type of meaning. OJ Simpson submitting but essentially beating the system is another. Both are examples of how the law is interactive with social forces.[48] Thus, it is not simply normativity that we have been describing. It is not simply views of right and wrong but of the law. George Michael being arrested for homosexual activity in a public bathroom sends messages about behavior and the power of police. It is part of how we know homosexuality, enforcing traditional views of surreptitious and seedy activity.

The influence of celebrities is greater in the less technical aspects of law. Thus, the authority of Dennis Franz, who plays Detective Sipowitz on *NYPD Blue,* is more evident with regard to the public perception we have about the authority of police than it seems likely to be in matters of police discipline such as the power of internal affairs divisions to subpoena records in their investigation. Similarly, we would expect Oprah, Larry Springer and Bill Moyers to contribute to how we feel about environmental pollution, divorce or even human rights laws but not a provision of the tax code that requires owners of real property to establish trust relations in order to liquidate their holdings.

Crimes such as the killing of seven year old Megan Kanka in New Jersey produce law. In this case, the murder and rape produced a national victim's rights movement 'Parents for Megan's Law, Inc' that has been responsible

[48] There is a correlation between market-economy forces of commodification which celebrities exemplify and the law itself.

for the widespread implementation of laws for registering sex offenders and notifying the community of their presence. President Clinton signed national legislation encouraging the states in this policy in 1996. We understand the law as coming from widespread knowledge of a particular event. The source of the legislation is a sort of celebrity crime. But the situation illuminates one of the aspects of this analysis that we are trying to develop. The celebrity and the law ought to not simply be seen instrumentally. Megan's Law, whether the national legislation or similar iterations in various states, embodies the celebrity of the murdered child. This contemporary development is similar to that surrounding the Mann Act in the early part of the twentieth century, although, then it was the perception that 'white slavery'[49] was a major social issue and the celebration of the individual was less central. With the passing of the white slavery issue from public consciousness has come the passing of the significance of the Mann Act although the prohibition against crossing state lines for immoral purposes has become a foundation for the national power to regulate affairs in the states.

We have relied on the work of the group of scholars at the University of Queensland who examine the cultural function of celebrity in the book *Fame Games*. Their project is represented on the cover by the seductive look and tarty smile of Australian singer Kylie Minogue. Introduced to a relatively clueless world as one of the icons of Australia during the closing ceremonies of the Sydney Olympics in 2002, Minogue's image migrates to the cover of the book as a marketing ploy and then it appears on the cover of the Cambridge University Press catalogue for 2001. There it functions, as the authors no doubt hoped it would for the book, like that of Julia Roberts or Princess Diana on the cover of *Time*. It draws attention to the product by association with the familiar and attractive. The once stodgy academic press uses the glitz and sexuality of the pop star to push its academic books for this season. It links Minogue to the products of the press, which become the treats inside the catalogue.

In *Fame Games*, Minogue's celebrity is linked to an analysis of the promotion industry and the production of the special place in the culture that is celebrity. In the societies we have been examining both celebrity and law are commodified.[50] Law shares cultural space and cultural form with celebrity and, where it is successful in influencing society, it is part of the 'culture industry.' Some of our colleagues in culture rather than law have argued that tabloids have replaced or become the fairytales of the 21st century.[51] Both are ways of defining and creating our culture's morality. Both are commodified. This is not new and the critique appears often in Western

[49] The kidnapping of women (emphasis on white women) and indenturing them into prostitution.

[50] Turner *et al* 2000 write of '... cultural industries whose interests are served by the celebrities promotion': above n 9 at 11. We think that law is this sort of cultural industry.

[51] Friedman 1999 above n 8 at 29.

culture. JD Salinger has Zooey talking about how knowledge, materialised as ego, can become just as much a possession as are cars, or money or houses. One aspect of celebrity as a source of law is in promotion.[52] We expect celebrity to be marketed and are only learning of the need to market law.

In articulating the ways celebrities act as sources of law it is important to describe how they act as participants in a policy making process. The AIDS work done by Princess Diana undoubtedly had an affect on public consciousness in regard to the disease by changing perceptions about its risks and how people who are sick should be treated. It also gave support to legislation, such as the Americans with Disabilities Act, which sought to protect those who had been infected.

Turner and his colleagues connect the production of celebrity with the construction of community.[53] It is an aspect of the fluid process that law as culture has to incorporate to fully comprehend governmentality.

V

CONCLUSION

When we say here that celebrity is a source of law we mean a number of things. Celebrities contribute alongside expected or traditional sources. At various levels and in various ways a reciprocal relationship may simply be a modern reality in which celebrity is as secular and non governmental as it was religious and governmental years ago. As once the law depended on the King and his court, it now depends on the celebrated in society in their many faceted forms.

[52] JD Salinger, *Franny and Zooey*: 'As a matter of simple logic, there's no difference at all, that I can see, between the man who's greedy for material treasure—or even intellectual treasure—and the man who's greedy for spiritual treasure' pp 147–48.

[53] Turner *et al* 2000 above n 9 at 15.

7

Writing Around the Censor: Gypsies, Thieves, and Rebels in Early Modern Spain

WILLIAM PENCAK

I

CENSORED WRITING: AN HISTORICAL OVERVIEW

CENSORSHIP HAS ALWAYS been an opportunity as well as an obstacle for critical thinkers throughout history. Even at the height of Stalinist repression in the Soviet Union, historians hostile to Stalin could express their thoughts indirectly by stressing the role of impersonal material forces, rather than personal agency, in their accounts of the French or Russian Revolutions.[1] A century earlier, Giuseppe Verdi became the hero of Italian nationalists by writing operas obviously hostile to Austrian and papal rule, transfering the contemporary situation to earlier periods of history and inferior political domains. (The King of Sweden became the 'Governor of Boston,' for instance, in *The Masked Ball*; nineteenth-century Austrian invaders were signified by Frederick Barbarossa in *The Battle of Legnano*.) Mozart and his librettist, Lorenzo Da Ponte, were able to avoid charges that they made the immoral Don Giovanni the most attractive character in the opera of that name by having the other characters warn the audience that villains inevitably go to hell—in a coda that is undoubtedly the most banal number in the entire score.

In *The Buried Mirror: Reflections on Spain and the New World*, Carlos Fuentes points out that the Spanish Inquisition of the sixteenth and seventeenth centuries was notoriously strict in the censorship of literature.

[1] The work of GM Enteen, who has regularly attended meetings of the Roundtable for the Semiotics of Law, has been crucial in establishing the semiotic coding of Soviet historical writing. See especially: 'The Rehabilitation of MN Pokrovsky' (1969) 20 *Soviet Studies* 306; 'Marxists vs. Non-Marxists: Soviet Historiography in the 1920s' (1976) 35 *Slavic Review* 91; and 'Writing Party History in the USSR: The Case of EM Iaroslavskii' (1986) 21 *Journal of Contemporary History* 321.

Paradoxically, the characteristically Spanish formality with which this censorship was enforced permitted authors to express critical thoughts as long as they tacked on a moralistic ending or made sure characters who subverted authority, however morally attractive, were roundly criticised by either the author or characters who upheld the existing order. In fact, so complexly written is much of this literature that it is frequently impossible to discern the author's 'intention': is Miguel de Cervantes' immortal Don Quixote hero, fool, or both, and what should Spain do, if anything, to correct its abuses?[2] Spanish censorship led to an outpouring of masterpieces by forcing writers, Fuentes notes, 'to evolve a comic, indirect language that went against the grain of official conformity.'[3]

In Spain at the turn of the seventeenth century, contrasts abounded. While historians Henry Kamen and David Ringrose have successfully refuted the stereotype of a perpetual Spanish 'decline,' it can neither be denied that imperial Spain was a world of paradoxes nor, as Kamen admits, that the period 1588–1658, when Spain produced its greatest literature, was one of nearly unmitigated disaster. The crown expelled the Jewish conversos, and numerous deadly plagues, decreases in trade and production, and military defeats afflicted the realm.[4] Much of the riches of the wealthiest and most far-flung empire in history wound up at the bottom of the sea in the Armada's wreck; a rigid aristocracy supported by an impoverished society lost four of its nine million people in the sixteenth century; enormous wealth was displayed alongside the presence of thousands of gypsies, bandits, and beggars. Writers had to juggle their defense of social hierarchy with a critique that could be interpreted as a plea for Christian Spain to live up to its own ideals, rather than as a cry for revolt and violence. 'Between official order and unofficial disorder,' writes Fuentes, 'a pictorial, verbal, and dramatic beauty' emerged, 'in this long tension between what was permitted and what was forbidden. Desire clashed with prohibitions, the visible with the invisible, and the said with unsaid.'[5]

Reflection on these two contrasting yet interlocking worlds is at the heart of Golden Age Spanish literature. Most notably, the character of Don Quixote, attached to an obsolete code of chivalry, mirrors an absurd aristocracy whose etiquette permitted King Felipe IV to fry to death in his chair

[2] Contrast, for example, the work of M McKenrick, *Playing the King: Lope de Vega and the Limits of Conformity* (London, Tamesis, 2000), who stresses the subversive nature of Lope de Vega's work, with that of ER Wright, *Pilgrimage to Patronage: Lope de Vega and the Court of Philip III, 1598–1621* (Lewisburg, Bucknell University Press, 2001), which shows his role as a favored court author and shows how his writings bolster royal authority. Also see Henry Kamen, 'Toleration and Dissent in Sixteenth-Century Spain: The Alternative Tradition' 19 (1988) *The Sixteenth Century Journal* 3–23.

[3] C Fuentes, *The Buried Mirror: Reflections on Spain and the New World* (Boston, Houghton Mifflin, 1992), at 176.

[4] Henry Kamen, 'The Decline of Spain: a historical myth?' (1978) 81 *Past and Present* 49. DR Ringrose, *Spain, Europe, and the 'Spanish Miracle,' 1700–1900* (Cambridge, Cambridge University Press, 1996).

[5] Fuentes, *The Buried Mirror*, above n 3 at 176.

because the proper official was not present to move it. Sancho Panza, the embodiment of the long-suffering populace, enables Quixote to survive. In addition to Cervantes' social commentary, he is also referencing Spain's picaresque literary tradition, where poor men of ill repute wander the realm, a cross between heroes and buffoons: Francisco Rico has pointed out numerous places in *Don Quixote* that bring up previous works in the genre, notably when the galley slave and scoundrel Ginès de Pasamonte declares that his own autobiography will leave *Lazarillo do Tormes*, the prototype of the picaresque novel, and all others in the dust. Here, too, Cervantes is ambiguous. Is he mocking his predecessors, genially sometimes, or paying tribute to them? All in all, as the scholar Martin de Riquer has entitled his short summation of his own life's work on Cervantes, at best we can hope for an 'approximation of *Don Quixote*.'[6]

In this essay, however, I turn to works less well known in the non-Spanish speaking world: two of Cervantes' *Exemplary Stories*—'La Gitanilla' (or 'The Little Gipsy Girl') and 'Rinconete and Cortadillo' published in 1613, eight years after the first part of *Don Quixote*—and Lope de la Vega's play *Fuente Ovejuna* written sometime between 1611 and 1618.[7] While paying lip-service to inquisitorial authority, all three speak up for a repressed yet vibrant populace while criticising their earthly superiors with the effectiveness of Goya's portraits, painted some two centuries later. In these great works of social commentary, imbecile royal faces emerge from the most elegant attire while the artist put his deepest emotions into powerful drawings depicting the horrors of Napoleon's invasion of Spain.

II

LITERARY DISCOURSE: A TOOL OF SUBVERSION

Two late-twentieth-century bodies of knowledge are especially helpful in examining the works of Cervantes and Lope de Vega: semiotic analysis (of both the Peircean and Greimasian variety) and subaltern studies. In the interest of clarity, I will first describe the plots and literary devices employed by Cervantes and Lope de Vega. Then I will apply each of these methodologies in turn.

Cervantes protects himself from the censor in his *Exemplary Stories* with a preface confirming the title's intention to provide behavioral instruction: 'some profitable example can be extracted from each of them.' Yet he then

[6] Francisco Rico, *The Spanish Picaresque Novel and the Point of View* (Cambridge, Cambridge University Press, 1984), esp 68; Martin de Riquer, *Aproximacion al Quijote* (Madrid, Salvat Editores, 1970), also traces *Don Quixote's* relations to the picaresque tradition and other elements of Spanish literature.

[7] M de Cervantes, *Don Quixote* in AF de Avellaneda (ed) (Madrid, Biblioteca Nueva, 2000); and following *Novelas Ejemplares I* in JB Avalle-Arce (ed) (Madrid, Castilia, 1982); Lope de Vega, *Fuente Ovejuna* in F Lopez Estrada (ed) (Madrid, Castilia, 1996).

compares the stories to 'a billiard table in the public square of our nation, where anyone may come and have fun without injuring anyone else.' Next he claims he would rather cut off his writing hand if even a single reader extracted one bad thought or desire from his work. Cervantes is vague as to exactly what is bad or profitable, but the vivid image of people shooting pool in public squares, the zocalos where state and church buildings majestically dominate Spanish cities, is certainly jarring.

By placing 'La Gitanilla' first in his collection, Cervantes is revalorising a despised, outlaw group. Gypsies were placed first in the Spanish law defining those considered vagabonds, subject to deportation or—if they were healthy males—rowing the galleys.[8] Not only is the gypsy girl—named 'Preciosa' or precious—beautiful, clever, and musical, Cervantes describes gypsy society as the very image of the vanished, mythical Golden Age depicted in chapter 11 of *Don Quixote*. Given the latter book's great popularity, nearly every reader of the *Exemplary Stories* could thus have interpreted the gypsies as representing an ideal society rather than, as was usual, the scum of the earth: they live in friendship, in harmony with nature, with little personal property but sustain general prosperity and happiness.

Cervantes, however, has again squared himself with the censors by appearing to condemn gypsies in the story's first paragraph. They were 'born into this world to be thieves' he reiterates several times:

> they are born of thieves, brought up with thieves, study to be thieves, and eventually become complete thieves themselves. The wish to steal and the act of stealing are instincts which stay with them until death.

As Dr Johnson might claim, 'He protests too much!' The action of the story subverts this claim: when a wealthy woman cannot seduce a gypsy man (actually, a young nobleman in disguise) who loves Preciosa, she plants her jewels among his belongings and falsely accuses him of stealing. He and the gypsy girl herself turn out to be members of the nobility, and the young man is pardoned for killing a soldier who comes to arrest him. True nobility appears in the young man's loyalty to Preciosa, even in the face of death, and in the behavior of the gypsies who are struggling to survive despite prejudice and persecution.

In 'Rinconete and Cortadillo,' much as organised crime and official authority coexisted amicably in his era and most others, Cervantes conflates rather than inverts the official moral order with the code of the outlaw. Two young men, in quest of a free and easy life, go to Seville to become

[8] JB Avalle-Arce, 'Novelas ejemplares: Reality, Realism, Literary Tradition' in H Bloom (ed), *Cervantes: Modern Critical Views* (New York, Chelsea House, 1987), at 136–37; IAA Thompson, 'A Map of Crime in Sixteenth-Century Spain' (1968) 21 *Economic History Review* 245.

criminals, only to find that not only is the city's underworld a tightly regulated hierarchy that mirrors the official order, the two are closely linked via payoffs and favors, a situation historian Henry Kamen has shown indeed existed.[9] Cervantes is right in sending the lads to Seville: as historian IAA Thompson writes of early modern Spain:

> Seville pullulated with foreigners, with disaffected *moriscos*, vagrants, ruffians, thieves, and the whole picturesque underworld of the picaresque ... Here, stimulated by the juxtaposition of fabulous wealth and massive poverty, and aided by the corruption and maladministration of justice and the anonymity and flux of the most populous city in Spain, crime flourished.[10]

This confusion of worlds appears most vividly in the confusion of words Cervantes uses to signify it. When he introduces Monopodio, the king of the crime syndicate, the latter terms his operation a 'hermandad' or brotherhood, thereby equating it to the great crusading, military orders of the realm. (These clerical orders, as Kamen has shown, themselves generated a great deal of crime and violence.)[11] Monopodio then utters a variety of malapropisms to describe his operations: estupdeno (stupendous) for estipendio (stipend—in this case paid by his organisation to a priest who says masses for deceased criminals); naufragio (shipwreck or disaster) for sufragio (aid—the effect of these masses); adversario (adversary relationship) for aniversario (anniversary) and popa y soledad (poop and sorrow) for pompa y solemnidad (pomp and solemnity). The last two mistakes appear in the concluding sentence of a speech that roughly translates 'Every year our brotherhood celebrates its adversarial relationship with all the above-mentioned [priest, lawyer, policeman, executioner, court officials, women who offer them aid, and their fathers and mothers] with poop and sorrow.' The established order is both incorporated into the underworld and brought down to its level through humor and linguistic subversion. Several words of Sevillian underworld slang in Monopodio's speech—lo que se garbea (what we steal—used to pay the priest); socorridas (women who help us); trena (jail); and guras (galleys)—the most common punishment for serious male criminals in Hapsburg Spain[12]—further implicate the clergy and benevolent women as supporters of organised crime. The criminals also mock the punishments inflicted on them—usually whipping or rowing the galleys—and those authorities who mete out what passes for justice.

[9] H Kamen, 'Public Auithority and Popular Crime: Banditry in Valencia, 1660–1714' (1974) 3 *Journal of European Economic History* 654.
[10] Thompson, 'A Map of Crime in Sixteenth-Century Spain' see above n 8 256.
[11] H Kamen, 'Clerical Violence in a Catholic Society: the Hispanic World 1450–1720' (1983) 20 *Studies in Church History* 201.
[12] *Ibid*, 246.

To escape the censor's wrath, Cervantes duly concludes that young Rinconete is ultimately convinced that the people of Seville lead evil, dangerous, libertine, and dissolute lives, and that his story should serve as an example and warning to all who read it. But even after realising the immorality of his ways, Rinconete continues to attend Monopodio's 'infamous academy,' as Cervantes calls it, for several more months. By use of the word 'academy,' Cervantes equates this school of crime with those of law and theology and once more subverts his argument even as he makes it.

In her book which plausibly describes Cervantes as a skeptic, Maureen Ihre notes that in the Spain of his day, 'definitions and proofs of honor elevated exterior appearances to the fore, de-emphasising actual inner truths and facts to the point of insignificance.'[13] With the possible exception of *Don Quixote* itself, no work of literature in history so scathingly deconstructs superficial and hypocritical pretenses of honor than the play *Fuente Ovejuna* by Lope de Vega. The action begins as the Comendador of the Order of Calatrava is in a huff because the 'discourteous' Master of his Order was not immediately present to greet him on his entry into town. (The Master is a younger man the Comendador dominates, much as the young King Felipe III was dominated by his chief minister the Duke of Lerma at the time the play was written.)[14] Yet it is this very Comendador who thinks it is an 'honor' for the village maidens of Fuente Ovejuna to yield to his sexual advances, and nothing less than rebellion itself when they insist on standing up for the honor they claim as their own. When he is the inferior, the Comendador insists on due respect, yet he refuses to offer comparable courtesy to others, including his own superiors, maintaining that honor is exclusively the prerogative of the aristocracy.

Justice, like honor, is also subordinated, it seems, to a double standard, as many Spaniards undoubtedly thought it was when in 1608 Felipe, at Lerma's request, granted military orders such as the one to which the Comendador belongs the exclusive right to judge the crimes of their members.[15] The Comendador and the Master of the Order are readily forgiven by monarchs Ferdinand and Isabella for having rebelled against them and supported the King of Portugal. Yet although the Comendador is a traitor, the monarchs do not forgive the 'unpardonable' resistance to him of the villagers he goads beyond endurance. They only escape with their lives after they all, young and old, male and female, are brutally tortured by the monarch's inquisitor. What saves them is their refusal to blame anyone except 'Fuente Ovejuna,' the community in its entirety, for the rebellion and the Comendador's death. The crown could punish some of its subjects, even unjustly, but it could hardly wipe them all out. Rebellion is justified when

[13] M Ihre, *Skepticism in Cervantes* (London, Tamesis Books, 1982), at 28.
[14] William R Blue, 'The Politics of Lope's *Fuenteovejuna*' (1991) 59 *Hispanic Review* 299.
[15] R Kagan, *Lawsuits and Litigants in Castile, 1500–1700* (Chapel Hill, University of North Carolina Press, 1981), at 30.

a community as a whole is aggrieved as opposed to rebellious individuals who might be venting personal issues.

Lope de Vega explicitly raises the question as to whether and how the words justice and honor can be manipulated from the very first. When the townsfolk greet the reprehensible Comendador, they praise him as a victor over the Moors in a city where no Moors live, worthy of the gifts of 'gansos' (badly written songs—'jingles') and 'cortezas' (hides) instead of courtesies, a word it closely resembles. Lope de Vega also treats the class specificity of justice and honor in a comic yet profound series of observations by two villagers, Frondoso and Laurencia, immediately after the Comendador has made his appearance. When Laurencia is amused that Frondoso has called her and a companion ladies ('damas'), he launches into a monologue making fun of euphemisms: the blind is called the blind in one eye, the student is called a graduate, the ignorant man a person of common sense, the coward is cautious, the person suffering from the plague has a cold, and so on at length. Laurencia then turns the table and shows how higher qualities in turn can be degraded, specifically how 'discourteous' language can be applied to 'courteous' activities. Thus, the serious man can be called tedious, the 'courteous' one a flatterer, the Christian a pretender, or the person who is justly rewarded a man of good luck. Her speech recalls the Comendador's insistence on courtesy in the previous scene, and carries the theme over to subsequent scenes where he will deny it to others. Note that it is the woman who deflates the pretences of the great, whereas the man displays society's euphemisms for undesirable qualities. The man excuses, the woman exposes.

Fuente Ovejuna is full of other meditations on what words best describe certain behavior. The Comendador uses 'perro' or dog, a particularly nasty Spanish word superiors used to dehumanise inferiors (in theory, whites in the New World were forbidden to apply it to Indians) to refer to the villagers. Laurencia, on the other hand, is changed from a 'lady' to an 'amazon' as she leads the village women in forcing their men to resist the Comendador with taunts of 'maricon' (or queer) and comparable words that question their masculinity. Identities shift according to circumstances: ordinary people have the potential to be heroes, whereas a warrior may be a brute in peacetime.

Lope de Vega is offering us either two contradictory or one paradoxical argument. He may be saying that justice and honor, like the string of terms Frondoso and Laurencia admit have double meanings, are words constructed by humans for ulterior purposes. Yet anyone who reads, or even better yet, sees the play, *knows* that true justice and honor are on the side of the villagers. If Lope de Vega's plays taken together argue the need for the united monarchy established by Ferdinand and Isabella to overcome the arrogant and quarrelsome aristocracy,[16] the message of *Fuente Ovejuna* is that

[16] D Ostlund, *The Re-Creation of History in the Fernando and Isabel Plays of Lope de Vega* (New York, Peter Lang, 1997).

a suffering populace must take action into its own hands to overthrow tyrannical rule that is not a matter of definition, but of blatantly obvious evil and repression. Right and wrong transcend the language games the characters have played throughout the drama with Wittgensteinian incisiveness.

III

SEMIOTIC ANALYSIS OF WRITING AROUND THE CENSOR

Peircean semiotics, as applied in Roberta Kevelson's pioneering work on legal semiotics, contrasting what a society records as legal with its legitimate *praxis*, can be incorporated into AJ Greimas's semiotic square in looking at how Cervantes and Lope de Vega use irony and wit to provide moral legitimacy for the lower-class and outcast groups of their age.[17] Imagine a semiotic square with the terms 'legal' and 'legitimate' on top, crossing over to 'not legal' (bottom left) and 'not legitimate' (bottom right). Legal and not legal stand for the (supposedly) enforced laws that (ostensibly) express the values and behavior of Spanish society. But as we in the twenty-first century also know from everyday experience, these legal rules only partially coincide with socially acceptable behavior. It is legitimate yet not legal to make phone calls on the corporate nickel, to drive an indefinite number of kilometers over the speed limit, and so forth. Similarly, it is legal yet not legitimate to voice certain doctrines—such as, c 2001/02, support for certain Third World liberation movements—or for poorly attired, destitute people of color to walk unchallenged through wealthy neighborhoods.

The world of Cervantes and Lope de Vega repeatedly tested the boundaries of legality and legitimacy, articulating the tension between the legitimate yet not legal (dis)order of criminals, ne-er-do-wells, and critical authors, on the one hand, and the legal order that maintained a social hierarchy steeped in illegally legitimate activity itself. Ironically, the gypsy society in 'La Gitanilla' that came closest to practicing Utopia was neither legitimate nor legal. The gypsy girl's behavior is 'noble,' which is legal yet not legitimate for a gypsy—the aristocrats in the tale cannot accept that a low-born person could behave so well—and thus she must be ancestrally legitimated, albeit through an unconvincing surprise ending that undercuts that very point. Similarly, Monopodio's underworld, while not legal, is certainly legitimate. Even the punishments his men suffer from time to time so the law can maintain a façade of respectability confirm two sorts of legitimacy. First, the convictions enable the authorities to point to their concern with legality, although they are normally in league with the criminals. This infrequent and unpredictable application of legality also helps to legitimate

[17] R Kevelson, *The Law as a System of Signs* (New York, Plenum, 1988); AJ Greimas, *Signs, Language, Culture* (Mouton, The Hague, 1970).

the criminals as criminals—the possibility of punishment confirms their reputation as bold spirits living outside the law.

In *Fuente Ovejuna*, Lope de Vega implicitly legitimates an illegal peasant rebellion as our sympathy turns toward the peasants whose honor has been impugned by the Comendador. On the other hand, the Comendador's rebellion, pardoned by the crown, is rendered illegitimate in the eyes of the reader because of his insufficient recognition of the honor of others and his extreme concern with his own. As Michel Foucault has written, the manner in which people in the early modern world suffered hardship served as a 'theatre' in which they exhibited their true nature. By bravely enduring torture, the villagers show their true honor as opposed to the ever-complaining Comendador. Similarly, the bravado with which Monopodio's men trivialise the harsh whippings and galley service they sometimes endure suggests their similar unconventional honor.[18]

Subaltern studies are also valuable in understanding Cervantes and Lope de Vega. Scholarship by Stephen Greenblatt and Tzvetan Todorov, among others, have shown the usefulness of applying this school of thought in the pre-modern world in which overseas colonialism and the forced relocation of massive numbers of poor folk within the colonizing powers' boundaries bears considerable similarity to recent experiences.[19] Originally developed in India in the 1980s to offer an alternative to the traditional historical narratives that stressed war, politics, and prominent people (almost always men), subaltern studies look especially at the literature in which oppressed peoples represent and attempt to overcome their situation.[20] There is, however, one major difference between the two eras. Modern subaltern writers can usually voice their insights authentically and directly, largely because their works can be published in countries that permit freedom of speech—ironically, mostly colonial or neo-colonial powers that would react with force if people tried to act on these ideas. Hence, a good deal of subaltern scholarship related to the early modern world looks at writers who had to encode their view in writings which could both express the situation yet avoid persecution.[21]

In seventeenth-century Spain direct criticism of authority was impossible. Hence, three key insights of subaltern studies apply: projection, or 'othering' on the part of the dominant group; psychological incorporation on the

[18] M Foucault, *Discipline and Punish: The Birth of the Prison*, A Sheridan(tr) (New York, Vintage, 1979) at 58.

[19] S Greenblatt, *Marvellous Possessions: The Wonder of the New World* (Oxford, Clarendon Press, 1991); T Todorov, *The Conquest of America: The Question of the Other* (New York, Harper, 1982).

[20] J Sharpe, 'Figures of Colonial Resistance' (1989) 35 *Modern Fiction Studies* 137; R Adorno, 'Reconsidering Colonial Discourse for Sixteenth- and Seventeenth-Century Spanish America' (1993) 28 *Latin American Research Review* 135; GC Spivak, 'Can the Subaltern Speak?' in C Nelson and L Grossberg (eds), *Marxism and the Interpretation of Culture* (London, Macmillan, 1988).

[21] J Jain, *Problems of Postcolonial Literature and Other Essays* (Jaipur, Printall, 1991).

part of the subaltern; and the powerful role of women is especially valuable in understanding Cervantes and Lope de Vega. As Edward Said has shown in *Orientalism*, Europeans project character failures they see within themselves on other groups.[22] Applied to seventeenth-century Spain, the aristocracy grew rich exploiting its tenants and the people of the Indies; practiced violence abroad in numerous wars and at home against the crown, each other, and the lower orders; and hardly did any work at all, which led it to take refuge in the minutiae of court etiquette and over-insistence on personal dignity. The elite thus projected its own flaws of idleness, theft, and viciousness onto the lower classes—the gypsies, the underworld, and peasants—along with Native Americans in New Spain.

On the other hand, the impoverished folk of early modern Europe were not, or were rarely, rebels. When they did take up arms, they almost always appealed to a traditionally sanctioned higher authority or law (the monarch or Christian principles) to justify opposing an obnoxious ruler who was himself viewed as the real lawbreaker.[23] In normal times, they, like colonial and post-colonial subjects, had at the very least to perform the social roles required of them, and outward performance can never be kept totally separate from the inner self.[24] So imitation of aristocratic behavior, as in the structure of underworld society or the insistence on a code of honor among peasants, also comes to characterise subaltern behavior. Hence so many revolutions turn against their own as some leaders assume traditional leadership characteristics while others try to remain true to their principles.

The appropriation and/or misuse of official language by sympathetically depicted criminals and rebels in both Cervantes and Lope de Vega also depict the very real struggle over language which occurred in their own time, and which continues today as one person's terrorist is another's freedom fighter. In Spain, as popular authors were playing outrageously with the meaning of words, Cristóbal de Villalón wrote treatises which sought to codify an official Spanish language—to be inculcated through education—designed to serve the absolutist state. Such linguistic battles were common in early modern Europe: the French essayist Michel de Montaigne told Frenchmen they could express themselves better in the language of Parisian fishwives than through the grammar taught in schools. In Italy writers such as Machiavelli favored the use of popular Italian dialects as one means of resisting the imperialistic claims of the papacy and foreign rulers.[25]

Women have not only been some of the most important subaltern thinkers: their work has underscored one of Charles Peirce's insights into

[22] E Said, *Orientalism* (New York, Pantheon, 1978).
[23] G Rudé, *The Crowd in History* (New York, Wiley and Sons, 1964).
[24] J Butler, *Excitable Speech: A Politics of Performance* (New York, Routledge, 1997).
[25] MJ Read, 'Cristóbal de Villalón: Language, Education, and the Absolutist State' in T Lewis and FJ Sánchez (eds), *Culture and the State in Spain: 1550–1850* (New York, Garland, 1999), 1; S Casciani, 'Ruzante: A Dissenting Voice in the Italian Renaissance' (1995/98) 11 *American Journal of Semiotics* 185.

history. It does not so much evolve as erupt 'cataclysmically'. In these moments new opportunities arise for previously suppressed historical actors to emerge.[26] From the French Revolution to the American civil rights movement, in the Iberian world from the days of *Fuente Ovejuna* to the Sandinistas and Zapatistas of the present, women have played a part in struggles for freedom that belies the role reserved for them in conservative society. Subaltern feminist literature, much like Cervantes' gypsy girl, demonstrates that such participation is in fact incipient in the non-traditional roles women must play simply to survive in repressive regimes. Their courage and resourcefulness—hidden as in the way black American women have held families and communities together for generations out of the sight of official history—has nevertheless been there all along for anyone who sought it out.

In this context, the women of *Fuente Ovejuna* become the prototype for their sisters over the next several centuries.[27] Furthermore, not only do these subalterns speak, and act, they point out the contradictions and absurdities in the language used to repress their bodies, but not their souls and minds. They deconstruct both the ideology and the structure of domination. Yet ironically, it is another woman, Queen Isabella, who orders them tortured, but then neither punishes them further nor forgives them. (Despite the tortures, she can't get the confession she needs.) The women freedom fighters retain their solidarity but fail to achieve liberation. At best, they will enjoy a somewhat more decent version of the *status quo ante*, further legitimated because one of their own, in the decidedly non-traditional role of ruler, has emerged as the savior of traditional society and champion of law and order. The queen too is a prototype, of Margaret Thatcher, Nancy Reagan, and Condoleeza Rice, who achieved their own place in history by denying the very history that made them possible.

Perhaps Don Quixote, like the women in *Fuente Ovejuna*, is also a prototype, a man of the future rather than of the past. It is all too easy to view the code of chivalry he represents as dysfunctional, outdated, or irrelevant; on one level, to be sure, he is a ludicrous figure. But he also fights to free slaves, which the King of Spain did by edict in 1541 with respect to the Native Americans, and most of the civilised world waited to do until the nineteenth century; he tilts at windmills, giants indeed which enabled wealthy landlords to monopolise the processing of grain and thereby exploit and dispossess the peasantry in early modern Europe; and he sees sheep as an army—sheep who did more to ravage the landscape of the early modern world than any army, forcing poor farmers into cities, into the factories, into the armed forces, or overseas. If one may laugh at Hapsburg

[26] For Peirce's ideas on history, see W Pencak, 'Charles Sanders Peirce, Historian and Semiotician' (1991) 83 *Semiotica* 311.

[27] HZ Ahmad, *Postmodern Feminism in Third World Women's Literature* (Boston, University of Massachusetts Press, 1998).

Spain in decline, culminating in the unfortunate King Carlos II who died in 1700, could not close his mouth, grieved incessantly in his ancestors' tomb, and probably could not perform the physical act required to perpetuate his lineage, no one laughs at the modern world's dark satanic mills and the landless peasants who still flock to them by the millions on several continents as capitalist agriculture continues its march.

The opposite of the Comendador in *Fuente Ovejuna*, Don Quixote stands for an absolute moral perspective that flies in the face of practical consequences. As any trip to Latin America or Spain will reveal, his persona is still cherished more than any other throughout the Spanish-speaking world—statues are available everywhere and can be found in nearly every home, along with those of his reality check and squire, Sancho Panza. We need a dose of Fuente Ovejuna's and Don Quixote's pre-modern idealism in our post-modern world to see rulers, windmills, sheep, and the wretched of the earth without the spectacles worn by the naked Emperor.

Part II

Cultural and Symbolic Analyses of the Law in Context

8

Subversion in the World of Order: Legal Deconstruction as a Rhetorical Practice

JOANNA JEMIELNIAK

I

INTRODUCTION

FOR A LONG time did the art of rhetoric seem to be a part of an eminent, though to a large extent forgotten, tradition. Sophisticated knowledge of the composition of convincing and touching speeches, 'ars bene dicendi,'[1] for a long time was treated as a ceremonious lesson given in the dead language. Classical handbooks of descriptive rhetoric were based mainly on two schemes: the theory of the parts of speech or on the Peripatetic model embracing the five tasks of the rhetoric. This art, codified in the times of yore, was incorporated into the medieval corpus of liberal arts and memorised by teenage adepts over centuries. In modern times rhetoric acquired the status of a rather exotic and fossilised discipline, known primarily to dedicated explorers of classical texts.

In this context, the current renewal of interest in rhetoric may seem unexpected and unusual to explain. Extensive catalogues of tropes and figures together with rules of their proper use and with detailed hints about how to orate seem to belong to a tradition long bygone. The statement by Fish ('hardly a novel one' as he emphasises) that 'we live in a rhetorical world'[2] might seem perhaps unexpected. This sentence becomes fully understandable only if we stop perceiving rhetoric as an arsenal of sophisticated, decorative, though rather rusty weapons, but instead notice the actual power of this art of convincing. The reason why this apparatus was invented

[1] Quintilian, after: M Korolko, *Sztuka retoryki. Przewodnik encyklopedyczny.* Reprint revised (Warszawa, Wiedza Powszechna, 1998. Original edition 1990), at 46.

[2] S Fish, *Doing what comes naturally. Change, Rhetoric, and the Practice of Theory in Literary and Legal Studies.* Reprint (Durham and London, Duke University Press, 1992. Original edition 1989), at 25.

was an everlasting human need for instruments of effective influence on the minds of others.

Rhetoric was described as an '*instrumental* use of language'[3], the art 'by which discourse is adapted to its end'.[4] Recognising the richness of this discipline, the following text concentrates on the persuasive aspect of rhetoric. The art of convincing as an essential part of rhetoric has been emphasised by numerous authors, from Cicero[5] and Bacon[6] to Burke[7] and Kristeller.[8] Adopting this perspective, this text aims at presenting legal deconstruction as a contemporary rhetorical practice, linked to the classical traditions. Currentness of this ancient legacy, discovered anew, is discussed in the context of Ong's theory of stages in the evolution of culture. The text discusses two basic versions of legal deconstruction (normative and non-normative) referring to the classical dispute on the necessity of the ethical groundings of rhetoric.

II

LEADING SOULS

The origins of rhetoric are traditionally connected with the development of the sophistic thought in Athens in the fifth century BC. Relativism and conventionalism proclaimed by the sophists resulted in the conviction that there is no absolute Truth, but just individual or local truths. The claim that a particular truth is common and binding is just the result of an agreement, custom or social consent. It is natural then to perfect ones skills of persuasion, as they enable the proliferation of our local truths.[9]

Trials over land properties in Sicily in the fifth century BC stimulated a codification of rhetorical rules. At that time the island belonged to the Greeks; its residents expelled the tyrants of the Teron and Hieron dynasty, but they also wanted to recover lands seized by them legally. In court praxis of the time every litigant had to prove his claims before the jury. Korolko points out that:

> for the virtually always uneducated clients the speeches were written by the sophists (for a suitable fee). Thus they gradually formulated the rules of

[3] GA Hauser, *Introduction to Rhetorical Theory* (Long Grove, Waveland Press, reprint edition 1991).

[4] G Campbell, *The Philosophy of Rhetoric* (London, William Tegg, 1850).

[5] MT Cicero, *De oratore,* Vol 1–2, H Rackham(trans) (Cambridge, Harvard University Press, 1969. Original edition 1914).

[6] F Bacon, *The Advancement of Learning* (New York, Modern Library, 2001. Original edition 1605).

[7] K Burke, *A Rhetoric of Motives* (Berkeley, University of California Press, 1969).

[8] PO Kristeller, 'Rhetoric in Medieval and Renaissance Culture' in JJ Murphy(ed), *Renaissance Eloquence: Studies in the Theory and Practice of Renaissance Rhetoric,* (Berkeley, University of California Press, 1983).

[9] See W Tatarkiewicz, *Historia filozofii,* Vol 1, Reprint (Warszawa, Wydawnictwo Naukowe PWN, 1998. Original edition 1931, revised 1968).

> *dialectics*, that is the art of conducting conversations and discussions in an attractive, suggestive and effective manner.[10]

An example of how this activity became professional are the logographs (*logographoi*). In ancient Greece there were rhetors who could be hired to write court speeches for their clients. The art of such an enterprise lied in the adjustment of arguments and style used to the personality of the commissioner. These ghostwriters of the classical world fulfilled in fact the contemporary functions of prosecutors and attorneys. Their present day descendants may yet easily be found in the retinues of politicians, composing suggestive orations for their patrons.

The judicial source of rhetoric echoes in the etymology of the term. The ancient Greek word *rhetón* referred to a strictly formulated legal rule. Such rigid norms, though officially authoritatively binding, were often hardly applicable to the changing everyday practice in the Greek *poleis*. Therefore arose a need for concrete and pragmatic solutions and models of social relationships which at the same time should not openly oppose the divine authority of *rhetón*. It resulted in the particularly innovative practice of the explication of legal rules leading to the distinction between norm and interpretation, *rhetón kai diánoia*.[11] It was the sophists who undertook this demanding task:

> the sophist, who managed to convince the Areopagus of the relativity of a so far immutable *rhetón*, was called *rhétor*. The technique applied to such a persuasive procedure was denominated as *rhetoriké*.[12]

As one could anticipate, rhetoric did not only awake enthusiasm. In Aristophanes' comedies the apprehensions of his contemporaries were depicted. The recurrent main topic of the plays was political quarrel hampering peace. The author pointed to the improper and immoral education of the Athenians as the main reason of the ruling chaos:

> The blame for the education, according to the comedy writer, was to be laid on the sophists, the teachers of wisdom. In the fifth century (BC) they massively came to Athens and propagated new disciplines of knowledge, of which rhetoric was the first and foremost, enabling them to turn white to black by means of quasi-logical reasonings.[13]

The argument that rhetoric as cultivated by the sophists served unethical ends was also the main point of its critique by Plato. The greatest power

[10] M Korolko, *Retoryka i erystyka dla prawnikow* (Warszawa, Wydawnictwa Prawnicze PWN, 2001).

[11] T Zielinski, 'O czytaniu mów sadowych Cycerona w Szkole' (1928) *Kwartalnik Klasyczny* 2.

[12] Korolko 1990/1998 above n 1, at 37.

[13] J Lawinska—Tyszkowska, 'Demokracja atenska i jej wielki przesmiewca' in Aristophanes, *Komedie*. Trans by J Lawinska-Tyszkowska (Warszawa, Prószynski i S-ka, 2001).

and at the same time the greatest danger of rhetorical practice relies on its ability to control peoples minds. The term *psychagogía tis dia lógon* (leading souls by words), used by Plato in the dialogue *Phaedrus* to describe this property, has been translated into English in various ways. In the translation by Jowett[14] it is said that 'it is the function of speech to lead souls by persuasion.' A more free and poetic translation provided by Fowler:[15] 'Oratory is the art of enchanting the soul', emphasises a delusive and perilous character of sophistic persuasion. In the same dialogue Plato (via a statement by Socrates) postulates on what he believes to be a real, not fallacious art of speech. This argumentation reflects Platonic idealism openly opposing the conviction of the sophists about the relativity of truth and values. An oration must therefore reflect the ultimate truth and enlighten people. Its goal is not a temporary victory in a particular dispute, not leading the souls without purpose but to make them aware of the absolute and transcendent values: justice, beauty and good.

The concept of an orator as a person who should meet highest moral requirements remained substantial in the further development of ancient rhetoric. For Aristotle, who systematised the theory of argumentation, the use of means of persuasion should be accompanied by the virtues of a speaker. It is the ethos of the orator who is able to gain the attention and amiability of his audience.[16] The glorification of the ideal speaker as a perfect man is a common motif of the Roman authors. In the dialogue *De oratore* by Cicero,[17] the adversaries unanimously recognise the internalisation of ethical norms as a requisite attribute of a rhetor. Though numerous other questions, including the details of the course of education, are a subject of their protracted dispute, the principle to betoken the truth stays supreme. A well-known expression of this belief is a definition by Cato: *orator est vir bonus dicendi peritus*—'an orator is an honorable man, proficient in the art of speech.'[18]

III

PRINT AND ORALITY

Cultivated throughout the medieval times, the art of rhetoric achieved the status of the obligatory part of education. The system based on seven *artes liberals* recognised rhetoric as one of the basic disciplines (together with

[14] Plato, 'Phaedrus' in *Selected Dialogues of Plato.* Trans by B Jowett. Reprint (New York, Modern Library Classics, 2001. Original edition of this translation 1871).

[15] Plato, 'Phaedrus' in *Euthyphro, Apology, Crito, Phaedo, Phaedrus.* Trans by HN Fowler. Reprint (Cambridge, Massachusetts and London, England, Harvard University Press, 1999. Original edition of this translation 1914).

[16] Aristotle, *The Art of Rhetoric.* Trans by H Lawson-Tancred. Reprint (New York, Penguin Classics, 1992. Original edition 1991).

[17] MT Cicero, edition 1969 above n 5.

[18] See Korolko 1990/1998 above n 1, at 183.

grammar and dialectics) taught in the frames of the first educational level: *trivium*. Acquiring this knowledge was perceived as necessary for continuing studies in *quadrivium* (in arithmetic, astronomy, geometry and music). Still, in the medieval scholastic tradition rhetoric had been by far dominated by dialectics. It was also developed largely in some specialized areas—as *ars dictaminis* (the art of dictating which was in fact the art of official correspondence) or *ars praedicandi* (the art of preaching).[19]

The further development of rhetoric seems significant. The findings of lost texts by Cicero and Quintilian in the fifteenth century increased interest in classical rhetoric and promoted it as a necessary part of the humanist, university education. The Renaissance revival of rhetoric took the form of ciceronianism. Studies on Cicero flourished in Italy already in the first half of the fifteenth century. A style imitating that by the author of *Brutus* became official in the pope's chancellery at the end of fifteenth century and was consequently adopted as a literary norm, especially in the epistolography.[20] The impact of rhetoric on literature and fine arts increased throughout the sixteenth and seventeenth century, as the discipline cultivated again harmonised with the expectations of the age of eloquence.[21]

The other important Renaissance stream in the studies on rhetoric was Ramism, named after its inventor Petrus Ramus (Pierre de la Ramée). Standing against the tradition of Aristotle and Cicero, Ramus perceived the scope of rhetoric in reduced form. In the Ciceronian theory rhetoric comprised five parts: inventio (invention, discovery of arguments), *iudicium* or *dispositio* (judgment or arrangement, assemblage or composition of the material discovered), *elocutio* (style) *memoria* (memory), and pronuntiatio (delivery). In his critique Ramus regarded invention and composition as parts of dialectic, not of rhetoric. From this area memory was also removed, as, according to Ramus, it underwent the general rules of development of thought and not the specific rhetorical ones. The field of rhetoric in Ramus' view was therefore limited to the issues of style and delivery. The concepts by Ramus, developed by his student and companion Omer Talon (Audomarus Talaeus) were widely adopted in Protestant countries as well as in France and served as the basis for a reform and simplification of education.

The ramist reduction of rhetoric has been criticised as cultural banishment of this discipline.[22] Still, for Walter J Ong the anti-Aristotelian and anti-iconographic approach by Ramus should be analysed in the context of dissemination of print. While classical rhetoric was oriented on oral communication, Ramism answered the problems of culture which became still more the culture of massively reproduced written word. Consequently Ong

[19] M Korolko 1990/1998 above n 1 at 187.
[20] *Ibid* at 189.
[21] M Fumaroli, *L'Age de l'Eloquence* (Geneva, Librairie Droz, 1980).
[22] Korolko 1990/1998 above n 1 at 189.

assumes that while classical rhetoric is agonistic (contest oriented), Ramism is quasi-monological.[23]

It seems worth to consider current renewal of interest in classical rhetoric in the context of theory of four stages in the evolution of culture provided by Ong.[24] According to this theory, Western Culture underwent the levels of primary orality, manuscript (chirographic), print (typographic) to the secondary orality (enabled by the means of electronic communications). Ramism was for Ong undoubtedly the result of the stage of print. Therefore contemporary interest in rhetoric could be interpreted as an effect of the cultural turn to the omnipresence of technologically advanced instruments of oral communication, from telephone to television.

IV

RETRACING RHETORIC

The hopes and fears of rhetorical power described by classical authors seem very current, and not only because we live in the rhetorical world. Certainly, as Clifford[25] points out, the increase of communication and intercultural flows means that it is even harder to define a person in the categories of a separate and independent culture than ever before. The particularities are produced in the process of creative syncretism rather than as an effect of strict defining. Clifford describes this condition in the terms of ambiguity, diversity or polyphony.

For the purposes of this text it seems useful to point out the problem of the relationship between rhetoric and semiotics. Close relationship between these two disciplines was stated already by Charles William Morris. In the same article where he introduces the classical division of semiotics into semantics, syntactics and pragmatics, he discusses rhetoric as 'an early and restricted form of pragmatics'.[26] In the Morris's concept rhetoric is perceived as a version of pragmatics and therefore establishes a part semiotics. Accordingly semiotic is treated as the framework for 'the modern equivalents of the ancient trivium of logic, grammar and rhetoric'.[27]

Ottmar Ballweg[28] disputes with this point of view. He claims that rhetoric should not be reduced to its pragmatic function and that it is not a

[23] W Ong, 'Fighting for Life' in *Contest, Sexuality and Consciousness* (Ithaca, Cornell University Press, 1981).

[24] W Ong, *Orality and Literacy: The Technologizing of the Word (New Accents)* (New York, Routledge, 1988).

[25] J Clifford, *Klopoty z kultura. Dwudziestowieczna etnografia, literatura i sztuka (The Predicament of Culture)*. Trans by E Dzurak, J Iracka *et al* (Warszawa, Wydawnictwo KR, 2000. Original edition 1996).

[26] Ch W Morris, 'Foundation of the Theory of Signs' in *International Encyclopedia of Unified Science*, vol 1 (Chicago, University of Chicago Press, 1938) at 30.

[27] *Ibid* at 56.

[28] O Ballweg, *Analytical Rhetoric, Semiotic and Law* in: *Law and Semiotics*, vol 1 (New York and London, Plenum Press, 1987).

subdiscipline of semiotics. From his perspective the relationship between both fields is opposite to the vision provided by Morris. Ballweg claims that semiotics is a special case of rhetoric. In the scheme of analytical rhetoric he presents this discipline as embracing the holistic, phronetic and semiotic perspective. In the holistic sphere he distinguishes ontotactics, axiotactics and teleotactics. Phronetic area consists of agontics, ergontics and pithaneutics. Finally he counts traditional parts of semiotics: pragmatics, semantics and syntactics.[29]

It seems however worth remarking that despite the broad concept of rhetoric, direct references to this discipline in semiotic analyses seem still to embrace firstly its pragmatic potential (as in the Eco's considerations on the reader).[30]

Adopting rhetorical perspective is yet connected with accepting epistemological assumptions as well. For Richard Rorty[31] cultivating a belief in an existence of some universal and absolute Truth (and in its accessibility to the human cognition) is a metaphysical illusion. In the polyphonic or rhetoric world the acceptance of such an illusion is probably even more naive or desperate than ever. But Rorty also emphasises an oppressive character of such systems: acting in the name of declared universal values excludes discussion or tolerance of different viewpoints. Consequently, it could be assumed that authoritative acts are acts of violence. This opinion is shared, among others, by Foucault[32] and Schlag.[33]

Schlag perceives law to be an area of inevitable and incessant violence, not simply because it must be enforced but because every judgment is a fulfilment of an imperative intellectual force: '(j)udges arrive at their decisions by killing off rival conceptions of law.'[34] According to Schlag, the final sentence is but one of possible, competing versions. Legal interpretation is not a linear process of sequential applying rule by rule and leading the reader safely to the final point. Traditions of legal reasoning based on the hierarchy and order of arguments become useless. Moreover, they are particularly inadequate as a consequence of a belief that there exists the ideal and only right final solution. This logocentric concept assumes that the divine letter of law should shine through all the particular decisions. Its procedural version is a theory by Montesquieu that a judge should be just the mouth that repeats the words of the law.[35] One of contemporary incarnations of

[29] *Ibid* at 30.

[30] U Eco, *Lector in fabula: wspoldzialanie w interpretacji tekstów narracyjnych*. Trans by P Salwa (Warszawa, PIW, 1994).

[31] R Rorty, *Przygodnosc, ironia i solidarnosc (Contingency, Irony and Solidarity)*. Trans by WJ Popowski. (Warszawa, Spacja, 1996. Original edition 1989). See also: *Obiektywnosc, relatywizm i prawda (Objectivity, Relativism and Truth)*. Trans by J Marganski (Warszawa, Fundacja Aletheia 1999. Original edition 1991).

[32] M Foucault, *Nadzorowac i karac. Narodziny wiezienia (Surveiller et Punir)*. Trans by T Komendant (Warszawa, Spacja, 1993. Original edition 1975).

[33] P Schlag, 'Clerks in the Maze' (1993) *Michigan Law Review* 91, at 2053–57.

[34] *Ibid* at 2053.

[35] C Montesquieu, *The Spirit of the Laws (De l'esprit des lois)* AM Cohler, BC Miller and HS Stone, eds (Cambridge, Cambridge University Press, 1989. Original edition, 1748).

this approach is the new textualism described by Eskridge, Frickey and Garrett:

> The meaning an ordinary speaker of the English language would draw from the statutory text is the alpha and the omega of statutory interpretation. When the text is relatively clear, interpreters should not even consider other evidence of specific legislative intent or general purpose.[36]

The new-textual model of interpretation requires therefore a creation of an ideal figure of an 'ordinary speaker of the English language.' It can be doubted whether such a representation of some universal cognitive abilities could be constructed at all. Rorty, who denies existence of general or typical attributes of the human nature,[37] would probably strongly oppose it. Yet even if such a figure is possible, the way it comes to life is absolutely arbitrary. The method does not in fact invoke an external criterion of common understanding because it is the judge who decides which meaning of the text he or she should accept as 'plain.' The belief that there exists a unique, unchangeable meaning coded for good in the text (and all we have to do is to discover it) is probably but a dream. A dream which would be even more understandable, as it would allow one to avoid a significant part of responsibility. It seems that there is no escape from the violent character of judging. Denying this characterisation of judgement through legitimisation procedures appealing to the 'common understanding' or through strict following the steps of argumentation is illusive.

V

THE SOPHISTS AGAIN

It is not just legal deconstruction that opposes the linear model of interpretation based on the hierarchy of arguments. Rules for finding necessary means, formulated as 'only if the shelf 1B is empty you can go to the shelf 5C', seem artificial and not working in practice. An interpreter would rather explore the whole warehouse to take and try out accessible instruments. Some of them could finally appear particularly useful. This idea is reflected, for example, in the pragmatic model by Frickey and Eskridge called 'funnel of abstraction.'[38] The funnel depicts the traditional hierarchy of interpretative arguments but also respects the dynamic character of the process. A practical interpreter:

[36] WN Eskridge, PP Frickey and E Garrett, *Legislation and Statutory Interpretation* (New York, Foundation Press, 2000).
[37] Rorty 1989/1996 above n 31.
[38] Eskridge, Frickey and Garrett 2000 above n 36.

> will slide up and down the funnel, considering the strengths of various considerations, rethinking each in light of the others, and weighing them against one another using conventional criteria.[39]

The model by Frickey and Eskridge could be placed halfway between the rigid textualism and the postulates of legal deconstructivists. It recognises the self-transforming powers in the process of interpretation, but it preserves the hierarchical structure of the indications. In this respect legal deconstruction can be perceived as a virtually free-style activity. The method, which tends to bring out still new readings of a legal text by placing it in changing contexts, is anti-hierarchical. It is also deeply rhetorical in its assumptions, since it perceives interpretation as a contest of persuasive forces of numerous possible variants of rendition. A solution which lacks such a force can not be maintained only for its hierarchical legitimacy.

Balkin[40] pays attention to the problem that Jacques Derrida, the initiator of philosophical deconstruction, openly resisted limiting it to a set of techniques.[41] Balkin argues that Derrida himself tends to treat deconstruction as a method. In the area of legal studies, which are pragmatic by virtue, deconstruction has been adopted naturally as a style of analysis. Balkin writes also about deconstructing the deconstruction, carried out by legal scholars:

> whatever deconstruction itself might be, deconstructive *argument* is, and always has been, a rhetorical technique used by scholars for pragmatic purposes.[42]

The texts by Balkin present not only a particular concept of deconstruction as used for the purposes of legal interpretation, but also a particular perception of rhetoric. They appeal to its sophistic origins rather than to the tradition of cultivating public virtues. Yet, when describing legal deconstruction as a rhetorical practice, Balkin refers to Aristotle:

> we might defend deconstructing argument in the same way that Aristotle defended rhetoric generally: Although deconstructive argument can be used for good or for ill, this does not mean that it cannot be a useful part of public life. It simply means that each of us becomes responsible for the ways in which he or she uses deconstructive argument.[43]

[39] *Ibid* at 241.
[40] JM Balkin, *Deconstruction's Legal Career* (http://www.yale.edu/lawweb/jbalkin/writings.htm 1998).
[41] J Derrida, *O gramatologii(De la gramatologie)*. Trans by B Banasiak (Warszawa, Wydawnictwo KR, 1999. Original edition 1967). See also: 'Psyché. Odkrywanie innego.' *(Invention de l'autre)* Trans by MP Markowski, in R Nycz (ed), *Postmodernizm. Antologia przek_adow* (Kraków, Wydawnictwo Baran i Suszczynski, 1996).
[42] JM Balkin 1998 above n 40, at 3.
[43] JM Balkin, 'Being Just with Deconstruction' (1994) *Social and Legal Studies* 3, at 400.

Adopting this point of view Balkin seems to pass over the normative aspect of Aristotelian concept of rhetoric. The defense of the use and teaching of rhetoric is not equivalent to a lack of ethical demands. In *The Art of Rhetoric,*[44] there easily can be found the echoes of Platonic idealism: human orations should first of all serve the truth; rhetoric is useful because it is true; just things by their nature predominate over the false and unjust ones, etc. Balkin's vision of legal deconstruction as a set of techniques which do not require establishing a preliminary ethical background seems closer to the sophistic origins of rhetoric. The usage of the deconstructive argument for defending good can be found rather in projects as Critical Legal Studies (CLS) movement.[45]

This distinction seems to resonate with the phases in the development of deconstruction as a method of legal analysis[46] and with the forms it takes. Deconstruction was initially introduced into legal theory by the CLS representatives and used as a normative tool. Instability of meaning, explicated by deconstructive arguments, was ascribed to the legitimisation of social and political structures. In this version deconstruction supported the CLS thesis on 'false necessity' of these structures (relying on law). They appeared to be reasonable, fair and obvious, while in fact functioned in oppressive way. Deconstruction in its normative version stood as an instrument for the CLS theorists (perceived as the new legal realists)[47] in their activity of unveiling hidden or disclaimed functions of law. Similar use of deconstruction can be found in the works connected with the feminist legal theory.[48] Normative use of deconstruction in legal analysis met with critique.[49] Its main points referred to the fact that though social and political structures are flexible, the meanings can not be freely ascribed to them or manipulated. For the deconstructionists meanings are social products and, as Derrida himself emphasises, the sign is inevitably limited in its play by structure.[50] The use of deconstructive argument as described above can be therefore perceived as an abuse of deconstruction. The liberation of legal deconstruction from the normative baggage was postulated as an alternative. Still legal deconstruction also in this sophistic version remains essentially pragmatic even if free from the tasks of 'defending good'.

[44] Aristotle 1991/1992 above n 16.

[45] R Unger, *The Critical Legal Studies Movement* (Cambridge, Harvard University Press, 1986). A Altman, *Critical Legal Studies. A Liberal Critique.* Reprint (Princeton, New Jersey, Princeton University Press, 1993. Original edition 1990).

[46] JM Balkin 1998 above n 40.

[47] R Kevelson, *Introduction to the First Round Table on Law and Semiotics* in: *Law and Semiotics* vol 1, ed by R Kevelson (New York and London Plenum Press).

[48] D Cornell, *Beyond Accommodation* (New York, Routledge, 1991).

[49] See JM Balkin 1998 above n 40; P Schlag, 'Le Hors' de Text, C'est Moi:' The Politics of Form and the Domestication of Deconstruction, 11 *Cardozo Law Review* 1631, 1990; P Schlag, 'The Problem of the Subject' 69 *Texas Law Review* 1627, 1991.

[50] J Derrida, *Structure Sign and Play* in: *Writing and Difference* (Chicago, University of Chicago Press, 1980).

VI

WITH A LITTLE HELP FROM MANY FRIENDS

The problem of ethical grounding of attacks and defences on rhetorics was particularly well recognised by Stanley Fish.[51] He rejects this perspective as he does not see the necessity of finding external justification for rhetorical practices, nor in their deconstructive manifestation. In the sophistic spirit he states:

> Derridean deconstruction does not uncover the operations of rhetoric in order to reach the Truth; rather it continually uncovers the truth of rhetorical operations, the truth that all operations, including the operation of deconstruction itself, are rhetorical.[52]

In the sphere of legal interpretation the acceptance of the concept of legal deconstruction has various consequences. It results in the adopting and recognising the force of arguments and figures formerly undervalued or denied in the official legal discourse—as metaphors, metonyms or irony.[53] On the other hand it enables one to draw inspiration from different disciplines such as literary studies,[54] psychoanalysis,[55] aesthetics,[56] or theory of music.[57]

Once having accepted the discursive rather than linear model of conducting legal interpretation, the reader is faced with the problem of criteria of the decision. Looking upon an interpretation (especially one which leads to the judgment) as deciding which version of the story should eventually prevail, can easily result in a suspicion that the final statement is totally arbitrary. For Fish[58] a good example of this approach is an opinion of Kenney Hegland in the case *Mills v Wyman*. Hegland opposes 'personal predilections' of the judge to the constraint of doctrine and explains that 'equally clear is the larger opposition of which this one is an instance: civilisation and order versus the anarchy of the individual will.'[59] Fish challenges this clear distinction as he deconstructs the purely conventional character of doctrinal principles. On the other hand he undermines a belief that what Hegland calls 'personal predilections' might be an exclusively individual

[51] Fish 1992 above n 2.
[52] *Ibid* at 493.
[53] See, eg: Balkin 1998; Eskridge, Frickey and Garrett 2000.
[54] Fish 1992 above n 2.
[55] P Goodrich, *Oedipus Lex. Psychoanalysis, History, Law* (Berkeley, Los Angeles, London, University of California Press, 1995).
[56] C Douzinas and R Warrington, *Justice miscarried. Ethics, aesthetics and the law* (New York, London, Toronto, Sydney, Tokyo, Singapore, Harvester Wheatsheaf, 1994).
[57] JM Balkin and S Levinson, 'Interpreting Law and Music: Performance Notes on "The Banjo Serenader" and "The Lying Crowd of Jews"' (1999) *Cardozo Law Review* 20, at 1513–72.
[58] Fish 1992 above n 2.
[59] *Ibid* at 11.

product. Fish's view harmonises with postmodern perception of the subject as a social construct.[60] In this context discrediting some predilections as personal or idiosyncratic seems to be an error.

Deconstructive scepticism concerning an *a priori* authoritative force of the hierarchy of arguments should not be misinterpreted as an approval for a complete lack of restraint. Legal deconstructivists recognise such limitations but reject their irrefutably superior character. The existence of such constraints is rather a matter of accepted conventions and as such can be freely discussed.

Another important issue concerns the problem of limits of conventional systems. The rhetorical power of legal deconstruction promotes the concerning of these systems as fluid and disputable rather than rigid. Instead of following strict rules of hierarchically planned interpretation the researcher now can explore an abundance of legal (and not only legal) topoi and tropes. Consequently, a concept of a flexible canon, as provided in the book *Legal Canons,*[61] seems more appropriate in this context than the construction of graded considerations, strict 'instruction of use' for legal interpretation. The authors of this tome demonstrate how the legal canon (or rather local canons in various disciplines, from constitutional to contract law) functions on different levels of conducted interpretation. The term 'deep canonicity' describes such forms of reasoning which are particularly difficult to be avoided, though the whole corpus of canon changes over time. In the introduction to the book Balkin and Levinson distinguish four forms of deep canonicity in legal reasoning: arguments, problems and approaches, narratives and examples.[62] The method used by the authors is analogical to the instruments of literary studies for the analysis of returning motifs, schemes and images. It also recalls classical rhetoric again, which to a large extent concentrated on the use of various means: from a proper choice of an order of compositions to the use of topoi and concrete figures.[63]

VII

CONCLUSION

The renaissance of interest in rhetoric in legal studies has manifold origins and manifests itself in various ways. It is present as an apparent and rather incontrovertible declaration of the rhetorical nature of legal deconstruction as a method of interpretation. In choosing concrete strategies by legal deconstructionists there revives an old dispute over the necessity of ethical engagement of the rhetoric. Appealing to the persuasive forces, which are

[60] Balkin 1998 above n 40.
[61] JM Balkin and S Levinson (eds), *Legal Canons* (New York and London, New York University Press, 2000).
[62] *Ibid* at 15–24.
[63] Korolko 1990/1998 above n 1.

the essence of rhetorical action, corresponds to the concept of legal interpretation as a discursive process. It also determines the assumption that legal reasoning is a non-linear process which does not necessarily base on the *a priori* taken hierarchy of arguments. A distinct issue is a problem of institutionalisation of legal interpretation and affecting this way its rhetorical potential. This institutionalisation can be analysed on different levels, including state, standard legal education and the discourse of legal academia. The discussion of this problem exceeds frames of this text, but it seems worth close examination in the future.

Perceived in a sophistic way, rhetoric provides the interpreter with instruments to help read the legal text without the necessity of obeying traditional patterns. Furthermore, it helps in undermining and challenging them. But it is exactly what rhetoric has always done. As we have seen, the first rhetors were persons who explored the duality *rhetón kai diánoia*. They were not alarmed by its existence but ready to examine it as a domain of invention and intellectual game. And this attitude remains unchanged to the present day.

9

The Substantive Issue and the Rhetoric of the Abortion Debate in Ireland

SOPHIE CACCIAGUIDI-FAHY

I

INTRODUCTION

'MNÁ NA HÉIREANN,[1] tell me about the land of saints and scholars ...'. 'An Irish solution to an Irish problem.' 'What is the substantive issue?' To understand the 'substantive issue' is to go deep down into Irish culture. It is to peel off the layers of years of nationalism, years of catholic hegemony, years of torturous political and legal debate of a nation's identity and culture. To understand the 'substantive issue' is to decode a cultural system still rooted in the past, desperately trying to 'leave' the future. Understanding the 'substantive issue' requires a certain amount of cultural knowledge of Irish society and its relationship with the law. Therefore the approach I have chosen to explain the 'substantive issue' is an exploration of legal culture, rhetorical strategies and pragmatic aspects of language used in the debate on abortion in Ireland.

It is now twenty years since the first referendum on 'the right to life of the unborn', which the Irish people enshrined into their Constitution in 1983. Twenty years of acrimonious public debate and court battles. Twenty years of confusing legal and political discourse with forces, both inside and outside Ireland, continuing to influence and shape the arguments. In 2003, the 'right to life of the unborn', 'the substantive issue', 'abortion', continue to raise controversial legal issues which are still defined in terms of rights: the right to equality, to privacy, to reproductive health, to family planning, to freedom of information, to freedom to travel, to adequate medical care, and human rights under European Union and United Nations agreements and treaties. As in other countries, the issues at stake delve into different

[1] Translated from the Irish language as 'Women of Ireland'.

complex legal, social, medical, and moral questions. The debate involves actors drawn from the medical, religious, political and legal communities. To date, the majority of research in the fields of abortion discourse analysis has focused on socio-legal feminist discourse, the aim of which has been to analyse the long-term implications of legal strategies designed to improve the position of women.

Public discourse is an important force that can shape legal and social frameworks to make them progress or regress. It can be used to investigate how interacting agents use cognitive and linguistic resources to understand and formalise arguments about a particular issue, such as abortion. The formation of rhetorical arguments in public discourse when discussing socio-legal moral dilemmas work because they can exploit culturally relevant semantic and pragmatic aspects of every day language understanding. They are paradigmatic in nature and use every day language to convey information that will subsequently shape attitudes.

This chapter presents an analysis of the changes in the rhetoric of the abortion debate since 1983 and traces the emergence of the euphemism 'the substantive issue' from its judicial origins to its widespread common use. As part of this analysis, I begin by examining the laws on abortion in Ireland and the role of the Constitution in Irish Society. After a brief discussion of the Eighth Amendment and the ways in which national identity was construed through abortion discourse until 1992, I go on to discuss the issues surrounding the X case, which gave birth to the euphemism 'the substantive issue'. I then examine the interaction between language and the law by analysing the arguments of the different protagonists and the manner in which they used this coded rhetorical euphemism to purposely avoid explicit association with abortion per se, which in fact lay at the centre of the proposed Twelfth Amendment in 1992.

The approach adopted will focus primarily on the Supreme Court decision rendered in March 1992 and public discourse taken from parliamentary debates and newspapers. By way of conclusion, I will consider whether the language used in relation to the abortion debate had become more upfront and less equivocal. This will lead to a consideration of whether there was a discernible shift in attitudes towards abortion evident from the language used in relation to the abortion controversies, reflecting a greater willingness to address the complex legal realities of the latest referendum (2002) concerning the 25th Amendment and the proposed insertion of the Protection of Human Life in Pregnancy Bill within the Constitution.

Through a reconstructive analysis, my aims are to show how the Irish judiciary dealt with the delicate task of shifting meaning in public discourse and the recursive impact the latter had on the redefinition of legal abortion. This discussion aims to illustrate how the interpretation of a particular sign, Article 40.3.3, in this case, adjusted to cultural and social upheavals through the medium of judicial interpretation. In turn, I propose to demonstrate the impact legal meaning had on public discourse (following the X case) and how public discourse subsequently borrowed signs from legal discourse to create, develop and use its own sign, 'the substantive issue' which it used as a mechanism to reframe the concept of legalised abortion. Finally, I intend to reveal that legal interpretation shows how law may reify social conventions and decide on social issues such as who can and who cannot avail of abortion and in what circumstances.

II

THE HISTORICAL CONTEXT

The criminalisation of abortion in Ireland dates back to pre-independence and is a statutory offence under the Offences Against the Person Act of 1861 (OAPA).[2] Section 58 of the Act makes self-induced abortion (or attempted self-induced abortion) a felony punishable by life imprisonment. Section 59 makes the assistance in an abortion or the supply of an abortifacient a misdemeanour. This was reaffirmed by the Health (Family Planning) Act in 1972. To date, the legal literature claims that there has never been a criminal prosecution in Ireland for the unlawful performing of an abortion while others argue otherwise.[3]

The first clue in decoding the rhetoric of abortion in Ireland is to realise that Irish law and politics are largely shaped by its Constitution[4] (*Bunreacht na hÉireann*). Today it is still considered by most constitutional lawyers as a theocratic 'living Constitution' in so far as, it institutionalises and legally formalises many values associated with Irish society: nationalism, Catholicism, traditional, rural, and family-orientated values. Suffice to read its preamble[5] and look at sections of Articles 40 and 41, to realise that the underlying legal philosophy of Irish law has embraced the principles of Catholic natural law philosophy.[6] The Irish judiciary has consistently recognised and upheld the influence of Catholic natural law when interpreting the Constitution,[7] emphasising the notion of 'common good, with due

[2] Offences Against the Persons Act, 1837 (7 Will 4 & 1 Vict C 85).

[3] J Casey, *Constitutional Law in Ireland* (Dublin, Sweet and Maxwell, 2000).
P Jackson, 'Abortion Trials and Tribulations' (1992) 18/1 *The Canadian Journal of Irish Studies* 112–20.

[4] Written by Eamon de Valera and adopted in 1937, at a time when Catholic identity was critical to the Irish State and its people who had just secured their independence from Protestant Great Britain.

[5] 'In the name of the Most Holy Trinity, from Whom is all authority and to Whom, as our final end, all actions both of men and States must be referred.' *Bunreacht na hÉireann* (Dublin, Brunswick Press, 2002).

[6] Its basic principle is to exalt God as the ultimate law order, clearly presenting the moral, social, and political teachings of the Catholic doctrine.

[7] See *McGee v The Attorney General* [1974] IR 284; 109 ILTR, where Walsh J cautioned the following: 'any action on the part of either the husband and the wife or of the State to limit family sizes by endangering or destroying human life must necessarily not only be an offence against the common good but also against the guaranteed personal rights of the human life in question'.

observance of Prudence, Justice and Charity ... so that may be ... true social order attained."[8]

The second clue and starting point for a legal semiotic analysis lies in the linguistic categorisation of the role of women as defined in the Constitution. The references made to women in the text are embedded in patriarchal nationalist discourse heavily influenced by previous historical events:[9]

> Article 40.3.3: The State acknowledges the right to life to the unborn and, with due regard to the equal right to life of the *mother*.
>
> Article 41.2.1: In particular, the State recognises that by her life within the home, *woman* gives to the State a support without which the common good cannot be achieved.
>
> Article 41.2.2: The State shall, therefore, endeavour to ensure that *mothers* shall not be obliged by economic necessity to engage in labour to the neglect of their duties in the home (emphasis added).

One realises immediately that the language used, defines the role of women as 'mothers'. It frames their function in a dual categorisation, restricting them to the domestic sphere, equating them to domesticity in the home, so as to secure a 'common good'.[10] In so doing, these Articles reinforce the hegemony of the Catholic doctrine, which revolves around the translation of religious preoccupations into law via the concept of natural law.[11] Furthermore, by assuming the interchangeability of woman with mother and domesticity,[12] women are made explicitly responsible for both the reproduction of the population and the transmission of the national identity through the practice of motherhood.[13] It is this tension between traditional ideologies and new emerging values systems due to progressive economic and social forces of changes in the 1980s, which first defined the praxis of the abortion rhetoric. Motherhood became the focal point of legal

[8] *Bunreacht na hÉireann*, Preamble.

[9] T Inglis, *Moral Monopoly—The Rise and Fall of the Catholic Church in Modern Ireland* (Dublin, University College Dublin Press, 1998). D Kiberd, *Inventing Ireland* (Cambridge, Mass, Harvard University Press, 1996). E Hynes, 'The Great Hunger and Irish Catholicism' (1978) 8/2 *Societas*, 132–56. E Larkin, *Historical Dimensions of Irish Catholicism* (New York, Arno Press, 1976).

[10] A ban on women's employment in any designated occupation was coupled with the marriage bar or legal permission for women to be fired from their job on marriage until the late 1960s. See P Conroy, 'Managing the Mothers: The Case of Ireland' in J Lewis (ed), *Women and Social Policies in Europe, Work, Family and the State* (Aldershot, Edward Elgar, 1993).

[11] J Fulton, *The Tragedy of Belief: Division, Politics, and Religion in Ireland* (Oxford, Clarendon Press, 1991).

[12] M Mullin, 'Representations of Irish Feminism and the Politics of Difference' (1991) 17 *Feminist Studies* 29–50.

[13] See what Pateman has called the 'sexual contract,' which depends precisely on this sharp distinction between public and private spheres in C Pateman, *The Sexual Contract* (Cambridge, Polity, 1998).

discourse when the Irish Constitution became the first one to enshrine the right to life of an unborn into law.

III

THE EIGHTH AMENDMENT, JUDICIAL INTERPRETATION AND THE START OF THE RHETORIC OF ABORTION IN IRELAND

In 1981, following Ireland's accession to the EEC, the legalisation of abortion in the United States,[14] and the Pope's visit to Ireland, the Pro-Life Amendment Campaign (PLAC), a lay organisation, began a crusade seeking to guarantee constitutionally the unborn's right to life. By advocating the insertion of a constitutional Amendment, it was campaigning not only to prevent the Irish courts from allowing abortion but making it almost impossible for the legislature to pass any bill legalising abortion. Its intention clearly was to prevent the legalisation of any form of abortion ever in Ireland. Following an acrimonious campaign[15] and a referendum,[16] the Eighth Amendment was carried and the following wording was inserted in the Constitution:

> Article 40.3.3: The State acknowledges *the right to life of the unborn* and, *with due regard to the equal right to life of the mother*, guarantees in its laws to respect, and, as far as practicable, by its laws to defend and vindicate that right (emphasis added).

The wording of the Eighth Amendment constructed the unborn as a separate entity, a person with rights that exists under natural law. It established a woman-foetus legal relationship raising possible legal conundrums by setting the rights of one against the other.[17]

Twice the Supreme Court, prior to the landmark X Case, interpreted the Eighth Amendment, the first time when the High Court heard the *Attorney General (SPUC)*[18] *v Open Door Counselling Ltd. and Dublin Well Woman Centre Ltd.*[19] SPUC sought to restrain the centres from counselling and

[14] *Roe v Wade* 410 US 113 (1973); 35 L Ed 2d 147.

[15] E O'Reilly, *Masterminds of the Right* (Dublin, Attic Press, 1988).

[16] For further information on the results of Irish Referenda, please refer to the following Government website: http://www.environ.ie/electindex.html. In the case of the 7 September 1983 Referendum, the results were: in favour, 841,233; against, 416,136.

[17] Concerns about the wording were raised at the time by the AG (Sutherland) regarding a definition of 'unborn' and a definition of the qualified right 'with due regard to'. Sutherland pointed that the words 'cohm cheart' in Irish means literally 'the same right', hence suggesting that the right to life of the unborn and the mother are equal. See T Hesketh, *The Second Partitioning of Ireland: The Abortion Referendum of 1983* (Dublin, Brandsma Books, 1990) 215.

[18] Society for the Protection of Unborn Children.

[19] *Attorney General (SPUC) v Open Door Counselling Ltd and Dublin Well Woman Centre Ltd* [1988] IR 593; [1987] IRLM 477 (HC); [1989] IRLM 19 (SC).

advising pregnant women on the availability and location of abortion facilities in England.[20] They argued that by providing non-directive information on pregnancy options, names of abortion clinics, and financial assistance to women travelling to England for abortions, the centres were violating the Eighth Amendment. The High Court issued an injunction finding that, 'the qualified right to privacy [and] the rights to association and freedom of expression ... cannot be invoked to interfere with such a fundamental right as the right of life of the unborn.' On appeal, the Supreme Court also favoured SPUC, holding that a woman's right to information, privacy, and freedom of expression was qualified by the fundamental right to life of the foetus.' Shortly thereafter, SPUC brought another action against three student groups that continued to publish abortion information despite the Open-Door decision. In *SPUC v Grogan*,[21] SPUC applied to the High Court to prevent the Students Union at University College Dublin (UCD) from distributing its 1988–89 Welfare Guide, which contained information on abortion clinics in England.[22] The pro-life lobby had gained access to judicial review and were patrolling constitutional protections granted to the unborn via civil litigation.[23] Critics have argued that the Supreme Court allowed the law to become 'an instrument for achieving fundamentalist goals.'[24]

How do people with different views, reflecting various dimensions, reflect a cultural, legal, social, and political system? How do people argue about abortion? The argumentative structure that public discourse uses in this case is coding schemas, which it encodes to mirror its various systems. In the case of Ireland, the law had codified the discourse on abortion in its Constitution and any subsequent discourse used, either in the public or in the political arenas, was therefore to be heavily influenced by legal discourse. Traditionally, pro-choice or pro-life discourse tends to be dogmatic and focuses on a single-issue dichotomy.[25] Techniques of semantic manipulations include the use of stereotyping, the elimination of neutral terms and their replacement by emotional value synonyms, the redefinitions of meaning to personalise the issue[26] while creating dualistic opposition, the alteration of meaning by replacing nouns or adjectives by punctuation.[27] In modifying terminology, the structure and thus the content of the discursive

[20] They never raised directly the issue of the lawfulness of article 40.3.3.

[21] *SPUC v Grogan* [1989] IR 753; [1989] ILRM 449.

[22] For a more complete analysis of the case see J Kingston and A Wheelan, *Abortion Law in Ireland* (Dublin, Roundhall Sweet and Maxell, 1997).

[23] S Bouclin, 'Abortion in Post-X Ireland' (2002) 133/13 *Windsor Review of Legal and Social Issues.*

[24] R Fletcher, 'Pro-life Absolutes, Feminist Challenges: The Fundamentalism of Irish Abortion Law 1986–1992' (1998) *36 Osgoode Hall Law Journal* 62.

[25] M Dillon, 'Argumentative Complexity of Abortion Discourse' (1993) 57/3 *Public Opinion, Quarterly* 305–14.

[26] In the case of Irish pro-life activist, the word 'foetus' was replaced by 'unborn child'.

[27] J Heinen and Matuchniak-Krasuska, 'Abortion in Poland: A Vicious Circle or a Good Use of Rhetoric: A Sociological Study of the Political Discourse of Abortion in Poland' (1995) 18/1 *Women's Studies International Forum* 27–33.

debate are altered. Critics when comparing the use of language by pro-life and pro-choice advocates have found that the latter use conventional and accepted terminology, both popular and comprehensible, while the former construct a special terminology, which clearly manifests their moral attitudes.[28] Use of poster and videos with selected images by acquiring the function of a message without a code also alter the perception of the audience.[29] In Ireland, from 1983 to 1992, public discourse on abortion moved from a more narrative based argument to an ideograph conception.[30] The pro-choice lobby used the ideograph of, choice = right = equality, equating the right to life of the unborn to the right to life of the mother.

Irish feminist strategies pragmatically concentrated on providing information and referrals to abortion clinics in the UK, while pro-life supporters, in their 1983 campaign, primarily focused on the redefinition of the foetus[31] as a person. They constructed it as a separate cultural sign, a manipulable political object used to articulate themes primarily based on notions of sectarianism and national unity.[32] As one protest poster from 1981 illustrated, 'The Abortion Mills of England Grind Irish Babies into Blood that Cries Out to Heaven for Vengeance', referring no doubt to the history of British oppression in Ireland and thus appealing to a very emotive issue.[33] The fact remains that it is difficult to ascertain that a debate actually took place as pro-choice activists came up with a very feeble strategy to counteract the pro-life discourse.[34] This is reflected by Judge Hamilton noting that,

> ideally, debate should have been confined to the merits of amending the Constitution in this fashion ... It is a pity that public discourse was diverted ... It is possible that the paucity of debate concerning the usefulness of the Amendment, its actual wording, and whether it was likely to achieve the object, contributed in no small measure to the problems which were to come.[35]

Once legal discourse had asserted the rights and the equality of rights of the 'unborn' in the Constitution, the debate shifted to safer grounds. The pro-life concentrated on constructing the foetus in medical discourse, which in

[28] *Ibid.*

[29] C Condit, *The Rhetoric of Abortion: Communicating Social Change* (Urbana, University of Illinois Press, 1990).

[30] As defined by Condit 'a word, a key sentence, that sums up a key social and moral commitment representing a culture' at 230.

[31] For a good analysis on the meaning of the foetus, refer to K Parsi, 'Metaphorical Imagination: The Moral and Legal Status of Fetuses and Embryos' (1999) 2/703 *DePaul Journal Health Care Law.*

[32] Above n 17, at 266, Hesketh.

[33] This poster is heavily inspired from the wrath of God in the Bible and shifts towards the IRA ideology of revenge, 'Tiocfaidh ár Lá' (our day will come).

[34] J Murphy-Lawless and J Mc Carthy, 'Social Policy and Fertility Change in Ireland' (1999) 6 *The European Journal of Women Studies* 69–96.

[35] L Hamilton, 'Remark Matters of Life and Death' (1996) *65/543 Fordham Review.*

turn, reinforced the construction of women as mothers as already defined in the Constitution. The debate moved from a hierarchical dichotomy to a more diametrical one and centred on cultural hegemony appealing to the construction of an Irish purity. Smyth suggests that this reflected the political concerns of the day and in particular the development of a national identity primarily concerned with controlling women's sexual behaviour and reproductive role. She defines one of the key-elements in pro-life discourse as the notion of the people standing as a united community against the disease of abortion coming from the outside world. PLAC usurped arguments deeply rooted in nationalism that envisioned outside influences as contamination that would inevitably lead to the disintegration and destruction of national identity, and the collapse of the nation and continuity.[36]

The decisions in the SPUC cases clearly established that the provision of information on abortion constituted a direct threat to the right to life of the unborn and as such was subject to restriction by the Courts. Therefore, the decision to travel to have an abortion would also represent a threat to the life of the unborn. To test this hypothesis, all that was required was a pregnant woman with a clear intention to have an abortion.[37]

IV

THE X CASE

The language of abortion was revitalised when the X case dominated the media and public debate in February 1992. In what has been considered the most contentious case ever to come before an Irish court,[38] the judiciary was forced to rule on 'the right to life of the unborn' and 'with due regard to the equal right to life of the mother.' The facts of the case were deeply disturbing. Following the rape of a fourteen-year-old girl, her parents approached the Gardaí (Police) and queried whether a DNA test could be carried out on the aborted foetus in order to obtain scientific evidence which could be used in a subsequent criminal prosecution. The Gardaí made enquiries with the Office of the Director of Public Prosecutions (DPP) and advised the parents that any such evidence obtained would be inadmissible in a criminal prosecution. Following a statement made to the Gardaí, the parents of the girl informed them of their intention to terminate the pregnancy. Meanwhile, the DPP had consulted with the Attorney General who then applied to enjoin X and her parents from travelling outside the jurisdiction.

[36] L Smyth, 'Narratives of Irishness and the Problem of Abortion: The X Case' (1998) 60 *Feminist Review* 61–83.

[37] P Ward, 'Ireland: Abortion: "X" + "Y" = ?!' (1995) 3/385 *University of Louisville Journal of Family Law*.

[38] It is commonly referred by the public as 'Bourne has arrived in Ireland' in reference to *R v Bourne* [1939] 1 KB 687; [1938] 3 All ER 615.

On February 7 1992, the High Court granted an *ex-parte* application for an interim injunction and issued orders restraining the girl and her parents from interfering with the right to life of the unborn, from leaving Ireland for nine months, and from procuring or arranging an abortion within or outside the jurisdiction.[39] While Judge Costello acknowledged that X was suicidal, he held that the risk of suicide was not 'one of those which may arise in the practice of medicine.' He applied the balancing test set forth in the Eighth Amendment and concluded that, 'The risk to the life of the unborn was of a far greater magnitude than the risk to the life of the mother'. The High Court also held that infringement of the EC right to travel was permitted in this case based on public policy and that the EC allowed national governments discretion on moral issues.

The reaction to the ruling was overwhelmingly convulsive. It prompted profound national and international outrage as it undermined the Republic's claim to be a modern liberal democracy. The media frenzy centred on the interrelationship between the state, the nation, and its women. The decision was viewed as endorsing sexual assault of women and children.[40] The question of rape, and child rape in particular, was a key turning point in the shift in popular opinion and state policy with respect to abortion.[41] In Dublin, protestors carried signs that read, 'Ireland Defends Men's Right to Procreate by Rape.'[42] Writing in the Irish Press, Emily O'Reilly remarked,

> the fact is that [the people] are appalled because such a horrendous case forces a re-examination of the national conscience about abortion and the abortion amendment—and the result of that examination is a queasy feeling that perhaps we got it wrong in 1983.

The discourse of shame, national mea culpa, was born.

A collective crisis of identity was looming on the horizon. Irish national identity is linked to radical populism where the notion of 'the people' is constructed as a homogeneous group, a community where conformism to the norms and values it holds, is essential to a sense of national belonging.[43] The President, Mary Robinson, reflected this when commenting:

[39] Judge Costello stated 'I am quite satisfied that there is a real and imminent danger to the life of the unborn and that if the Court does not step in to protect it by means of the injunction sought its life will be terminated ... I am strengthened in this view by the knowledge that the young girl has the benefit of the love and care and support of devoted parents who will help through the difficult months ahead.' In *Attorney General v X* [1992] 1 *IR*, 12

[40] L Oaks, 'Abortion is part of the Irish Experience, it is part of what we are: The Transformation of Public Discourse on Irish Abortion Policy' (2002) 25/3 *Women's Studies International Forum* 315–33.

[41] Smyth above n 36.

[42] See JA Weinstein, 'An Irish Solution to an Irish Problem: Ireland's Struggle with Abortion Law' (1993) 165/173 *Arizona Journal of International and Comparative Law* 191.

[43] B Walter, 'Irishness, Gender and Place' (1995) *Society and Space* 35–50.

> we are experiencing as a people a very deep crisis in ourselves. I hope we have the courage, which we have not always had to face up to and look squarely and say this is a problem we have got to resolve.[44]

For the first time in its history, Ireland as a nation state found itself in the position of the 'barbaric other', personified by a Court deciding that it was

> appropriate ... that a citizen of Ireland can be prevented from travelling abroad for purposes that are entirely legal in the jurisdiction abroad ... the State is right to intervene in ... an entirely private family affair.[45]

The largest Union in the country, SIPTU, alleged that X and her parents had been 'virtually interned' in Ireland,[46] invoking images of the British government's policy of internment without trial, introduced in Northern Ireland in 1971. On 23 February 1992, an opinion poll found that sixty-six per cent wanted to change the Constitution to allow abortion in limited circumstances.[47] As Buckley points out, it appeared that the former moral absolutism of Irish citizens and the judiciary began to collapse under the particularly heart-rending facts of this case.[48] X became the symbol of abortion narrative in the national press when questioning the state authority, through her position within the nuclear family, the redefinition of motherhood and of women's sexuality.

As observed by Smyth, the Pro-life lobby responded to the X case by accusing pro-choice and the media of exploiting an innocent victim for their own purposes. They characterised the excessive exploitation of young Irish women travelling to England for abortion as part of the British capitalist system that was taking advantage of them for mere financial gain.[49] They reverted to the language of the enemy of the State used in relation to terrorism and sectarianism in Northern Ireland. Their response was that the State was not guilty of cruelty and totalitarianism, but was in fact, the last bastion of humanity in a barbarous world.[50] This discourse was part of a deep-seated rhetoric, which constructed Ireland as a great Christian culture with exceptional forms of morality, the 'land of saints and scholars' spreading the message of the more traditional moral values of society across the world:

[44] *The Irish Times*, 20 February 1992.

[45] Dáil Éireann Volume 415, 18 February, 1992 'Ban on Termination of Young Girl's Pregnancy: Statement'.

[46] *The Irish Press*, 21 February 1992.

[47] FX Beytagh, *Constitutionalism in Contemporary Ireland: An American Perspective* (Dublin, Round Hall Sweet and Maxwell, 1996).

[48] A Buckley, 'Other International Issues: The Primacy of Democracy over Natural Law in Irish Abortion Law: An Examination of the C Case' (1998) 9/275 *Duke Journal of Comparative and International Law*.

[49] Smyth above n 36.

[50] *Ibid*. This notion is also reflected in the dissenting judgment of Judge Hedeman in the Supreme Court.

> We must have the pride and the courage to be ourselves and instead of us becoming like the rest of Europe, it is more than likely that within the lifetime of many persons now alive, Europe will want to become like us.[51]

Amidst the angst of a cultural crisis, the entire country held its breath waiting for the Supreme Court's ruling on the appeal by the girl's parents.[52] Under national and international scrutiny,[53] it ruled that X could return to England for the purpose of an abortion because there was a 'real and substantial threat to the life as distinct from the health of the mother,' which could 'only be avoided by the termination of the pregnancy.' In a majority decision, the Supreme Court held that, if it were established, as a matter of probability, that there was a 'real and substantial risk to the life, as distinct from the health, of the mother which can only be avoided by the termination of her pregnancy, such termination is permissible.' As a result, the injunction granted by the High Court was lifted. In its *dicta*, the Supreme Court also indicated that the constitutional right to travel could be restrained so as to prevent an abortion taking place in circumstances where there was no threat to the life of the mother. Accordingly, the right to travel *simpliciter* did not take precedence over the right to life.

The decision in the X case gave rise to the following conclusions:

(1) If it is established as a matter of probability that there is a real and substantial risk to the life, as distinct from the health, of the mother, which can only be avoided by the termination of her pregnancy, such termination is permissible (the so-called *substantive issue*);

(2) The dissemination of information with regard to abortion services available outside the State was unlawful (the *right to information*) and;

(3) Travel abroad for the purpose of obtaining an abortion was unlawful and could be restrained (the *right to travel*).

The decision raised various concerns. The Supreme Court had found for the first time, that the so-called pro-life Amendment enacted in 1983, allowed for a lawful abortion, where it was necessary to avert a 'real and substantial risk to the life of the mother' (the substantive issue of the case). It also raised concerns about a possible abuse of suicide risk as grounds for

[51] *The Irish Independent*, 21 February 1992.

[52] It is worth noting that the parents of X filed an appeal on the advice of the Government and that the latter agreed to pay all legal costs. See G Whyte, 'Abortion and the Law' (1992) 25/261 *Doctrine and Life*.

[53] The Government was also concerned that the X Case would derail the impending vote on the Maastricht Treaty with pro-life activists suggesting that the more liberal European law would supersede Ireland's abortion ban. In a highly embarrassing volte-face the Government sought to amend Protocol 17 to take cognisance of the judgment. Following the EU refusal to re-open the debate on the Protocol, the Government had to settle on a Solemn Declaration. See 'Protocol Annexed to the Treaty on European Union and to the Treaties Establishing the European Communities, 1992' OJ (C 224) 130.

obtaining an abortion. However a large number of commentators[54] raised concerns about the willingness of the Court to restrain persons from travelling outside Ireland for the purpose of having an abortion. In November 1992, three constitutional amendments were put to the people dealing with the three different legal questions raised by the judgment as outlined above. Whether intentionally or not, the Supreme Court had created a new frame in the history of Irish women. It reconstructed another definition of the legal status of women by distinguishing between 'types' of women: acceptable and unacceptable candidates for abortions. Tormented X, the archetypal 'worthy' victim-candidate was found to be eligible for abortion services. Her status was raised to that of an icon: 'Mother Ireland' for which the people of the island have great passion had just been re-incarnated in a fourteen-year-old pregnant rape victim.[55] The discourse of shame had just given birth to the discourse of sorrows which underlying nationalistic representation, in a perverse twist of fate, rejoined the discourse advocated by the pro-life campaigners.

V

THE SUBSTANTIVE ISSUE

The phrase 'the substantive issue' first emerged in the abortion context in the immediate aftermath of the Supreme Court Judgment. While legal discourse normally uses 'substantive issue' to distinguish the central or primary issue of a case from subsidiary or secondary consideration, in the post-X Ireland, the phrase surreptitiously became corrupted and became a euphemism for distinguishing the Twelfth Constitutional Amendment (dealing with the issue of abortion) from the 13th and 14th Amendments dealing with the rights to travel and information, respectively. While it is difficult to accurately pin point the first use of the phrase, in the abortion context, it appears to have been initially used in the Parliament's (Dáil Eireann) debates in an attempt to preserve neutrality and depolarise the legal and political catastrophe, which had arisen. From there on, it acquired increasing authoritativeness to be adopted subsequently by the media and from there into the general political vernacular.

On April 28th, Alan Shatter[56] raised a question concerning legislation 'dealing with the substance of the issue'. In a moment of utter frustration the Taoiseach (Prime Minister) stated, 'It would be helpful if Fine Gael indicated if they had any views on the substantive issues'.[57] The following day, still under pressure, he indicated, 'The Government are continuing their consideration and deliberations on the very complex and substantive issues

[54] See A Wheelan (ed), *Law and Liberty in Ireland* (Dublin, Oak Press Tree, 1993) 113–48.
[55] See Howlin (below) for an explication of the iconicity of 'Mother Ireland'.
[56] A Fine Gael TD (Member of Parliament) and a lawyer specialising in Family Law.
[57] Dáil Éireann Volume 418, 28 April 1992 Order of Business.

arising from the Supreme Court decision on Article 40.3.3.'[58] On May 5th, Lawlor (Fianna Fáil TD) pointed, 'Nobody disagrees with the need to clarify the issue but the substantive one is whether the difficulty should be resolved by referendum or amending legislation.'[59] On May 13th Dick Spring, commented, 'If we want to address the substantive issue arising from the X case'.[60] Subsequently on October 7th, the Taoiseach stated, 'As to issues arising from the Supreme Court decision ... the Government have decided that the three issues, namely travel, information and the substantive issues, will be dealt by referenda.'[61] Within weeks the phrase was in widespread and sometimes erroneous use by lawyers, media pundits,[62] politicians,[63] church leaders[64] and other protagonists in the debate regularly substituting 'the substantive issue' for the more explicit language of abortion. It was equally used to refer to the matter of reconciling the rights of the mother and the unborn. More specifically it became a widely used if somewhat ambiguous way of referring to the limited abortion regime, which would come into effect in the event of the amendment being adopted. As such the expression achieved a certain ironic status and seems to have reflected the discomfort of mainstream politicians (usually male) with the whole issue of abortion and the reproductive rights of women.

A clear passing of the euphemism from the political to the public domain can be found in the period leading up to the Referendum from October to December 1992. On October 13th the Taoiseach explained that 'What the substantive issue is about is to ask the Irish people whether they want to accept the Supreme Court decision ... as the basis for legalised abortion in Ireland.'[65] The Minister for Justice, Pádraig Flynn, further legitimised the use of the euphemism when he submitted, in his official speech, his proposal for a new referendum on October 15th, 'separate referenda will be held on December 3rd to deal with the questions of travel, information and the substantive issue.'[66] On October 20th, the opposition lashed back with Labour TD, Brendan Howlin, stating 'they cannot even bring themselves to use the

[58] *Ibid.*
[59] Dáil Éireann Volume 419, 05 May 1992 Eleventh Amendment of the Constitutional Bill, 1992: Second Stage (Resumed).
[60] Dáil Éireann Volume 419, 13 May 1992 Eleventh Amendment of the Constitutional Bill, 1992: Second Stage (Resumed).
[61] Dáil Éireann Volume 423, 7 October, 1992 Questions, Oral Answers.
[62] *The Irish Times Editorial*, June 20 1992, 14: 'There is a commitment to tackling the substantive issue of abortion.'
[63] D Coghlan, *The Irish Times*, 5 June 1992. The Government was asked about the protocol and the 'substantive issues' concerning abortion which arose from the Supreme Court judgment.
[64] D Walsh, *The Irish Times*, 20 June 1992. The Hierarchy, in its statement of May 26th, said: 'We accept there is a sincere intention in Government to address the substantive issue of the right to life of the unborn child after the Maastricht referendum.'
[65] Dáil Éireann Volume 423, 13 October 1992 Order of Business.
[66] Dáil Éireann Volume 423, 15 October 1992 Questions, Oral Answers Constitutional Referenda.

word abortion, they prefer to hide behind a meaningless euphemism like the substantive issue. Abortion is used only as a term of abuse and anyone who opposes a blanket ban is accused of advocating on demand.'[67] Soon the proposed Twelfth Amendment was to be identified with the substantive issue as mentioned by the Minister for Health, Dr O'Connell, 'the Government intention in relation to the Twelfth Amendment, that is, the amendment on the substantive issue itself'.[68] Flynn coined the use of the euphemism because there were to be three separate issues submitted to the people and to ensure that people knew what they were voting for. The 'substantive issue' as identified by the Minister for Justice in his speech[69] was referring to the substantive issue of abortion in the State, sanctioning it into political vernacular, and identifying it with the Twelfth Amendment[70] which stated:

> It shall be unlawful to terminate *the life* of the unborn unless such termination is necessary to save *the life*, as distinct from the health, of the mother where there is an illness or disorder of the mother giving rise to a real and substantial risk to her *life*, not being a risk of self-destruction (emphasis added).

Subsequently, the debate raged on in the Dáil on the wording of the amendment. Since three referenda were needed, three ballot papers were required. The Thirteenth and Fourteenth amendments respectively had a head note with the words 'travel' and 'information' while the Twelfth head note was to be 'the right to life', implicitly indicating to the electorate the Government position. On October 27th, Proinsias De Rossa accused the government of using an

> emotive and simplistic slogan which has been hijacked by one side in the current controversy and it has been used in such a way as to suggest that anyone who opposes their narrow view of the abortion issue is in some way anti-life.[71]

The manipulation of the word 'life' was self-evident. Appearing three times in the amendment, it raised highly emotive feelings and appealed to the emotions of the electorate. The nouns 'unborn,' 'termination,' 'disorder' and the adjective 'substantial' were also left to open interpretation and

[67] Dáil Éireann Volume 423, 20 October 1992 Twelfth Amendment of the Constitution Bill, 1990: Second Stage (Resumed).
[68] *Ibid.*
[69] Dáil Éireann Volume 423, 15 October 1992 Twelfth Amendment of the Constitution Bill, 1990: Second Stage.
[70] The Thirteenth amendment concerned the right to travel and proposed that, 'this subsection shall not limit the freedom to travel between the State and another state.' This amendment was carried. The right to information amendment provided: 'This subsection shall not limit freedom to obtain or make available, in the State, subject to such conditions as may be laid down by law, information relating to services lawfully available in another State.'
[71] Dáil Éireann Volume 424, 27 October 1992 Private Members' Business Referendum (amendment) (No 2) Bill, 1992: Second Stage.

future challenges. The Supreme Court had just removed the ambiguity of the Eighth Amendment and there was a Government re-introducing ambiguous verbiage by failing to legally define the above-mentioned words. Ex-Taoiseach Garrett FitzGerald objected to the use of the verb 'save' as opposed 'to protect' indicating an act of violence, the adverb 'necessary' and the phrase 'as distinct from the health of the mother' implying that women's health is different. As a linguistic point it is worth noting that he formally debated that 'if one is to change the order of the sentence as put the third first and the first last, the sentence makes no sense.'[72]

On October 27th during a debate of the Private Committee at the final stage of the opposed bill, the Opposition Labour party suggested, that the Amendment itself be titled 'the substantive issue'. Since the euphemism was now in such widespread use, Ferris (Labour TD) explained that

> one of the reasons the Labour Party decided to put forward the words 'substantive issue' [as a head note for the Bill] as opposed to any other terminology was that we knew there would be disagreement between all sides about whether this amendment is what it purports to be.

He continued by saying that 'rather that try to be derogatory, as Gaeilge nó as Béarla[73] we would say the substantive issue.'[74] As a result of the use of that terminology by the Taoiseach, the Government, Ministers, Spokespersons for all parties, it was simultaneously integrated in public discourse by both sides of the debates. As Ferris points out,

> the moment the phrase 'the substantive issue' is mentioned, there is no doubt in people's mind that what is being addressed is the real issue, whether there is a right to termination of pregnancy to save a mother's life.[75]

Proinsias De Rossa disagreed with the statement and recorded that, 'the term "substantive issue" is media terminology, which the government promoted to avoid the use of the word "abortion" or "pregnancy termination".'[76] Several other TDs supported the use of the euphemism 'substantive issue' as they viewed it as a neutral term and felt that the electorate knew what was being referred to. However its primary function was to become a substitute for the word abortion, which Brendan Howlin had stressed earlier.[77]

[72] Dáil Éireann Volume 423, 15 October 1992 Twelfth Amendment of the Constitution Bill, 1990: Second Stage.
[73] Translated as 'in Irish or in English'.
[74] Dáil Éireann Volume 424, 27 October 1992 Private Members' Business Referendum (amendment) (No 2) Bill, 1992: Committee and Final Stage.
[75] *Ibid.*
[76] *Ibid.*
[77] Dáil Éireann Volume 423, 20 October 1992 Twelfth Amendment of the Constitution Bill, 1990: Second Stage (Resumed).

A sample analysis of Ireland's newspaper of record, *The Irish Times*, found that in the period of October to December, twenty-two letters to the Editor used the euphemism 'the substantive issue'. It had become a standard part of the lexicon. A similar pattern was to be found in media reporting on the proposed referenda. On November 25th, the country went to the polls and rejected the Twelfth Amendment while accepting the Thirteenth and Fourteenth Amendments.[78] The Irish people, by reframing their conception of permitted abortion in the debate, had opened up a breach in the abortion ban. The law on abortion was now operating under the conditions of the X case.[79]

VI

THE C CASE

The X case brought about a sea-change in Irish public attitudes to abortion. However, despite Government promises to introduce legislation to give effect to the X case ruling, nothing was in fact done for several years until another court case involved, yet again, a suicidal pregnant teenager. Five years after the X case, the Courts allowed another young rape victim to travel to the UK for an abortion. Like the X case, the C case was placed at the centre of political and media attention. However, it evolved in a more complex manner as the Court had to remove the child from parental custody and place her into the care of the Eastern Health Board in accordance with her wish.[80] Though the X case had established the right to travel abroad for an abortion, the C case, established that the Fourteenth Amendment was not intended to confer a right to travel abroad for an abortion, 'it merely prevents injunction against travelling for that purpose.'[81] This case refuelled the debate and pointed desperately to the fact that legislation was needed. The Supreme Court was no longer in a position to arbitrate the debate of the 'substantive issue'. The existence of the right to life of the unborn was now solely dependent on judicial interpretation unless the Government brought forward legislation.

[78] The results were for the Twelfth Amendment (white ballot): in favour, 572,177; against, 1,079,297. For the Thirteenth Amendment (green ballot): in favour, 1,035,308; against, 624,059. For the Fourteenth Amendment (pink paper): in favour, 992,833; against, 665,106.

[79] See A McFarlane, 'No to Abortion Tribunals', *The Irish Times*, 5 October 1992 for a contribution on the legislative options opened to the Government.

[80] R Lentin, 'Responding to the Racialisation of Irishness: Disavowed Multiculturalism and its Discontent' (2001) 54 *Sociological Research Online* (http://www.soresonline.org.uk/5/4/lentin.html).

[81] *A and B v Eastern Health Board & Ors* [1998] 1 IR 464.

VII

ANOTHER REFERENDUM: ANOTHER DISCOURSE?

Following the C case,[82] the Government set up a Cabinet Committee to oversee the drafting of a Green Paper,[83] prepared by an Inter-Departmental Working Group of officials. Its mission was to consider how to deal with the 'substantive issues' dilemma in a more positive discursive framework. The public was invited to make submissions to the Working Group and over 10,000 submissions were received in response to advertisements in the National Press.[84] The Green Paper was published and sent to the All-Party Oireachtas[85] Committee on the Constitution in September 1999. Having reviewed legal, medical and other submissions put forward, seven possible ways of dealing with abortion were identified.[86] The recommendation of the Constitution Review Group in May 1996 was that no further referenda should be held and that legislation to give effect to the Supreme Court's ruling on abortion in the X case should be introduced was ignored.[87] The All-Party Oireachtas Committee also invited submissions from the public and received some 105,000 submissions. Having taken oral evidence at a series of public hearings between May and July 2000, the Committee suggested, in November 2000, three possible options: (i) retention of the status quo; (ii) legislation to give effect to the Supreme Court decision on abortion in the X case; and (iii) a constitutional amendment to prohibit termination of pregnancy in cases of risk to the life of the pregnant woman arising out of suicide.[88] The Government chose to go for a constitutional amendment, partly due to political pressure from a small number of Independent TDs on whom it was dependent for its majority. Despite significant concerns among

[82] One must also mentioned that in between the X case and the C case, another X-case like, was heard in the High Court as reported in the front page of *The Irish Times* on 27 June 1994. The Y case as it became to be known was pregnant and the victim of incest.

[83] *The Green Paper* (Dublin, Government of Ireland Press,) 10 September 1999.

[84] 'Green Paper on Abortion: Chapter 5' *The Irish Times on the Web*, 10 September 1999. http://www.ireland.com.newspaper/special/199/abortion.

[85] 'Oireachtas' means 'Senate'.

[86] '(i) Introducing an absolute constitutional prohibition on abortion; (ii) permitting abortion where the life of the woman was put at risk by the continuation of pregnancy, except where the risk was one of suicide; (iii) retaining the status quo; (iv) retention of the constitutional status quo, but with a new criminal prohibition on abortion to replace the 1861 Act; (v) enacting legislation to give effect to the Supreme Court decision on abortion in the X case; (vi) repealing Article 40.3.3; and (vii) permitting abortion on wider grounds than those specified in the X case, such as risk to the mental or physical health of the pregnant woman, in cases of pregnancies arising out of rape or incest, in cases of foetal abnormality, on socio-economic grounds or on request'. 'Green Paper on Abortion: Chapter 5' *The Irish Times on the Web*, 10 September 1999. http://www.ireland.com.newspaper/special/199/abortion.

[87] *The Need for Abortion Law Reform in Ireland: The case against the Twenty-Fifth Amendment of the Constitution Bill, 2001* (Dublin, Irish Council for Civil Liberties, 2002) http://www.iccl.ie/women/abortion/abortion_paper 2002html.

[88] 'Green Paper on Abortion: Chapter 5' *The Irish Times on the Web*, 10 September 1999, http://www.ireland.com.newspaper/special/199/abortion.

its own party, it insisted on reopening the referendum option on abortion issues. After almost twenty years of debate, the country braced itself to go back to the polls for the third time.

This time however Ireland had changed. With the arrival of the Celtic Tiger, the return of its emigrant population, new visions, new structures in Irish society had emerged. The pillars of the old community were crumbling. Four figures symbolised the traditional role of rural Ireland: the Church, the law, the medical practitioner and the teacher. At the bottom of the scale, due to economic pressures, the teachers of the country lost their leading role following an acrimonious industrial action with the Government. At the top of the scale, the moral authority of the Church collapsed with the sex scandals, which rocked its foundation. The two figures left were the Law and the doctor. The Law had already chosen to erode the principles of natural law fundamental to the Constitution with the two abortion cases put to her by practising what is known as judicial activism.[89] The medical profession was now to enter the debate and become an intrinsic part of the new amendment. In fact the relationship between a woman and her medical practitioner was a central point of the Bill. Bertie Ahern, the Taoiseach, urged that we

> must, by every reasonable means at our disposal, strive to reduce the incidence of crisis pregnancy. Law is only part of the picture; education, advice, care and compassion are, in many ways, much more important.

He continued:

> I want to end by expressing the hope that the inevitable far-reaching public debate on these proposals will be informed by a spirit of reason, tolerance and open-mindedness.[90]

This statement seems to signal an important change in both perceptions of the Irish abortion issue and the Irish Government's responsibility to address it, and, further, suggests a broadening of the definition of 'abortion politics' from the limited realm of legal discourse to that of a more progressive social discourse.

This inclusive new discourse, the discourse of 'the people' can be construed as an attempt to avoid the divisiveness of the 1980s and 1990s referenda. By appealing to a collective voice born out of a collective conscience and a collective past, rather than using the language of 'pro-life' versus 'pro-choice', whereby opposing firmly entrenched camps, with no

[89] D Gwynn-Morgan, *A Judgment Too Far? Judicial Activism and the Constitution* (Cork, Cork University Press, 2001).

[90] 'Letter from the Taoiseacht to the Fine Gael leader concerning the abortion issue' *The Irish Times on the Web*, 19 October 2001, 2. http://www.ireland.com/newspaper/special/2001/abortion/.

common language or interest, negotiations remained impossible. This emphasis on the need for 'the people' to face up to the failures of the past, was an important rearticulating of 'the people's' will, and a reminder of past Irish populism. After twenty years, the construction of abortion moved from discourses of morality towards discourses of public policy with the 'pro-life' amendment wording itself used as a justification for adopting a more pragmatic approach to the role of the State in policing abortion practice. The discursive shift from legal discourse into social policy arose subsequent to clear indications from the Supreme Court that it was not prepared to fill the vacuum in the absence of Government legislation on abortion. At the heart of the issue was simply the old question of the separation of powers. A key feature to this was the fear that the Law would be brought into 'disrepute', which almost twenty years earlier, John Bruton of the Fine Gael Party, had already warned:

> It was arguable that what was happening in law enforcement of the ban on abortion might go well beyond what was 'practicable'—to use the word in the pro-life amendment. If this happened, it might bring the law on this subject into disrepute, and have the perverse and unintended effect of promoting abortion.[91]

What is interesting is the manner in which the Referendum Commission Booklet explained to the public the inherent difficulties allowing discourse dealing alone with the issue. It appealed to a more pragmatic approach from the people:

> The issues involved in this referendum are complex. Law is not a science. It is expressed in words which may be interpreted differently by different people and at different times. It is often not possible to be absolutely certain exactly what the effect of a new constitutional wording or a new law will be. However, in most cases it is possible to say what the likely effect will be. If you are undecided about how to vote the arguments presented on television and radio programmes and in press articles may help you to make up your mind. You may consider that neither the present situation nor the proposed changes are perfect. If that is the case, you should decide which is the better situation and vote accordingly even if it is not perfect from your point of view.[92]

The distinguishing features of the new *Act for the Protection of Human Life in Pregnancy* were first to eliminate the threat of suicide as grounds for legal

[91] Dáil Éireann Volume 415, 18 February 1992 Ban on Termination of Young Girl's Pregnancy: Statement.

[92] 'Use your Vote' *Twenty-Fifth Amendment of the Constitution (Protection of Human Life in Pregnancy) Bill* (Dublin, Referendum Commission 2001).

abortion in Ireland, second to legally term 'abortion'.[93] However, the Government was also accused of trying to redefine legally the term 'unborn' by using the expression 'unborn human life after implantation.'[94]

The Twenty-Fifth Amendment Bill, as it was called, consisted of a constitutional amendment within a constitutional amendment, containing a piece of legislation which itself was to be enshrined within the Constitution. This was an unprecedented format for amending the Constitution. If Irish voters accepted the Government's proposals and the Oireachtas passed the law, the Irish Constitution would have included new subsections providing that the life of the foetus was to be protected in accordance with the *Protection of Human Life in Pregnancy Act*; and that any future proposal to amend or repeal the Act will have to be approved by way of referendum. As such, the 'unborn' would have continued to be protected by Article 40.3.3 and in addition by the Act which contained a specific prohibition on abortion. Contrary to what he had indicated earlier, the Taoiseach's approach amounted to a rollback of the X and C decisions, as evidenced by his statement when launching the Bill on October 2nd:

> I think that to legislate for the decision in the X case, and in particular, to make complex legal provision and control for the suicide risk as a ground for abortion, would commence an inevitable slide to freely available social abortion in Ireland.[95]

His use of the term 'social abortion' refuted suicide as grounds for a lawful abortion and denied the realities of the abortion problem in Ireland. It was a subtle way to influence the polls and shift back the frame prior to X. The allusion to an 'inevitable slide' revealed a government's view that women could not be trusted to make decisions that affect every aspect of their lives:

> At present the only real defence against wide spread use of the X case as a basis for 'social abortion' in Ireland is the ethical consensus in the medical profession.[96]

The people defeated the proposal by a narrow margin (50.42 per cent to 49.58 per cent).

[93] The proposed definition was 'the intentional destruction by any means of unborn human life after implantation in the womb of a woman.' This definition of 'after implantation in the womb' was chosen to allow the use of the morning pill and IUD as well as the genetic testing industry to continue research.

[94] 'Letter from the Taoiseacht to the Fine Gael leader concerning the abortion issue' *The Irish Times on the Web*, 19 October 2001, 2, http://www.ireland.com/newspaper/special/2001/abortion/. Here, it must be noted that in the event of a constitutional interpretation challenge, the Irish text takes precedence. As it stands, the Irish version of article 40.3.3 'na mbeo gan breith' is a collective plural and was translated in 1983 by 'unborn' when it means in fact 'not yet born'.

[95] 'Speech by the Taoiseacht Mr. Bertie Ahern' *The Irish Times on Line*, 2 October 2001, http://www.ireland.com.newspaper/special/2001/ahernabortion/index.html.

[96] *Ibid.*

VIII

DISCUSSION

Framing socio-legal contexts creates and provides opportunities where new lexicon acquires strategic functions to describe new situation and engender debates. Balkin suggests that legal semiotics can teach us much about legal culture.[97] He argues that

> political and legal ideas can change their political valence over time from progressive to conservative and aback again ... Ideological drift occurs because political, moral and legal ideas are and can only be made public through signs that must be capable of iteration and reiteration in a diverse set of new moral, legal and political context.

In Ireland, elements of ideological drifts, which facilitated the emergence of a new set of moral legal and political contexts can be observed. Beginning with the so called 'pro life' amendment of 1983, PLAC sought to enshrine in the Constitution the rights of the unborn setting them in direct competition with the rights of the mother. In the aftermath of this amendment public discourse became more complex and multifaceted. It influenced the emergence of a rhetorics of competing legal rights, which Habermas labelled as 'the moral discourse about the impartial consideration of competing claims'.[98] Barak-Erez *et al* argue that the concept of a rights strategy relies primarily on the notion of symmetry and is concerned with symmetry between positive rights and negative rights. They point out that

> deception of this concept is obvious when engaged in a discourse such as procreation rights and particular in the context of abortion or euthanasia. Whenever a conflict arises between two rights, the first question to answer is to see which one has been recognized as a legal right, and if both parties have acquired legal rights, which one takes precedence over the other.[99]

They further contend that the creative interpretation of these rights merely represents the political activity of a particular interest group.[100] This is the case of the 1983 frame. Indeed, the Eighth Amendment is still referred to as the 'sectarian Amendment' as it was clearly representing the one-sided argument of Catholic teaching on abortion.[101] The Protestant Churches did not support it.[102]

[97] JM Balkin, 'The Promise of Legal Semiotics' (1991) 1831 *University Texas Law Review*.

[98] B Peters, 'On Reconstructing Legal and Political Theory' in M Deflem (eds), *Habermas, Modernity and Law* (London, Sage Publications, 1996) 101–34.

[99] D Barak-Erez & R Saphira, 'The Delusion of Symmetric Rights' (1999) 19/297 *Oxford Journal of Legal Studies*.

[100] *Ibid.*

[101] In 2002, Judge Hanlon who was deeply involved in the campaign against the 25th Amendment wrote to his S. Em. Cardinal Battista and described it as 'intrinsically evil'. His letter can be found at http://www.theflanagan.com/abortionreferendum2002/frames/rory-ohanlan2.htm.

[102] Above n 17, at 266, Hesketh.

As mentioned earlier, 1983 epitomises a staleness of discourse, as not only was there little opposition to the construction of PLAC discourse, but there was a clear indication from Irish society that the issue of abortion could not be raised in public, let alone the word mentioned. This was unambiguously stressed by Paddy Harte (Fine Gael TD) who insisted that abortion should not even be discussed, and that members of the party who supported it should be expelled.[103] However, it must be noted that PLAC never used the violent speech acts of American discourse. It was more concerned to be 'viewed by the Government as a responsible and determined organisation.'[104]

The major organising themes of the 1983 debates, terrorism, sectarianism, national purity, and the related construction of women in the nation as overwhelmingly subordinate and instrumental signs, shifted in 1992 in response to the X case, while continuing to reflect the form of the 1983 debate. In the X and the C cases, the language of public discourse changed to address issues such as victim-hood, the language of privacy and the State's intervention in the family, the language of national identity and collective morality, leading to a distinction between 'totalitarian' and 'modern' states as part of a more general discourse of progressiveness and liberalism in international politics. The ensuing soul-searching of the legal and political debates in which constitutional principles were scrutinised against social realities ended any illusion that moral views on abortion were uniform. Framing and reframing abortion discourse allowed for a shift in constitutional discourse which is now set in the highest written record of the land. The language of Article 40.3.3 defined for a long time the normative base of Irish law on abortion.[105] However, through the medium of judicial interpretation, the language used in the decision of the landmark X case contributed to redefine the legal norm. The concept of 'the people' as 'a collective identity' and the notion of 'the way of life' at stake were reconstructed, through an engagement of what Habermas calls the 'ethical-political discourse'.[106] For a long period of time, the highly selective euphemism the 'substantive issue' was used as a coding schema for integrating the complexities of the debate. It encoded a significant degree of abstraction away from reality, the purpose of which was to hide the true nature of abortion realities in Ireland. It served to hide the legal bipolarity of competing rights as set out in the Constitution. At best it allowed for an open dialogue, at worse it was used to deceive public discourse by using language to camouflage foetal protectionism.

By the late 1990's, abortion was being framed as a health care matter, and the discourse of the Government's Green Paper was explicitly rooted in

[103] *Ibid.*
[104] *Ibid.*
[105] Above n 24, at 227, Fletcher. Fletcher calls it the 'fundamentalist narrative of Irish abortion law'.
[106] Peters above n 98.

the language of legal pluralism and social policy, using a more dialectic paradigm to set out the legislative and constitutional options. While on the surface the debate appeared to have reached Habermas's 'pragmatic conception of discourse,'[107] the Taoiseach of the day continued to reflect the older 'moral discourse' of competing rights when he voiced his concerns about 'social abortion.'

Abortion issues are a classic example of discursive dichotomy between law and social order. In interpreting Article 40.3.3 we saw how Constitutional Law anchored the meaning of lawful abortion into an absolutist interpretation of the unborn rights. How, penultimately, it had to alter that sign and reframed it in a more pragmatic context in response to a shift in the external context of public discourse. This shift however may have undermined one of the basic principles of natural law as stipulated in the preamble of the Irish Constitution and raised serious questions as to the influence of public discourse over the judiciary.

But the question to ask remains. Has the debate really moved on from legal discourse to social discourse? Has the frame really shifted? The debate is based on a triangle, set by the people, the judiciary and the legislature. The first frame was an absolute ban on abortion where the law and legal discourse were used to institutionalise the concept of competing rights in an authoritative text. The second frame was a breach in the abortion ban, which allowed access to information and travel abroad for the purpose of an abortion. Again the law and legal discourse, with the nudge of the discourse of shame and sorrows, were used to institutionalise concepts in the authoritative text. The third frame was built upon pragmatism and appealed to the discourse of the common good. However it still used the law and legal discourse in an attempt to restrict parts of the second frame. By throwing it back to the judiciary, the people chose to regress back contextually into the second frame but with a different discourse. Abortion discourse in Ireland does not seem to be able to move from the realms of the law. But if the Irish were told back in 1983 that one day women could travel to England for an abortion, that magazines would advertise abortion clinics, that doctors would refer patients for an abortion and that abortion would be allowed on the grounds of suicide, they would have never believed it.

IX

CONCLUSION

It is clear from the Irish experience that legal reforms which frame social changes may have an impact on the way in which we view fundamental values and institutions representing them. The power of judicial interpretation is striking and is particular to a semiotic of changing meaning. The rulings

[107] *Ibid.*

in the X and C cases undoubtedly struck the nation when it recognised that there was now an exception to the constitutional provision prohibiting abortion. Legal discourse shifted from the static of article 40.3.3 to a more unstable discourse. As a consequence, we are now left in a situation where a pregnant woman, if suicidal as a result of her pregnancy, is not only free to travel abroad for an abortion, but can also legally seek one in the Republic.[108]

Both cases framed a general debate on the legitimacy and the appropriateness of the law dealing with social issues such as abortion. Indeed, the practice of having recourse to the courts to address social issues is not uncommon in Ireland but the Supreme Court in both cases made it clear that it was an inadequate forum to solve the abortion debate. This was unmistakably expressed in the dicta of the X ruling by Justice McCarthy:

> in the context of the eight years that have passed since the Amendment was adopted ... the failure by the legislature to enact the appropriate legislation is no longer just unfortunate; it is inexcusable. What are pregnant women to do? What are the parents of a pregnant girl under age to do? What are the medical profession to do? They have no guidelines save what may be gleaned from the judgments in this case. What additional considerations are there? Is the victim of rape, statutory or otherwise, or the victim of incest, finding herself pregnant, to be assessed in a manner different from others? The Amendment, born of public disquiet, historically divisive of our people, guaranteeing in its laws to respect and by its laws to defend the right to life of the unborn, remains bare of legislative direction.

The abortion debate is the most divisive issue in Irish contemporary culture. It is in part what makes the Irish, Irish. It is an example of what shapes not only the political and social landscape but also the rhetoric and representation of contemporary Irish legal culture. The historical background set the stage in which to understand the Court decision and the impact of its application in the daily life of its citizens. The effects produced by the legal discourse, the wording used, the lexical choices made and taking into account the semantic investment or disinvestments of a word were subsequently used by the politicians to convince and exert pressure on the electorate on the issue of abortion. As Brendan Howlin stated:

> the function of maternity is so venerated that it is identified in our Constitution as the focal point of the family, and therefore Irish society'. Ironically the very symbol of our nation is one linked to fertility, 'Mother Ireland' in her suffering, a recurrent symbol in the folklore of independence and nationalism.[109]

[108] However, it is important to note that the practical reality is that there can be no legal abortion performed in Ireland by a medical practitioner as it is prohibited by the Irish Medical Council's ethical guidelines.

[109] Dáil Éireann Volume 423, 20 October 1992 Twelfth Amendment of the Constitution Bill, 1990: Second Stage (Resumed).

10

Wealth of Terms—Scarcity of Justice? Term Formation in Statutory Definitions

RICHARD FOLEY

I

INTRODUCTION

IN A COMMUNITY governed by the rule of law, citizens must be able to ascertain, in their own language and from sources accessible to the general public, what the State and other public authorities expect of them.[1] In the EU, this right is guaranteed by Regulation No 1,[2] which, as the Community's first regulation, can be construed as a meta-legal message[3] indicating who the law is for. The legislation demonstrates that the language issue is central to the Community's conception of itself.

Clearly, directives are among those sources which the general public is entitled to consult.[4] Like other legislation, directives should be reasonably comprehensible to an intelligent citizen with an enquiring mind and an interest in the subject—not just to lawyers, politicians, and trade associations.[5] Although not applicable in the Member States before being transposed into national legislation, directives allow citizens to compare the purposes of Eurolaw and the transposition.[6]

[1] T Schilling, 'The labelling of foodstuffs in a language easily understood by purchasers' (1996)1 *European Food Law Review*, at 57.

[2] Official Journal 1958, at 385.

[3] R Sullivan, 'Some Implications of Plain Language Drafting', 22:3 *Statute Law Review* at 179.

[4] Legislation in the EU consists of primary and secondary legislation. The first category comprises the Treaties, eg, the Treaty of Rome, the second directives, regulations and decisions. Regulations and decisions are directly applicable in the Member States. Directives set out provisions which must be implemented in the national legislation of the Member States.

[5] M Cutts, *Clarifying Eurolaw* (Plain Language Commission, 2001), at 7. Available at http://www.plain-language-commission.com/PDFS/EUROLAW.pdf.

[6] Sullivan above at n 3.

The notion of 'own language' underpinning Regulation No 1 is rendered problematical by the distinctive character of legal discourse. The legislator's knowledge of generic conventions—including definitions—constitutes power and privilege vis-à-vis the lay reader:

> [The matching of writer's and reader's intentions is] possible only when all the participants share, not only the code, but also the knowledge of the genre, which includes the knowledge of its construction, interpretation and use. A necessary implication of this shared genre knowledge is that it is not routinely available to outsiders, which creates kind of a social distance between the legitimate members of a discourse community and those who are considered outsiders.[7]

The legislator and lay reader thus belong to different semiotic groups.[8]

The implications for democracy of this distance between professional and lay contexts in the EU have been addressed under the issue of transparency. It is a two-pronged effort embracing the aims of broader public access to information and EU documents and more easily readable instruments.[9]

While clearly a laudable goal politically, transparency is a challenging ambition linguistically. With reference to social legislation in Canada, Bowers notes:

> a vicious spiral of substance, expression and readership set in whereby the greater the readership, the greater the complexity of the law and the greater the need for intelligibility.[10]

This is clearly applicable to the EU, where juridification also proceeds apace.

Over the past decade a concentrated effort has been made to establish a market guaranteeing the four freedoms, but this has meant a wealth of European legislation. Simplifying this mass of law has now become a priority in order to ensure that Community action is transparent and effective.[11]

The most visible attempt to address the issue of the intelligibility of legal language is the Plain Language Movement.[12] In the EU, the principal manifestation of this movement is the Translation Service's 'Fight the Fog' Campaign. At its best, plain language holds out the promise of a new literacy, embodied in a

[7] VK Bhatia, 'The power and politics of genre', (1997) 16:3 *World Englishes* at 364.

[8] B Jackson, *Making Sense in Law* (Liverpool, Deborah Charles Publications, 1995), at 96–8.

[9] ScadPlus glossary under 'Transparency' at http://europa.eu.int/scadplus/leg/en/cig/g4000.htm.

[10] F Bowers, *Linguistic Aspects of Legislative Expression* (Vancouver, University of British Columbia Press,1989), at 332.

[11] Scadplus glossary, above n 9, under 'Simplification of legislation.'

[12] For a detailed review of the Plain English Movement, see P Tiersma, *Legal Language* (Chicago, University of Chicago Press, 1999), at 211–30.

process of translation[13] that would produce a single text melding the purposes of the legislator and lay audience. However, many of the accounts of plain language seem bottom-up, focusing on simplification or correction of legal language. The style sheets and drafting guides written in this vein[14] do a disservice to the ultimate aim of transparency in that they assume the primacy of a traditional, obscure legal text that is then improved. The many do's and dont's available, such as 'Use *by* not *by means of* and *carry out* in preference to *implement*', seem to cry out for implementation as a legal spelling checker[15] and clearly urge an untenably superficial notion of readability.

Among the proposals for bridging the gap between legislator and lay reader are those elaborated by Bhatia[16] or Cutts[17] in which the lay audience would be provided with non-normative versions of legislation in plain language. This approach is criticised by Jackson,[18] however, who observes that 'the popular audience which relies on such [plain language] documents is no less engaged in a game whose rules it does not know than when it relies on lawyers and expostfacto court judgements.' Non-normative documents would presumably reinforce the untoward meta-legal message that the public requires an intermediary after all in order to interpret the law.

Sullivan asserts that the promise of plain language lies not so much in the prospect that the public will begin reading or be better able to read legislation but in the fact that plain language undermines 'the simple equation of [law]=[rule]=[text]=[meaning] and draws attention to the improvisational character of the law.'[19] Plain language drafting blurs the conventional distinction between text and context. Sullivan asserts: 'Different readers bring different levels of competence and different contexts to their reading. These differences play a crucial role in constructing meaning from a text and inferring the intentions of the speaker.'[20] This opens up opportunities for the audience, the reader, to contribute to the interpretation of the text.

Statutory definitions are demonstrably crucial elements of the genre of legislation but as yet have received comparatively little attention in plain language circles. To address this shortcoming, the article examines the term-formation processes in two data protection directives as a reflection of how the generic power of interpretation is distributed among legislator, linguist and lay reader. This is particularly salient where personal data protection is concerned, for the legislation in that field articulates and regulates the rights of national authorities to compile information on every citizen and distribute this to third parties, including commercial interests.

[13] *Ibid* at 222–27.

[14] See, eg, R Dick, *Legal Drafting in Plain Language* (Toronto, Carswell, 1995), at 154–59 and http://plainlanguage.gov/library/smpl1.html.

[15] Tiersma 1999 above n 12, at 225.

[16] VK Bhatia, *Analyzing Genre: Language Use in Professional Settings* (London and New York, Longman, 1993), at 113.

[17] Cutts 2001 above n 5, at 6.

[18] Jackson 1995 above n 8, at 134.

[19] R Sullivan, 'The Promise of Plain Language Drafting', 47 *McGill Law Journal* 97 at 128.

[20] *Ibid* at 179.

II

STATUTORY DEFINITIONS

While the drafting process in the Community ensures that the conceptual fields for professionals working in any of the eleven official languages will coincide, varying term-formation strategies, coupled with the translation process, produce a diversity of linguistic forms. The focal question here is whether the resulting forms enhance or detract from the intelligibility of the text for the average citizen. Given the multilingual context of the EU, the analysis must include a cross-linguistic perspective to determine whether speakers of one language might be at a disadvantage vis-à-vis speakers of another.

In directives, statutory definitions are typically set out in Article 2. They are governed by the enactment clause[21] and operate on a metalinguistic level to bring about new lexical and legal states of affairs in the instrument.[22] The Definitions section can be seen as a forum where legislator, linguist and lay reader come together to negotiate meaning. The genre accords considerable power to the drafter.

> The attempt to define terms to their extremity removes the need, or at least withdraws the invitation for the receiver to play his interpretive part; the extreme of definition usurps the shared language to the sender alone.[23]

Only two authorities—both drafters—take up the implications of statutory definitions for intelligibility. Thornton[24] discusses definitions in a chapter entitled 'Intelligibility' and Dick[25] covers them extensively in his 'Legal Drafting in Plain Language.' Both caution against the excessive use of definitions. Two types of definition are distinguished: lexical and stipulative. The first states the meaning corresponding to actual usage, eg, specifying the intended sense from among those in common usage. The second sets down a meaning that is different from actual usage, giving 'certainty to an otherwise vague term by using specifications of measurement.'[26]

As a terminological entity, a statutory definition consists of three elements: concept, term and definition. The concept is the abstract representation of the knowledge of domain experts. The term is a form devised by the linguist with due regard for economy, precision, and appropriateness.[27] The concept and term are linked through the definition, which serves as an articulation of the concept for the reader.

[21] The preamble of a directive typically begins 'THE EUROPEAN PARLIAMENT AND THE COUNCIL OF THE EUROPEAN UNION' and ends with the enactment clause 'HAVE ADOPTED THIS DIRECTIVE,' which signals the beginning of the operative section of the legislation. This bracketing of the preamble, highlighted through the use of uppercase, can be seen as a semiotic device accentuating the differential legal status of the two sections.

[22] Bowers 1989 above n 10, at 167.

[23] *Ibid*, at 176.

[24] GC Thornton, *Legislative Drafting* (London, Butterworths, 1970), at 55–9.

[25] Dick 1995 above n 14, at 78.

[26] *Ibid.*

[27] J Sager, *A Practical Course in Terminology Processing* (Amsterdam/Philadelphia, John Benjamins, 1990), at 107–13.

Terminology is the first and most obvious way to regulate a domain of social experience.[28] Special lexis is distinctive of discourse communities[29] and is as exclusive of the lay reader as other aspects of the genre. As a special language, the language of the law uses:

> terms in addition to words, ie linguistic expression forms endowed with special reference as distinct from the general reference of words.... Only if both interlocutors in a speech act know the special reference of a term, and, by implication they are using terms rather than words, can special communication succeed.[30]

The distinction between term and word is further reflected in the avoidance of synonymy in legal language. Drafters state categorically that different words or expressions should not be used to denote the same thing and that the same word or expression should not be used with different meanings.[31]

Thus there are two codes or conceptual worlds encoded in the same linguistic forms, which the legislator as both specialist and lay reader is able to distinguish but which the average citizen cannot. Moreover, the lay reader does not have the generic discipline to read a term consistently in the sense set out in the definition.[32] It is this duality of term and word in the mind and singularity of linguistic form on the page which jeopardises the transfer of the power of interpretation from the professional to the lay person. Bowers proposes a solution to the dilemma:

> because more difficulties have arisen in the case of legal vs. non-legal polysemy than in other cases, it might be wise to have some specific mark—a superscript of the registered trademark kind—to indicate that a word is being used in its strict legal sense, whether this is one of judicial notice or of other authority. *The purpose is not to alert lawyers so much as other consumers of an Act* (emphasis added).[33]

The meta-legal message of such a system would clearly amount to informing the lay reader of yet another game.

Yet the words on the page are likely to be the lay reader's principal resource when he or she takes directive in hand. In terms of schema theory, reading can be described as an interactive process in which the reader tests his or her emerging understanding of a new text against previous knowledge in the form of content and formal schemata.[34] In the present case, the first comprises

[28] Y Maley, 'The Language of the Law' in J Gibbons (ed), *Language and the Law* (London, Longman, 1994), at 22.
[29] J Swales, *Genre Analysis* (Cambridge, CUP, 1990), at 26.
[30] Sager 1990 above n 27, at 105.
[31] Dick 1995 above n 14, at 86.
[32] Thornton 1970 above n 24, at 59.
[33] Bowers 1989 above n 10, at 146.
[34] PL Carrell and JC Eisterhold, 'Schema Theory and ESL Reading Pedagogy' in PL Carrell, J Devine & D Eskey (eds), *Interactive Approaches to Second Language Reading* (Cambridge, Cambridge University Press, 1998), at 79.

background knowledge on data protection, the second an awareness of generic conventions such as the provision of definitions of terms within the instrument itself. The less background knowledge or experience of the genre the lay reader has—and none can be assumed—the more he or she will rely on the text itself.

III

MATERIALS AND METHODS

The terms to be discussed below are drawn from two directives on data protection: the Personal Data Directive and the Privacy in Telecommunications Directive[35] (hereinafter PDat and TCom respectively). Interestingly, while definitions are normally characterised by fluidity[36] between instruments and contexts, the terminologies of the two instruments are explicitly linked intertextually through the following phrase at the beginning of Article 2 in TCom: 'In addition to the definitions given in Directive 95/46/EC, for the purposes of this Directive...'.

Of the twelve terms defined in the directives, the following have been chosen for closer analysis: *data subject* (65), *controller* (59), *processor* (10), *recipient* (38), *third party* (11), *user* (15), *subscriber* (54). (The figures in parentheses give the absolute frequencies of the terms in the directives.) The choice has been restricted on a functional basis to terms that potentially address the reader; that is, they represent roles that are likely to engage the lay reader, who tends to search for the implications the text has for a matter of interest to him or her rather than as a key to the meaning intended by the author.[37]

The impact of the terms on intelligibility of the texts will be assessed with reference to polysemy[38] between technical and non-technical senses of the words, opacity and transparency of compounds, and the relationships among terms and concepts both within and between languages. The frequency and meaning of the words and phrases in general usage will be assessed using a standard dictionary and data from the British National Corpus (BNC). A corpus such as the BNC is the only resource that makes it possible to assess the meaning of compounds.[39]

[35] Directive 95/46/EC of the European Parliament and of the Council of 24 October 1995 on the protection of individuals with regard to the processing of personal data and on the free movement of such data and Directive 97/66/EC of the European Parliament and of the Council of 15 December 1997 concerning the processing of personal data and the protection of privacy in the telecommunications sector.

[36] A Wagner, 'The Legal Discourse of the Common Law: A Game of Chess' 15:4 *International Journal for the Semiotics of Law,* at 354–56.

[37] Sullivan above n 3, at 103.

[38] Following Bowers, the relation between legal and non-legal senses will be described as polysemous in what follows. From a strictly terminological standpoint, the relation is one of homonymy. M Cabré, *Terminology: Theory Methods and Applications* (Amsterdam/Philadelphia, John Benjamins, 1999), at 108–09.

[39] On the promise of corpus techniques in investigating lexical meaning in law, see J Gibbons, *Forensic Linguistics* (Oxford, Blackwell, 2003), at 49–50.

IV

ANALYSIS

The definitions of the focal terms are provided in Table 1 below.

Table 1 Definitions of Analysed Terms

data subject (PDat)	'personal data' shall mean any information relating to an identified or identifiable natural person ('data subject'); an identifiable person is one who can be identified, directly or indirectly, in particular by reference to an identification number or to one or more factors specific to his physical, physiological, mental, economic, cultural or social identity;
controller (PDat)	'controller' shall mean the natural or legal person, public authority, agency or any other body which alone or jointly with others determines the purposes and means of the processing of personal data; where the purposes and means of processing are determined by national or Community laws or regulations, the controller or the specific criteria for his nomination may be designated by national or Community law;
processor (PDat)	'processor' shall mean a natural or legal person, public authority, agency or any other body which processes personal data on behalf of the controller;
third party (PDat)	'third party' shall mean any natural or legal person, public authority, agency or any other body other than the data subject, the controller, the processor and the persons who, under the direct authority of the controller or the processor, are authorized to process the data;
recipient (PDat)	'recipient' shall mean a natural or legal person, public authority, agency or any other body to whom data are disclosed, whether a third party or not; however, authorities which may receive data in the framework of a particular inquiry shall not be regarded as recipients;
user (Tcom)	'user` shall mean any natural person using a publicly available telecommunications service, for private or business purposes, without necessarily having subscribed to this service;
subscriber (Tcom)	'subscriber' shall mean any natural or legal person who or which is party to a contract with the provider of publicly available telecommunications services for the supply of such services;

Data subject has 18 attestations in the BNC, but with all clearly restricted to legal contexts, the term can be considered a neologism and therefore not polysemous to the average reader. The compound gives rise to two plausible comprehension scenarios. In the first, the reader will treat the term as a whole and associate it with the definition as such, for there is 'no evidence that in the effort of comprehension, we decompose a terminological unit into constituent parts in order to understand it better.'[40]

In the second scenario, the reader will proceed analytically, attempting first to determine the intended sense of the polysemous *subject* and then to establish the relation between this and *data*. He or she must rely on general usage here, inasmuch as neither the intended sense nor the relationship is specified in the definition.

As *subject* clearly refers to a person (in contrast to 'topic'), the following four of eighteen senses distinguished in Webster's *Encyclopedic Unabridged Dictionary of the English Language* might be considered salient candidates here:

11. one who or that which undergoes or may undergo some action
12. a person or thing under the control or influence of another
13. a person as an object of medical, surgical or psychological treatment or experiment
16. (Philos.) that which thinks, feels, perceives, intends, etc[41]

The first three senses suggest that the 'identifiable natural person' is in fact the object of data collection, with all of its untoward political connotations; the last views the person as the source of and presumably the one to control—through intention—the flow of data. As attractive as the latter interpretation may be, it is marked as a philosophical term of art and is thus unlikely to be part of the competence of the average reader. If the ambiguity is resolved in favor of 'object,' *data subject* can be interpreted on the analogy of *research subject*, ie, n_2 [is_for] n_1[42], as 'a person being used for the purpose of data collection' (sense 13) or 'a person undergoing, being subjected to data collection' (sense 11).

As an essential and frequent term in the legislation, *data subject* yields an instructive opportunity for cross-linguistic comparison. Following are its equivalents in the other official languages:

es	el interesado
it	persona interessata
fr	personne concernée

[40] Sager 1990 above n 27, at 103.

[41] Webster's *Encyclopedic Unabridged Dictionary of the English Language* (New York, Portland House, 1989), at 1415.

[42] RJ Quirk, J Svartvik, G Leech and S Greenbaum, *A Comprehensive Grammar of English* (Addison-Wesley, 1985), at 451.

pt	pessoa em causa
de	betroffene Person
nl	betrokkene
fi	rekisteröity
sv	den registrerade
da	den registrerede
el	το πρόσωπο στο οποίο αναφέρονται τα δεδομένα ('the person with respect to whom data is reported')

A first observation is that English and Greek are the only languages in which the equivalents contain the word *data* and thus an overt link to the term *personal data*; moreover, these are the only two terms that can be considered well formed in being context independent.[43] In contrast, the equivalents in the Romance languages, Dutch, and German—'the affected person, person concerned'—are skeletal, forcing the reader to rely on the context to answer the question 'affected by what?' The Danish, Swedish and Finnish 'registree' falls in between the two, inasmuch as registration implies an exchange of information. However, the past passive participles define *data subject* very much as 'data object.'

Controller and *processor* broaden the perspective by highlighting how term formation may affect intelligibility in masking or making explicit the relationship between two concepts. *Controller* is well attested in general usage in animate senses, eg, 'air traffic controller'; *processor*, however, occurs almost exclusively in inanimate senses, eg, (computer) processor, 'word processor', 'food processor.' If the animate sense for the latter in the definition can be considered term-formation through sense extension,[44] no antagonistic readings[45] or ambiguity are likely.

However, it is the hierarchical relationship between the concepts that is the crux where intelligibility is concerned, as can be seen in their warranting an 'exegetical' section of their own in the IDA Data Protection Compliance Report.[46] Here, term formation across a cluster of terms can be seen as contributing to or detracting from comprehension; the success or failure of the strategy in English will be analysed in cross-linguistic perspective with reference to the following table of equivalents:

[43] Sager 1990 above n 27, at 59.
[44] Cabré 1999 above n 38, at 93.
[45] DA Cruse, *Meaning in Language* (Oxford, Oxford University Press, 2000), at 108.
[46] IDA Report, at 12. Available at http://europa.eu.int/comm/internal_market/en/dataprot/studies/idareport.pdf.

Table 2 Cross-linguistic Comparison of *Controller* and *Processor*

en	processing of personal data	personal data filing system	controller	processor
sv	Behandling av personuppgifter	register med person-uppgifter	register-ans-varig	register-förare
de	Verarbeitung von personenbe-zogenen Daten	Datei mit personen-bezogenen Daten	fuer die Verarbeitung Verantwort-licher	Auftrags-verarbeiter
fr	traitement de données à carac-tère personnel	fichier de données à caractère personnel	responsable de traite-ment	sous-traite-ment

English lacks any formal connection between *personal data filing system* and *processor* and *controller*. Swedish keeps the relationship explicit through use of *register* throughout, although the relationship between 'processing' and 'processor' is obscured. German and French can be considered the most transparent terminologies here, as they maintain 'processing' throughout and indicate the crucial hierarchical relationship of the concepts 'controller' and 'processor' quite explicitly with the distance between 'responsible for' and '(sub)contractor.'

With 1237 attestations in the BNC, many relating to contracts or treaties, *third party* might be considered a familiar technical term shared by the professional and lay person. However, as defined in the directive the term cannot be considered technical, for it does not rely directly on specific professional knowledge. It is in fact defined negatively: a third party is neither the data subject nor the party comprising the controller and processor. With the exception of the transparent Finnish *sivullinen*—literally 'side (person), by-stander'—all of the other official languages use the same potentially technical equivalent 'third person'

As a linguistic form, *recipient* is straightforward, ie, one who receives information. However, the addition of the formulaic 'a natural or legal person, public authority, agency or any other body' gives it a forbidding, technical aspect. An additional shortcoming is the mention of *third party* in the definition, which gives *third party* more status and suggests more specific content than its negative definition warrants.

User and *subscriber* also seem straightforward at first sight: a 'subscriber' is defined as a 'user with a contract', a relation that is certainly consonant with general usage; ie, one can use a newspaper or telephone without subscribing to it. From a legal point of view, however, 'user' in excluding 'legal person' seems to be a hyponym of 'subscriber.' The liability of inverting hyponyms and superordinates is noted by Bowers.[47]

In the light of the analysis, what have been referred to above as term-formation strategies seem unworthy of the name, at least if strategy is taken to mean purposeful pursuit of a goal, eg, intelligibility. Some terms, such as *third party* and *recipient,* seem to be translated unproblematically 'across the board' while others, such as *data subject*, and *controller* and *processor* vary inexplicably in terminological well-formedness across the languages.

V

DISCUSSION

The variation identified above within and between languages sends the meta-legal message that where terms and words coincide, it is more by accident than by design: in other words, intelligibility for the lay reader has not been and is not a consistent concern of the drafter in formulating definitions in the EU context.

Paradoxically, it is only when directives are transposed into national legislation—and drafters may modify supranational terminology and definitions as they see fit—that distinct strategies emerge. Some reflect principled commitments to the interests of the lay reader; others are less encouraging.

Table 3 below illustrates the 'evolution' of the terms *personal data* and *data subject* in the transposition process. The data for Finnish, German and Swedish are based on the English translations of the national implementing legislation; the translations are literal and faithful to the original.[48]

Particularly striking is the complication of the definition in its being transposed into British English. Not only is it appreciably longer than the original, it has become partly dependent on another term, *controller.* Definitions should be self-contained.[49] The other languages have simplified the original formulation, Swedish appreciably so. Indeed, Cutts asserts that the translation of the Swedish implementation is easier for a Briton to understand than his or her 'own.'[50] A second noteworthy development is that the Swedish translator has created a new term, 'registered person', which could compete favorably with *data subject.* Finnish and German adhere to the term used in PDat.

[47] Bowers 1989 above n 10, at 169.

[48] On the translation of legal texts which will have no legal effect in the target language, see Sarcevic, *New Approach to Legal Translation* (The Hague, Kluwer Law International, 1997), at 276–79.

[49] Thornton 1970 above n 24, at 59.

[50] Cutts 2001 above n 5, at 3.

Table 3 Definitions of *Personal Data* and *Data Subject* in PDat and Certain National Implementations

Directive (en)	UK	FI	DE	SV
(a) 'personal data' shall mean any information relating to an identified or identifiable natural person ('data subject'); an identifiable person is one who can be identified, directly or indirectly, in particular by reference to an identification number or to one or more factors specific to his physical, physiological, mental, economic, cultural or social identity;	'personal data' means data which relate to a living individual who can be identified- (a) from those data, or (b) from those data and other information which is in the possession of, or is likely to come into the possession of, the data controller, and includes any expression of opinion about the individual and any indication of the intentions of the data controller or any other person in respect of the individual;	(1) personal data means any information on a private individual and any information on his/her personal characteristics or personal circumstances, where these are identifiable as concerning him/her or the members of his/her family or household;	(1) 'Personal data' means any information concerning the personal or material circumstances of an identified or identifiable individual (the data subject).	Personal data All kinds of information that directly or indirectly may be referable to a natural person who is alive.
	'data subject' means an individual who is the subject of personal data;	(5) data subject means the person to whom the personal data pertains;		The registered person A person to whom the personal data relates.

VI

CONCLUSION

A first conclusion to be drawn from the analysis and discussion above is that the Plain Language Movement should add statutory definitions to its many areas of concern. Progress towards principled term-formation strategies for definitions could start with the conceptualisations of the professional, which for reasons of space have been considered largely inviolate here. For example, one might ask whether *recipient* and *subscriber* merit explicit definition or whether such definitions merely serve to juridify the language and reinforce the legislator's ownership of the genre. Where definitions are warranted, interdependent definitions and formulaic, overwrought elements such as 'natural or legal person, public authority, agency or any other body' clearly detract from intelligibility.

On the level of the term, legally significant hierarchical relationships, such as that between *controller* and *processor,* should be made explicit in all languages. Context-independent neologisms remove the potential distraction of competing senses (*data subject* is at most politically flawed). The greatest liability lies in a conscious confounding of term and word, as seen in the establishment of a legally significant distinction between *user* and *subscriber,* whose frequency in the general language makes them poor candidates for the principled assignment of term to concept.

The evolution of definitions and terms, exemplified above, suggests that strategies will emerge to rectify shortcomings such as those cited where the intelligibility of legislation is a concern. Indeed, it seems that there are jurisdictions in which the legislator and linguist have succeeded in sharing the code with the lay reader more equitably. To sustain and encourage such development, the Plain Language Movement in general, and linguists in particular, could tap the wealth of language in the EU on all levels with a view to articulating successful strategies for legislative drafting at Union level in the future.

11

Enduring Signs and Obscure Meanings: Contested Coats of Arms in Australian Jurisdictions

RICHARD MOHR

I

INTRODUCTION

IN THE AUSTRALIAN state of New South Wales judges have sat under the coat of arms of the British monarchy since the nineteenth century (figure 1). Having been accustomed to seeing this symbol over the course of many years doing research in New South Wales courtrooms, I was surprised to notice during some research into the physical form of courts in 2000, that a different coat of arms had appeared above the bench in a new court building. This was the State arms of New South Wales. This change had been officially introduced into new courtrooms by an executive decision in 1995, in the midst of a controversy over Australian republicanism and allegiance to the British monarchy. Further developments saw a bill supporting the use of the State arms introduced into the New South Wales Parliament in 2002, and the whole matter referred to a parliamentary committee which took public submissions on the subject and reported in December 2002.

In January 2002 aboriginal protestors removed the Australian coat of arms, which features the native kangaroo and emu, from the old Parliament House, located in the centre of the national capital, Canberra. They objected to the use of sacred animals on the symbol of Australian government sovereignty, while this government does not recognise the prior rights and sovereignty of the Indigenous people of the continent.

These events provide the cultural background and framework within which I interpret the meanings of these contested coats of arms. Coming across these contemporary contests over coats of arms in a short space of time, I became interested in the meaning of these ancient and obscure symbols. They offer the possibility of investigating the ways in which meanings change over time. This investigation in turn suggests some insights into the relationship between signs, their objects and their interpretive context. Coats of arms endure over long periods of time, as a result both of their formalised specificity and their material existence. While the sign remains (physically) the same, the context in which it is interpreted and hence its meaning can change.

The process of interpreting a sign may be understood through the context of meanings by which a sign is connected with various other cultural manifestations. The changing cultural, social and political context refigures the meaning which we attribute to a sign. In other words, its meaning depends on the associations, cultural contexts and broader meaning frameworks by which we interpret it. Some of these contexts derive from referents to other words, symbols and objects. In the case of heraldic symbols these may be well documented, if not widely understood. For instance, the harp on the British coat of arms refers to Ireland, by long historical association.

In the pragmatic semiotic tradition signs can also be understood by their effects. Following Peirce, Eco observes that we may best understand a military command by observing how the troops respond to it.[1] Likewise, we can find valuable clues to the social role of signs by considering the uses to which they are put. The process of connecting the sign to various other meanings is a complex semiosis which may expand infinitely.[2] Since this cultural context changes over time and between cultures, situations where meanings change or are contested are particularly instructive for semiotic research. The following discussion examines the changed and contested meanings surrounding some unchanging physical symbols. Their meaning is considered from the point of view of their cultural referents, including both antecedent associations and actual or intended effects.

The cultural specificity and political salience of these interpretants draws attention to the social dimension of interpretive communities. In social semiotics, we may gain considerable insight into different people's interpretations if we can analyse the cultural baggage they bring to bear on an interpretive task. Looking at the New South Wales coat of arms (figure 2), classically trained lawyers may read the Latin motto, while indigenous people may recognise the kangaroo as a sacred totemic animal. Neither of these interpretants may be in the least relevant to the issue of republicanism which, from another point of view, may appear to drive the recent debate over courtroom symbolism. This discussion leads through the various ways

[1] U Eco, 'Peirce's Notion of Interpretant' (1976) 91 *MLN*, 1457–72.

[2] 'At this point there begins a process of *unlimited semiosis*, which, paradoxical as it may be, is the only guarantee for the foundation of a semiotic system capable of checking itself entirely by its own means.' U Eco, *A Theory of Semiotics* (Bloomington, Indiana University Press, 1976), at 68.

in which coats of arms are interpreted and used in the context of New South Wales law courts, to conclude with some reflections of the different ways they may be interpreted. It is suggested that a discrepancy between the cultural associations of particular signs and their pragmatic impact may present a 'gap', or a certain obscurity, which may in itself have semiotic significance.

The value of coats of arms as objects of semiotic study derives from their physical existence and their old and well documented provenance. Physical objects persist over long periods of time and may acquire various different interpretations. Coats of arms exist in many physical forms, etched into metal, or made of painted iron or wood. More recently they have taken new forms, such as plastic film or bytes on a government computer server. They follow ancient conventions of heraldry, and they may depict mythical beasts or long past events as well as more modern conventions.[3] The original interpretive context of heraldic symbols of ancient origin may well be quite obscure to contemporary observers. So they are notable both for their persistence over time and for their semiotic obscurity. However, as will be seen, they also come to be invested with different meanings as a result of changing historical contexts and political projects. The meaning of coats of arms may be understood by their history, by the political contests to which they are enlisted, and by their impacts within particular social settings. To the extent that there is a hiatus between the ancient referents of coats of arms and their contemporary political and social roles, it is possible to investigate the part played by obscurity and endurance in their interpretation.

II

LOST TRADITIONS

To try to 'read' any of these coats of arms in a literal sense leads to several difficulties. We find their languages—visual or verbal—obscure. What are we to make of these lions and kangaroos; of old French and Latin mottos? Even if we understand the words, some of the mottos seem to make little sense, and convey no sense of the power they wield or any apparent meaning of the symbols. A natural response to this obscurity is to try to understand the interpretive framework of the time and mentality which created them. There are cues to this and it is possible to discover quite a lot of their original referents, some of which are considered below. I also inquire into the shifts of meaning which the same symbol can undergo in moving to a new context in time and in place.

[3] The old coat of arms of the Basque province of Gipuzkoa depicts cannons seized in a battle in 1512. See R Mohr, 'Territory, Landscape and Law in Three Images of the Basque Country' in W Taylor (ed), *The Geography of Law: Landscape, Identity and Regulation* (Oxford, Hart, 2005). On the other hand, submissions to the Standing Committee on Law and Justice (2002) proposed that the New South Wales coat of arms be 'updated' in ways discussed below.

First I will consider the content of the two coats of arms which are the subject of the New South Wales Government's change of courtroom symbolism, and the Legislative Council's Inquiry into Regulating the Use of Coats of Arms in New South Wales.

Figure 1 British Royal Coat of Arms displayed in a NSW courtroom (c 1880s)[4]

The coat of arms of the British monarchy, currently still displayed in most courtrooms in the State, depicts animal and floral emblems of the constituent 'nations' over which it rules in the British Isles. For instance, the lion and the rose are English; the unicorn and thistle, Scottish. The Irish get a harp and a shamrock, while the Welsh must make do with the Prince of Wales.[5] 'Honi soit qui mal y pense' is written on a garter (naturally) because it is the motto of the Order of the Garter. 'Dieu et mon droit', at least, makes sense to a legal semiotician. The possessive tells us that the monarch is the source of right, and whatever the connective 'et' signifies exactly, she is obviously connected in some way with God.

Experts in heraldry who gave evidence to the Inquiry into the Use of Coats of Arms in New South Wales pointed out that the British monarch has distinct arms in her capacity of Queen of Scotland and of Canada. The arms used in New South Wales courts are those of Great Britain and Northern Ireland (as can be seen by the symbolic references to those places). One witness, Michael McCarthy, maintained that arms are 'territorial and

[4] Photograph by Richard Mohr, with the assistance of the Law and Justice Foundation of New South Wales.

[5] 'The special position of Wales as a Principality was recognised by the creation of the Prince of Wales long before the incorporation of the quarterings for Scotland and Ireland in the Royal Arms. The arms of the Prince of Wales show the arms of the ancient Principality in the centre as well as these quarterings.' *The Monarchy Today*, http://www.royal.gov.uk/output/page400.asp (website of the British Royal Family, accessed 22 April 2002). In evidence to the public hearings of the NSW Standing Committee on Law and Justice (12 August 2002), Michael McCarthy put it less delicately in referring to the bloody English conquest of Wales, by comparison with the merger of the English and Scottish kingdoms.

specific to certain places only'. In his view, to use British arms in New South Wales is to risk the most populous Australian state being mistaken for 'one of the lost counties of England' (evidence, 12 August 2002). On the other hand, the Garter King of Arms (the chief officer of heraldry in England) maintains that this coat of arms is the 'Arms of The Queen as Sovereign of Australia: they are used throughout the Commonwealth where The Queen is Head of State.' He adds that Scotland and Canada are exceptions.[6]

These interpretations of the Royal coat of arms may have been available to the educated classes at the time of its inception, hundreds of years ago, and still exercise a few heraldic experts today. However, as I am emphasising in this discussion, the interpretive world we live in, and over which this coat of arms may still preside, has changed. When I discussed this research with a magistrate from South Australia, another state where the Royal coat of arms is displayed above the bench, he told me of a fellow magistrate who had been sitting in a remote South Australian town. There he observed that an Aboriginal child who was appearing on a criminal charge had his gaze fixed throughout the proceedings on the ornate coat of arms above the bench. The magistrate hearing the case concluded that this symbol was making a profound impact on the child. Whatever impact this object of rich colours, mythical animals and an unknown language had on the child, it would have had nothing to do with the interpretants or semiotic framework of the originators of the symbol. Through the continuing processes of colonisation to the other side of the earth, that symbol of British unity and Royal power has persisted and been transported into a completely different interpretive world.

Figure 2 New South Wales Coat of Arms, from the Government's website (2001)[7]

[6] P Gwynn-Jones, Garter King of Arms, to F Nile MLC, 8 May 2002.
[7] Digital image by the New South Wales Government.

The New South Wales coat of arms, which the State Arms Bill 2002 NSW proposes should replace that of the monarchy, is of comparatively recent origin (1906). There are Australian symbols (the kangaroo and the stars of the Southern Cross) and the British lion. The economic bustle of the brash young state comes across in the symbols of agricultural prosperity (wheat and sheep) and the self-congratulatory motto ('Recently risen how brightly you shine'). It has only been in the past generation that the primary industries depicted here have been overtaken by tertiary ones. Even though education now earns more foreign currency than does wheat, and Sydney is a centre for foreign currency exchange, it may be demeaning to have the sheafs replaced by an academic 'mortar board' hat, and the sheep by dollar signs.

Here I have presented interpretations of the coats of arms which I am discussing based on historical research and a little translation from Latin. From this analysis we can see that a lion represents England, a unicorn, Scotland and the whole arrangement represents the British monarchy. These interpretations are available to the scholar of iconography or heraldry, but have little resonance with the interpretive frameworks of the majority of citizens of New South Wales. However, the conflicts and polemics over these symbols suggest that they may be viewed at another level.

III

POLITICAL PROJECTS

The polemics associated with these coats of arms, and the alternative versions discussed, indicate that people are identifying these symbols with particular causes. As the State coat of arms is enlisted in support of a republican campaign, the British coat of arms is seen as royalist. Despite their sometimes obscure and ancient symbolism, they have meanings of another type. These cannot be read by simply delving into the historical origins, but must be deduced from the contemporary contexts in which the symbols appear, and from the disputes which they represent.

These disputes are about sovereignty, allegiance, and ethnic identity. In New South Wales a republican project seeks to replace one symbol, representing Royalty, by another which does not. Reaction to this move emphasises an embattled British heritage threatened by multiculturalism. In drawing attention to the prior sovereignty of Australia's Aboriginal inhabitants, Indigenous interests have objected to the cooptation of indigenous animals for a colonising project.

The courts in New South Wales (the first Australian colony) have displayed the Royal coat of arms since they were empowered to do so by the King of England in the nineteenth century. With one anomalous exception, they did so until at least 1995, when the State Premier proposed a number of changes aimed at modernising the referents of executive power. The

Premier, Bob Carr, represents the Labor Party which campaigned for a 'yes' vote in the referendum of 2000 on Australia becoming a republic. While he has sometimes played down the republican motives behind his 1995 moves regarding references to the Crown (in the face of criticism), they must be seen in the light of this recent Australian political history.

Although the last legal and constitutional ties to British institutions were severed by the Australia Act 1986, the Queen of England remains the Australian Head of State. In fact, the responsibilities of this office are carried out by a Governor General who is appointed by the Queen on the recommendation of the Prime Minister. However, the continuing ties to the British monarchy constitute an irritation to Australian republicans, and a comfort to monarchists and Anglophiles. Changing these arrangements requires a constitutional amendment to be achieved by approval of a majority of voters in a majority of states in a referendum. Changing the Australian Constitution is difficult at the best of times, for procedural and sociopolitical reasons. On the question of Australia becoming a republic, a variety of constitutional reforms was canvassed. At a minimum, a constitution would need to specify a process for selecting a President. Republicans were split between popular election and appointment by the legislature. The referendum on a 'minimalist' republic with an appointed President was defeated in 2000. Some of the passions behind this symbolic move may also be seen in the debate over the New South Wales coat of arms.

Similar constitutional arrangements apply to the Australian States such as New South Wales, with heads of State called Governors appointed by the Queen on the advice of the head of government, who is called a Premier. The role of and many of the references to the Queen are largely symbolic. When the New South Wales Premier Bob Carr introduced the Oaths and Crown References Bill into Parliament in 1995 he was explicit in his reference to republican sentiments. This bill, he said, was intended 'to make a number of symbolic changes to remove some of the obvious and significant references to the Crown in State legislation and administration.'[8] Accused by opponents of representing 'republicanism by stealth', the bill was defeated in the Parliament.

The bill did not mention the Royal coat of arms in courtrooms. The Attorney General (the Minister responsible for the courts) raised this issue in a letter to the Premier accompanied by seven pages of advice from the State's Solicitor General. The Attorney General, Jeff Shaw, proposed

> In light of the Government's moves to remove references to the monarchy and the Solicitor General's advice on this matter it would seem preferable for the State Coat of Arms to replace the Royal Coat of Arms in New South Wales court rooms.[9]

[8] Second reading speech 23 May 1995. Hansard p 50–1. www.parliament.nsw.gov.au/prod/la/lahans51.nsf? open (accessed 21 June 2001).

[9] JW Shaw, Attorney General, to RJ Carr, Premier, 10 July 1995.

The Premier agreed to replace the Royal coat of arms with those of the State 'over time, whenever refurbishment of the various court rooms takes place.'[10] Courts built or refurbished since 1995 were to have displayed the State coat of arms, but usage has been inconsistent. Currently all New South Wales courts display a coat of arms behind the bench, and very often at the entrance, but this may be either the State or the Royal coat of arms.

The most interesting source of considerations regarding the appropriate symbol of the court's authority can be found in the Solicitor General's advice. Taking issue with arguments in favour of the Royal coat of arms in other documents, the Solicitor General, Keith Mason[11] made several points in support of its replacement:

— the historical and outdated nature of references to the State's 'British heritage';

— the independence of Australian and New South Wales laws from those of Britain, initiated by the *Colonial Laws Validity Act 1865* (UK) and established finally by the *Australia Act 1986* (Cth);

— the provision of the 1986 Act that 'unless Her Majesty is personally present in New South Wales, Her powers and functions are exercised by the Governor, on the advice of the Premier'.

In response to a view that the Royal coat of arms signified the independence of the judiciary and the separation of powers, the Solicitor General concluded, 'The judiciary is indeed an independent and separate arm of government. But it is nevertheless an arm of government of New South Wales.'[12]

This is a succinct statement of the social, legal and political sources of judicial authority: it is to be in line with our culture and heritage; it represents the source of laws and the executive power which enforces them; and it is represented as an arm of that same government, while being independent of it.

Submissions to the Public Inquiry into Regulating the Use of Coats of Arms in New South Wales raised several other issues, many of them relating to the referents of the symbols.[13] Submissions opposing the use of the State arms couched their concerns as a defence of British traditions. While several submissions decried the State Arms Bill as a form of 'creeping

[10] RJ Carr to JW Shaw, 31 August 1995.
[11] Keith Mason, (NSW Solicitor General), 1995. *Displaying the New South Wales Coat of Arms*, SG 95/47 (photocopy of opinion provided to the Attorney General).
[12] *Ibid*, at 5–6.
[13] Forty nine submissions were received by the Public Inquiry between March and May 2002. My references are to those submissions, all of which were made public by the Committee. I have identified the source of those submissions made on behalf of a named organisation.

republicanism'[14] or 'republicanism by stealth'[15]—they were typically keen to protect British heritage rather than the monarchy as such. They opposed multiculturalism, 'Britain bashing', and 'vandalism against British heritage'. One suggested that the government should devote more attention to 're-establish law and order amongst ethnic communities'. Another referred to 'the likelihood [sic] that yet another part of the Anglo-Celtic culture is to be wiped out, ie the Coat of Arms from all buildings', and asked, 'is the English language to go, also??'

Those in favour of the State arms sought more appropriate local references. The New South Wales coat of arms includes a kangaroo and the stars of the Southern Cross, as well as the lion and symbols of a colonial economy. Several submissions called for a redesigned coat of arms. For instance, George Poulos of the Australian Iconography Foundation advocated that the State arms should be 'more intrinsically New South Welsh'; they should be non British and possess 'intrinsic unequivocal State uniqueness'. As an example he suggested that the dexter lion rampant guardant might be replaced by the distinctive Australian duck billed monotreme, a platypus rampant. The submission of the Flag Society of Australia stated, 'The current state arms portray sufficient symbols of European provenance, but none specifically of the original peoples,' and cited several local and territorial government arms which do.

This too could be contentious. Aboriginal representatives have opposed the use on Australian arms of indigenous animals which have a special significance and totemic power. Australia Day, 26 January 2002 marked the 214th anniversary of white settlement, and the thirtieth anniversary of the establishment of an Aboriginal Embassy in front of the old Parliament House in the heart of the national capital, Canberra. A distinguished Aboriginal leader wrote, under her preferred nickname Mum Shirl[16] that this Embassy 'was to mean that we were treated as strangers in our own country.' During celebrations to mark the embassy's thirtieth anniversary, protestors removed the Australian coat of arms from the old Parliament House. That coat of arms has an emu as well as a kangaroo. Kevin Buzzacott, one of the protestors, called for the removal of these native animals from the coat of arms. He suggested replacing them with more appropriate introduced species, such as a monkey or a rabbit. 'It's about taking back what's ours. ... These judges, these coppers ... are trying to use our sacred animals for their power, their mad power.'[17]

[14] Submission of Australians for Constitutional Monarchy.

[15] Submission of Reverand Fred Nile, Christian Democratic Party.

[16] Mum Shirl, 'The Tent Embassy' in *Voices of Aboriginal Australia: Past, Present, Future*, edited by I Moores (Springwood, NSW, Butterfly Books, 1995) at 117.

[17] Katharyn Brine, 'Tent Embassy Protestors Have their Day in Court' *Canberra Times*, 7 February, 2002 at 1.

IV

THE POWER OF THE OBJECT

Why is it that coats of arms, as physical objects of ancient origin, come to be associated with sovereignty and state jurisdiction? Do they bring any additional authority to the government, court or political project which they represent? Apart from the traditional symbolism of these objects, their physical presence in places of power suggests they may play other roles. Having considered, above, some of the historical associations of these symbols, and their enlistment in political projects, I now turn to another aspect of the effects of these symbols.

It appears that in New South Wales court rooms the physical presence of coats of arms invokes authority. The coat of arms is always displayed above the judge or magistrate. In older courts this was often on a canopy which projected out from the wall above the judge (as seen in figure 1). In newer courts it is usually on the wall behind the judge so it is seen above his or her head from the body of the court. The coat of arms occupies a unique place in most New South Wales courtrooms as the only ornament or symbol. Unlike the courts of many countries, there are no flags and no portraits or pictures of any kind. What is more, the position of the coat of arms unambiguously identifies it with the power of the judge. Controversy over the State Arms Bill mainly surrounds the use of the coat of arms in courts.

The power of this symbol has been noted in two official documents and has further been suggested to me by magistrates. A New South Wales magistrate who generally sits under the Royal coat of arms said that it represents the authority which the community invests in the magistrate.[18] Referring to a copy of a document which he had been involved in drafting, and which he endorsed, headed 'Standards of Court Design'[19] we may find a slightly different interpretation: the (Royal) coat of arms indicates 'the sovereignty of the court' (4.6). The Solicitor General finds that the New South Wales coat of arms represents the independent and separate judicial power of the government.

Magistrates, the Solicitor General and a group responsible for drafting court design standards have found various diverse sources for the power of the coats of arms: that of the community, of the sovereignty of the courts' power, or of a separate judicial power of the State. These interpretations reflect the symbolic position of the coat of arms above the judge. However, whether they are referring to the State or the Royal coat of arms, and whatever the source of the power they see it as symbolising, all identify the coat of arms with power.

One of the motivations behind the State Arms Bill appears to be the profusion of coats of arms in New South Wales courts. While it was approved

[18] Interview, 2 February 2001.
[19] Undated photocopy, probably from the 1980s.

practice until 1995 to use the Royal arms, a major refurbishment of several courts in 1975 used the State arms.[20] Since 1995 heritage buildings use Royal arms, while new buildings use State arms. At least one major refurbishment since 1995 has used the Royal arms.[21] The Chief Judge of the District Court wrote to the Public Inquiry into Regulating the Use of Coats of Arms in New South Wales:

> I advise that the criminal business of this Court is conducted, under the present constitutional arrangements, on behalf of the Crown. For that reason, it is my view that the coats of arms as presently used are appropriate and the use of the State coat of arms would be inappropriate.

The submission was written on letterhead bearing the New South Wales coat of arms.

In furnishing every court with one or the other coat of arms above the judge it is clear that interchangeable symbols are made to do the job of invoking the authority of the court. Whether the symbol is the Royal or State coat of arms, and however it is interpreted, it takes the same place and is seen to be indispensable to the exercise of judicial power.

How is it that the coat of arms, whether that of the British monarch or that of the State of New South Wales, acquires this power? What is apparent about the coat of arms is its presence, whatever it represents. In the spatially loaded but iconographically sparse New South Wales courtroom the coat of arms is powerfully conspicuous, simply by being there: *there*, above the judge's head. The use of a particular symbol is decided by practice, or occasionally by some controversy, and continues by custom. As a physical object, the coat of arms is an enduring presence over time. It appears that a physical object conveys messages rather differently to other signs, particularly verbal ones.

Some of these differences may be observed by comparing the ways in which the New South Wales Government and the Parliament have approached the different issues of the physical coat of arms and the verbal judicial oath. The 1995 decision to change the coat of arms in New South Wales courtrooms was a relatively informal process compared with that required to change the oath or the other references to the Crown, proposed by the Premier around that same time. The Oaths and Crown References Bill 1995 failed to pass into law, and New South Wales judges still swear allegiance to the Queen even though they may now sit under the coat of arms of the State. In legal terms, this is explained by the fact that the use of one or another coat of arms was a simple executive decision not requiring legislation.

The current inconsistency in the use of various coats of arms shows that executive decisions can be ignored by members of the executive government,

20 Level 5, Downing Centre, Castlereagh Street.
21 Land and Environment Court, Mena House, Macquarie Street.

especially if they are advised by the head of the jurisdiction for whom they are building or refurbishing courts. The introduction of the State Arms Bill 2002 by a private member of the Legislative Council calls attention to an otherwise quiet but incomplete process. In response the Legislative Council referred the bill to its Standing Committee on Law and Justice, in the hope of gauging public reaction rather more carefully than in 1995. The possibility of quietly introducing the new physical coat of arms, and of then using an earlier version on various occasions may be compared with the formal legislative change to the judicial oath, drawing attention to the weight which that legal system places on words compared with visual symbols.

The difference in fortunes of the verbal oath and the physical coat of arms points to some interesting aspects of the use of symbolism and text in contemporary law. The words of the oath can be written out and debated by legislators. The coat of arms is more elusive. Its meanings are more ambiguous, its presence perseveres over time in a particular place. However, it is not an event enacted at a specific point in time like the swearing of an oath. Gagliardi has suggested that these are characteristics common to physical objects:

> The possibility that artefacts evade censorship depends on two intrinsic features present in different measure in the various artefacts: the tendency, proper to matter, to endure over time—something not always easy to manipulate—and the characteristic they have of being 'ornament', of being 'innocent forms', apparently without influence on the 'important things' which are said and done.[22]

The persistence of the Royal coat of arms in most New South Wales courts is an example of this endurance over time. The decision to change to the State coat of arms was made relatively easily—they were more 'innocent' than the wording of an oath—but the objects will last for many decades. Hence, as Pasquale Gagliardi points out, physical objects have qualities of innocence as well as endurance. Their innocence, in his terms, derives from their lack of explicit influence on important utterances and actions. This in turn derives from the facts that objects are inert (and thus not active) and their meanings are inexplicit, or less amenable to exegesis than texts. The meaning of the coat of arms is all the more obscure through its tangential reference to ancient interpretants. A judicial oath of allegiance to the Queen is more explicit than a coat of arms in the court room because it uses the English language to pledge that allegiance. It is more immediate since it is spoken in the here and now—in 'real time'—it is a current commitment rather than an enduring presence. Apparently the coat of arms as a physical object acquires power from both these qualities, of endurance and of obscurity.

[22] P Gagliardi, 'Artifacts as Pathways and Remains of Organisational Life' in P Gagliardi (ed), *Symbols and Artifacts: Views of the Corporate Landscape* (Berlin, Walter de Gruyter, 1990) at 26–7.

V

OBSCURITY

Australian lawyers commonly believe that the obscurity of the symbols of the common law adds to their mystique and to the authority which they wield. This viewpoint was illustrated in my earlier discussion of the magistrate who believed that an Aboriginal child was suitably impressed by the coat of arms. Lawyers of a more modern or critical persuasion find these arcane ancient symbols, including the wigs and gowns of many Australian judges and barristers, to be an embarrassment: the law should be expressed in plain English and lawyers should dress like anyone else. Even distinguished Aboriginal leader Mum Shirl,[23] invited to the Prime Minister's Lodge, was turned away by this symbol of authority:

> I looked around the outside a bit; it was a big and fancy place, and I was curious about it. When I walked in, though, there was this big coat of arms and it didn't feel like a house at all, so I just turned around and walked right back out of there.[24]

This suggests that these symbols may be effective in impressing those who are expected to submit to imperial or judicial power. There is also evidence that the powerful believe that they are effective. The Solicitor General's advice and the political debate which formed its context discussed the referent of the symbols, ie the British monarch or the State government, which I considered above. What was left out of his discussion, indeed of any of the debate around which coat of arms should be used in New South Wales courts, is the seeming necessity to have *some* coat of arms. The different symbols of the State and the Royal arms signify different places (Britain or New South Wales) and different sovereign powers (the Queen or the New South Wales government). What is it about a coat of arms which makes it, as I noted above, the sine qua non of judicial power in New South Wales?

I have already argued that physical presence is an important attribute of *any* coat of arms. I want now to emphasise another characteristic common at least to these two coats of arms, their ancient and relatively obscure iconography: both heraldic and linguistic. Neither the Solicitor General nor the Ministers nor the magistrate compared unicorns with kangaroos, rising suns with crowns, nor harps with sheep. Nor did they discuss the content of the mottos or their preferences for Latin or old French. These are the elements which differ between the two symbols, yet they are also share the

[23] Mum Shirl n 16 above at 121.

[24] Mum Shirl here describes her arrival at the Lodge in response to an invitation from the Prime Minister Gough Whitlam and Margaret Whitlam to a tea party on the lawns of the official residence.

common element of heraldic symbols and dead languages. An oath expressed in contemporary, albeit legal or ceremonial, English has contemporary meaning and reference which is avoided by the use of obscure languages.

Both coats of arms are characterised by their relative obscurity, and their curious relationship to law courts and sovereign power. Even translating the mottos from the old French or the Latin, they are senseless in the context of contemporary New South Wales law. The unicorn, lions and the kangaroo only become meaningful when they are identified with a specific monarchy, with a State and its republican aspirations, or with the totemic power of an indigenous animal. The reliance of Australian law officers, from magistrates to the New South Wales Solicitor General, on obscure symbols of State or Royal authority, suggests that their very obscurity adds to their power.

The gap between the literal referents of the components of these coats of arms (unicorns, dead sheep) and any tangible relevance they may have to sovereignty or judicial power leaves an area of uncertainty. Some social groups or expert interpreters may have access to an interpretive framework in which unicorns indicate Scotland and dead sheep the economic might of a rural colony. Others will be faced with obscurity, or draw on new referents for the interpretation of symbols.

In New South Wales the contested territory of ethnic identity, British heritage, republicanism and Australian cultural symbolism has been fought out over the coat of arms and the appropriate symbol of the power of the state and its courts. Signs have consequences as a result of the meanings which audiences may read into them. While the contest over *which* coat of arms to use indicates the depth of feeling which each can arouse, it has blurred the significance of the coat of arms as such. Indeed the inconsistent usage in recent court buildings and refurbishments highlights the interchangeability of these purportedly distinct symbols.

The gap between the symbol and its apparent, contemporary meaning provides an opportunity for interpretive plurality, and yet obscurity may have other outcomes. Obscurity, like meaning, has consequences. The symbol may be powerful as much for what cannot be interpreted as for what can. Georg Simmel associated secrecy with social power:

> The secret gives one a position of exception ... It is basically independent of the content it guards. ... From secrecy, which shades all that is profound and significant, grows the typical error according to which everything mysterious is something important and essential.[25]

[25] Georg Simmel, *The Sociology of Georg Simmel* translated and edited by Kurt H Wolff (New York, The Free Press, 1964). First English edition 1950, at 332–3.

Eco uses other parts of this passage in his attack on Hermetic interpretation, ie overinterpretation.[26] It seems to me that this misses Simmel's point, which is not that obscure symbols may suffer an excess of interpretation, but rather that they gain a certain form of social power through a paucity of interpretants, which leads the powerless to doubt their ability to interpret them. Interpretations may be part of a political project, particularly one which seeks to capture the power of a traditional or ancient symbol and to invest it with new meanings. However, the obscurity of ancient objects, symbols and languages may also gain political power through their lack of contemporary interpretants, and hence their obscurity.

While competing factions of Anglophiles and republicans have recently fought out their causes under the banners of the Royal and the State coats of arms, as symbols of judicial power these symbols have another purchase on political symbolism. Signifying power itself, in ways which appear ancient and obscure to the majority of people, the coats of arms continue to exist as signs. But, as signs which are interpreted through the *gaps* in their referents rather than through some transparent interpretive pathway, they are signs of themselves, signs of their own power.

VI

CONCLUSION: ENDURANCE

If the efficacy of physical symbols in invoking authority derives from their obscurity, as Simmel suggests of the secret, the analysis of ancient heraldic traditions and of dead languages indicate that obscurity in turn derives from the longevity of objects. Endurance has other effects which are not directly related to obscurity, but rather to physical presence itself.

In discussing the difference between the verbal oath and the physical coat of arms I pointed out that the former is only uttered in real time, while the latter persists. This is also a function of human agency. The oath must be uttered by a person; it is their commitment to allegiance. It is a performative like the judicial decision. The human agent who carved or painted the coat of arms, or the one who fixed it to the wall of the courtroom, may be long gone from that place, yet the sign remains. It is not apparent who made it or who put it there. In this way it acquires a semiotic power which is not linked to any individual sign-maker.

The impersonal object manifests that basic aporia of jurisprudence, the rule of law and not of men. Should we then conclude that the coat of arms has the effect of masking human agency? If the judge pronounces judgment only in the presence of this obscure and ancient object, it appears that the object lends its impersonal and enduring authority to the performance. In

[26] Umberto Eco, Richard Rorty, Jonathan Culler, and Christine Brooke-Rose, *Interpretation and Overinterpretation* (Cambridge, Cambridge University Press, 1992) at 38.

identifying this authority with the state, Michael Taussig calls one of the communicative uses of signs 'state fetishism', and he quotes Philip Abrams:

> [T]he state is not the reality behind the mask of political practice. *It is itself the mask* which prevents our seeing political practice as it is. ... The confusing figure of the mask is helpful only so long as, instead of trying to rip it off, we recognize and even empathize with its capacity to confuse, which means we take stock of the fact that what's important is not that it conceals but that it makes truth.[27]

The sign's meaning is immanent in its effects. If the sign is found to constitute a social reality regardless of its associations (ancient or contemporary), we know it by its works. Where the sign is the mask which constitutes the power of the state, what does the mask conceal if it is doing this work in front of our eyes?

The symbol which constitutes state power is only a mask if it has a hidden meaning. Interpretation such as that offered by the Solicitor General sees the constitution of power in a semiotics which discovers in the State coat of arms a transcendent meaning of indivisible separation no less mysterious than the Holy Trinity: the judiciary is part of the combined power of the three arms of government, yet independent. And yet this is not what the object does in the courtroom. The object itself may mean nothing or anything: the monarch, the state or the independent judiciary. If the symbolic object means nothing beyond its invocation of power, then it is a transparent manifestation of power constituted in the here and now of each actually existing courtroom.

To say, as Taussig does, that the symbols which invoke state power are 'fetishes' is to associate the modern state with the objects of 'primitive' religions. This was Marx's rhetorical move in associating the bourgeois means of production with the commodity fetish.[28] It is mirrored in the Aboriginal accusation that 'these judges [and] coppers' have stolen sacred animals for their own power. I say mirrored, however, and not reproduced, because the Aboriginal protest does not try to diminish the bourgeois order by an association with 'fetishism', but rather tries to reclaim the objects themselves. In the present analysis I have recognised the power of objects and tried to explain it. Used in suitably powerful social contexts, objects are equally efficacious in Aboriginal society and in the colonising society. Indeed the parallels clarify this efficacy, without debunking or denigrating the objects or the beliefs they sustain.

I said above that consequences may flow from the interpretation of meanings. If a sign means a monarchist or a republican New South Wales

[27] M Taussig, *The Nervous System* (New York, Routledge, 1992) at 113.
[28] WJT Mitchell, *Iconology: Image, Text, Ideology* (Chicago, University of Chicago Press, 1986) at 190ff.

we understand the content of the sign by the context in which it is used, and the polemics surrounding its use. Yet I have discussed here a case in which it seems that a sign's efficacy has become detached from its denotation of different sources of authority or allegiance. Different symbols can be used interchangeably to invoke judicial power, even though the signs may 'mean' allegiance to a British Queen or a republican cause. In this situation we see that different signs may have the same effect—the invocation of judicial power—despite various different prior associations.

To return to the ways of interpreting signs with which I began this discussion, of course meaning is constituted through both cultural association and pragmatic effect. This example of symbols bearing different associations with the same effect suggests the possibility of disjuncture between the interpretive regimes of antecedent association and consequential effect. By drawing attention to the obscurity of the associations behind these signs, together with the immanence of their physical presence and invocation of power, I have tried to explore the relationship between an exegetical approach to meanings (from prior association) and a pragmatic approach (understanding their effects). Where effect can stay the same despite variations in association, this suggests that the very obscurity of those associations may be contributing to the effect.

The physical coat of arms is an object which endures over long periods and is used to invoke judicial power. Its meaning is apparent in this use. As a physical object of early provenance it not only has ancient, obscure, or ambiguous associations, but also represents the power of entities that are not present. Whether this is the power of a monarch, of the state, or of an independent judiciary, it is not the power of the individual judge qua individual. While judicial decisions may only be pronounced by such an individual, the invariable association of this performative with the coat of arms serves to attach the immediate power of the judge to the enduring power of the object. Likewise, the enduring power of the object invokes an impersonal authority with every judicial pronouncement.

12

Critical Race Reggae: The Sound of a Narrative

AARON RS LORENZ

I

FOR LEGAL SCHOLARS enthralled by the impact of jazz music on race, the emergence of critical race theory marked the death of racism in the law. Professor Jonathan A Beyer, invoking the work of Archie Shepp, Miles Davis, and Duke Ellington, described death to the Lucifer of the law and the funeral that ensued.[1]

Beyer narrated a funeral procession composed of citizens, scholars, clergy, judges, lawyers, and elected officials. The slow moving procession was accompanied by a slow bass drum sprayed with a soulful trumpet. The burial was marked by the words of a judge who explained what the law could and should have been.[2] As the crowd understood what the law was capable of, the trumpet began a louder blast. Beyer describes this metamorphosis as the end of the funeral and the beginning of a carnival.

The faith that racism in the law died with the jazz metaphor as critical race theory emerged is one worthy of adherence. However, death and life in this context should be understood further. The goal of jazz music is certainly marked by the burying of racism in American law. While jazz music attempted, and continues to attempt, to act as the metaphor for critical race theory through reconstructing a pluralist justice from the ashes of racism in the law, I argue that reggae music is the metaphor better suited to convey 'the repulsion with racism and the optimism shared by critical race scholars.'[3]

[1] JA Beyer, 'The Second Line: Reconstructing the Jazz Metaphor in Critical Race Theory' (March 2000) *Georgetown Law Journal* 537. This paper is a response, of sorts, to Beyer's work which methodically and sophisticatedly describes jazz music as a metaphor for critical race theory. I argue that Beyer's work is incomplete in that reggae music better suits the reconstructive nature of critical race scholarship.

[2] *Ibid.*

[3] *Ibid*, at 563.

II

CRITICAL RACE THEORY: AN INTRODUCTION[4]

Critical Race Theory emerged as a response to the Critical Legal Studies movement of the 1970s. However, critical race scholars have been furthering their stance on race and law in the United States since the inception of the civil rights movement. Critical Race Theory (CRT), for the purposes of this piece, has six main elements.

First, CRT recognises that racism is endemic to United States society. The question is not about eliminating racial discrimination and preserving the status quo for the elites. Rather, CRT argues that the traditional interests and values serve as tools for racial subordination. Law remains the mechanism for socially constructing both race and racism.

Second, CRT is extremely skeptical of legal claims of neutrality, color blindness, and meritocracy. These claims are devoid of social meaning and are ahistorical. Claims that societal problems regarding race can be solved through race neutrality is a myth.

Third, CRT challenges ahistoricism and insists on a contextual analysis of the law. Current inequalities can be linked to earlier periods in which the law was fashioned to create a dominate race and subordinate another. Most importantly, CRT scholars argue that race has infested all aspects of group advantage and disadvantage.

Fourth, CRT insists that people of color be part of the analysis and story telling. Their experience is immeasurable. Knowledge, for a CRT scholar, is gained from critical reflection through the experience of racism and active political practice toward eliminating racism.

Fifth, CRT is interdisciplinary. Since it borrows from various traditions like liberalism, law and society, critical legal theory, and pragmatism, the numerous methodologies effective enable the voice for advancing the cause of racial justice.

Lastly, CRT works toward the elimination of racial oppression as a broader goal for ending all forms of oppression. Racial oppression can be linked to other oppressive experiences regarding class, gender, and sexual orientation. The interests of all people are taken into account because they are subordinated and their consciousness of that subordination is the key to effecting sociolegal change.

[4] The introduction to Critical Race Theory is taken from M Matsuda, C Lawrence III, R Delgado, K Williams Crenshaw, *Words That Wound, Critical Race Theory, Assaultive Speech, and the First Amendment* (Boulder, CO, Westview Press, 1993), at 6–7. See Richard Delgado and Jean Stefancic, *Critical Race Theory: An Introduction* (NY, New York University Press, 2001).

III

THE FIRST VERSE: REGGAE AS REVOLUTION

Reggae music has embarked upon the mission of protecting the oppressed; of making the world aware of the downtrodden; presenting the people a vision of life through the eyes of a Jamaican raised on the mean streets of Kingston. Critical race scholars attempting to protest racial inequity within American jurisprudence have often turned to jazz music to find their identity. Contemporary scholarship seems to address the impact of rap music and hip-hop music on racial designation. However, scholars seem to be disregarding reggae music, which I argue captures critical race theorists' reconstructive criteria.

Reggae music originated, as best as one can prove, from the West African beats of the indigenous people brought over as slaves to the Caribbean. Molded from rock-steady with its pulsating mid-beats and ska with its faster overtones and rebellious lyrics, reggae music emerged in the 1960s. To believe that reggae was born in 1968 when Toots Hibbert of Toots and Maytals recorded the driving number 'Do the Reggay,' is to believe a myth. Toots is quick to point out that he didn't invent the term; 'reggae' was just an expression circulating in the streets meaning, roughly, 'raggedy, everyday stuff.'[5] But the popular tune captured the term on vinyl and coined the phrase for contemporary use. Reggae incorporated the raw sound of the streets of Jamaica (and other Caribbean islands) with the more polished sounds of Motown artists such as Marvin Gaye, James Brown, and The Temptations. The music seemed to capture the move away from colonial control—as Jamaica gained independence from Britain in 1962—with recognition of past inequalities and hope for repatriation, redemption, peace, and a return to their homeland, Mama Africa.

By the early 1970s, reggae had evolved into a regional force. Its message included revolution and peace, politics and religion, and of course, race. The emergence of Bob Marley and Wailers, led by the musical prophet Marley, catapulted reggae into an international phenomenon. Exported from the streets of Trenchtown, Jamaica, a ghetto outside the capital Kingston, Jamaica was no longer solely known for its beautiful beaches. Marley helped push issues of law and politics into the national and international debate.[6] Marley's message, best used here as an example of reggae's protesting spirit, was one which responded to the past and present inequities that plagued not only those of African descent, but those subjected to colonialism and imperialism. In 1973, Marley addressed in song the violence that encompassed Jamaica surrounding the 1972 election of democratic socialist Michael Manley. Marley wrote:

[5] S Davis and P Simon, *Reggae International* (New York, Random House, 1982), at 45.

[6] NW Keith and NZ Keith, *The Social Origins of Democratic Socialism in Jamaica* (Philadelphia, Temple University Press, 1992), at 196.

This morning I woke up in a curfew
Oh god, I was a prisoner too—yeah
Could not recognise the faces standing over me
They were all dressed in uniforms of brutality
How many rivers do we have to cross
Before we can talk to the boss...
(That's why we gonna be) Burnin' and a-lootin' tonight
(Say we gonna burn and loot) Burnin' and a-lootin' tonight
(One more thing) Burnin' all pollution tonight
(Oh yeah, yeah) Burnin' all illusions tonight
Give me the food and let me grow
Let the roots man take a blow
All them drugs gonna make you slow now
It's not the music of the ghetto.[7]

Commenting on the curfew imposed by the Jamaican government, Marley described a Jamaica where political leaders used the Jamaican people as pawns to fight their battles for power. The result was an international spotlight on a small Caribbean island and its political struggles. Marley used that spotlight to continue his musical revolution.

Similar to jazz music, reggae music permeated white culture as well as African-American culture. Instead of rejecting Marley's claims of racial injustice, many in white culture supported reggae's foundation that colonialism led to the underdevelopment of Africa and the African Diaspora. Marley was not the only reggae musician involved in the reggae revolution. One of Marley's friends, and founding member of the Wailers, Peter Tosh left the Wailers in 1974 to pursue a solo career. Tosh, along with Jimmy Cliff, Toots Hibbert, Joe Higgs, Dennis Brown, Dilinger, and various other artists combined to produce reggae music as both celebration and revolution.

Reggae's beat, easily recognisable and often uplifting, is usually coupled with stinging lyrics that draw the link to critical race theory. The revolution link that I am beginning to outline is both the radical nature of the message as well as the connection of the concept of reconstruction that critical race theory describes. Marley sang 'Revolution' in 1974:

It takes a revolution (revolution) to make a solution Too much confusion, so much frustration, eh! I don't wanna live in the park (live in the park)
Can't trust no shadows after dark (shadows after dark), yeah-eh!
So, my friend, I wish that you could see,

[7] Bob Marley and the Wailers, 'Burnin' and Lootin'', *Burnin'* (New York, Island Records, 1973).

Like a bird in the tree, the prisoners must be free, yeah! (free)
Never make a politician grant you a favour
They will always want to control you forever, eh! (forever, forever)
So if a fire make it burn (make it burn, make it burn)
And if a blood make ya run (make ya run, run, run),
Rasta de 'pon top, can't you see?
So you can't predict the flop. Eh-eh![8]

Marley's message in this song in particular, seemed to anger the Jamaica Labour Party (JLP) which was the traditional capitalist party. Led by Edward Seaga, affectionately referred to by followers of reggae as 'C-I-A-ga' because of his ties to US President Ronald Reagan, the JLP viewed Marley's message as subversive. With the Peoples National Party (PNP) in power from 1972–1980, led by Prime Minister Michael Manley, Marley and reggae music seemed to have an ally.

The mid 1970s and late 1970s produced profound and influential reggae music. Dominated by Bob Marley's tunes, more reggae artists began to involve themselves in the process—the revolution grew. Regardless of the artists, the predominant message continued to be racial equality. During the post World War II period in the US, African Americans, who had fought equally to defend America, sought to increase attacks on legalised social and economic racism.[9] Jazz musicians responded accordingly and developed an intense, eccentric, and revolutionary style known as 'bebop.'[10] During the 1950s, 1960s, and into the 1970s, reggae musicians paralleled bebop's creation by capturing the same rage and discontent. They deconstructed traditional jazz, blues, and rhythm and blues and then reconstructed a new sound: reggae. By arranging a mid-beat into the song, the traditional drum intersection was severed and the new tune created a slower, methodical sound. The revolutionary and reconstructing effort did not stop at the sound or the lyrics.

Reggae musicians, generally speaking, hold a strong connection with Rastafarians. Rastafarians emerged from the streets of Kingston, dreadlocked, in the early 1930s as a religious response to Jamaica's racial history.[11] Due to the legacy of slavery and colonial oppression combined with the prophesies of Marcus Garvey, young Jamaicans began to embrace the religion of Rastafari. Based on the premise that Emperor of Ethiopia Haile Selassie I is God, Rastas redefine and reinterpret the Bible. Born as Ras Tafari Makonnen in 1892, Selassie ruled Ethiopia from 1930–1974. Rastas

[8] Bob Marley and the Wailers, 'Revolution,' *Natty Dread* (New York, Island Records, 1974).
[9] Beyer 2000 above n 1, at 541.
[10] *Ibid*, at 542.
[11] Davis and Simon 1982 above n 5, at 59.

view Selassie as Jah Rastafari and Ethiopia as their homeland. The attempt was for Jamaicans, and all in the African Diaspora, to have a God in their own light. Marcus Garvey implored,

> Since the white people have seen their God through white spectacles, we have only now started out (late though it be) to see our God through our own spectacles. ...That is the God in whom we believe, but we shall worship him through the spectacles of Ethiopia.[12]

Thus, the destiny of reggae music is forever tied with Rasta culture. Within that culture, which I will subsequently refer to as either Reggae or Rasta, included the withdrawal from popular culture.

Inherent in that withdrawal is gradual departing from conventional culture. Reggae musicians, like their bebop counterparts, revolted and restructured their own society. Adopting patterns of dress and speech unique to themselves, Rastas separated themselves from much of mainstream society. Their dreadlocked hair signifies their religious commitments and beliefs. Their dialect, a unique patois, includes various phrases that are purely Rasta. Rasta's use 'I' instead of 'me' or 'I and I' instead of 'we' to signify their individuality. They use terms like 'overstand' instead of 'understand' to reconstruct the framework that is used in society. The distinctions to jazz music and the metaphors to critical race theory are evident. As Professor Beyer writes:

> In addition to the music, members of the bebop revolution also adopted distinctive patterns of dress and speech to further separate themselves from dominant America society. In its musical and cultural separatism, bebop replaced dominant norms with dissonant expression. Through cultural disengagement, bebop challenged contemporary styles in the same way black militancy attacked conventional politics. Similarly, critical race scholars separate themselves from the culture of the legal academy and voice a protest of cultural discrimination analogous to bebop jazz musicians.[13]

Reggae musicians were not neutral. During a time when race neutral rhetoric dominated the national debate in America, Rasta culture introduced an answer: reggae.

IV

THE SECOND VERSE: CRITICAL RACE THEORY AS REGGAE MUSIC

Critical race scholars find 'black jazz' or 'fire music' of the 1960s to be the period of jazz history most representative of their attack on institutional

[12] Davis and Simon 1982 above n 5, at 60.

[13] Beyer 2000 above n 1, at 542. Beyer notes that bebop musicians, similar to reggae musicians, assigned positive connotations to terms for mental instability such as 'crazy' and 'insane.' Reversing the meaning is a classic hallmark of the revolutionary.

racism.[14] The explicit political purpose of jazz musicians like Archie Shepp, whose recording titled 'Fire Music,' meshes well with reggae. Fire musicians, like reggae musicians, sought to deconstruct traditional jazz and inject African styles. Reggae music, like its counterpart fire music, is unique because it exclaims a political as much as a musical purpose.[15]

Like reggae music, critical race theory emerged as a response to the enduring political, social, economic, and legal inequities of African Americans. Critical race theories' revolutionary approach is its effort to deconstruct law and legal concepts. Just as Rasta's redefined and reinterpreted the Bible and reggae musicians deconstructed the legacy of colonialism, critical race theorists use the same techniques. The commonality that they both share deconstructionist experiences amplifies the reconstructionist aspect of reggae music as a metaphor for critical race theory.

Reggae music best exemplifies the voice of protest in critical race theory because, like critical race theory, reggae's goal is political reform. Rastafarians may argue that 'politricks,' as they term politics, has no place in their reality; that their role is to do Jah's work. However, Selassie's message, arguably, was one of world racial harmony, based on Ethiopians maintaining their political, social, and legal power. More appropriately, reggae musicians and critical race theorists share the common objective of dismantling the status quo. In an interview, Marley once said:

> My music fights against the system that teaches to live and die ... music is the biggest gun, because it saves. It nuh kill, right? The other gun lick off ya head ... the revolution is a mechanical thing you know—they've planned it ... revolution is not planned. It just happens and you can see it going on around you ... not like the Cuban revolution—the whole universe is involved in this revolution.[16]

Marley, uncomfortable with his fame, considered himself a messenger of Jah and here on Earth to do Jah's work. That work included what critical race scholars would term 'deconstruction.'

In order to deconstruct, both reggae musicians and critical race scholars need to have a grasp of the past. Just as Rastas look to the history of colonial control, critical race scholars look to the roots of slavery and discrimination. In John O Calmore's poignant essay on fire music and critical theory, he writes:

> It [critical race theory] is concerned with redressing conditions of oppression and subordination which exist beyond their narrow translation into judicially recognisable claims and relief. Historical discrimination and its legacy merge more definitively and symbiotically with the present to provide the

[14] *Ibid*, at 544.
[15] *Ibid*.
[16] I McCann, *Bob Marley: In His Own Words* (London, Omnibus Press, 1993), at 39–41.

> temporal context. While not abandoning a faith in rights strategy, Critical Race Theory recognises that such strategy cannot be divorced from the larger economics and politics of things. It recognizes that whatever the specific issues of legal cases and controversies may be, the overriding issues of social justice and institutional legitimacy always lurk nearby.[17]

Rastas recognise the need to explain their history. 'Don't forget your history, know your destiny,' Marley sang in 1976.[18] Affected by the teachings of Dr. Walter Rodney—a Guyanese born historian who traveled the Caribbean teaching 'the people' how Europe underdeveloped Africa—Rastas deconstructed, with the help of Rodney, the racist assumptions that plague world history. Rodney wrote:

> the regime has been forced into carrying out a crude manipulation of the symbols of national black pride. Marcus Garvey and Paul Bogle were enshrined as 'National Heroes,' when the methods and achievements of these Black Liberators point the way ever more clearly toward Black Resistance today.[19]

Rodney's message, often used as a foundation piece by reggae musicians, draws the metaphor to critical race theory by connecting the motif that historical inequities have existed yet institutional legitimacy remains a major theme.

V

THE CHORUS: A REGGAE REPUBLIC[20]

In April of 1980, Bob Marley received a distinction that catapulted him to honor within the world community. Marley was invited to headline at the independence celebration in Zimbabwe as it gained independence from Britain and shed the name Rhodesia. When soldiers of the revolutionary struggle learned of Marley's concert, they broke down gates to hear and witness their idol.[21] Marley's message had been clear and powerful many times before. But I argue that it was here that the reggae republic—the

[17] JO Calmore, 'Critical Race Theory, Archie Shepp, and Fire Music: Securing an Authentic Intellectual Life in a Multicultural World' in K Crenshaw, N Gotanda, G Peller and K Thomas (eds), *Critical Race Theory: The Key Writings That Formed the Movement* (New York, The New Press, 1995), at 320.

[18] Bob Marley and the Wailers, 'Rat Race,' *Rastaman Vibration* (New York, Island Records, 1976).

[19] W Rodney, *The Groundings with My Brothers* (London, Bogle-L'Ouverture Publications, 1969), at 12.

[20] This idea has been adopted from Beyer's piece. By republic, I am referring to a political community where both the needs of the individual and the needs of the community are balanced for the greatest good.

[21] R Steffens, 'Bob Marley: Rasta Warrior' in NS Murrell, William D Spencer, and AA McFarlane (eds), *Chanting Down Babylon: The Rastafari Reader* (Philadelphia, Temple University Press, 1998), at 262.

reconstruction with regard to race—truly began. Marley sang in front of a defeated Prince Charles:

Every man got a right
To decide his own destiny
An in this judgment
There is no partiality
So arms in arms, with arms
We will fight this little struggle
'Cause that's the only way
We can overcome our little trouble[22]

Those that witnessed Marley's performance claim that the evening was magical. A man, Marley, born to a Black mother from a White father, returned to Africa to construct a societal discourse based on new, oppositionist accounts of race.

Critical race theory deconstructs existing social norms and reconstructs a new foundation: the reggae republic. Critical race scholarship is not neutral or objective. The legal scholarship about race has been neutral which has led to debates where race is not considered. Critical race scholarship notes that legal scholarship cannot be written objectively or with detachment.[23] Understanding that race is constructed through legal power, legal scholarship about race is best understood through reconstruction. Just as reggae addresses racial power and the foundations of race, so to does critical race scholarship. There is no position outside of the discourse of racial power from which one can view race. Race must be an immersable activity. Both critical race scholarship and reggae musicians grasp that importance.

Professor Beyer claims that no objective discourse on race exists because conversations involving race inevitably include political positions.[24] One need only look to critical race scholarship regarding color-blind standards in education and employment. Viewing color-blind standards as an actual bias toward reinforcing the status quo concerning racial power, critical race theorists advocate that such political positions simply mask racial identity through a false neutrality. Rastas, with their disenchantment with politricks, reconstruct a new racial identity through race consciousness and radical political reform. Dr Walter Rodney connects reggae's message and critical race theory:

[22] Bob Marley and the Wailers, 'Zimbabwe,' *Survival* (New York, Island Records, 1979).

[23] K Crenshaw, N Gotanda, G Peller, and K Thomas (eds), *Critical Race Theory: The Key Writings That Formed the Movement* (New York, The New Press, 1995), at xiii. See Richard Delgado and Jean Stefancic, *Critical Race Theory: An Introduction* (New York University Press, 2001).

[24] Beyer 2000 above n 1, at 546.

> The white world defines who is white, and who is black. In the USA if one is not white, then one is black; in Britain, if one is not white then one is coloured; in South Africa, one can be white, coloured or black depending upon how white people classify you. Actually I've found out that a lot of whites literally cannot tell one black from another. Partly this may be due to the fact that they do not personally know many black people, but it reflects a psychological tendency to deny our individuality by refusing to consider us as individual human beings ... there is nothing with which poverty coincides so absolutely as with the colour black—small or large population, hot or cold climates, rich or poor in natural resources—poverty cuts across all of these factors in order to find black people. That association of wealth with whites and poverty with blacks is not accidental. It is the nature of the imperialist relationship that enriches the metropolis at the expense of the colony.[25]

Race consciousness, while not a new idea, is revolutionary because it has been considered taboo by many in mainstream politics. Malcolm X understood the need for a new interpretation. He wrote, 'the old interpretation excluded us. It kept us out.'[26] Mutabaruka, a reggae musician, Rasta philosopher, and Jamaican radio personality, exemplifies reggae's connection to critical race theory in his 1991 album 'Blakk wi Blak...k...k...'[27] Asserting race as integral to the struggle, is both in the style of reggae and critical race scholarship.

Critical race scholarship notes that race has traditionally been understood through an integrationist lens. The conventional result has been defining racial oppression through prejudice and stereotyping based on skin color, and identifying progress by the transcendence of racial consciousness.[28] Reggae and critical race scholarships reconstruct. The process of racial designation has not been simply a linear one. Promoting it as linear implies racial equality as both a goal and inevitable. However, viewing integration as such, implies it as the only solution. Reggae and critical race scholarship redefines the boundaries of race and racism. There is a simultaneous treatment by critical race scholarship and Rastas to treat people as both individuals as well as by racially grouped identification.

The solution to discrimination, according to traditional thought, is equal treatment through neutral norms. Yet, once neutrality replaced discrimination, equal opportunity would follow. Peter Tosh would term such logic as 'foolish, part of the Babylon shitstem.' The integrationist would argue that race is inconsequential except as an unfortunate historical occurrence. I argue that disregarding race is irrational and neither reconstructive nor

[25] Rodney 1969 above n 19, at 16–19.
[26] G Peller, 'Race-Consciousness' in K Crenshaw, N Gotanda, G Peller and K Thomas (eds), *Critical Race Theory: The Key Writings That Formed the Movement* (New York, The New Press, 1995), at 127.
[27] Mutabaruka, *Blakk wi blak...k...k...* (Kingston, Jamaica, Shanachie Records, 1991).
[28] Peller 1995 above n 26, at 127.

deconstructive; it simply maintains the status quo. Professor Patricia Williams, in *Seeing a Color-Blind Future*, writes:

> Race is not a cipher for the whole of life. When I speak of race, you must bear in mind that this not the same thing as saying that race explains everything. Race does not explain all forms of misfortune any more than it explains the color of one's socks. Yet conversations about race so quickly devolve into anxious bouts of wondering why we are not talking about something—anything else, like hard work or personal responsibility or birth order or class or God or the good old glories of the human spirit. All these are worthy topics of conversation, surely, but ... can we consider, for just one moment, *race*.[29]

The confounding problem is that race is a legally constructed norm. Race is neither an essence nor an illusion, but rather a continuous, contradictory, self-reinforcing, plastic process subject to the macro forces of social and political struggle and the micro effects of daily decisions.[30] It is human interaction that has defined race, not biological differentiation. Racial meanings arise from social forces, legal in this sense, creating the racial classifications. While I am not positing that all Rastas or reggae musicians view race in the same complex legal terms that Professor Haney Lopez[31] does, the music shows that they view race as a construct of law. This construct is what they appear to be reconstructing.

Attempting to understand race from a biological standpoint is illusory. Yet, when one looks at race through the lens of a socio-legal microscope, race becomes better understood. Rastas note that race has been a point used to contest their past enslavement. Once such abhorrent treatment is recognised, the inverse seems to be the traditional argument; arguing that equality is based upon race becoming indistinguishable. Critical race scholarship, along with reggae musicians, argues that race must be embraced; it simply must be embraced from a different standpoint. The invocation of leaders like Malcolm X in reggae music exemplifies the reconstructionist components. During the civil rights struggle in the 1950s and 1960s, Malcolm X spoke on the concept of segregated schools. His ingenious remarks, certainly one of a critical race theorist, addressed the heart of race in America. He summarised the integrationist argument to claim that as long as whites were in schools with blacks, then the black children would receive better a education, simply due to the white presence.[32] Malcolm X analysed, dissected,

[29] PJ Williams, *Seeing a Color-Blind Future: The Paradox of Race* (New York, The Noonday Press, 1997), at 63.

[30] IF Haney Lopez, 'The Social Construction of Race' in R Delgado (ed), *Critical Race Theory: The Cutting Edge* (Philadelphia, Temple University Press, 1995), at 193.

[31] *Ibid*, at 196. Due to the infancy of this study, it is impossible to determine if Rastas and self-pronounced critical race scholars both understand race in the same academic/scholarly ways. However, it is my attempt to draw comparisons and avoid judging gradations of knowledge.

[32] Peller 1995 above n 26, at 128.

deconstructed, and reconstructed. He proposed all-Black schools, staffed with 'the type of teacher who has our good at heart.'[33] Critical race scholarship draws upon this notion and so does reggae music.

During the 1960s in Jamaica, color and race were debated. With the election turmoil of the 1970s beginning to fester and PNP leader Michael Manley visiting Ethiopia, race consciousness was at the forefront of national discourse. Rastafarians effectively used their condition (race and class) to dramatise their disagreement with Jamaican politicians.[34] The tone of the demands was rooted in the spirit of the Black Power Movement:

> 'In Jamaica true Black power does not attack white as white, brown as brown. All men are equal. The attack is on white, brown or black as oppressing Afro-Jamaican and as an oppressive and social class.' This position is extremely close to mainstream Rastafarianism.[35]

The Rasta philosophy follows critical race scholarship. For both, race is a legally constructed norm that has assisted in oppressing Blacks throughout the world. Recognising race, embracing it, is a both reggae and critical race scholarship.

One of critical race theories' cornerstones is its incorporation of personal narratives into the scholarship. Reggae music uses the same such narratives. Culture, one of Marley's favorite new bands in the 1970s, sang:

> Oh, what a happenin'
> Pain on the slaveship
> We have been robbed of our
> Even my sister has been stripped
> Still rest on my heart
> Can you imagine the way the people felt
> Travelling from home to Jamaica ...
> After a hard days labor, they took my neighbor
> Place him down his knees, hear me now
> And then the slavemaster climb on his back,
> And mount onto his horse
> That burns into my soul.[36]

[33] *Ibid.*
[34] Keith and Keith 1992 above n 6, at 202.
[35] *Ibid*, at 203. It is worth noting that Rastafarians do not refer, and explicitly deny the reference, that their religion is an 'ism.' They view Rasta as reality and 'isms' as man-made creations.
[36] Culture, 'Still Rest My Heart,' *Three Sides to My Story* (Kingston, Jamaica, Shanachie Records, 1991).

The crux of the message is the result of race as a legal construct, in this case, slavery. Derrick Bell, one of the founders of critical race theory, incorporates narrative into his work and like Rastas, introduces the chord of race consciousness.[37]

Many mainstream critics dismissed black jazz as nonmusical. Various complaints have been lodged against critical race theory as unscholarly.[38] However, just as black jazz and reggae music do not follow conventional tones and meters, and critical race theorists do not follow traditional academic paths, it is the revolutionary nature that is intriguing, similar, and worthy of study. The metaphor of reggae captures the resistance movement within critical race theory. Critical race theorists have created a reggae republic.

VI

LINER NOTES: CONCLUSION

The first verse of critical race theory is the revolutionary tone with which the theorists describe the past. Giving a history of race unlike contemporary scholars, critical race scholars use the history as their weapon. The death of racism in law that jazz music envisioned has been assisted by reggae artists. The oppositional aims of the Rastafarians have changed the legal and political discourse on law and music. Deconstruction was the answer.

The second verse of critical race theory involves the continuous deconstruction coupled with new reconstructive efforts. From the narrative approaches, critical race scholarship has created a republic: the reggae republic. The republic consists of race conscious scholars and musicians who have expanded the metaphor in order to bring about significant and meaningful change. The rules, which have been social constructs, are not followed by critical race theorists. This, by no means, makes the work less scholarly, simply more unsettling to the status quo.

The reggae metaphor in critical race theory reflects the revolutionary aspect of both genres. The music teaches us the communal aspect of meaning-making, a notion that legal thinking should take into account.[39] Music becomes the truth—truths about culture, law, tolerance, belonging—race.[40] Reggae music, like critical race theory becomes the protector, not simply of rights, but of legal consciousness, specifically with regard to race. Critical race theorists absorb societal variables and develop a legal theory from the culture. Reggae musicians absorb societal norms and comment on them.

[37] Beyer 2000 above n 1, at 547.

[38] *Ibid* (citing Mark Tushnet's criticisms of narrative scholars such as Patricia Williams).

[39] D Manderson and D Claudill, 'Music and Legal Theory: An Interdisciplinary Workshop Introduction' (May-July 1999) *Cardozo Law Review*, 1328.

[40] *Ibid.*

They both incorporate society's inequalities and give poignant criticism of the imbalance. I have argued, cursorily, that the incorporation by reggae musicians is in fact an aspect of critical race theory. Ziggy Marley, following in the footsteps of his famous father, sings:

From the slaveship to the chain
From the taskmaster's whip to my brain
Kidnapped and slaved, raped and killed
By the lynch Klan again and again.
Now I know you don't care about me.
I'm just a nigger walking down the street
Code of silence is there
Yet your actions speak so loud and clear.
Diallo's killer is going free
Paid by society.
Now I know you don't care about me.
... Amadou Diallo they killed him for nothing
No crime he did not do.
And just like him they suffer for no crime they did not do.
Amadou Diallo, Amadou Diallo, reggae music knows your name.[41]

Marley's message here is one that critical race scholarship should be aware of. Marley seems to be arguing that once reggae becomes part of the equation, change occurs. Wailing to the spirit of Amadou Diallo, the unarmed black man shot 41 times on his doorstep in New York City, the song seems to embody an effort by Marley to calm Diallo (in spirit) and society that his death shall not be in vain. It is a form of reconstruction.

Reggae music is legal revolution, as is critical race theory. Both refuse to continue the cycle of traditional discourse on race. Race, understood as a legal construct, can be reassessed and through that assessment, education based on new definitions of race are introduced. In 1979, Bob Marley sang of the concept of race in one of his most rebellious songs before his passing in 1981. He wailed:

We refuse to be
What you wanted us to be
We are what we are
That's the way it's going to be.

[41] Ziggy Marley and the Melody Makers, 'I Know You Don't Care About Me,' *Live Vol I* (New York, Elektra Entertainment Group Inc, 2000).

You can't educate I
For no equal opportunity
Talking about my freedom
People's freedom and liberty.[42]

Critical race theory can do more than speak in narratives, it can sing.[43]

[42] Bob Marley, 'Babylon System,' *Survival* (New York, Island Records, 1979).
[43] This theme has been taken from a symposium held in 1998 at the Benjamin N Cardozo Law School.

13

Cromer's Olde England and the Dome's New Britain: Two Same/Different Imageries of the Law of Britain's Empire

RONNIE LIPPENS

I

INTRODUCTION

NATION, IN BENEDICT Anderson's words, is a work of imagination.[1] As such, it does not—if one is to accept Lacan's distinction of human orders of communication[2]—belong as much to the symbolic order, ie the order of signs and language, in short: the realm of cognition, as it does to the imaginary order, ie the order of images, senses and affect, in short: the realm of emotion. Nation, one might think, is first and foremost (a) *matter* of beating hearts and secreting glands, of vision and scenery, of images and imagery, indeed of *imagination*. Nations, somewhere in-between Anderson and Lacan, are forced/forged, first and foremost, with materials of imagination; with images of rolling hills and undulating fields and spires and your everyday baker shop; with images of smiling faces and waving hair; pictures of school and holiday outings and the sensation that comes back, again and again, when one evokes, again and again, the scenery of one's favourite, loved and much-visited town. Nation is a matter of imagination, and imagination is a matter of imagery and images. These bring us lines of identity/difference. This may be all the more so in an age of 'un-reason', of un-fixing and floating signs.

This essay will compare two imageries of nation—*(imagi)nations*—that have emerged on the British Isles, a place where considerable hostility

[1] B Anderson, *Imagined Communities* (London, Verso, 1982).
[2] Eg in J Lacan, *Télévision* (Paris, Editions du Seuil, 1974).

towards images, has such deep historical and cultural roots.[3] The first of these imageries is a textual one that lurks in a passage that was written around the turn of the last century. Written during the first decade of the twentieth century by Lord Cromer, at the height of Empire, it imagines a thriving colonial nation which he, Cromer, confidently and fearlessly calls 'England' (note: not 'Britain'). The second image of Britain is one that was seen around the time of the latest Millennium on and below the Millennium Dome's canvas: the Dome, declared expression and aspiration of what some have called 'New Britain'. Note that the Dome talks about a 'Britain'. Not the old Britain of Empire and domination, not Cromer's Britain, that is, 'England', no, a 'New' Britain, some space beyond domination and past wrongs, but, nevertheless, once again expressing/aspiring nothing less than the Best. How can we imagine the Dome's imagery, looking at its material lines of identity/difference? What was the *matter* at the Dome? Those are the questions of this essay.

There's almost a century of imagination that lies between Cromer's and the Dome's imageries. This essay, then, tries to see (or, to *imagine*, one might say) whether Cromer's and the Dome's imageries are similar, or different, and to what extent they are. Seeing lines of identity/difference is a matter of images, of imagination, a matter of emotion, dislike and affection, and pumping hearts. The reader is advised to imagine this when reading what is about to follow.

II

CROMER'S OLDE ENGLAND: EARTHY NOMADICS OF DIVINE BELONGING

Edward Said, in *Orientalism,* quotes Lord Cromer, Britain's chief colonial administrator in Egypt around the turn of the last century, at length. It's worthwhile to have a close look at this extended quote, since it evokes a particular imagery of England and Englishness. Lord Cromer writes in the first decade of the twentieth century:

> Can it be any matter for surprise that the Egyptian, with his light intellectual ballast, fails to see that some fallacy often lies at the bottom of the Frenchman's reasoning, or that he prefers the rather superficial brilliancy of the Frenchman to the plodding, unattractive industry of the Englishman or the German ? Look, again, at the theoretical perfection of French administrative systems, at their elaborate detail, and at the provision which is apparently made to meet every possible contingency which may arise. Compare these

[3] See eg P Goodrich, Y Hachamovitch, 'Time out of Mind: An Introduction to the Semiotics of Common Law' in P Fitzpatrick (ed), *Dangerous Supplements* (London, Pluto Press, 1991); P Goodrich, *Oedipus Lex: Psychoanalysis, History, Law* (Berkeley, University of California Press, 1995).

features with the Englishman's practical systems, which lay down rules as to a few main points, and leave a mass of detail to individual discretion. The half-educated Egyptian naturally prefers the Frenchman's system, for it is to all outward appearance more perfect and more easy of application. He fails, moreover, to see that the Englishman desires to elaborate a system which will suit the facts with which he has to deal, whereas the main objection to applying French administrative procedures to Egypt is that the facts have but too often to conform to the ready-made system.[4]

Apart from reading some blatant disdain in this *orientalist* text, we may be able to learn something here about the way members of the British imperial *élite* liked to imagine Britain and Britishness. Cromer, however, expressly refers to 'Englishmen', even in a text on the role of Britain in its Empire. Let us continue with 'Englishmen' here, bearing in mind, however, that the Empire Lord Cromer wrote for, was British. It is interesting to note that Cromer imagines England not only in contrast to Egypt, the land of 'half-educated' Egyptians, but also in sharp contrast to France, place where administrative systems of 'theoretical perfection' are being made. England, according to Cromer, is neither a place of theory nor a place of perfection. But it is a place of education, and this, education, seems to set it apart from places like Egypt. Education is no business of theory or perfection, still less of theoretical perfection. On the contrary, education, like administration, if it is to suit Englishmen, is likely to be a practical business whereby only a 'few main points' may be sufficient to lead pupils into the realm of Englishness, and into the realm of Empire. This realm is one where 'a mass of detail' is to be left to 'individual discretion'. In a way, Lord Cromer was evoking an image of England as a place of incessant movement, a place where a multitude of little individual moves occur and end up 'suiting' whichever 'facts' one 'has to deal with'. An uncomplicated place, Cromer's England, full of little wriggling facts and moves, a stream of practicalities flowing in-between a few main rules and points. This England is unlike Egypt's empty desert of ignorant immobility. It's also different from the sterility of France's 'theoretically perfect' impracticality and uselessness. Cromer's imagery has much in common with John Ruskin's imagination of gothic architecture (especially with regards to its unsteady, somewhat shaky lines and forms) as the most important space of and for Englishness. As Ian Baucom has recently argued, in his insightful *Out of Place*, Ruskin recognised Englishness in the trembling hands of his imagined builders of gothic buildings; trembling hands that are prepared to produce asymmetrical figures and zigzagging lines if 'the facts' demand it; trembling hands that only need a few rules and main points from where to start on a winding, bumpy road of imperfection and ad hoc adaptations.[5]

[4] E Said, *Orientalism* (London, Penguin, 1995), at 212.
[5] I Baucom, *Out of Place* (Durham, Duke University Press, 1999), at 41–74.

Note also that Egypt, or the Orient in general, in Cromer's imagination, is a more or less feminised creature. A *courtisane* perhaps, uneducated or half-educated at the most, incapable even of building and asserting herself, who therefore has to choose between the steady feet-in-the-earth sturdiness of 'the Englishman' on the one hand, and the more or less whimsical vanity of the 'theoretically perfect' Frenchman. Also 'the Frenchman', in Cromer's imagination, seems to appear as somewhat feminised. No wonder, then, that in Cromer's imagination, there's that constant threat of uneducated Egyptians, who by definition seem to lack the ability to distinguish the things that really matter from superficial decoration, and who are drawn towards all those luring but utterly useless theoretical niceties and perfections of 'the Frenchman'. France, and Frenchmen, in Cromer's imagination, are on the verge of being orientalised, while Orientals and Egyptians, uneducated as they are, seem to emerge as even lesser versions of French superficiality. And indeed, listen to what Cromer writes about 'the vivacious and cosmopolitan Frenchman, who', in sharp contrast to the Englishman, 'does not know what shyness means, and who in ten minutes is apparently on terms of intimate friendship with any casual acquaintance he may chance to make'. The half-educated Egyptian stands by, 'looks coldly on the Englishman, and rushes into the arms of the Frenchman'.[6]

The Englishman, Cromer imagines, is he who is in no need of too many rules ('just a few main points' will suffice) when he goes on with his daily feet-on-the-ground, feet-in-the-ground work. Standing on firm ground, far away from theoretical niceties that blind him with their seeming perfections, the Englishman works facts. He builds his world and his self with solid facts. Who he is, and what he is, he is because he himself made it out of raw, solid facts. He did it all by himself, fully independent from surroundings. He did not have and does not have any need for theoretical perfections in order to do the job. What he is, and what he does, he is and does by his own discretion. He is his own alpha and omega, and both these are made of undeniable, concrete, solid facts. Unlike the Frenchman, who dishonestly uses theoretical brilliance to blind others and to lure them into his nets, the Englishman is of the honest, *what-you-see-is-what-you-get* kind.

England, in Cromer's imagination, is not only the space where Englishmen live. It is also *like* the Englishman. If it has fashioned an Empire, then it has done so because other peoples and nations have joined it through a recognition of England's solid honesty. They joined the Empire because, watching the Englishman at work, they came to realise that the facts of Empire speak for themselves, and cannot be denied or avoided. This is why pink is the predominant colour in atlases. Other peoples and nations have ultimately chosen to join the Empire, because they realised that this is an inevitable fact of life, that speaks for itself. No tricks, no perfection, no brilliance, no theory, no ruse was necessary to build this Empire. The

[6] E Said, above n 4, at 211.

Empire is the result of inevitable pragmatics, of inevitable facts of life. Experts in working the solid facts of life, the English have fashioned an Empire that is entirely the inevitable result of their working the facts of life. Unlike the French colonial system, which is the unstable result of volatile theoretical perfections, lures and tricks, the Empire simply *is* a fact of life. The French system is dependent on the lures and tricks (brilliant and showing perfection, yes, but volatile and superficial nevertheless) through which it manages to keep the system together. The Empire isn't dependent on anything except itself. The Frenchman, as well as France, ultimately, are the passive recipients of others' choices, of the latter's willingness to let themselves be blinded by the brilliance of French theoretical perfections. The Englishman, as well as England, are the active originators of their Empire: by working the mere pragmatics of life, Empire emerged.

What is it that articulates the Englishman and England? Something has to bind their enormous diversity. In Cromer's imagination, this 'something' seems to boil down to a few rules, to 'a few main points'. A few lines, perhaps a few broad strokes, then, allow for a dazzling variety of acts of life, and the equally diverse Englishmen working them, not only to articulate England, but Empire as well. Those few lines and points are probably not just plain facts of life. They have to be stated, they have to be forged somewhere. Ultimately, they will have to be forced. What is this thing? It could be force, and the forms of domination it takes: perhaps hierarchical force is that un-English thing that keeps Englishmen apart/together (that keeps them apart precisely by bringing them together, and that brings them together, precisely by keeping them apart), that binds nations into Britain and glues peoples into an Empire. This, hierarchical force, authority and domination, could be the possibly un-English thing, that has to be stated, that has to be forced somewhere, in order to let Englishmen keep on going with the daily pragmatics and with the workings of inevitable facts of life, in order also to let England be England, and Empire be Empire. This thing has to be forced from somewhere and onto somewhere. 'Just a few main points' ... Cromer does not want to go into much detail here.

The essence of England, in Cromer's imagery, remains largely unspoken. Perhaps it needn't be spoken, after all? Perhaps it *is* a fact of life, too obvious to mention, after all? Unlike the French, whose essential characteristic is the lure of *égalité, fraternité, et liberté,* the English (or so Cromer's imaginary seems to suggest) do seem to have an uneasy relationship with hierarchical force that lies at the very heart of Englishness. 'Just a few points', says Cromer, and apparently it only takes just a few words to say it. Saying more, perhaps, would have been problematic: force might have shown through *as* force, unsettling a delicate balance. Saying less might have been equally problematic: no force at all might have shown through *as* force; nothing might have been able to articulate Englishmen, England, or Empire. In Cromer's imagination, only 'a few points' may be able to articulate the Englishman.

Cromer's England appears as a space of sturdy pragmatists, each of whom works the real, perfectly clear, unmediated facts of life, wandering through a *green and pleasant* landscape (Cromer's England probably is the countryside), flexibly forging paths while reproducing a space that, apparently, only needs a few words, a few main points to emerge. It's a space of openness and opportunity (it only takes of few main points ...), a space of force (it takes a few main points !). It appears as a space that is wandered by sturdy workers of the facts of life, who may use its openness to roam and expand, forge new paths, cope with obstacles and hindrances, and rework the wilderness of theoretical niceties and mediations into an orderly, divine garden of plain and inevitable, practical facts of life.[7] Something nomadic lurks in Cromer's imagery. Like nomads who roam empty deserts, in-between scarce resources and sparsely scattered beacons, or like nomads who roam plains and jungles of relative abundance, in-between a myriad of beacons and points of reference, Cromer's Englishmen seem to go on with life somewhere in-between rout(in)es of flexibility and flexible rout(in)es. Their time is Now. They are in no need of theoretical niceties as those will in no way help them in or through life, in or through the daily pragmatics of the inevitable. They don't need big ideas that build towards grand futures. Just a few words will do. Just a few main points will set the stringent parameters of harsh and sturdy, nomadic life.

Nomadic life seems to run its course through a series of sturdy routines that, however, at a second glance, seem to be made of intricate webs of little opportunities and obstacles. A nomad's life often consists of innumerable little occurrences along the road that need to be flexibly coped with and turned, as it were, into routines which, in turn, it is hoped, may then offer renewed strength and resources for further flexible *routinisations*. During such often highly inventive routinisations, all kinds of novelties that get thrown up along nomadic tracks tend to be de-invented towards routine, towards an *order*, towards a silent *command* of (but also a command *from*) tradition. A nomad's Now often has an eye on the past. The past is where selves and futures are shaped. The past is where nomads often go back to when they build and shape Now, each and every time they have to cope with the never-ending occurrences their wandering life of rout(in)e is made of. Somehow, the orderly and forceful routines of nomadic life are forged, every minute of the day, through countless little, inventive wanderings and flexible de-inventions. Something of these nomadics lingers on in a much practised English pastime, *rambling*, or roaming the English countryside. Ramblers make use of routinely produced 'public footpaths' that snake and mesh across the green and pleasant properties and public lands of England. They forge their own path through a dazzling variety of possible trajectories.

[7] See also E Darian-Smith, 'Legal Imagery in the 'Garden of England' (1995) *Indiana Journal of Global Legal Studies* 2.

So many tracks and routines have produced this labyrinthine mesh of winding, criss-crossing 'public footpaths'. So many tracks and routines have come out of this labyrinthine mesh of wanderings. So much order has come out of so much roaming. So many *roamings* have reproduced the orderly routines, the *commands* of the network of 'public footpaths'.

In a recently published essay, the late Raphael Samuel recalled the many countryside walks he used to make with his mother. Like so many others, they seemed to have no specific interest in plants or wildlife, or 'nature' as such. 'In short', Samuel says, 'we had no historical sense of the countryside, no feel for natural history. Our reverence for nature was quite abstract',[8] as if the landscape were a series of meandering and meshing *surfaces,* the roaming of which, as such, in itself, would be the thing that's sought after, something down-to-earth, far away from the niceties, novelties and images of the city and the suburb. The mere muddling through, the mere roaming and wandering, 'in the abstract', the mere feet-in-the-ground (re)producing of tracks, the mere flexible reproductions of routine, the mere routinely coping with the intricacies of sudden occurrences, the mere pragmatics of life: this is what ramblers, such as Samuel, seem to be attracted to. They want to roam, 'in the abstract', on and in-between mere surfaces. They seem to want to flexibly *routinise*, 'in the abstract', as close as possible to the soil. They seem to want to roam as close as possible to the orders, the flexibly reproduced orders, the routinely reproduced orders, of the countryside; as close as possible to the orders of *the country* ... Roaming the English countryside only takes a few words. A few main points, a few signposts will do. A few main points enable one to roam across the landscape in labyrinthine ways and to work the inevitable, earthy, *common*sensical facts of life. A few main points will force a dazzling number of labyrinthine wanderings into (but also *onto*) the orders and routines of a few signposts.

Nomads are often advised to travel light. A few words, a few main points suffice. The openness between those points enables them to proceed with their meandering life and will allow them to swerve into the tracks of the maze of life. A few words, a few main points ... the *force* of their closure will push nomads towards established routines of flexibility; will command them *into* the orders and rigidity of past traditions; will ultimately lead them back to the core, to the inevitable core of the maze. Travelling light should facilitate such swervings. It should equally come in handy during *routinisations* of niceties and novelties that have popped up along the winding roads of nomadic life.

Cromer's image of England, of Olde England, resembles the one Peter Goodrich has been at pains to trace in his many historical and iconographical writings on English 'common law'.[9] This common law, unwritten,

[8] R Samuel, 'Country Visiting : A Memoir', in *Island Stories. Unravelling Britain* (London, Verso, 1999), at 141.

[9] P Goodrich, *Oedipus Lex: Psychoanalysis, History, Law* (Berkeley, University of California Press, 1995).

elusive, of labyrinthine enigma, it was alleged amongst 16th century legal scholars, originates in the nebulae of times immemorial. Common Law, the ways of Olde England, are eternal. Like a divine soul it resides at the core, at the heart of the maze of England. It allows Englishmen to wander and roam their lives, while it also forces them to naturally work the facts of life from and towards a divine order. Probably since Henry's Act of Supremacy (since Elizabeth, says Samuel), the King's order, the King's command, 'just a few words', *force* (both expression *as well as* factory of common law), turned into eternal divine order. Since that moment, Englishness and England ceased to be a matter of ethnicity, Samuel goes on to claim, but 'attached instead to those of rule and superiority'.[10] Elusive, and largely unwritten (who, asks Goodrich, needs to write, to fix or to grasp something which is known to come divinely naturally to a chosen people?), this common law turned into a divine law, and housed the eternal, ever-ungraspable soul of England, of eternal England, of God's kingdom. England, the home of God; England, the home of gods; god-like England, all-powerful; all-rightful, where superiority comes divinely *naturally*, in and through everyday routines, ie the unmediated pragmatics of nomads. Common Law does with as few words as possible ... just a few words ... just a few main points. A divine order indeed, Olde England, where life can and inevitably, naturally will (be forced to) do as much as possible without images, representations, signs, 'theoretical perfections' (it's all just 'superficial brilliancy', says Cromer), novelties and niceties, and other lures.

Fragments of this imagery of Olde England have slipped into Cromer's imagination of English superiority. However, not only Cromer's imaginations proved unable to resist this image of Olde England. In Hyndman's early search for socialism, *England for all*, for example, which was written some 25 years before Cromer's text, one is able to read not only very critical remarks on Britain's colonial policy, but also lines that state that 'ordinary Englishmen were conquering an empire just in the way of everyday business'.[11] Also in Hyndman's view, Empire came naturally. It may be needless to stress here that also to Hyndman, the socialist future, back in 1881, lay in the past, in a rural, mediaeval England, where 'sturdy freedom was based upon property and good living'.[12] These are nomadics of earthy, divine imperfection, and they seem to be light-years away from France's 'theoretically perfect', 'superficial brilliancy', from its 'administration' of idolatry and other ungodly lures and tricks. Cromer's image of Olde England (to use Baucom's words here) is one that sketches an England of *belonging*, less one of becoming. Un-mediated workers of the inevitable facts of life, living and reproducing the eternal, divine order of England, Englishmen *belong* to that space that allows them to live their meandering

[10] R Samuel, above n 8, at 48.
[11] HM Hyndman, *England for All* (London, Gilbert & Rivington, 1881), at 132.
[12] *Ibid*, at 8.

lives the orderly, eternal, divine, English way. They *belong* there: living in that space, on that soil, is what being English is all about. One cannot be English if that space, that soil, this earth, that feet-in-the-ground space, is not around—which, as Baucom has illustrated, was probably why English colonials made a tremendous effort to mimic England, complete with cricket pitches (just a few rules and main points and lines on the pitch), gothic architecture (trembling, imperfect, divine order), greens and village scenery (the workings of everyday factual life), throughout the Empire. With an eye on the elusive, though eternal past of belonging, highly suspicious of all kinds of novelties, niceties, theoretical perfections and other *becomings*, the Englishman works the facts of life towards the stable, eternal core that lies at the centre of the maze of life. No words, no images, just a few main points.

III

THE DOME'S NEW BRITAIN: GRAVITY-DEFYING NOMADICS OF MEDIOCRE EVASION

Let us now have a look at the Millennium Dome. The first impression one may have when looking at the Dome, is that it very much resembles a tent. Quickly pitched by New Britons, a very temporary home, its destiny in 2000 was unsure. The Dome hovers about ten metres above ground level, as if it will not, can not or should not touch the earth.

THE NEW MILLENNIUM EXPERIENCE 19 October 1998 Photo ref: MX(A)191098.1/10 Aerial view of the Millennium Dome on the Greenwich Peninsula* (NMEC/QA Photos)

The Dome hovers; it is unlikely to settle down. It threatens, no, has already announced that it will leave very shortly. To be pitched elsewhere, or to be forgotten. For the time being, it just hovers: a temporary, open, white canvas, a quickly pitched shelter for New Britons. A place of belonging, yes, where New Britons may express themselves, a place where New Britons *have* expressed themselves. A place where New Britons belong, yes, but also a place where New Britain may *become*. In other words, a factory of and for New Britain ... a highly mobile, hovering factory, quickly pitched and quickly gone. Gone are the days of solid, rock-solid, earthy systems of welfare.[13] 'Gravity-defying' may be a word that can be used to describe the factory of-for New Britain. This may be so for various reasons. Of course, at the time of the Millennium, Britain was the scene of an immense yearning for cyberspace and e-commerce (quickly pitched, quickly gone) while investments in manufacturing, down-to-earth manufacturing, were on the decrease, gradually causing images of industrial Britain to fade away. But there's another sense in which the Dome's defiance of gravity seems to have been so much a part of its image. In the Millennium Commission's publicity leaflet on the Dome, issued the night before the Dome opened its attractions to the public, one could read about the 'gravity defying' Mind Zone. It is the mind that, according to New Britons, is, or has to be gravity defying. It is the Mind that has to defy earth and earthy matters. It is the Mind, that volatile, flexible, ever-moving zone of words and thoughts and images, that gravity-defying Mind, that has come to lie at the heart of New Britain.

IV

MIND ZONE

THE MILLENNIUM EXPERIENCE— Computer generated illustration of the 'Mind' zone in the Dome, centrepiece of the UK's millennium celebrations (Copyright Hayes Davidson)

This may remind one of Paul Virilio's reading of Howard Hughes, powerful ex-centric. Hughes flew aeroplanes and gathered speed. In other words, he defied gravity, and this he did in order 'not to be identifiable',[14] 'not to inhabit'[15] a specific, fixed place, least of all earth, down-to-earth earth.

[13] I'm grateful to Nick Lee who has suggested to me this link: 'Dome-tent-temporary' versus 'welfare state'.

[14] P Virilio, *The Aesthetics of Disappearance* (New York, Semiotext(e), 1991), at 23.

[15] *Ibid*, at 25.

Hughes spent the last years of his life as a recluse, as an unidentifiable, absent, *gravity defying*, nameless power, as a pure surface of force, as an enigmatic (labyrinthine) ghost that works behind the scenes. The Dome, the white canvas, white space of New Britain, may have something of Hughes' unidentifiable, nameless, speed-gathering, absent power. Mere force seems to flow on its surface; an unearthly, gravity-defying force; an elusive force that seems to evade all earthy fixities. A force that seems to want to whirl in the elusive world of Baudrillard's hyperspace, a zone of mediation and image, where each and every origin or end, each and every core or centre, only plays illusory games.[16]

Upon entering the Dome, one quickly got enmeshed in its labyrinthine intestines. 'An empty space, packed with light, sounds and shapes', the Millennium Commission's leaflet said about the Rest Zone. One wonders whether this phrase had not been originally coined for the Dome as a whole. Under its huge, near-open, hovering canvas, a huge empty space was filled with moving shapes and lights, sounds, queues and flows. One would perhaps be lured into saying: packed with images. Upon closer inspection, however, this may be illusion. Images, in the Dome, seemed to appear as mere surfaces, not unlike the Dome's white, egg-shaped hovering canvas. Mere light, mere sounds, mere shapes, mere surfaces, mere movement of criss-crossing surfaces: this is what the Dome's labyrinthine space looked like. A rambler, roamer of England's network of 'public footpaths', may have had a similar experience walking the Dome's internal labyrinth. 'Quite abstract', said Samuel, when he described his mother's (as well as his own) interest in the English countryside and the surfaces they moved in and through or past, during long and winding walks. Quite abstract indeed was the Dome's interior: moving shapes and light, moving surfaces, sounds that have caused so many commentators to complain about the blandness and bleakness, about the *superficiality* of it all. Surfaces. Superficiality. And labyrinthine movement in a centreless, gravity-defying, evasive Dome. New Britain.[17]

Something of Olde England's elusive, divine common law also seems to have lingered in the Dome, on its surfaces. Some of Olde England's common lawyers' hostility towards images and imagery and signs of idolatry (which Peter Goodrich has been able to evoke so strikingly) seems to have gushed on the Dome's surfaces. Surprisingly little in the Dome was allowed to crystallise. Movement and *unfixity* were predominant; images and signs were not allowed to fix something, least of all meaning. Fixing meaning, or just plain fixity might go against New Britain, this realm of gravity-defying unfixity. Images in the Dome tried to appear as surfaces, as mere surfaces. The products of nomadic New Britons, the working stations for the

[16] Eg J Baudrillard, *The Illusion of the End* (Cambridge, Polity, 1994).

[17] R Lippens, 'Greenwich, 1 January 2000. De-inventing the Law of Britain in a Tent' 13 *International Journal for the Semiotics of Law* 3.

production of New Britons and New Britain, they seemed to hold all and nothing, all *and* nothing. The body in the Body Zone (actually it looked like two bodies) was not allowed to be a clear image of a body: a sexless, polished surface, it was supposed to attract all identities inside (although none in particular). It allowed for all kinds of difference, though none really.

IV

BODY ZONE

THE MILLENNIUM EXPERIENCE—Computer generated illustration of the 'Body' zone in the Dome, centrepiece of the UK's millennium celebrations (Copyright Hayes Davidson)

As a 'blank space' of pure movement, pure 'motility'[18] it allowed flux, and prevented fixity and closure. Visitors who climbed (gravity-defying indeed) into the body's equally bland and bleak, surface-like interior, passed a giant pumping heart (the seat of emotion; birthplace of nation and community) that may have reminded them of the need to move along. In the Faith Zone, they walked past a life-size drawing of the child Christ, whose genitalia were polished away, leaving the child more naked than naked.

V

FAITH

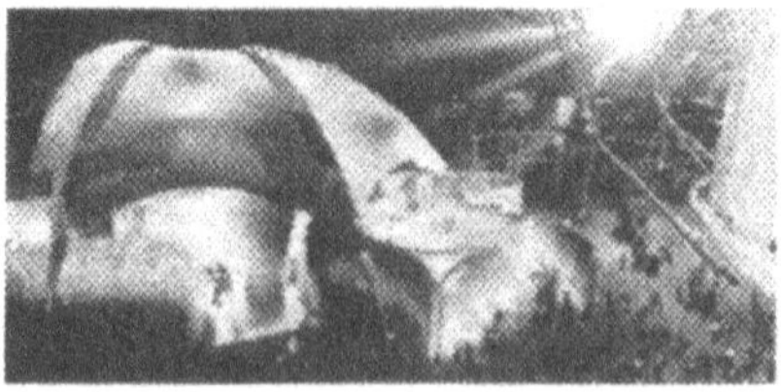

THE MILLENNIUM EXPERIENCE—Computer generated illustration of the 'Faith' zone in the Dome, centrepiece of the UK's millennium celebrations (Copyright Hayes Davidson)

[18] K Hetherington and N Lee, 'Social Order and the Blank Figure', 18 *Environment and Planning* D.

This may have been Olde England's divinely superior hostility towards images showing through. Perhaps it was just a politically correct way (the New British way) of emasculating divinity. Or else it was part of the Dome's gravity-defying force that was desperate to show itself on unidentifiable, unnameable surfaces, and that used this *non-identifiability* to steer and control, to govern forcefully, like Howard Hughes, allowing for all and everything, but nothing really, allowing for all *and* nothing, in labyrinthine ways.

The Dome had no real centre. In that it was different from the old Celtic maze, the remnants of which are still visible about one mile to the south, at Maze Hill station, South Greenwich. Old Celts, Ancient Britons, used to walk the maze, trying to find the 'path of wisdom',[19] that is, they tried to find that *one* path to that *one* wisdom, ie an elusive wisdom that supposedly lay at the origin of all, somewhere at the heart of life, in the centre of the maze. Walking the maze of life towards this origin, towards this centre, for ancient Celts, was walking backwards. It meant walking towards that one Final, eternal destination that lay in an almost unreachable past. Walking the maze, then, was ultimately about finding and walking one road, towards one ultimate, central space, while, in the process, losing all kinds of novelties and niceties, losing all imageries, and hoping to emerge from the maze re-born, that is, re-born into the One, though ever-elusive final truth of a past, eternal origin.

Some of this Ancient Britain survived in Olde England's divine common law, and, ultimately in images, like Lord Cromer's, of a nation of down-to-earth Englishmen who free themselves from novelties, niceties and 'theoretical perfections'. Some of this *Old Britishness* re-appears in ramblers' meandering, criss-crossing wanderings and swervings which reproduce an age-old network, 'just a few main points', just a few posts, a network of 'public footpaths', the ultimate, final backbone of Olde England's country(side). Something of this Ancient Britain slipped onto and into the Dome as well. Could it have been otherwise, in a place that wanted to hold all (and nothing)? But there was difference. The Dome, indeed, had no real centre, and neither did its empty space ('packed with sounds, light and shapes') have an ultimate 'path of wisdom' in it. The Dome did not have a network of fixed signposts for visitors to use in order to trace their individual, labyrinthine tracks. There seems to have been *only* labyrinthine possibilities on surfaces. There was no centre in the Dome. Well, yes, there was a central area, but it was nothing like a Final destination. Actually, it was a stageless stage (there was no fixity there either) where, high above ground level, a gravity-defying show of trapeze artists took place. 'Five times a day', said the Millennium Commission's leaflet. In the Dome's central area, there seems to have been nothing but 'an empty space', 'packed with light, sounds, and shapes' of a moving, gravity-defying, 'dramatic, love story of a boy of

[19] J Attali, *The Labyrinth in Culture and Society. Pathways to Wisdom* (Berkeley, North Atlantic Books, 1999).

dreams and a girl of action as epoch-making events overtake their worlds'. No world was allowed to remain, or just to be. No world was allowed to fix into or onto some kind of centre. All had to be overtaken in and through gravity-defying, earth-evading swings and swerves.

Who needs to write and who needs images, when the labyrinthine meanders of dreams, when the swinging actions, when pure movement, when the *blankness* of superficialities are being put to work to express as well as reproduce the New greatness of Britain. 'One amazing day', the leaflet said, 'inside the millennium's most awe-inspiring, eye-opening, mind-boggling day out'. One amazing day. One *mazing* day. In a way, in labyrinthine ways, some of Olde England's imaginations of superiority were still around in the Dome. Their *force*, however, was not so much centred anymore. This force seemed to rush restlessly, scattering in and on surfaces. It looked as if the eternal, divine soul of Olde England, in the Dome, in a gravity-defying *move*, gushed out of its elusive, unspoken and unspeakable though earthy core, into and onto labyrinthine, superficial nooks and crannies, where it scattered and splintered all over the place, though nowhere in particular. If New Britons are still to work the facts of life, in the Dome, they were likely to do so, they were lured to do so, they were commanded to do so, they may have chosen to do so in a gravity-defying manner, watching and walking surfaces, following no specific tracks, going to no specific centres, in an empty space that holds all, and nothing. All *and* nothing. This, perhaps, was the centre of the Dome (mind : *not* the centre *within* the Dome) : its ever-moving centrelessness, its unearthy and unbounded divinity that was present everywhere but nowhere in particular.

There's something else to be said about the Dome. There's something else about New Britain. The Dome was pitched on Greenwich peninsula. A *meridianal* place, Greenwich. The navel of the world, where all and everything converges, and where all and everything comes from. A meridianal place indeed, where day and night meet. An interstitial place, perhaps, that possibly holds both, and none, both and none. An absolute centre (divine, superior, forceful, luring irresistibly, commanding the inevitable) while, at the same time, also a boundary to all places imaginable. A place (again) fit for a divine Immovable Mover? An inevitable origin, and a final destiny it may be, and yet, at the same time, it's just a passageway, a zone of transition from the past to the future, from the one to the other, indeed a zone in-between zones, a zone where the one is present (though not quite) while the other is not there yet (though its presence is felt everywhere).

The Dome (New Britain) is also a meridianal place in another sense: it's located right in-between the City (place of flexible financial nomadics; place of possible plenty; place of routinised flexibility) and the South East of London (place of a nomadics of scarcity; place of desperate tracks amongst scarce resources; place of flexibilising routines). The Dome wanted both. And none. It wanted to (dis)connect both and none. It wanted to (dis)connect histories and geographies of despair and opportunity. The interstitial space which it occupies on Greenwich peninsula does this work of (dis)connection (this work probably *is* New Britain) through a labyrinthine mesh of gravity-defying, evading, elusive surfaces. In an era of widening gaps between North and South, between the country and the city, between the City and the South East, between the 'four nations' of a trembling and devolving unity, the force of New Britain can, apparently, only express or show itself, and can only aspire to be force, to force itself, to *force,*[20] in and through the spins of a mind-boggling, labyrinthine, awe-inspiring Dome. It is this force that seems to be articulating New Britain, that seems to keep it apart/together. New Britain, in the imagery of the interstitial Dome, appears as a space of mediocrity, that is, on the one hand a space of *meridianality*, a space of (dis)connection in-between the one and the other, and, on the other hand, a space of gravity-defying superficiality. The Dome: tent of mediocrity. New Britain: mediocre Britain, divinely spinning Britain. High-flying, superior Britain, once again. In order to assume this role of superiority and rule this force had to leave the earth: since the loss of Empire, Cromer's Empire, that is, since rule and superiority cannot be imagined anymore through the everyday workings of down-to-earth Englishmen who just work the naked, inevitable facts of life, the only way for the phoenix Britain to arise from its ashes seems to be up and out, into the mind-boggling surfaces of mediocrity. Superior superficiality, as it were. Superficial superiority. This may be New Britain's *newness*: a novel leap into sameness. A same/different spin, imagine, somewhere in-between, but not quite.

VI

CONCLUSION

Paul Watzawick and colleagues, psychologists and therapists, once argued that *real change*, let's call it *newness*, or just *difference*, which they termed 'first order change', can only come about from impulses that emanate from the *outside.*[21] If there's no such impulse, all which one is left with is 'second order change', or, more prosaically, just more of the same. The builders and guardians of the Dome may have assumed something along those lines when they imagined the Dome as a hovering canvas, with a rough, jagged edge some ten meters above ground level, and with huge tent poles (aerials for receiving impulses? masts for transmitting impulses?) that seem to reach into whichever possible, whichever imaginable 'outside'. Hoping, perhaps commanding impulses to slip in, and to bring some real change, some

[20] T Luke, *Shows of Force. Power, Politics, and Ideology in Art Exhibitions* (Durham, Duke University Press, 1992).

[21] P Watzlawick, *et al*, *Change* (New York, Norton, 1974).

newness, something like a 'New' Britain. One may perhaps be forgiven for thinking or imagining that, especially in a rhizomic age which Deleuze and Guattari once characterised as one in which 'intérieur et extérieur, moi et non-moi, ça ne veut plus rien dire'[22], that is, when the without is (at least potentially) already within, and vice versa, real change, *newness*, is neither thinkable, nor imaginable. Is New Britain really New? Is it different, is it beyond Olde England? Newness, in the Dome of New Britain, one might safely assume, is not so much a space beyond, as it is a space of uneasy hybridity and of mediocre in-betweens. Images flow in same/different worlds. They're never really, completely beyond; they're never the same either.

Images of Olde England, like Cromer's, evoke a *green and pleasant* space, where autonomous, fully-fledged, self-sufficient, complete subjectivities roam and wander. Partakers of, and bearers of a divine, natural, earthy order, an elusive order (only few words are spoken about it, *can* be spoken about it, *need* to be spoken about it) they work 'a mass of details', unmediated facts of life, and in doing so, they reproduce this divine, natural, earthy order. Olde England is the space of naturally, orderly converging god-like subjectivities. The gaze of Olde Englishmen, in Cromer's imagery, is backwards, towards an eternal, immovable divine origin that, though elusively, lurks and hides and shows through in each and every of the Englishman's wanderings and roamings. Complete, full, self-sufficient subjectivities, Englishmen can only lose some of this self-sufficiency, and will thus be unable to reproduce their divine, eternal order, if they let themselves be lured into the deceptively perfect mediations, words and images, of courtisanes, of untruthful and disorderly Frenchmen and Egyptians, gypsies and strangers. Life, for self-sufficient subjectivities, is one of a permanent, labyrinthine struggle against and hostility towards unearthy words and images, against awfully corrupt and dangerously excessive images, France and Egyptians/gypsies. Life is about *losing* or getting rid of words and images. It's a labyrinthine mesh of criss-crossing tracks in, on, and especially, *towards* surfaces. It's a voyage towards the surfaces of an *immovable*, eternal origin. A divine, earthy force is guiding this journey in everyday facts of life, as they come naturally. Cromer's colonial Britain: imagine God's Olde England.

In New Britain, at the Dome, subjectivities were lured as well as commanded. Life, at the Dome, did not come naturally. Not the divine, earthy, eternal way. The Dome was not just, in Luke's words, an expressive *show of force*, it was also, and perhaps more so, a space where force was aspired to. New Britain is not so much a space of expression, as it is a space of aspiration. The gaze of New Britons is not particularly backwards, nor is it directed towards some dawning horizon. The Dome wanted to express all and nothing, both and none, both *and* none. It aspired both *and* none.

[22] G Deleuze and F Guattari, *Anti-Oedipe* (Paris, Les Editions de Minuit, 1972), at 7.

Through its labyrinthine windings, it invited, lured and commanded broken and shattered subjectivities to learn and to acquire while it simultaneously invited, lured and commanded these broken and shattered subjectivities to lose their burden. It wanted both and none. It wanted subjectivities to reproduce its enigmatic, labyrinthine trajectories of movement, where nothing was allowed to fix or solidify. New Britain at the Dome was a space of movement, where the one was allowed to enter, but invited and commanded to move on, and where the same went for the other. It was a gravity-defying and mind-boggling space, New Britain. But once again, it was a labyrinthine mesh of criss-crossing tracks in, on, and especially, *towards* surfaces.

14

Law in the Age of Images: The Challenge of Visual Literacy

CHRISTINA O SPIESEL, RICHARD K SHERWIN, NEAL FEIGENSON

The process of changing back and forth from conception as paramount, to the actual visual document as paramount, [is] the key learning process ... It is the way in which the students learn to see.[1]

I

INTERDISCIPLINARITY IS THE sign of our times. The widespread recognition that meanings are socially (as well as psychologically and culturally) constructed entails a turning away from hegemonic theorising and an increasing need for multiple systems of interpretation. Meaning-making and understanding become more complex precisely because no one interpretive frame or expert discourse can be taken for granted. Visual communication epitomises this trend: our culture is flooded with images whose import may be simultaneously overdetermined and indeterminate, whose layers of significance can be teased apart only by means of a varied array of interpretive tools.

What is true of the culture at large is true of law as well.[2] Mass mediated images, conveyed through television, film, video, CD-ROM, DVD, the Internet, and traditional print media, are infusing law practice just as they have come to dominate our entertainments, our politics, our news, and our methods of education. Law is both a co-producer and a by-product of today's visually preoccupied society. We see this inside the courtroom, the law office, and the court of public opinion. For example, American jurors today are increasingly turning to electronic screens. They are looking at visual evidence in the form of digitised graphics and video documentaries showing the injuries and personal suffering allegedly caused by accidents. They are

[1] Sol Worth, quoted in L Gross, 'Introduction' in S Worth, *Studying Visual Communication* (Philadelphia, University of Pennsylvania Press, 1981), at 2.

[2] Our analysis of visual rhetoric in legal practice and pedagogy pertains mainly to the Anglo-American legal systems, in which proof is gathered and presented adversarially and in which (in America) juries decide both facts and 'mixed questions' of law and fact (eg, the reasonableness of a party's behavior) in roughly half of all trials. Although we are unaware of any empirical studies of the matter, anecdotal evidence leads us to believe that visual displays are

looking at witnesses testifying from a distance, at accident and crime reconstructions, and at police surveillance tapes. They are also looking at PowerPoint slide shows and videos that serve as legal arguments. In all of these instances, what audiences believe is heavily influenced by what they see; but how do the advocates who construct the images capture those beliefs?

The specific challenge we face is how best to maximise the benefits of a multidisciplinary approach to legal rhetoric and practice given the specific constraints and demands of legal argumentation. To prepare lawyers both to deploy images in the service of their cases and to critique them effectively when they are in play, we have devised a course, 'Visual Persuasion in the Law.' Our task is to describe something of the contemporary visual practice of law and to explain how students can best be acculturated into this polysemous world in an educational program that is not only multidisciplinary but multimodal, embracing the experience of making visual arguments as well as studying and reading about them. Given this premise, what follows is an exercise in semiotic complexity. First we set the technocultural scene of the contemporary interpenetration of law and visual culture. Then we shift the focus to law students' efforts to work within this world, creating images that persuade on multiple levels. Finally we explore the pedagogic theory and practice that allows students to flourish in a world of polysemy and uncertainty.

II

THE INTERPENETRATION OF LAW, MEDIA, AND POPULAR CULTURE

Legal semiotics provides a methodology for the sociology of legal knowledge. It offers a stable platform for the descriptive and critical tasks of legal

at present used much less often in Continental than in Anglo-American legal proceedings. It might be expected that the perceived need for and effects of visual communication and persuasion would differ in Continental adjudication, in which fact-finding is dominated by legal officials rather than the parties and many of the critical factual determinations are made before trial (M Damaška, *The Faces of Justice and State Authority* (New Haven, Yale University Press, 1986)). Decision making under different procedures implicates different cognitive and other psychological dynamics (M Damaška, 'Epistemology and Legal Regulation of Proof' 2 *Law, Probability & Risk* 117 at 119–22), so image-based communication would be expected to play different roles. For instance, in Continental legal systems in which documentary records produced by official investigations before trial guide later proceedings, there would seem to be less malleability in the determination of facts for visual displays to exploit, although lay participants may well need the kinds of visual representations that can enhance understanding of technical forensics, and these might be provided before rather than during trial. At present, methods of proof and fact-finding vary across the Continent; however, the development of the European Union and larger globalisation forces have increased the importance not only of global markets, but also of transnational criminal and civil legal issues that call for a harmonisation of forensic expertise (see JF Nijboer and WJJM Sprangers, *Harmonisation in Forensic Expertise, An Inquiry into the Desirability of and Opportunities for International Standards* (Amsterdam, Thela Thesis, 2000)). Moreover, the increasing influence of Anglo-American visual culture in general around the world is altering laypeople's views of what happens in the law. Under these pressures, some European legal systems may soon come to resemble the Anglo-American in their receptivity to visual rhetoric.

pragmatics. Rather than commencing with a body of rules or general principles, characteristic of the legal positivist tradition,[3] legal semioticians start with actual behavior: What forms of discourse are being used, by whom, when, and with what effect within the legal system?

This pragmatic semiotic perspective has historic roots in the twentieth-century Legal Realism movement.[4] Scholars associated with critical legal studies subsequently advanced its semiotic thrust.[5] Currently, a broader, multidisciplinary approach to the pragmatics of meaning-making is taking shape under the rubric of cultural legal studies.[6] This emerging body of legal scholarship takes as an important point of departure the insight that law is not an autonomous domain.

To be sure, law continually generates it own highly specialised forms of discourse together with rule- and custom-driven processes (or rituals) of usage. However, the border separating law from the culture at large has always been highly porous. Just as the specialised culture of law exports storytelling forms and content for popular consumption, so too does it import a wide range of shifting meaning-making practices from society at large. The legal semiotician's task, therefore, is to look at law from within and without in order more fully to understand and descriptively capture the complex relationships that form between the domains of popular and legal culture.

Tracing the diverse ways in which legal meaning-making occurs, or breaks down, or remains occluded, requires a broad array of disciplinary tools. Visual tropes and genres, audio cues, and nonlinear digital editing, among numerous other rhetorical offshoots of screen-based communication practices, must now take their place among more traditional rhetorical, linguistic, and cognitive mappings of the terrain of meaning. As new signs proliferate within society, legal semiotics must meet the challenge of providing an adequate typography of emerging patterns of discourse. New tools must be grasped if we are to describe and assess systematically the meaning-making processes in which we are now situated.

[3] HLA Hart, *The Concept of Law* (Oxford, Oxford University Press, 1961).

[4] '[A]lthough Pierce's enormous contributions are rarely directly discussed, they do actually constitute the basis of realism in law and its related movements': B Kevelson, 'Interpretation and Discovery in Law from the Perspective of Peirce's Speculative Rhetoric' 61 *Indiana Law Journal* 355 at 357.

[5] D Kennedy, 'Form and Substance in Private Law Adjudication' 89 *Harvard Law Review* 1685. 'What one discovers, then, when one studies the forms of legal discourse, is that the basic styles of argument do not vary as one moves from one set of rule choices to another ... I call this the crystalline structure of legal thought': J Balkin, 'The Hohfeldian Approach to Law and Semiotics' 44 *University of Miami Law Review* 1119 at 1132.

[6] 'In the last fifteen years ... legal scholars have come regularly to attend to the cultural lives of law and the ways law lives in the domains of culture': A Sarat & T Kearns, 'The Cultural Life of Law' in A Sarat & T Kearns (eds), *Law In the Domains of Culture* (Ann Arbor, University of Michigan Press, 2000), at 5; see also A Amsterdam & J Bruner, *Minding the Law* (Cambridge, MA, Harvard University Press, 2000), at 18 [noting the 'ubiquitousness and power of categories, narratives, rhetorics, and culture in law as in the rest of life'].

The present work represents a first step in the effort to grapple with this new semiotic challenge. First we address the interrelationship among law, mass media, and popular culture. More specifically, we wish to examine the various ways in which the rise of visual mass communication is changing the practice, theory, and teaching of law in contemporary western society. Our thesis may be simply put. Law today is traveling down the same path as journalism and politics. In our media-saturated world, advertising may be the most important paradigm for communication and persuasion.[7] In a visually literate society, effective storytelling requires immediacy, familiarity, and the illusion of transparency, which is to say, it must operate within the available bandwidth of popular culture. To be sure, lawyers have always tapped popular cultural forms in their efforts to persuade lay juries. In today's wired courtrooms, however, the spoken and written word must now compete with sounds and images on ubiquitous electronic screens.

The implications of this development are profound. The ways people think about law, the ways law is practiced, and the ways legal meanings, including substantive policy decisions, are produced, are changing. One reason for these changes is that communication technologies are providing people with new cognitive tools for making sense of actions and events in the world. These days, most people get their news in visual form, from television. Likewise, most people get their legal knowledge not from direct experience, but vicariously—by watching notorious trials, like the OJ Simpson case, and by watching documentaries, docudramas, and feature films.

What is interesting about this, as recent social psychology studies have shown, is that these different sources are not always kept neatly separated in people's minds.[8] Truth readily intermingles with fiction. The important thing, in terms of affecting real-world judgments, is the strength of the association between the story concept and pre-existing world-knowledge concepts. Our world-knowledge is often scripted by a mixture of fictional and non-fictional sources.[9] Indeed, the credibility of a particular image or story may depend on its faithful emulation of fictional storytelling techniques that fulfill popular expectations about what reality looks like on the screen.

Consider in this regard the credibility of a 'home video' aesthetic. A few years ago, this low-tech style was exploited in a popular American horror film called *The Blair Witch Project*. In this film, three amateur filmmakers go off into the woods in search of a fabled witch. The rough, ill-lit images produced by an unsteady camera, off-centre framing, and seemingly unscripted exchanges all contributed to an enhanced sense of immediacy

[7] R Sherwin, *When Law Goes Pop* (Chicago, University of Chicago Press, 2000).

[8] D Prentice & R Gerrig, 'Exploring the Boundary Between Fiction and Reality' in S Chaiken & Y Trope (eds), *Dual-Process Theories in Social Psychology* (New York, Guilford Press, 1999).

[9] R Gerrig, *Experiencing Narrative Worlds: On the Psychological Activities of Reading* (New Haven, Yale University Press, 1993).

and visual truthfulness. What began as a distinct cinematic visual style may have serious consequences outside the realm of popular entertainment—particularly when the chief evidence in a law case is a film. Consider, for example, a recent criminal case prompted by an 'amateur' video that was made by several college students who used a camcorder to film what American prosecutors are calling a kidnapping and assault of a young woman, and what defense lawyers describe as nothing more than an amateur horror film. In due course a jury will be called upon to watch and judge for themselves the 'truth' or 'simulation' of what they see. Is it real horror, or is it staged? Here, then, we encounter a criminal case that essentially turns on a jury's response to aesthetic cues.

In our view, the point worth emphasising is that when people are persuaded or moved by an especially compelling image or story, they do not always know why it is persuasive, or whether the source of its credibility comes from fact or fiction. Indeed, governments and television networks are well aware of this confusion and have shown little compunction about exploiting it. Consider, for example, *JAG*, a fictional American TV series about military justice.[10] In a recent episode, producers and writers worked closely with the United States defense department to show that the newly created, post-9/11 'military tribunals' for alleged terrorists operate in a fair and trustworthy manner. In essence, the story was scripted to highlight the legitimacy of this as-yet untested, and highly controversial, legal procedure. As the chief writer and consulting producer put it, 'War is terrible, conflicts are terrible, but somebody has to do it and so it's necessary, maybe not completely honest, but necessary to imbue those things with glory.' Clearly, the producers understood, and apparently were banking on the expectation that by *confusing* fictional images with the real thing, viewers might adopt the scriptwriter's values.

Trial lawyers, judges, jurors, and the lay public must deal with similar challenges as visual evidence and visual storytelling become more commonplace in courtrooms and everywhere else legal meanings are being disseminated. Of course, successful trial lawyers have always been good storytellers. It is through stories that people make sense of fragmentary bits of evidence, linking the salient facts of the case (or perhaps finding no link at all) with the relevant rules of law. Popular culture is a major supplier of familiar story genres, metaphors, plot lines, and character types. These are the materials that shape and inform popular expectations about how a particular kind of story is supposed to go, and when one story, rather than another, best fits the circumstances. Trial lawyers need to take this cultural knowledge seriously. How else can they hope to cue, and tap into, people's narrative expectations?

[10] K Seelye, 'TV Drama, Pentagon-Style: A Fictional Terror Tribunal' *The New York Times* (March 31, 2002).

Today, those expectations more often than not are based on the visual codes of film and television. In modern visually literate societies, these codes have become a part of our visual common sense, which is to say, they have been unconsciously assimilated. People understand cross cutting and parallel editing. They do not need anyone to explain these storytelling techniques. Put bluntly, the camera is inside our heads. Consider, for example, Ridley Scott's now famous TV commercial introducing the first Apple computer in 1984. The ad agency that made it describes it this way:

> Open on an Orwellian vision of the future. Mindless, hollow-eyed people march in lockstep toward assembly hall, where big brother harangues them with the party line in a huge video screen. As the crowd stares, unseeing, an athletic young woman, pursued by guards, runs into the hall, wielding a sledgehammer. The woman runs toward the screen, winds up and throws the sledgehammer with all her strength. The screen explodes in a blinding flash of light which sweeps over the staring uncomprehending crowd. An announcer's voice then proclaims: 'On January 24th Apple Computer will introduce Macintosh. And you'll see why 1984 won't be like '1984.'[11]

This ad was broadcast only once, during the 1984 Super Bowl. Apple's sales exceeded all expectations. One minute was all it took for Scott to set up a familiar story: a tale of David and Goliath. The giant is, of course, 'Big Blue,' the monolithic IBM. The young upstart is Macintosh. The ragged, walking dead are all those who have been imprisoned by Big Blue's tyranny. They are liberated by the vibrant female athlete, the life force. She alone appears in living color.

We get the message because the iconic images of oppression, of big brother and technocratic dehumanisation from George Orwell's classic novel, *1984*, are now stock images in the popular imagination. We need only a little stimulation to recognise the genre, and we are only too happy to fill in missing details. This is something that advertisers know well. They know that it is far easier to prompt and then piggyback onto what is already in someone's mind than to introduce something new. This is also what experienced litigators teach other trial lawyers. We submit that it is what law teachers should be teaching their students. Like filmmaker Ridley Scott, students need to understand that legal conflict is often expressed in mythic terms: good vs. evil, man vs. nature, big vs. small, innocence vs. deceit. They must also recognise how to use the raw materials that popular culture supplies—materials out of which lawyers, like advertisers, will craft the right story for their clients. To paraphrase Aristotle, students need to know which tools in their storytelling toolkit are best suited for the problem at hand.

Perhaps it will be a detective story, like the one Marcia Clark told the jurors in her summation for the prosecution in the OJ Simpson case. In Clark's hands

[11] http://www.uriah.com/apple-qt/1984.html (accessed 25 June 2002).

the case became a whodunit, and in the end the pieces of the puzzle fit neatly into place. Indeed, this is literally what the jurors saw on a large electronic screen inside the courtroom during the state's closing argument. As the prosecutor rattled off each clue, a fragment of Simpson's face clicked into view: his opportunity to kill (click), his motive (click), the victim's blood on his socks and glove (click), the blood trail that he left at the scene (click). Until there he is. The face of OJ Simpson is revealed; the crime has been solved.

Or perhaps it will be a hero quest story, a subjunctivised narrative (as cognitive psychologist Jerome Bruner has put it)[12] that casts the jurors themselves as protagonists, making them the true heroes of the tale told in court. This is the story that Johnny Cochran told jurors in his summation for the defense in the OJ Simpson case. Cochran launched the jurors on a heroic quest against 'genocidal racism.' 'If you don't stop it [ie, the state's cover up],' Cochran urged, 'then who? Do you think the police department is going to do it? ... You police the police through your verdict.'[13] Once the defense rests it will be up to each individual juror to complete the lawyer's tale by bringing home the holy grail of justice, something each juror can achieve, but only if he or she reaches the right verdict.

Today, the stories about law and politics that people carry around in their heads frequently come from television and film, the chief generators of popular culture. Notably, visual stories use a different code for making meaning than do written texts or oral advocacy. They are non-linear and they work by association. Often, their meanings are implicit. They are also rich in emotional appeal, which is deeply tied to the communicative power of imagery. This power stems in part from the impression that visual images are unmediated. They seem to be caused by the reality they depict.

But visual images not only enhance their credibility by masking the way they mediate reality. They also often prompt the same emotional response as experience in real life. Watching on the screen is like being there. Consider, in this regard, the amateur videotape shot by George Holliday of Los Angeles police officers surrounding and beating motorist Rodney King. In presenting the state's case against the officers, the prosecutor repeatedly told the jurors to just watch the tape. What more was needed? The state was banking on the credibility of Holliday's 'low-tech' film aesthetic. But in this case the prosecutor's confidence was misplaced. In fact, the prosecutor was so locked into his own literal viewing that he missed the defense's digitised re-narration of the scene. By changing the flow, and rhythm, of images, the defense *reversed causation*. 'Look,' defense experts urged, as they pointed to still frame images moving slowly across a large screen. 'You see, he's getting up. His knees are cocked. He's like a linebacker getting ready to run.'[14]

[12] J Bruner, *Acts of Meaning* (Cambridge, MA, Harvard University Press, 1990).
[13] R Sherwin, 'Law and the Myth of the Self in Mass Media Representations' 8 *International Journal of Semiotics of Law* 299.
[14] Sherwin above n 7.

Only when he rises up do the police batons come down. And when they do, King appears to move back down.

This is the way the eye and the brain construct causation: When two bodies meet and one moves away, the still object seems to have caused the other object's movement.[15] By the end of the trial, when the jurors watched the tape, as the prosecutor had instructed them to do, they saw police officers 'escalating' and 'de-escalating force' in response to Rodney King's aggressive resistance of arrest. By getting up, instead of lying prone, as the police commanded him to do, King *caused* the batons to come down. As jurors told journalists after their acquittal of the officers, Rodney King was in control.

Making legal meaning is more than simply showing data or reciting facts; it is more than merely reading the applicable rules of law (as all too many litigators do—much to the distress of the poor, distracted juror). We make meaning by turning information into a compelling story that captures and organises popular images and character types, the stuff of popular imagination. Notably, the dramatic nature of visual metaphors often masks, and in so doing diverts attention away from, its technical imprecision. As we remarked previously, visual images not only prompt strong emotional responses, they also effectively convey *implicit* meanings. As teachers of law it is not enough for us to demonstrate to our students that legal semiotics provides a theoretical master key to understanding the movement from the spoken and printed word to audiovisual constructs on the screen—interesting and challenging as that is. We believe that it is of even greater scholarly interest to researchers, and of greater practical value to our students, to engage in a semiotic analysis of the visual rhetoric actually generated by everyday legal practices in the digital era. Applied theory is the hallmark of our course, Visual Persuasion in the Law.

III

CONSTRUCTING LEGAL VISUAL RHETORIC

Successful legal rhetoric involves not only mastery of relevant legal texts and accepted modes of interpretation, but also mastery of stylistic forms of communication that are strategically crafted to appeal to specific audiences. It must also effectively address particularised problems within the constraints of evidentiary rules and in the face of aggressive testing by opposing views.

[15] 'There is a celebrated monograph, little known outside academic psychology, written a generation ago by the Belgian student of perception, Baron Michotte. By cinematic means, he demonstrated that when objects move with respect to one another within highly limited constraints, we *see* causality': J Bruner, *Actual Minds, Possible Worlds* (Cambridge, MA, Harvard University Press, 1986), at 17. A classic reference is David Hume: 'I find that in the first place, that whatever objects are consider'd as causes and effects, are contiguous...': D Hume, *A Treatise on Human Nature*, Ernest Mossner (ed) (Middlesex, England, Penguin Books, (1739–40) 1969), at 123.

Electronic images introduce interesting and complex elements into this rhetorical culture. Yet, the traditional emphasis in law school classrooms on the printed word persists. This raises important pedagogical issues. For example, can law students be acculturated into the multivalent world of persuasion through many modalities? Can they learn, in the span of a few short months, to complement their almost exclusively text-based training with the substantive and strategic training required to construct persuasive arguments using sound and images? After three years of experience teaching Visual Persuasion in the Law, we are inclined to answer this question in the affirmative: Students can bridge this pedagogic gap. In an effort to explain further how this cultural shift occurs, we turn now to the design of the course. First we will describe the work product of the students in our course and illustrate how students draw on the multidisciplinary resources we offer to construct persuasive visual displays. Next, we will discuss the particular pedagogic strategies that we use to get them there.

We ask our students to create two major pieces of legal visual rhetoric. The first is a still visual display (graph, photo array, etc) for use as demonstrative evidence at trial. The second is a digital video for use during closing argument. Both projects are anchored in highly detailed and realistic case simulations. Together, they challenge students to explore the persuasive potential of both static and time-based images, and to construct visual rhetoric first within and then without the tight constraints of rules of evidence.

Whether arguing in words or images, the successful advocate must discover and refine a *theory of the case*, which is 'a simple, plausible, coherent, legally sufficient narrative that can easily be integrated with a moral theme.'[16] Figuring out a compelling theory of the case requires the advocate to grasp not only the law and the facts, but also the audience's likely 'common sense' response to the case: What will strike them as most important about it? Where is the emotional impact? What important values can be upheld only by a decision in the client's favor?

To think through these questions and find the moral/emotional crux of the case, our students draw on readings in several disciplines. From classical rhetoric, they gather the insights that persuasion works on both the audience's thoughts and their feelings, and that audiences can be persuaded by the form as well as the content of the message; from cognitive and social psychology, an awareness that the audience's intuitive understandings of 'how things go,' the way the world is, play a critical role in how they receive the message; from narrative theory, the recognition that people use stories to organise their understandings and that narrative forms help cue their emotional and cognitive responses; and from advertising and public relations, the importance of focusing the persuasive message into a single point, like a sound bite or tag line (which can then be effectively envisioned).

[16] R Burns, *A Theory of the Trial* (Princeton, Princeton University Press, 1999), at 37.

As outlined above, our students' first major project is to create a non-moving visual display for use as demonstrative evidence in a trial. Demonstrative evidence includes any visual display—photographs, movies, and diagrams, for instance—used to illustrate oral testimony. Generally speaking, it is admissible at trial as long as the judge believes it can help the jury (and the judge) to understand the case and is not substantially more prejudicial than probative.[17] A typical example would be an accident reconstruction expert's use of a diagram, computer animation, or model to show how the accident occurred. Perhaps the most difficult rhetorical task posed by the use of demonstrative evidence generally is how to use it to further the theory of the case without appearing to argue. (If an advocate uses demonstrative evidence to argue rather than illustrate the facts, opposing counsel can object, prompting a judge to rule the display inadmissible.)

A particularly challenging task is to make quantitative evidence both meaningful and persuasive. In 2001, using a hypothetical juvenile justice case, we asked our students to represent a black youth trying to avoid transfer from juvenile court to adult court—where, if convicted, he would face a longer sentence and, if incarcerated, would do the time in adult prison. We asked the students to argue that statistical disparities in the treatment of white and black youth offenders violate the Equal Protection Clause of the Fourteenth Amendment to the US Constitution. (For example, in one jurisdiction blacks are more than twice as likely as whites who commit the same type of offense to be tried as adults.) It is a difficult legal argument: The Supreme Court has held that the Equal Protection Clause forbids only intentional racial discrimination, and that (with few exceptions) an intent to discriminate (here, on the part of prosecutors and/or juvenile court judges who make the transfer decision) cannot be inferred from mere statistical differences (here, eg, in the rates at which white and black youth, respectively, are transferred).[18]

How might the lawyer present the relevant statistical data? The statistical expert might simply testify, saying something like: 'White youth make up 45 per cent of the general youth population and 24.7 per cent of those arrested but only 5 per cent of those tried as adults. Black youth, by contrast, make up only 8 per cent of the general youth population but 12.6 per cent of those arrested and, most strikingly, 30.1 per cent of those tried as adults.' But purely verbal representations of quantitative information are notoriously difficult for laypersons to understand and remember. So the lawyer might have the expert augment the oral testimony with a table of the relevant numbers, providing at least some visual anchor for the audience. A well-designed chart, however, featuring simple visual representations of quantities (eg, by bars of differing heights), would make the essential contrasts (eg, between black and white youth transfer rates) even easier to grasp and retain. Thus, the design challenge our students faced was to educate the judge by

[17] Federal Rule of Evidence 403 (St Paul, MN, West Publishing Company, 2002).
[18] *Washington v Davis*, 426 US 229 (1976); *McCleskey v Kemp*, 481 US 279 (1987).

presenting the expert's statistical information in clear, intelligible visual form, but also, if possible, to do it in a compelling way that linked the numbers to something the judge would be inclined to identify as wrongful discrimination—and yet to do this without explicitly arguing.

One student used colorful pyramids (blue for white youth, red for black youth), instead of the usual bars or columns, to represent the chosen data: the percentages of whites versus blacks in the general youth population, youths arrested, and youths transferred to adult court, respectively (Figure 1).[19] The shapes and colors attract interest and hold attention, while still managing to present clearly a considerable amount of information (three different paired comparisons of white and black youths in percentage terms). More importantly, read from left to right (the natural pattern for English and European readers), this student's graphic representation of the data *tells a story* about what happens to young men as they move from the general population through the juvenile justice system. And following the tips of the blue pyramids down (from left to right) and the red pyramids up, the viewer sees the student's theory of the case, the equal protection narrative: As youths progress through the criminal justice system, whites systematically get fewer bad outcomes and blacks get more.

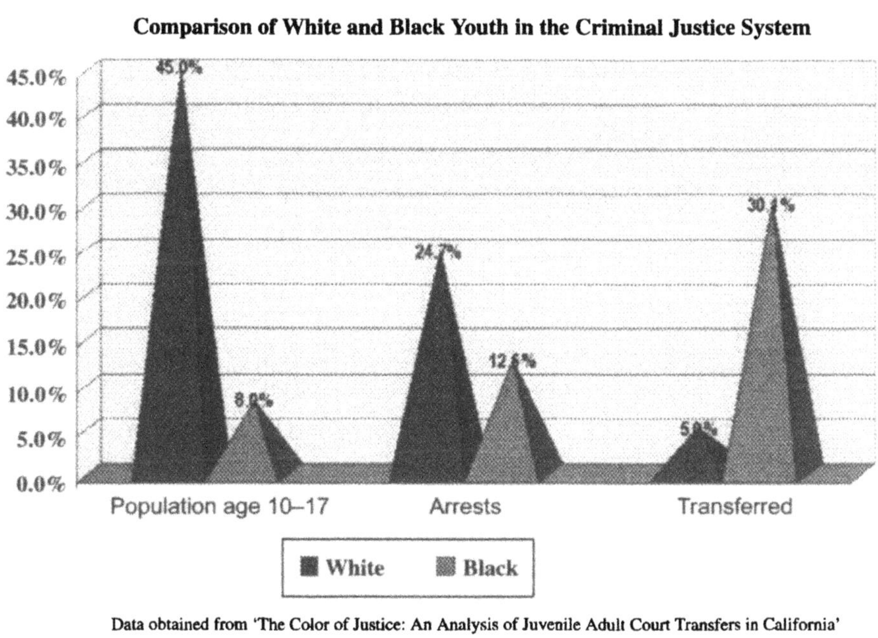

Figure 1. Demonstrative evidence: graph of juvenile justice statistics (by Catherine Esposito)

[19] All illustrations are of work created by students in the Visual Persuasion in the Law course in spring 2001.

A second student transformed the standard graphic display of (a similar set of) data to communicate a simple, powerful story of inequality (Figure 2). The difference between white and black youths' outcomes in the juvenile justice system can be expressed not only in simple percentage terms (eg, in one jurisdiction, 60 per cent of young black felony offenders are tried as adults, compared to 36 per cent of white youth who commit similar offenses), but also as the 'advantage' that white kids have over blacks (eg, white youth in that jurisdiction have a '24 per cent advantage' in avoiding transfer to adult court). This student had a brilliant visual insight: Instead of the usual bar chart method of setting the y-intercept of the x axis at zero and the bars for different values (eg, percentages of kids of each race transferred) at different heights (this is what the first student's graphic, like most bar charts, did), he set the zero value at the *midpoint* on the y axis, converting values above to plus-per cents and below to minus-per cents. The midpoint, the zero value, represents equal treatment, the law's ideal—no advantage for one race over the other. Now the black and white values do not merely differ in height; they go in different directions: The white bar representing white youth, who have the advantage, goes up from the midpoint; the black bar goes down. This makes more visually salient the narrative theory of the case: when white and black youth, otherwise equal, enter the juvenile justice system, they head in different directions—to an extent that can be explained only by racial discrimination. And the visualisation of the directions—up is good, down is bad—fits with one of our culture's deep cognitive metaphors.

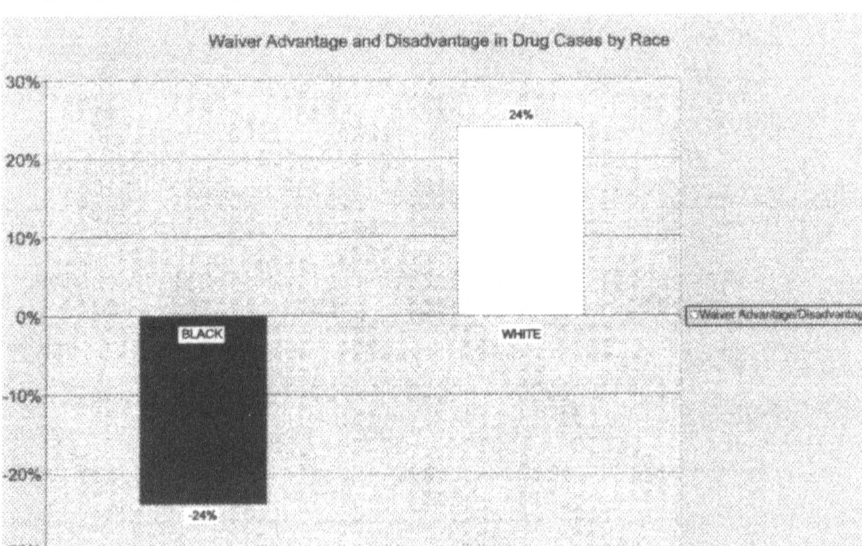

Figure 2. Demonstrative evidence: graph of juvenile justice statistics (by Christopher Major)

A third student's visual display confronted a different rhetorical challenge. How can the lawyer who makes a statistical argument of racial inequality present the data clearly and yet also make visible that behind the aggregate percentages stand individual white and black boys, the individual victims of the alleged discrimination—including the lawyer's client? This student broke up the aggregate to represent the individuals who comprise it. Instead of using bars of different heights (or other shapes) to represent the different outcomes for white versus black youth at different stages of the juvenile justice process, she created two square grids, each filled with over a thousand small white and black circles, and placed them side by side; the one on the right, representing the racial composition of the population transferred to adult court, shows far more black circles than the one on the left, representing the racial composition of those arrested for comparable offenses. The display visually persuades by using immediately understood visual signs (circles indicating heads, which signify people) and by signaling quantitative detail that gives an impression of accuracy. The viewer's eye immediately registers the sheer number of circles, their arrangement into grid-like arrays making overall patterns, and the contrast between the two arrays, which is the main point of the display.

The students' final project is to make a video closing argument. Video arguments use a full array of media sources (including edited videotapes of testimony, re-enactments, news or feature film footage, and animations) in a single presentation—in essence, a persuasive documentary for the client's position. The most apt analogy may be the American political campaign film (eg, Ronald Reagan's 'A New Beginning' or Bill Clinton's 'Man From Hope'). Video arguments are already used in negotiations (video settlement brochures) and administrative proceedings, and while not yet commonly used at trial, they may very well be in the near future.

To make their videos, students work in groups of three or four, shooting their own footage if they want to (eg, to simulate expert testimony that would have been introduced at trial), adding documentary or other sources of information available through the mass media, and then using digital video editing software to create their own texts and graphics and assemble the entire movie. They complete the entire job—from first learning about the case to screening their videos—in six to seven weeks. We are not looking for high production values (especially given the students' lack of prior training and time constraints), but rather for the visual thinking embodied in their work.

We will briefly describe (as best we can within the medium of print) how two groups of students used the medium of digital video to envision the same legal argument in very different ways. In this case, students were assigned to represent inmates in a 'supermax' prison in a hypothetical lawsuit against prison officials. In a supermax (or 'secured housing unit' within a larger prison), persons whom prison authorities consider to be disciplinary risks are assigned to indefinite solitary confinement and extreme sensory deprivation (sometimes lasting over a decade). The legal argument is that supermax imprisonment inflicts 'cruel and unusual punishment' in violation of the Eighth Amendment to the US Constitution. The legal argument is difficult to win: The test for deciding whether a punishment is cruel and unusual—whether it falls short of 'evolving standards of decency'[20]—is itself defined partly in terms of current practices, so if a majority of states use supermax imprisonment,[21] it becomes hard to argue that supermaxes are cruel and unusual.[22] But the visual rhetorical challenges are at least equally daunting. How can the advocate, in just a few minutes, convey to the judge and jurors what long-term solitary confinement and sensory deprivation are really like, making this treatment seem so repugnant that jurors will want to reject it as unconstitutional?

One group of students made a video that emphasises the expository style, presenting an ostensibly objective point of view with a consistent 'voice of God' narration. This relatively dispassionate 'discourse of sobriety'[23] locates the argument in what the students expected the judge and jurors would accept as the world of fact. In several respects this video closing argument is 'by the book,' a kind of an illustrated text driven by a traditional verbal argumentative structure: The structure itself is consistent with readings on closing arguments taken from a leading trial practice text; crucial scenes consisting of photomontages (of prison exteriors, of cartoons about torture) with text represent the screen as flat surface, like a page (Figure 3); and historical references to earlier forms of imprisonment rely on shots of still images taken from books or book-like web pages. The video's visual narrative style effectively communicated the students' theory of the case: Supermax conditions are the equivalent of punishments from earlier eras once found acceptable but later found to be cruel and unusual—the pillory, water torture, and the sweat box.[24]

A second group of students envisioned the same legal argument very differently. While addressing the legal basis for their claim as precisely and thoroughly as did the first group, these students framed their argument as a (largely) subjective account anchored in the prisoner's point of view, designed to heighten jurors' empathy and hence sympathy for the clients (Figure 4). They sought to convey a personal and emotional truth that

[20] *Rhodes v Chapman*, 452 US 337, 346 (1981).

[21] More than 30, as of 1999 (US Department of Justice, National Institute of Corrections, *Supermax Prisons: Overview and General Considerations* (1999), at 6).

[22] C Haney & M Lynch, 'Regulating Prisons of the Future: A Psychological Analysis of Supermax and Solitary Confinement' 23 *New York University Review of Law and Social Change* 477.

[23] B Nichols, *Representing Reality* (Bloomington, IN, Indiana University Press, 1991).

[24] This convincingly addresses one of the most difficult aspects of the Eighth Amendment argument—how to get around the apparent devolution of American 'standards of decency' regarding what prisoners should be expected to put up with.

Figure 3. Closing argument video on supermax confinement (by Todd Schulze, Ryan Trought, Leticia Crespo)

would elicit the audience's imaginative participation in the case. How did they accomplish this? Like the makers of the first video, these students tried to achieve credibility for their images by using the visual language of popular media, which they presumed their audience would recognise and immediately understand. But they emphasised a different vocabulary, that of cinema vérité. They used ambient sound, but also, and more importantly, the amateur video aesthetic—the shaky, hand-held camera style—popularised by *The Blair Witch Project*, the George Holliday videotape of the police beating Rodney King, and a variety of 'reality' television shows.

Taken together, these two different video arguments indicate law students' intuitive grasp of at least some of the variety of visual language in contemporary culture, and their skill in adapting the forms of visual persuasion, so effective in the world at large, to the precise demands of legal argumentation.

IV

THE PEDAGOGY OF VISUAL PERSUASION

How do we get our students to put theory into practice in the thirteen short weeks of a semester in the United States? Our teaching methods evolved out of some assumptions about what skills would best serve our students in the long run, and about the relationship of the pedagogical model to the desired outcome.

Figure 4. Closing argument video on supermax confinement (by Edwin Farrow, Matthew Stachowske, Aaron Kanar, Philip Kent)

Just what is it that law students need to know when it comes to images? In its simplest formulation, law students need to learn what images are, how they are perceived and interpreted, and how they propagate through the culture like sporulating fungi. Legal professionals rarely understand the images they use because visual literacy has not been part of their education; it has not been regarded as an essential skills set. Many people reach adulthood maintaining the naive and fundamentalist assumption that a picture is simply its subject matter. Yet visual texts are different from printed words, and to learn the possibilities for both forms and ranges of meaning, our students need to decode them more consciously and more completely.

Verbal text is time-based, moving from one word and one sentence to the next. Words are understood to be abstractions, signs for something else. Pictures are first seen whole; only later are their parts decoded and understood in relation to the initial interpretive gestalt. When they are photographic they carry an additional indexical charge. The problem is that in everyday life such critical analysis occurs only infrequently. Consequently, the totalised visual gestalt remains, and the picture is identified with its subject matter just as text is first experienced as its semantic meaning. The ways in which the picture has been constructed, and the various perceptual, cognitive, and cultural elements that contribute to the meaning of the whole, tend to be ignored. Of course, such economy of perception makes sense. If we were to think about such things with regard to every percept and every visual text we encounter it would become impossible for us to conduct our lives.[25] Yet, in order to understand how images are made meaningful, such an exploration cannot be avoided.

All images are signs of one kind or another; and they may also be made up of many signs. But the first perception of the image is a non-verbal one. To make that perception available socially, we must translate our non-verbal experience into words that can be shared. Like the compression of files on a computer, some aspects of the image will be sharpened and clarified in the move to the verbal; other data will be lost. The efficiency of the verbal translation is such that it quickly can become the basis for all further discussion in ways that lead the viewer far away from the image text itself; viewers may dispute the meaning of verbal constructions (rather than the image in all its complexity). One way to look at our double task is that we must increase the amount of 'original' information taken in as we read the image so that our translations can be fuller—when we have more to work with, we can then make more meanings consciously available through verbal construction. In a Peircean sense, we will have more abductions, hypotheses, available to sort through. We can say with Floyd Merrell that

> in spite of the many incursions into the depths of signs, their meanings have remained elusive, meaning flows within the *semiosic* process, resisting any and all artificial pigeon-holes. It is, as a result of this flow, plurality not singularity; it is many not one; continuous not discrete.[26]

Perhaps it is best to say that our goal is to make students both more comfortable and more conscious of the semiosic process itself. 'To learn to see anything well is a difficult undertaking. It requires the activity of the whole personality.'[27] Little in legal training asks for the engagement of the whole personality.

Our students display a wide range of capabilities. Some come to our schools directly after graduation from college from their early to mid-twenties; others are mature adults in their fifties with grown families and successful careers. They take this elective at the end of their legal education; spring semester students are anticipating graduation as soon as the course is completed. This means that we teach them as they are about to go from being students to being professionals. They have thoroughly assimilated the skills and culture of law school.

[25] For a description of the scale of our routine image encounters, see M McCullough, *Abstracting Craft* (Cambridge, MA, MIT Press, 1998). He begins his summary with an MIT Media Lab dictum that '[i]n the course of a single day, you will see more artificially constructed images that a seventeenth-century Englishman would have seen in his entire lifetime' (McCullough 1998 at 42).

[26] F Merrell, *Peirce, Signs, and Meaning* (Toronto, University of Toronto Press, 1997), at x.

[27] J Dewey, A Barnes, L Buermeyer, V de Mazia, & M Mullen, *Art and Education* (Philadelphia, The Barnes Foundation, 1947), at 7.

We had to work within obvious constraints. For example, we had to confine our efforts to a single semester. We also had to be sure that what we did was securely anchored in the culture of the law even as we stepped into new territory. Finally, whatever we did, we had to overcome what we assumed would be the shyness and resistance of law students when asked to work in unfamiliar ways. After all, they were admitted to law school because they enjoyed, among other strengths, a facility with words. Nowhere in the application process were they asked to demonstrate skill in making visual representations.

And yet making such representations is precisely what we had decided to do as a first move in pedagogical strategy. There are two assumptions at work in this here. The first is that people are more committed and more engaged when their own work is being discussed. The second is that in confronting real design problems and making decisions themselves, students can begin to anticipate how the design professionals with whom they may eventually work engage in real problem solving. Students encounter the questions and think generally about how to approach them—which is far more important in the long run than knowing a few particular design answers. We enable untrained students to embrace information design and high-level video graphics computing even though we lack the time to train them in sophisticated design skills. The 'hands-on' practice in visual analysis and production builds skill sets targeted to the specific problems the students will confront in practice. By using the power of the peer group and creating a micro-culture that supports and enhances the goals of the class, we plunge them into a classroom environment that is itself a multi-media, semiotic creation.

Although a number of assigned texts contain images, the primary image texts used in class are those made by the students themselves. Their investment in making these images increases their confidence in their knowledge about them, which in turn guarantees their interest in responses from other group members. The six or so exercises that lead up to the projects move from word-image collages from the newspaper, to photographic images arranged to tell stories, to real objects accompanied by invented stories from made-up legal cases, to image-only 'books' and, finally, a storyboard exercise. Our first exercise doesn't seem to involve any personal material at all. By the fourth one, students have acculturated to the class and their books are often highly suggestive as snapshot self-portraits. For instance, a recent book had a black cover with a small title. Inside, every page illustrated scenes from sports. The inside pages, though, were not rectangular like the cover but were, instead, shaped like the ball used in the game illustrated—footballs, basketballs, baseballs, and soccer balls, two for each of these sports. The maker was a young man, very quiet in class—like his book, he was 'covered' by an inscrutable demeanor but repeatedly surprised us with the way he solved his problems in the projects.

We bring all our visual exercises to class, put them out for all to see/read/explore, and then discuss them together, mostly without specific reference to who made what. We model exploring what is seen and read these exercises in a wide-open way. These assignments directly prepare students in ways of thinking they will need when producing their videos, but we do not tell them that until the second project is introduced and we can make visible the connections between the assignments and their new work. The professors join the students in producing and sharing their work on these exercises because it is important for the professors to model the behavior that they wish to elicit.[28]

The work of learning to talk about perceptions of pictures begins here: in showing the range of readings/responses and non-judgmentally discussing what we have all made. Knowing that their work will be 'published' within the group leads students to take the production process seriously. The experience of making also sensitises them to the pedagogy of mutual interpretation and critique. Students experience this process of making, interpreting, and critiquing as very empowering, and this enables them to take further risks. Laterally sharing power over the reading of visual texts enhances the development of peer relations within the group and internalises the decentralised and collaborative pedagogy of the course. This subsequently carries over to their response to written texts as well. We encourage students to share their thinking rather than to withhold their 'good' ideas for the sake of some sort of competitive advantage. In this way, students come to regard the class as a model of the kind of collaborative process of case development and critique that goes on in the real world of legal practice.

As faculty we have to be prepared to respond in the moment—we never know what the students are going to bring in. We are not controlling the text. [29] Some pedagogues would take this exercise in the direction of naming various kinds of signs and engaging in taxonomy. We follow a different path. We want our students to begin to trust the validity of their perceptions, and then to test them. We aim to show them both broad cultural themes and the realities of atypical, unexpected responses from individuals. While learning to use their own responses as tuning forks, they need to experience how very differently others may encounter the same material. As lawyers they will have to make just these kinds of judgment calls about likely audience reactions to their arguments, and they need this practice.

If we assume, then, that the goal is to make self-conscious engagement with visual meaning-making possible, with the understanding that absolute

[28] This is true for all forms of professional training; when there are calls for change, it is often because of pressure to produce new styles of authority.

[29] Faculty of course retain control over the syllabus and have the power to grade, with all its attendant consequences. Our classroom practice is not an abandonment of all authority but its reconfiguration.

and stable meanings cannot be constructed, then we must create a classroom where pluralities of meanings are tolerated and experienced as non-threatening. The students must become active agents and not just passive receivers, comfortable with the absence of conclusive answers.[30] They need to enjoy liminality, the entrance of thoughts and feelings just below the threshold of consciousness, while at the same time thinking critically: They must both lower barriers and be more conscious. If, as suggested above, pictures provide a particularly powerful way for lawyers to exploit implicit meanings in making their arguments, the only way to explore what those meanings might be in any one image is to test people's direct responses to the images. Such explorations put visual legal training on a collision course with traditional law school pedagogy. This is so not because law teachers regard text as transparent, but because the students' responses to texts or other materials are sharply controlled by teachers who generally seek to elicit specific answers, which they already have in mind upon entering the classroom. Students in law school learn to read texts differently than they do outside law school. According to Elizabeth Mertz,

> the classroom discourse [in a traditional law classroom] is a semiotic disciplining to a new form of reading and discursively organizing texts, and this reading can of course be multiply recontextualised in the various speech settings of legal practice.[31]

First-year law students often find this retraining of reading stressful and they depend upon faculty and faculty's authority to make this transition; it is non-obvious from the materials themselves. We are introducing yet different habits of mind that require the cultivation of creative, nonlinear thinking and more active, decentralised, and collaborative participation than the traditional law teaching model allows. We have had to reconfigure the traditional law school paradigm.

We signal the different culture of this classroom immediately. Two professors, coming from very different disciplines—law and fine arts—share authority (more about this later). The group is small enough (between twelve and sixteen students) so everyone can have face-to-face contact. The professors use their first names. Unlike other law school courses, we do not

[30] G Hess & S Frideland, *Techniques for Teaching Law* (Durham, NC, Carolina Academic Press, 1999), at 108–09, while asserting that '[m]odern professional practice is characterised by complexity, uncertainty, and value conflict,' state immediately thereafter that 'student experiences are most likely to promote significant learning if they are carefully planned, monitored, and structured to achieve specific learning goals.' While we believe that careful teaching is important, our model is more wide open, the goals of any one class more a moving target. Maybe this is due to the fact that we are engaging in a non-linear curriculum where constant themes move between the warp and the weft and we look for recursiveness both to reinforce those themes and to build the group.

[31] E Mertz, *Recontextualization As Socialization: Text and Pragmatics in the Law School Classroom* (Chicago, American Bar Foundation, 1993), at 36.

post the readings for the first class in advance. Students arrive with no orientation apart from the various expectations that the course description may have sparked. This highly practical classroom structure may be unconventional for American law schools, but it has enabled students to bring their individual interests and experiences into the classroom, often supplementing the planned materials in important ways. For example, one student with experience in the District Attorney's Office taught us how drug dealers in Connecticut do their accounting. A former corrections officer taught us about adolescents in prison. A psychotherapist moved our discussions to levels of counter-intuitive sophistication that students might have otherwise missed. Finally, a master player of the popular video game 'Doom' showed us what we needed to know to pursue a hypothetical case against the game's publishers in litigation deriving from the shootings at Columbine High School. These contributions of what anthropologists call 'local knowledge'[32] have, each time, expanded the content available for use in the class and enhanced the development of our classroom micro-culture.

Once faculty realise that the small group dynamics are producing a micro-culture, it becomes relatively simple to cultivate this dimension more deliberately. With all members of the group freely engaging a variety of materials—both verbal and visual—we develop a system of reference to the formal elements of the course as well as to jokes arising from our common experiences and some knowledge about our personal lives. These references, not unlike the private language of family life, can be evoked and deliberately invoked by faculty as part of classroom communication. Such gestures toward group bonding contribute to the overall sense of the class as a self-contained discourse community.

Patterns are already emerging after four iterations of the course. At the beginning of the semester, when confronted by thick packets of interdisciplinary materials—not just those of the law and facts of the hypothetical case, but also those drawn from social psychology, cognitive science, philosophy, literature, art history, history of science, media studies and so on—students often panic. Their initial uneasiness is exacerbated by our not telling them why or how to argue (although we give them everything they need to make their arguments). Responses range from groans to 'Can't we just settle the case and be done with it?' or 'What do I do—I dislike my client?' As the mid-term looms, there are more and more questions about the formal written requirement—what form do we want, how long, etc.—seemingly reflecting a fear of having no boundaries when, in fact, we give clear guidelines but more than the usual latitude. We have provided extra class time to work as a committee of the whole in thinking through the issues. A student last fall noticed the general anxiety in the classroom and

[32] C Geertz, *Local Knowledge: Further Essays in Interpretive Anthropology* (New York, Basic Books, 1983).

said: 'The project is big, lacking definition. We have to swallow without sufficient chewing.'

Just as students voice their anxieties, outside of class, so do the professors. 'Are we losing them?' comes up when we see how anxious they are. 'Are we letting them down by not dealing with every dreading in detail?' 'Am I, a non-lawyer, on target or not?' 'Will they take my thinking seriously?' About three quarters of the way through each semester (or nine to ten weeks into it), the law-trained member of the team usually begins to be really concerned, and so plans a little structured presentation or two—very useful, pulling together the various intellectual threads we have in play, weeding the garden a bit. And each time, in slightly different versions, the students have manifested resistance to going back to a more conventional classroom style. They become inattentive, sometimes even engaging in side conversations during the professor's presentation on the law. Our students have brought food and drink to share with the class. This too can be seen as an aspect of rebellion ('we are going to nurture ourselves, the leaders aren't the only source of feeding') but when this occurs at the end of the course, it is a celebration and a sharing of leadership, a mature self-definition of the group.[33] It is not uncommon for students to ask to bring guests to class for the project presentations at the end, opening and extending that boundaries that we faculty have so carefully protected.

Rebellion also occurs just around the time we are asking them to work seriously on the video project as a small group activity. They have to take on the mantle of authority to do this project and set out into the unknown, with their grade depending upon the collaboration. Their rebellion can be seen as furthering the goals of the course as well as a stage in the maturing of the group. Our students are adults and the course has many real task-oriented demands. The drama of the group is a subtext. Nevertheless,

> a *deliberate* group action enormously strengthens group confidence, group self-awareness, and internal differentiation. This is one of the reasons why the group revolt so often marks a major advance in group consciousness.[34]

The video projects are accomplished in six weeks after two hours of video production training and two hours of editing training. All it takes is the experience of lifting a sound track from one clip and attaching it to another for students to know with certainty that everything on film is constructed

[33] In the context of this short paper, it is not possible to lay out a complete group dynamics analysis. This reading of the group's behavior is carried out under the analytical frame of P Slater, *Microcosm* (New York, John Wiley & Sons, 1966).

[34] Slater 1966 at 246. What is unknown, and would be interesting to study, is what effect having two professors has on the revolt of the group. Does this automatically diffuse some of the leader's power without any abandonment of it? Also unknown is how important it is that the two are a man and a woman in our working contexts. We certainly repeat visually images of the two parent, two gendered family. Unlike some families, there is a full sharing of authority between these two 'parents.'

and that they can be builders in this medium. We teach them just what they need to know to do the project. Our bottom-up approach—'here's a tool; 'use it' rather than, 'you need to know this and this and this before you can use it'—works. It works because people are empowered; it works because they call upon other knowledge they have—one student said, 'I see, it's a word processor for film!'—and it works because they discover, when they sit in front of the computer and perform the simplest operations with it, that whatever they don't know about computers pales beside everything that they do know about film and video. Students have displayed a fluency and sophistication in their editing that is often lacking in the written portion of their midterm projects. While visual literacy has been neglected as a component of formal education, American students have been unwittingly assimilating a complex knowledge of film language simply from watching television and going to the movies. Not having to draw upon that knowledge, or think about it in a more self-conscious and critical manner, they didn't realise they had it. However, once they begin to apply this body of knowledge, they feel competent and able—and patient—with the technology. They also have the support of their peers both as team members and as an audience.

In what follows we will pull together the foregoing observations about course pedagogy and content in an effort to summarise how the Visual Persuasion course reflects the value of an interdisciplinary approach to legal visual rhetoric. We offer five brief observations about how the course reflects the value of an interdisciplinary approach to legal visual rhetoric.

First, to persuade in any medium, both the content and form of a message must mesh with what the audience is prepared to understand and believe. Readings in rhetoric, the psychology of persuasion, and cognitive and social psychology introduce students to this basic idea (among many others). Narrative theory shows them that audiences are more likely to accept an argument packaged as a story that resonates with familiar themes of right vs. wrong, good vs. evil, man vs. nature, big vs. small, innocence vs. deceit.

Second, in a visual culture, students who are to succeed in discovering the possible means of persuasion in any situation need to know about the psychology of perception, information design, art history, advertising, and media studies, among other fields. In addition to these intellectual tools, students also need to practice making and responding to images, which is what visual exercises (and examples of legal visual rhetoric shown in class) provide.

Third, students' efforts to argue using images as well as words reflect deep, intuitive understandings of modern visual culture, from movies to documentaries to advertising. But to integrate the persuasive techniques of popular culture effectively with the demands of real legal arguments, that intuitive knowledge must be made (at least partly) self-conscious and explicit. Interdisciplinary readings give students many ways to articulate what they already know, and thus to develop a common vocabulary for creating and critiquing modern visual rhetoric. Visual exercises and larger projects make their understanding active. And students are much less likely to forget what they have done themselves, for their experiential knowledge is but an extension of who they are (or have become).

Fourth, making digital videos allows students to discover how easy it is to access and manipulate information today (it's all zeroes and ones), and how easy it is to represent reality in multiple ways. This in itself makes them more critical consumers of mass media. As students tell us: 'I'll never watch TV the same way again.' Readings in digital media and communication enhance students' appreciation of what it means to use digital technology to persuade—as well as how audiences accustomed to computer interfaces and digital interactivity may respond differently to visual appeals than do audiences comfortable only with analog media.

Fifth, and finally, a highly multidisciplinary approach increases the connections among law, media, and culture that students visibly realise in their work. This encourages a new visual ethnography of legal communication, allowing us to observe how the coming generation of media-savvy lawyers is primed to creatively and strategically import into descriptive and adversarial legal discourse the contents and styles of popular culture. Studying how these new lawyers use the latest visual technologies may ultimately help us to reconceive the theory and practice of legal rhetoric itself.

V

CONCLUSION

Close to the end of the semester, one of our students said, 'I thought we were supposed to learn the rules and apply them and now you are leading us down a different path altogether.' We answered, 'Laws and rules are interpreted, facts arranged into a theory of the case. How are you going to convince people that your position should be adopted without thinking about persuasion?' Yet, we can understand the student's quandary. Classical rhetoric is rarely taught any more in the law school curriculum, and the move to the visual leaves us exploring unknown territory where images evoke not just visions of reason and justice but also encounters with difficult emotions and the imponderables of audience reception. All three of us believe that the empowerment of rhetorical speech which we try to foster will do more than make students smarter and more thoughtful about pictures; it will also enable them to be more active participants in public rhetoric and more sophisticated observers of how mass media shape and inform how people think and feel.

The empowerment and critical sharpening of their speech have also led to a sense of greater personal integration. Many students have told us at the end of the course that they feel the course has helped them to rescue parts of themselves that had remained dormant. They never realised that they could use more of themselves in their professional work. In this course, we have constructed a semiotic environment in which our materials, assignments, and practices are indexical for the very thing we wish to teach, just as the 'recontextualisation, [of legal texts] to a significant extent, performs the semiotic mediation of social praxis.'[35]

What we did not anticipate was how our course might help to fulfill the most fundamental purpose of Martha Nussbaum's call for the literary imagination to be incorporated into the practice of the law. She defines this as the development of empathy for the other. When students make their video projects, they are left completely free to decide whether they wish to film original footage or just appropriate existing material to be used as part of their arguments. When they film original footage, some cast themselves as professionals, which they are becoming; others as citizens, with whom they must be comfortable; and still others imagine themselves as outsiders, convicts, tricksters. We believe that this is demonstrative evidence that these new lawyers are 'capable of entering imaginatively into the lives of distant others and to have emotions related to that participation.'[36] It is our hope that this experience of empathy, combined with the sturdiness of legal testing in the adversarial setting of the law, will help to constrain the adverse effects of rhetorical manipulation while making our students effective communicators of the facts and narratives of their cases.

Visual literacy presents lawyers, especially trial lawyers, with new communicative power. Complex events can be translated into clear and easily accessible images without sacrificing accuracy. At the same time, however, this power introduces new challenges: technical, strategic, and ethical. In the long run, there is no choice but to confront these challenges. As law, like the rest of our social and cultural institutions, increasingly uses visual means to communicate, legal practice will look increasingly like politics, advertising, and TV journalism. It, too, will assimilate the fluid reality of images moving across an electronic screen. This is our vernacular, the popular bandwidth of an increasingly global culture in which lawyers will operate. In recent years, as the technologies of visual communication have proliferated, the pace of change has accelerated rapidly. As academics, it is up to us to teach our students how to self-reflectively tell and critique the visual stories and visual arguments that are being presented in the courtroom, and that circulate within the popular legal imagination in the culture at large. With its potent integration of theory and practice, we believe that legal semiotics provides the tools that are needed for this descriptive and critical task.

[35] Mertz 1993 above n 31, at 5.
[36] M Nussbaum, *Poetic Justice* (Boston, Beacon Press, 1997), at xvi.

Selected Bibiliography

BOOKS

ALLEYNE, MD, *International Power and International Communication* (London, MacMillan 1995).

AMSTERDAM, A, and BRUNER, J, *Minding the Law* (Cambridge, MA, Harvard University Press 2000).

ANDERSON, B, *Imagined Communities* (London, Verso 1982).

ARISTOTLE, *The Art of Rhetoric.* Trans by H Lawson-Tancred. Reprint (New York, Penguin Classics 1992 Original edition 1991).

ATTALI, J, *The Labyrinth in Culture and Society. Pathways to Wisdom* (Berkeley, North Atlantic Books 1999).

BAKHTIN, M, *Teoria Y Estetica De La Novela, Trabajos De Investigacion* (Madrid, Taurus 1989).

BAUCOM, I, *Out of Place* (Durham, Duke University Press 1999).

BAUDRILLARD, J, *The Illusion of the End* (Cambridge, Polity 1994).

BEATTY, D, *Constitutional Law in Theory and Practice* (Toronto, University of Toronto Press 1995).

BERGER, RAOUL, *Government by Judiciary: The Transformation of the Fourteenth Amendment* (Cambridge, MA, Harvard University Press 1977).

BERNS, W, *Taking the Constitution Seriously* (New York, Simon and Schuster 1987).

BHATIA, VK, *Analyzing Genre: Language Use in Professional Settings* (London and New York, Longman 1993).

BORK, R, *The Tempting of America: The Political Seduction of the Law* (New York, Macmillan 1990).

BOWERS, F, *Linguistic Aspects of Legislative Expression* (Vancouver, University of British Columbia Press 1989).

BRIGHAM, J, *The Cult of the Court* (Philadelphia, Temple University Press 1987).

BRIGHAM, J, *The Constitution of Interests: Beyond the Politics of Rights* (New York, NYU Press 1996).

BRUNER, J, *Acts of Meaning* (Cambridge, MA, Harvard University Press 1990).

BURKE, K, *A Rhetoric of Motives* (Berkeley, University of California Press 1969).

BURNS, R, *A Theory of the Trial* (Princeton, Princeton University Press 1999).

BURTON, F, and CARLEN, P, *Official Discourse: On Discourse Analysis, Government, Ideology and the State* (London, RKP 1979).

BUTLER, J, *Excitable Speech: A Politics of Performance* (New York, Routledge 1997).

CAMPBELL, G, *The Philosophy of Rhetoric* (London, William Tegg 1850).

CAMPBELL, TD, *The Legal Theory of Ethical Positivism* (Aldershort, Dartmouth 1996).

CHEN, A, *An Introduction to the Legal System of the People's Republic of China* (Singapore, Butterworths 1992).

CHEN, JIANFU, *Chinese Law: Towards an Understanding of Chinese Law, Its Nature and Development* (The Hague, Kluwer Law 1999).

COOK, G, *The Discourse of Advertising* (London and New York, Routledge 1992).

CUTTS, M, *Clarifying Eurolaw* (Plain Language Commission 2001).

DAMAŠKA, M, *The Faces of Justice and State Authority* (New Haven, Yale University Press 1986).

DAVIS, S, and SIMON, P, *Reggae International* (New York, Random House 1982).

DELEUZE, G, and GUATTARI, F, *Anti-Oedipe* (Paris, Les Editions de Minuit 1972).

DELGADO, R, and STEFANCIC, J, *Critical Race Theory: An Introduction* (New York, NYU Press 2001).

DERRIDA, J, *Structure Sign and Play* in: *Writing and Difference* (Chicago, University of Chicago Press 1980).

DICK, R, *Legal Drafting in Plain Language* (Toronto, Carswell 1995).

DIXON, M, *The Imaginary Australian: Anglo-Celts and Identity—1788 to the Present* (Sydney, UNSW Press 1999).

DOYLE, B, *English and Englishness* (London, Routledge 1989).

DWORKIN, R, *Taking Rights Seriously* (London, Duckworth 1977).

DWORKIN, R, *Law's Empire* (London, Collins 1986).

EAGLETON, T, *Literary Theory: An Introduction* (Oxford, Blackwell 1983).

ECO, U, *A Theory of Semiotics* (Bloomingtion, Indiana University Press 1976).

ECO, U, RORTY, R, CULLER, J, and BROOKE-ROSE, C, *Interpretation and Overinterpretation* (Cambridge, Cambridge University Press 1992).

ESKRIDGE, WN, FRICKEY, PP, and GARRETT, E, *Legislation and Statutory Interpretation* (New York, Foundation Press 2000).

FAIRCLOUGH, N, *Language and Power* (London, Longman 1989).

FISH, S, *Doing What Comes Naturally. Change, Rhetoric, and the Practice of Theory in Literary and Legal Studies* (Durham and London, Duke University Press reprint edition 1992).

FOUCAULT, M, *Discipline and Punish: The Birth of the Prison*, tr A Sheridan (New York, Vintage 1979).

FUENTES, C, *The Buried Mirror: Reflections on Spain and the New World* (Boston, Houghton Mifflin 1992).

FULTON, J, *The Tragedy of Belief: Division, Politics, and Religion in Ireland* (Oxford, Clarendon Press 1991).

FUMAROLI, M, *L'Age de l'Eloquence* (Geneva, Librairie Droz 1980).

GEERTZ, C, *Local Knowledge: Further Essays in Interpretive Anthropology* (New York, Basic Books 1983).

GÉNY, F, *Science et Technique en Droit Positif, 3 volumes* (Paris, Recueil Sirey 1922).

GIBBONS, J, *Forensic Linguistics* (Oxford, Blackwell 2003).

GOODRICH, P, *Languages of Law: From Logics of Memory to Nomadic Masks* (London, Weidenfeld and Nicolson 1990).

GOODRICH, P, *Oedipus Lex. Psychoanalysis, History, Law* (Berkeley, Los Angeles, London, University of California Press 1995).

GREIMAS, AJ, *Signs, Language, Culture* (Mouton, The Hague 1970).

HALLIDAY, MAK, *Language as Social Semiotic. The Social Interpretation of Language and Meaning* (London, Edward Arnold 1978).

HART, HLA, *The Concept of Law* (London, Oxford University Press 1961).

HAUSER, GA, *Introduction to Rhetorical Theory* (Long Grove, Waveland Press reprint edition 1991).

HESKETH, T, *The Second Partitioning of Ireland: The Abortion Referendum of 1983* (Dublin, Brandsma Book 1990).

HILTUNEN, R, *Chapters on Legal English: Aspects Past and Present of the Language of the Law* (Helsinki, Suomalainen Tiedeakatemia 1990).

HYNDMAN, HM, *England for All* (London, Gilbert & Rivington 1881).

JACKSON, B, *Making Sense in Law* (Liverpool, Deborah Charles Publications 1995).

JAUSS, HR, *Aesthetic Experience and Literary Hermeneutics* (Minneapolis, University of Minessota Press 1989).

KAHN, PW, *The Cultural Study of Law: Reconstructing Legal Scholarship* (Chicago & London, University of Chicago Press 1999).

KEITH, NW, and KEITH, NZ, *The Social Origins of Democratic Socialism in Jamaica* (Philadelphia, Temple University Press 1992).

KEVELSON, R, *The Law as a System of Signs* (New York, Plenum 1988).

KEVELSON, R, *Flux, Complexity, and Illusion, Sixth Round Table on Law and Semiotics* (New York, Peter Lang, 1992).

KEVELSON, R, *Conscience, Consensus, and Crossroads in Law, Eighth Round Table on Law and Semiotics* (New York, Peter Lang, 1993).

KLEIN, N, *Fences and Windows: Dispatches from the Front Lines of the Globalization Debate* (New York, Picador 2002).

KURZON, D, *It Is Hereby Performed ... Explorations in Legal Speech Acts. Pragmatics and Beyond VII: 6* (Amsterdam, John Benjamins 1986).

LACAN, J, *Ecrits: A Selection* (New York, Norton 1977).

LARKIN, E, *Historical Dimensions of Irish Catholicism* (New York, Arno Press 1976).

LEWIS, F, *The Context of Judicial Activism: The Endurance of the Warren Court Legacy in a Conservative Age* (Lanham, MD, Rowman and Littlefield 1999).

LIBBY, R, *Hawke's Law: The Politics of Mining and Aboriginal Land Rights in Australia* (Perth, WA, UWA Press 1990).

LINDON, R, *Le Style, L'éloquence Judiciaire* (Paris, Albin Michel 1968).

LINELL, P, *Approaching Dialogue: Talk, Interaction and Contexts in Dialogical Perspectives* (Amsterdam/Philadelphia, John Benjamins Publishing Company 1998).

LUHMANN, N, *A Sociological Theory of Law* (London/Boston, Routledge and Kegan Paul 1985).

LUKE, T, *Shows of Force. Power, Politics, and Ideology in Art Exhibitions* (Durham, Duke University Press 1992).

MATSUDA, M, Lawrence III, C, Delgado, R, and Williams Crenshaw, R, *Words That Wound, Critical Race Theory, Assaultive Speech, and the First Amendment* (Boulder, CO, Westview Press 1993).

MCCANN, I, *Bob Marley: In His Own Words* (London, Omnibus Press 1993).

MCILWAIN, CH, *Constitutionalism: Ancient and Modern* (Ithaca, Cornell University Press 1947).

MCQUAIL, D, *Mass Communication Theory: An Introduction* (London, Sage 1983).

MELLINKOFF, D, *The Language of the Law* (Boston, Little Brown and Company 1963).

MENAND, L, *The Metaphysical Club: A Story of Ideas in America* (New York, Farrar Straus and Giroux 2001).

MERRELL, F, *Peirce, Signs, and Meaning* (Toronto, University of Toronto Press 1997).

MERTZ, E, *Recontextualization as Socialization: Text and Pragmatics in the Law School Classroom* (Chicago, American Bar Foundation 1993).

MITCHELL, WJT, *Iconology: Image, Text, Ideology* (Chicago, University of Chicago Press 1986).

MO, HONGJI, *Zhengfu yu gongmin xianfa bidu: Zhonghua renmin gongheguo xianfa xiuzhengan quanjing touxi* (*Compulsory Readings for the Government and Citizens: A Complete Analysis of the Chinese Constitutional Amendments*) (Beijing, Zhongguo renmin gongan daxue chubanshe 1999).

MONTESQUIEU, C, *The Spirit of the Laws (De l'esprit des lois)* AM Cohler, BC Miller and HS Stone (eds) (Cambridge, Cambridge University Press 1989. Original edition, 1748).

MORRIS, Ch W, *Foundation of the Theory of Signs* in *International Encyclopedia of Unified Science*, vol 1 (Chicago, University of Chicago Press 1938).

NICHOLS, B, *Representing Reality* (Bloomington, Indiana University Press 1991).

NUSSBAUM, M, *Poetic Justice* (Boston, Beacon Press 1997).
ONG, W, *Fighting for Life* in *Contest, Sexuality and Consciousness* (Ithaca, Cornell University Press 1981).
ONG, W, *Orality and Literacy: The Technologizing of the Word (New Accents)* (New York, Routledge 1988).
POWE, L, *The Warren Court and American Politics* (Cambridge, MA, Harvard University Press 2000).
RAWLS, J, *A Theory of Justice* (Oxford, Oxford University Press 1974).
RODNEY, W, *The Groundings With My Brothers* (London, Bogle-L'Ouverture Publications 1969).
ROSENBAUM, AS, *Constitutionalism: the Philosophical Dimension* (New York, Greenwood Press 1988).
SAGER, J, *A Practical Course in Terminology Processing* (Amsterdam/ Philadelphia, John Benjamins 1990).
SAID, E, *Orientalism* (London, Penguin 1995).
SAMUEL, R, *'Country Visiting: A Memoir', in Island Stories. Unravelling Britain* (London, Verso 1999).
SARCEVIC, S, *New Approach to Legal Translation* (The Hague, Kluwer Law International 1997).
SHERWIN, R, *When Law Goes Pop* (Chicago, University of Chicago Press 2000).
SWALES, J, *Genre Analysis*, (Cambridge, CUP 1990).
TANNER, MS, *The Politics of Lawmaking in Post-Mao China: Institutions, Processes and Democratic Prospects* (Oxford, Clarendon Press 1999).
TAUSSIG, M, *The Nervous System* (New York, Routledge 1992).
THORNTON, GC, *Legislative Drafting* (London, Butterworths 1970).
TIERSMA, P, *Legal Language* (Chicago, University of Chicago Press 1999).
TODOROV, T, *The Conquest of America: The Question of the Other* (New York, Harper 1982).
VAN DIJK, TA, *Racism and the Press* (London, Routledge 1991).
VIRILIO, P, *The Aesthetics of Disappearance* (New York, Semiotext(e)1991).
WAGNER, A, *La Langue de la Common Law* (Paris, L'Harmattan 2002).
WALLERSTEIN, I, *The End of the World as We Know It, Social Science for the Twenty First Century* (Minneapolis, University of Minnesota Press 1999).
WATZLAWICK, P, WEAKLANO, J and FISCH, R, *Change* (New York, Norton 1974).
WIDDOWSON, HG, *Exploration in Applied Linguistics* (Oxford, Oxford University Press 1979).
WILLIAMS, PJ, *Seeing a Color-Blind Future: The Paradox of Race* (New York, The Noonday Press 1997).
WORTH, S, *Studying Visual Communication* (Philadelphia, University of Pennsylvania Press 1981).
XU, CHONGDE, *Xianfa* (*Constitutional Law*) (Beijing, Zhongguo remin daxue chubanshe 2001).

YNGVESSON, B, *Virtuous Citizens, Disruptive Subjects* (New York, Routledge 1993).

ZIZEK, S, *Enjoy Your Symptom! Jacques Lacan in Hollywood and Out* (New York, Routledge 1992).

CHAPTERS IN EDITED VOLUMES

BAKHTIN, M, 'The Problem of Speech Genres' in C Emerson and M Holquist (eds), *Speech Genres and Other Late Essays*, VW McGee, trans (Austin, University of Texas Press 1986).

BAZERMAN, C, 'Performatives Constituting Value: The Case of Patents' in BL Gunnarsson, P Linell and B Nordberg (eds), *The Construction of Professional Discourse* (London and New York, Longman 1997).

BRINER, R, 'Globalization and the Future of Courts of Arbitration' in M Pfeifer (ed), *The Internationalization of the Practice of Law* (The Netherlands, Kluwer Law International 2001).

CALMORE, JO, 'Critical Race Theory, Archie Shepp, and Fire Music: Securing an Authentic Intellectual Life in a Multicultural World' in K Crenshaw, N Gotanda, G Peller and K Thomas (eds), *Critical Race Theory: The Key Writings that Formed the Movement* (New York, The New Press 1995).

CAMPBELL, KK, and JAMIESON, KH, 'Form and Genre in Rhetorical Criticism: An Introduction' in KK Campbell and KH Jamieson (eds), *Form and Genre: Shaping Rhetorical Action* (Falls Church, VA, The Speech Communication Association 1978).

CARRELL, PL, and EISTERHOLD, JC, 'Schema Theory and ESL Reading Pedagogy' in Carrell, PL, J Devine and D Eskey (eds), *Interactive Approaches to Second Language Reading* (Cambridge, Cambridge University Press 1998).

CHEN, JIANFU, 'Unanswered Questions and Unresolved Issues: Comments on the Law on Law-Making' in JM Otto, MV Polak, Jianfu Chen, Yuwen Li (eds), *Law-Making in the People's Republic of China* (The Hague, Kluwer Law International 2000).

DF VAGTS, DF, 'The Impact of Globalization on the Legal Profession' in M Pfeifer (ed), *The Internationalization of the Practice of Law* (The Netherlands, Kluwer Law International 2001).

DOWDLE, M 'Constructing Citizenship: The NPC as a Catalyst for Political Participation' in M Goldman and EJ Perry (eds), *Changing Meanings of Citizenship in Modern China* (Cambridge MA, Harvard University Press 2002).

FRADE, C, 'Introduction to the Legal System in Brazil' in VK Bhatia, CN Candlin, J Engberg and A Trosborg (eds), *Multilingual and Multicultural Contexts of Legislation: An International Perspective* (Hamburg, Peter Lang GMBH 2003).

GOODRICH, P, and HACHAMOVITCH, Y, 'Time out of Mind: An Introduction to the Semiotics of Common Law' in P Fitzpatrick (ed), *Dangerous Supplements* (London, Pluto Press 1991).

HANEY Lopez, 'The Social Construction of Race' in R Delgado (ed), *Critical Race Theory: The Cutting Edge* (Philadelphia, Temple University Press 1995).

HASAN, R, 'Contexts for Meaning' in JE Alatis (ed), *Language, Communication and Social Meaning, Georgetown University Round Table on Languages and Linguistics 1992* (Washington, DC, Georgetown University Press 1992).

HOUTTE, H van, and Wautelet, P, 'International Lawyers and Uniform Law' in M Pfeifer (ed), *The Internationalization of the Practice of Law* (The Netherlands, Kluwer Law International 2001).

JACKSON, BS, 'Narrative Theories in Legal Discourse' in C Nash (ed), *Narrative in Culture: The Use of Storytelling in the Sciences, Philosophy and Literature* (London, Routledge 1990).

KELLER, P 'The National People's Congress and the Making of National Law' in JM Otto, MV Polak, Jianfu Chen, and Yuwen Li (eds), *Law-Making in the People's Republic of China* (The Hague, Kluwer Law International 2000).

LINELL, P, 'The Power of Dialogue Dynamics' in I Markovà and K Foppa (eds), *The Dynamics of Dialogue* (Hemel Hempstead, Harvester Wheatsheaf 1990).

MARTINS, P, 'Arbitragem através dos Tempos. Obstáculos e Preconceitos à sua Implementação no Brasil'['Arbitration through Times. Obstacles and Prejudice to its Implementation in Brazil'] in AN Pucci et al (eds), *A Arbitragem na Era da Globalização [Arbitration in the Era of Globalisation]* (Rio de Janeiro, Editora Forense 1999).

PELLER, G, 'Race-Consciousness' in K Crenshaw, N Gotanda, G Peller and K Thomas (eds), *Critical Race Theory: The Key Writings That Formed the Movement* (New York, The New Press 1995).

PETERS, B, 'On Reconstructing Legal and Political Theory' in M Deflem (ed), *Habermas, Modernity and Law* (London, Sage Publications 1996).

RAZ, J 'On the Authority and Interpretation of Constitution: Some Preliminaries' in L Alexander (ed), *Constitutionalism: Philosophical Foundations* (Cambridge, Cambridge University Press 1998).

VERNON, J, 'Narrating the Constitution' in James Vernon (ed), *Re-reading the Constitution: New Narratives in the Political History of England's Long Nineteenth Century* (Cambridge, Cambridge University Press 1996).

VON SENGER, H 'Ideology and Law-Making. Law-Making in the People's Republic of China' in JM Otto, MV Polak, Jianfu Chen and Yuwen Li (eds), *Law-Making in the People's Republic of China* (The Hague, Kluwer Law International 2000).

YU, Xingzhong 'Citizenship, Ideology, and the PRC Constitution' in M Goldman and EJ Perry (eds), *Changing Meanings of Citizenship in Modern China* (Cambridge, MA, Harvard University Press 2002).

JOURNAL ARTICLES

BALKIN, JM, 'The Promise of Legal Semiotics' (1991) 1831 *University Texas Law Review*.

BEYER, JA, 'The Second Line: Reconstructing the Jazz Metaphor in Critical Race Theory' (March 2000) *Georgetown Law Journal* 537.

BRIGGS, CL, and BAUMAN, R, 'Genre, Intertextuality, and Social Power' (1992) 2 *Journal of Linguistic Anthropology* 131.

BRINE, K, 'Tent Embassy Protestors Have Their Day in Court' *Canberra Times* (7 February 2002).

CAI, DINGJIAN, 'Development of the Chinese Legal System Since 1979 and its Current Crisis and Transformation' (1999), 11:2 *Cultural Dynamics* 135.

CAMPBELL, L, 'Drafting Styles: Fuzzy or Fussy?' (1996) 3 *E-Law Murdoch University Electronic Journal of Law*.

CAMPBELL, TD, 'The Point of Legal Positivism' (1998) 9 *The King's College Law Journal* 63.

CIOFFI, JW, 'Governing Globalization? The State, Law, and Structural Change in Corporate Governance' (2000) 27 *Journal of Law and Society*.

DARIAN-SMITH, E, 'Legal Imagery in the 'Garden of England'' (1995) *Indiana Journal of Global Legal Studies* 2.

DASCAL, M, and WRÓBLEWSKI, J, 'The Rational Law-maker and the Pragmatics of Legal Interpretation' (1991) 15 *Journal of Pragmatics*.

DERRIDA, J, 'The University in the Eye of its Pupil' (1983) Fall *Diacritics* 3.

DOWDLE, M, 'Of Parliaments, Pragmatism, and the Dynamics of Constitutional Development: The Curious Case of China' (2002) 35:1 *New York University Journal of International Law and Politics*.

DUNCANSON, I, 'Mr Hobbes Goes to Australia: Law, Politics and Difference' (2000) 13 *International Journal for the Semiotics of Law*.

ECO, U, 'Peirce's Notion of Interpretant' (1976) *Media Lawyer Newsletter* 91.

ERICSON, RV, 'Mass Media, Crime, Law and Justice' (1999) 31(3) *The British Journal of Criminology*.

FRADE, C, 'Mitigating Conflict in Arbitration Clauses Through Language' (2002) 2 *LSP & Professional Communication*.

FRADE, C, 'The Legal Cooperative Principle: An Essay on the Cooperative Nature of Contractual Transactions' (2002) 15 *International Journal for the Semiotics of Law* 4, 338.

HART, HLA, 'A Description of Responsibility and Rights' (1963) *Essays in Logic and Language* 146.

KAMEN, H, 'Public Authority and Popular Crime: Banditry in Valencia, 1660–1714' (1974) 3 *Journal of European Economic History.*

LENTIN, R, 'Responding to the Racialisation of Irishness: Disavowed Multiculturalism and its Discontent' (2001) 54 *Sociological Research Online* (http://www.soresonline.org.uk/5/4/lentin.html).

LIPPENS, R, 'Greenwich, 1 January 2000. De-inventing the Law of Britain in a Tent', 13(3) (2000) *International Journal for the Semiotics of Law.*

MALEY, Y, 'The Language of Legislation' (1987) 16 *Language in Society.*

MATHEWSON, GC, 'Outdoing Lewis Carroll': Judicial Rhetoric and Acceptable Fictions' (1998) 12 *Argumentation.*

MCCORQUODALE, R, FAIRBROTHER, R, 'Globalization and Human Rights' (1999) 21(3) *Human Rights Quarterly.*

MOONEY, A, 'Human Rights, Linguistics and the Law: The UK and Beyond' (2002) 15:4 *International Journal for the Semiotics of Law.*

PARSI, K, 'Metaphorical Imagination: The Moral and Legal Status of Fetuses and Embryos' (1999) 2/703 *DePaul J Health Care L.*

PEERENBOOM, R 'Ruling the Country in Accordance with Law: Reflections in the Rule and Role of Law in Contemporary China' (1999) 11:3 *Cultural Dynamics* 315.

PENCAK, W, 'Charles Sanders Peirce, Historian and Semiotician' (1991) 83 *Semiotica* 311.

RATNAPALA, S 'The Idea of a Constitution and Why Constitutions Matter' (Summer 1999/2000) *Policy* 3.

SCHILLING, T, 'The Labelling of Foodstuffs in a Language Easily Understood by Purchasers' (1996) 1/96 *European Food Law Review.*

SCHLAG, P, 'Clerks in the Maze' (1993) *Michigan Law Review* 91.

SHARPE, J, 'Figures of Colonial Resistance' (1989) 35 *Modern Fiction Studies.*

SULLIVAN, R, 'The Promise of Plain Language Drafting' (1997) 47 *McGill Law Journal.*

TURENNE SJOLANDER, C, 'The Rhetoric of Globalization: What's in a Wor(l)d?' (1996) 51 *International Journal.*

VAN DIJK, TA, 'Structure of Discourse and Structures of Power' (1989) 12 *Communications Yearbook.*

VARENNES, F De, 'Law, Language and the Multicultural State' (1996) 16(3) *Language and Communication.*

WAGNER, A, 'The Legal Discourse of the Common Law: A Game of Chess' (2002) 15:4 *International Journal for the Semiotics of Law.*

WANG, GUANGHUI, 'Xianfa wei genben fa zhi yanjin' (Constitution as a Basic Law and its Evolution) (2000) 2 *Faxue yanjiu* (*CASS Law Journal*) 127.

Index

Abortion
Ireland. *see* Ireland, abortion debate in
Abu-Jamal, Mumia
celebrity status 106–7
Alexy, Robert
argumentative theory of law 6
Aristophanes
rhetoric, and 129
Aristotle
language, on 2–3
rhetoric, and 130, 135–6
Arnold, Matthew
British constitution, on 23–24
Asylum seeker
meaning. *see* Refugee meanings
Australia
refugee meanings. *see* Refugee meanings
Australian coats of arms 179–95
appropriate symbol of authority of court 186
British monarchy 179, 182–3
connection with other cultural manifestations 180
constitutional arrangements, and 185
cultural association 195
effects of signs 180
endurance 193–5
ethnic identity, and 192
'fetishes' 194
heraldry, and 182
hidden meaning 194
inconsistency in use of 189–90
interpretation 179–95
lost traditions 181–4
masking human agency 193–4
obscurity of meaning 190–3
effectiveness 191
heraldic and linguistic iconography 191–2
Hermetic interpretation 192–3
interpretative plurality 192–3
political projects 184–7
power of the object 188–90
pragmatic effect 195
Queen of England as Australian Head of State 185
referents of symbols 186–7
republican project 184
social dimension of interpretative communities 180–1
State arms of New South Wales 179–84
indigenous animals 187
power of symbol 188–9
verbal judicial oath, and 189
use of symbolism and text in contemporary law 190
value as objects of semiotic study 181

Bakhtin, M
genre, on 60–1
Balkin, JM
philosophical deconstruction, on 135–6
Ballweg, Ottmar
rhetoric, on 132–3
Blair, Tony
May Day protests 2001, on 50–1
Blair Witch Project 234–5
Borges, Jorge Luis
garden of forking paths 1–2

Boutros-Ghali, Boutros
  media, on 52
Brazil
  international arbitration, and 64–5
Brazil's Arbitration Law 9.307/96 57–69
  Brazilian law-making process, and 65
  'capable', meaning 67
  courts, voice of 66
  dialogistic nature of 57–69
  equity, meaning 68
  'general principles of law' 68
  interpretation 66
  multitude of voices 65–6
  President, voice of 66
  'resources with potentials' 67
  responsiveness to prior or subsequent legislation 66–7
  semitechnical words 67–8
  technical terms 68
Brest, Paul
  theories of constitutional interpretation, on 93
Brigham, John
  celebrities, on 14
Britain
  imageries 213–29
    Millenium Dome. *see* Millenium Dome
    rambling 218–9

Cacciagiudi, Sophie
  rhetoric, on 15
Cantor, Georg
  infinity, on 1
Cao, Deborah
  Chinese constitution, on 13
Celebrity 95–112
  A Time to Kill 103
  Abu-Jamal, Mumia 106–7
  authority, as 104–8
  authority in law, as 95–112
  authority, meaning 107–8
  complexity of status 102
  conflict with law 102
  convergence of politics, law and public relations 105
  Eminem 109–10
  Fame Games 111
  feeling about law, and 109
  fluidity in law, and 106
  gag orders 107
  hip-hop 109–10
  homosexuality, and 109–10
  identification with discredited ideology 102–3
  importance of 97
  influence in matters of policy 101
  instability of 101–2
  judges 104
  legal practice 108–12
  less technical aspects of law, and 110
  Megan's law 110–1
  multi dimensional authority 110
  political aspects 99
  Princess Diana 103–4
  rap 109–10
  Saving Private Ryan 108
  Sleepers 103
  social quality of authority in law, and 103
  status 98–104
  traditional authority, and 100
Censorship 113–24
  Cervantes, 115–19. *see also* Cervantes
  decline of Spain, and 114
  Don Quixote 114–5
  early modern Spain 113–24
  Golden Age Spanish Literature, and 114–5
  historical overview 113–5
  semiotic analysis of writing, and 120–4
    appropriation and/or misuse of official language 122
    boundaries of legality and legitimacy 120–1
    chivalry, and 123–4
    colonization, and 121
    Don Quixote 123–4
    rebellion, and 121–2
    women, and 122–3
  Spanish Inquisition 113–4
Cervantes 115–9
  censorship, and 115–9
  Exemplary Stories 115–9
  gypsies, on 116
  Lope de Vega 119–20
  organised crime, on 116–7
  Sevillian underworld slang 117
  skeptic, as 118
Chinese Constitution 71–84
  amendment 1999, 79–81
  basic constitutional principles 78–9
  common communist ideology 77–8
  contents 75–6

entrenched position of Chinese Communist Party 76
legal entrenchment 79
Party norms 82
ethical positivism, and 83
features of 74–81
first 80
four fundamental principles 77–8
fundamental rights and duties of citizens 75
General Principles 75
inherent defects in legal system, and 83
legal document, as 81
legal scholars, and 80–1
legislative expression 79
making sense of 81–4
National People's Congress 75–6
political association 75
political document, as 81
restraint of executive government, and 84
rule governance, and 83
second 80
separation of branches of government 76
socialist market economy, and 82
socio-political environment, and 84
Soviet influences 76–7
stability of 81
structures of state 75–6
supremacy of 81–2
supreme legal force 78
third 80
xianfa 74–5
Cicero
rhetoric, and 130, 131
Civil law
language of 62
Clark, Marcia
prosecution in OJ Simpson case 236–7
Clifford, J
rhetoric, on 132
Clinton, President Bill
Health Care proposal 91
Coats of Arms
Australia. *see* Australian coats of arms
Cochran, Johnny
OJ Simpson case, and 237
Common law
Goodrich, Peter on 219–20
legal language 62
Constitutions 72–4
central features 73–4
characterisation 72–4
democratic 72
differences in understanding and practices 72–3
fundamental laws, as 72
jurisprudential ramifications 82–3
Raz, J on 73
thin and thick senses 73–4
Constitutive Approach 7
Crapanzaro, Vincent
Serving the word: Literalism in America from the Pulpit to the Bench 92–3
Critical Legal Studies Movement 7
Critical Race Theory 198
Cromer, Lord 214–21
British Empire, on 216–7
diversity of Englishness, on 217
Egypt, on 216
England as green and pleasant place 228
England as space of sturdy pragmatics, on 218
Englishness, on 214–21
imagery of Old England 220
images of England 214–21
Cultural and symbolic analyses of law in context 14–6

Darian Smith, Eve
garden, image of 108–9
Dialogism 59–61
nature of 59
'voice', theory of 61
Diana, Princess
celebrity status 103–4
Don Quixote
censorship, and 114–5
Duncanson, Ian
refugees, on 12–3
Dworkin, Ronald
homogeneity, on 27

Eagleton, Terry
homogeneity, on 27
Eastwood, Clint 98, 101, 103
Eminem
homophobic lyrics 109–10
European Court of Human Rights
immigration law, on 39–40
local culture and values, on 54

Feigenson, Neal
visual imagery, on 16

Fish, S
  rhetoric, on 127, 137
Foley, Richard
  legislation, on 15
Frade, Celina
  legislation as genre, on 13
Friedman, Lawrence
  celebrity, on 96, 98, 99–100, 106

Garden of forking paths 1–16
Genre 59–61
  addressee 61
  nature of 60
Geny, F
  analysis of free interpretation of law 5
  law as a symbol, on 3
Globalisation 11–4
  international arbitration, and 64–5
Goodrich, Peter
  common law, on 219–20
Gourevitch, Philip
  law and celebrity, on 103
Greimas, AJ
  verification, on 8
Gypsies
  Cervantes on 116

Habermas, Jurgen
  argumentative theory of law 6
Hart, HLA
  philosophy of language 7–8
Hayes, Rutherford B
  awarded US Presidency 90
Hegland, Kenney
  deconstruction, and 137–8
Holliday, George
  Rodney King videotape 237–8
Homosexuality
  celebrity, and 109–10
Hughes, Howard
  defiance of gravity 222–23
Human Rights Act 1998, 35–55
  aliens, and 45–6
  immigration law 35–46
  proportionality 35–8
  'reasonableness' 35–6
  rights limited by law 37–8
Hyndman, HM
  Olde England, image of 220

Immigration law 35–46
  Ahmadi religion 45
  'balancing', rhetoric of 44–5
  countries not covered by ECHR 45
  entry clearance 40–1
  EU Member States, and 40
  European Court of Human Rights on 39–40
  human rights, and 35–46
  medical grounds cases 42–3
  objective test 41–2
  proportionality
    objective test 42–4
  public interest, and 44
  right to family and private life, and 40–2
  Secretary of State, and 42
  'Wednesbury' test of reasonableness 41
Interdisciplinarity
  images, and 231–2
International arbitration 64–5
  Brazil 64–5
  globalisation, and 64–5
International Association for the Semiotics of Law 9–11
International Round Table for the Semiotics of Law 9–11
Ireland, abortion debate in 141–64
  C case 156
  Catholic natural law 143–4
  Celtic Tiger, and 158
  changes in language of public discourse 162
  changes in pillar of old community 158
  coding schemas 146–7
  Constitution, importance of 143–4
  Constitution of 1983, 141
  counselling centres 145–6
  discursive dichotomy between law and social order 163
  Eighth Amendment 145
    judicial interpretation 145–8
  feminist strategies 147–8
  frame shifted, whether 163
  Green Paper 157
  health care matter, as 162–3
  historical context 143–5
  ideological drifts 161
  importance of public discourse 142
  Irish culture, and 141
  judiciary, and 142–3
  legal semiotics 161
  major organising themes 162
  maternity, function of 164

motherhood, importance of 144
PLAC 145
public policy discourses 159
Referendum Commission Booklet 159
rights strategy 161
role of women as defined in Constitution 144
semantic manipulations 146–7
semiotic of changing meaning 163–4
'social abortion' 160
substantive issue 152–6
Dail debate 153–5
'life' 154–5
media terminology 155
Referendum 153–4
'unborn' 159–60
X case 148–52
conclusions 151–2
facts 148–9
pro-life lobby, and 150
radical populism, and 149–50
rape, and 149
Supreme Court decision 151–2
Ito, Judge
celebrity status 104

Jackson, Bernard 9–10
Jemialniak, Joanna
rhetoric, on 15
Johnson, President Andrew
impeachment 90
Judges
celebrity status 104

Kelsen, H
theory of legal structure 5
Kennedy, JF
celebrity, as 101
Kevelson, Roberta, 9–10
communication, on 3–4
King, Rodney
visual images 237–8
Korolko, M
rhetoric, on 128–9

Law
visual imagery, and 231–2
Law, media and popular culture 232–8. *see also* Legal visual rhetoric
Apple TV commercial 236
confusion of 235
detective stories 236–7
'home video' aesthetic 234–5
implications 234
intermingling of 234
Legal Realism movement, and 233
Orwell, George, and 236
Rodney King case 237
trial lawyers, and 235
visual codes of film and television 236
visual evidence and storytelling 235
Law and morality 4
Legal Consciousness Studies 7
Legal deconstruction. *see also* Rhetoric
Critical Legal Studies movement 136
limits of conventional systems, and 138
method of legal analysis, as 136
Legal dialogism 61–4
civil law 62
common law 62
manifestation 69
responsiveness 63
Legal illocutionary act
categories of 57
Legal language 2–3
Legal semiotics
function of 232–3
Legal visual rhetoric 238–45
classical rhetoric, and 254
constructing 238–45
demonstrative evidence 240
Equal Protection Clause 240
graph of juvenile justice statistics 242
grids 243
pyramids 241
pedagogy of visual persuasion 245–54
anxieties of professors 252
assumptions 248
capabilities of students 247
construction of film 252–3
empowering of students 249
images as signs 247
learning about images 246
manipulation of information 254
multidisciplinary approach 254
nature of pictures 246
patterns, emergence of 251–2
persuasion 253
pluralities of meanings 249–50
primary image texts 248–9
rebellion of students, and 252
small group dynamics 251
traditional law school paradigm, and 250–1

understandings of modern visual culture 253–4
power of visual literacy 255
quantitative evidence 240
statistical data 240–1
theory of the case 239
video closing argument 243–5
personal and emotional truth 244–5
prison inmates 243–5
'voice of God' narration 244
Legislation
asymmetrical 58–9
monological 58–9
nature of 57–9
vocabulary of 63
Lewis, Frederick
US Constitution, on 13–4
Lippens, Ronnie
Englishness, on 15–6
Livingstone, Ken
May Day protests 2001, on 49
Lope de Vega 119–20
censorship, and 119–20
justice and honour, on 119
Lopez, Jennifer 99
Lorenz, Aaron
reggae, on 15
Luhmann, Niklas
law as subsystem of social system 6–7

McIntyre, Stuart
late colonial bourgeoisie, on 24
McVeigh, Timothy
celebrity status 101
Madonna 98
Malcolm X
segregation, on 207–8
Marley, Bob 199–200, 203–4, 210–1
Zimbabwe independence celebration 204
Marley, Ziggy 210
Mass media
influence on public opinion 53
May Day protests London 2001, 46–51
'flashpoint' 48
'fluffies' 47–8
globalisation, and 47
Ken Livingstone on 48–9
police preparations 51
press portrayal of victims 46–50
'spikies' 47–8
'stand off' 49
Tony Blair on 50–1
treatment of protestors 46–7
'zero tolerance' 48
Megan's Law 110–1
Metaphor
part of conceptual system, as 53
Meyers, Jill
celebrities, on 14
Millenium Dome 221–7
articulation of New Britain 226–7
body zone 224
Celtic maze compared 225
Faith zone 224
'gravity defying' 222
Greenwich peninsula 226
labyrinthine nature of 226
lack of centre 225
meridianal place, as 226–7
mind zone 222–4
Rest zone 223
space of aspiration, as 228–9
tent, as 221–2
unfixity of 223–4
Minogue, Kylie
Fame Games 111
Mohr, Richard
coats of arms, on 15
Mooney, Annabelle
human rights, on 13
Morris, Charles William
rhetoric, on 132

Nation
meaning 213
Neo-Kantianism
language and law, and 4–5
Nomadic life
nature of 218–9
Nussbaum, Martha
development of empathy for the other, and 255

Ong, Walter J
rhetoric, on 131–2
Orwell, George
images 236

Pencack, William
Spanish censorship, on 14
People's Republic of China. *see* Chinese Constitution
Plain Language Movement 166–7, 177
Plato
rhetoric, on 129–30

Positivism
  law and morality, and 4–5
Proportionality
  meaning 37–8

Racism
  reggae, and. *see* Reggae
Radbouch, Gustav
  supralegality, on 6
Ramism 131–2
Rastafarians
  reggae, and 201–2
Rawls, John
  'veil of ignorance' 27
Raz, J
  senses of constitution, on 73
Reagan, Ronald
  celebrity, as 100–1
Realists 7
Refugee meanings 19–34
  Aborigines, and 20–1
  alien character of detained asylum seekers 30–1
  'asylum seeker' 29
  Australia, meaning 29
  Australian nation state, and 20
  barred subject of refugee 32–4
  cheap labour 33–4
  Chinese labour 24–6
  class, and 22–6
  class interests, and 25–6
  community 27–8
  contagion, theme of 30
  globalisation, and 33
  military threat, designation as 31
  'national security', and 33
  official positionings of asylum seeker 29–32
  official response to refugees, and 21
  privileged meaning 19
  public discussion of class, and 26
  Tampa 32
  tradition 27–8
  UN human rights organisations, and 31–2
  for whom 29
  workplace rights, and 33
Reggae 197–211
  Bob Marley 199–201, 210–1, 203–4
  Critical Race Theory 198, 202–4
    continuous deconstruction 209
    equal opportunity 206
    legal revolution 210
    not neutral or objective 205
    political reform, and 203
    race consciousness 206
    race as legally constructed norm 207
    revolutionary tone 209
  dialect, and 202
  lyrics 200–201
  Malcolm X, and 207–8
  message of racial equality 201
  origin 199
  personal narratives 208
  racism, and 197–211
  Rastafarians, and 201–2
  reggae republic 204–9
  regional force, as 199
  revolution, as 199–2
  white culture, and 200
  Ziggy Marley 210
Renaissance
  rhetoric, and 131
Rhetoric 127–39
  Aristophanes, and 129
  Aristotle, and 130, 135–6
  art, as 127
  artes liberals 130
  Balkin, JM on 135–6
  Ballweg, Ottmar on 132–3
  Cicero, and 130–1
  Clifford, J on 132
  codification of rules 128
  current renewal of interest in 127–8
  ethical grounding of attacks and defences 137
  Fish, S and 137
  'funnel of abstraction' 134
  instrumental use of language, as 128
  judicial source of 129
  legal deconstruction, and 127–39
  logographs 129
  medieval scholastic tradition 130–1
  Morris, Charles William on 132
  Ong, Walter J on 131–2
  origins 128
  Plato on 129–30
  Ramism 131–2
  Renaissance, and 131
  Rorty, Richard on 133, 134
  Schlag, P on 133–134
  semiotics, relationship with 132–4
  sophists, and 128–9
Right to family and private life
  immigration law, and 40–2
Rodney, Dr Walter

reggae and critical race theory, on 205–6
Roman law
significance of 3
Roosevelt, Franklin
attempt to 'pack' US Supreme Court 90–1
Rorty, Richard
rhetoric, on 133–4
Ruskin, John
gothic architecture, on 215

Samuel, Raphael
rambling, on 219
Santa Ana, O
cognitive linguistics, on 53–4
representation of immigrants, on 37
Saving Private Ryan
celebrity, and 108
Schlag, P
rhetoric, on 133–4
Scott, Ridley 236
Semiotics 2, 9–11 ,16, 60, 120, 132–3, 161, 180, 194, 232–3, 238, 255
rhetoric, relationship with 132–4
Sherwin, Richard K
visual imagery, on 16
Simpson, OJ
stories told in trial 236–7
Singh, R
judiciary, on 54
Spain
early modern, censorship in. *see* Censorship
Spanish Inquisition
censorship, and 113–4
Spiesel, Christina O
visual imagery, on 16
Statutory definitions 165–77
distinction between term and word 169
drafting process in EU 168
elements 168
EU Regulation No. 1 165
implications for intelligibility 168
materials 170
methods 170
'own language' 166
Personal Data Directive 170–6
controller 173–5
data subject 171–173, 175–6
defined terms 170–5
personal data 175–6
personal data filing system 174
processor 173–4
recipient 174
subscriber 174–5
third party 174
user 174–5
Plain Language Movement 166–7, 177
Privacy in Telecommunications Directive 170–6
defined terms 170–5
schema theory 169–70
Sullivan, R on 167
term formation in 165–77
transparency 166
Sullivan, R
plain language, on 167

Terrorism Act 2000
scope of 36
Theweleit, Klaus
German Freikorps, on 29–30
Turner, Graeme
celebrity, on 97

US constitutional scholarship 85–93
Bush v Gore 87
certainty, quest for 85–93
constitutional 'creativity', practice of 85–93
historical reality of constitutional 'creativity'
Civil War, and 89
Clinton, President, Health Care proposal 91
composition of Supreme Court 90–1
Hayes, Rutherford B 90
Johnson, President Andrew 90
legal gender distinctions 91–2
racial segregation 90
Roosevelt, Franklin 90–1
two-term presidential tradition 89
US Constitution as 'living' document 89
normative and theoretical concerns 92
original intent 85–93
ambiguous language, and 88
difficulties with 87–8
Equal Protection Clause 87
historical reality, and 88
US Supreme Court, and 86

Van Dijk, TA
mass media, on 53

Vernon, J
English constitution, on 23
Victorian Britain
bourgeois perception of bourgeois self 22–3
Visual literacy 231–55

Watzawick, Paul
change, on 227
Weber, Max
sources of law, on 105
Welzel, Hans
outological structures, on 5–6
Williams, Professor Patricia
race, on 207
Wolfe, Alan
jurisprudence of original intent, on 92–93
Woods, Tiger 99

Zizek, Slavoj
homogeneity, on 27

www.ingramcontent.com/pod-product-compliance
Ingram Content Group UK Ltd.
Pitfield, Milton Keynes, MK11 3LW, UK
UKHW020246290926
15470UKWH00002B/777

9 781841 135458